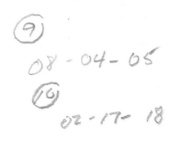

⑨
08 - 04 - 05
⑩
02 - 17 - 18

Enchanted Evening

BY THE SAME AUTHOR

The Far Pavilions
Trade Wind
Shadow of the Moon

Death in Berlin
Death in Cyprus
Death in Kashmir
Death in Kenya
Death in the Andamans
Death in Zanzibar

The Ordinary Princess
Murder Abroad
House of Shade

The Sun in the Morning
Golden Afternoon

Enchanted Evening

Volume III of the Autobiography of M. M. Kaye

M. M. Kaye

St. Martin's Press ✖ New York

www.stmartins.com

ISBN 0-312-26581-6

First published in Great Britain by the Penguin Group, Penguin Books Ltd

First U.S. Edition: December 2000

10 9 8 7 6 5 4 3 2 1

For
Tacklow,
who once told me that
on a clear day, from a
certain hillside above the
road to Simla, one could 'see
forever'.

Contents

List of Illustrations

~ᶻᶜᵛᶜᵛᶜᶻ~

Foreword

~※※※~

Having finally got down to writing my autobiography instead of thinking about doing so, and managing to complete the first volume, I imagined that writing the next one would be a piece of cake. After all, it was not as though I had to invent characters or worry about a plot, as one had to with novels. This was just remembering the past and writing it down as it happened. Simple.

Sadly I had omitted to make any allowance for advancing years and what they can do to you. I had managed to keep arthritis within bounds if not at bay, but angina at its nastiest was a bolt from the blue, and meant that Volume 2 of *Share of Summer* had to be put on hold for several years. When at last I started to write again it was only because I knew that if I once said: 'I can't do it,' I would never be able to write again. So I made myself a solemn promise to write something every day, even if it was only a line. Even if I knew that I would rub it out next day! Anything – *anything* – that would keep the book inching forward.

I kept that promise faithfully. But the result was, to say the least of it, entirely unexpected, for when at last I was able to say (as I handed the final chapter to Margaret, the noble girl who manages with the aid of a word processor to make sense out of my sheaves of pencilled foolscap) 'Well, that's Volume Two finished,' she replied with some asperity: 'You mean Volumes Two and Three; you can't *possibly* compress this lot into a single book. Have you any *idea* how much you have written?'

Well, I hadn't, of course. And Margaret was right again when I protested that it wouldn't cut in half successfully, and she pointed out that on the contrary, it would cut very neatly – where Tacklow* decides to take himself and his family off to China. It did. Which is how I found myself

---

* Family nickname for my father.

in the curious position of someone who has written an entire book by mistake; practically a candidate for the *Guinness Book of Records*.

And now I come to think of it, any reader who has not read *The Sun in the Morning* or *Golden Afternoon* will have no idea what I am doing on an Italian passenger ship, *en route* across the Indian Ocean to North China. Why China of all places? Well, anyone who has read either of the two previous volumes will know, and can skip the rest of this preface, which I will try to make as short as possible . . .

My dearly loved father, having retired with a knighthood after a term of years as Director of Central Intelligence, had been recalled by the Government of India to revise Aitcheson's Treaties – treaties that had been made back in the previous century between Britain and the princely states of India. When that job was completed he had been urged by the ruler of Tonk to stay on as his President of the Council of State. I don't think my father had any desire to do so. But since Mother, my sister Bets and myself were all for it, and he could never refuse Mother anything that was in his power to give her, he accepted; and at first everything went like a marriage bell. But alas, the old Nawab died and the whole thing fell apart in an incredible welter of lies and palace intrigue that ended in darling Tacklow being dismissed in the shabbiest manner by the Nawab's successor.

Convinced that after a long and distinguished career he had been publicly disgraced, he planned a second retirement. Not to England this time, but to China. Which was something he had always dreamed of doing because, long ago in the dawn of the twentieth century, his regiment, the 21st Punjabis, had been sent to China to help clear up the shambles that had been made in that land by the Boxer Rising.

Since he happened to be a language buff – he spoke nine major languages and seventeen dialects, Mandarin and Cantonese among them – he was immediately at home and at ease in China and with the Chinese. He fell in love with the country from the moment he set foot on it. And with my mother the moment he first saw her, on the Tientsin railway station platform. Her father, known to the family as 'the Grand-dadski', was a Scottish missionary, and Tacklow had a hard time getting himself accepted as a son-in-law. It took him the best part of three years, but he won her at last and they were married and spent a halcyon honeymoon in Pei-tai-ho, a little seaside town on the Gulf of Pei-chih-li. It was the happiest time of his life, and when he talked to me of China it was always as though he was remembering paradise. As for Mother, he adored her to the end of his days.

That was why, when he had been so bitterly hurt by the débâcle of Tonk, he felt, like Tennyson's King Arthur, that if he could go back there, back to that almost legendary land in which he had found such happiness, he could forget the bitter wound that India had dealt him. Hence the SS *Conte Rosso*, *en route* to the Far East.

❧ I ❧

China: Spring 1932

❧❧❧❧

Chapter 1

The *Conte Rosso* was one of an Italian line of passenger ships that plied between Genoa and the Orient, and though in the interests of economy Tacklow* had booked us to travel Tourist Class, we ended up travelling in great luxury in first class. For which we had to thank the fact that in those far-off times anyone who had a handle to their name – particularly a British one – was automatically a 'Milord'. And, naturally, all Milords must be rich.

This drew attention to the fact that Tacklow and his family were travelling 'rough' and the Captain was curious. He went out of his way to be gracious to Tacklow and, on discovering that he spoke Italian with great fluency, leapt to the conclusion that he must have been born and brought up in that country.

Tacklow disabused him of this idea, but in the course of conversation mentioned an old friend of his, an Englishman named Wyatt who during the First World War had served as a liaison officer, or something of that sort, with the Italian army, and been so taken with the country and its people that he had retired there and become a citizen.

Well, we all know that it's a small world, so you will not be too surprised to learn that the Captain's home town was the one in which Commendatore Wyatt had settled, and that the two were old friends. And, since the ship happened to be half empty, the Captain insisted on moving us up to two vacant first class cabins. The Italian-speaking members of the crew took Tacklow to their bosoms, and for the remainder of that voyage we were treated like royalty.

It was a marvellous voyage, for since my sister Bets† had just become

---

* See dedication and Foreword.

† Bets also had the nickname 'T' for Trainer. We had a game when young that I was a performing mouse and she my trainer. My family always called me Mouse from then on, and I always called her 'T' for Trainer. I still do.

engaged to a young man in Burma-Shell's India section, I was secure in the knowledge that with Bets's future decided, even if my parents did decide to settle in China, there would always be somewhere in India that I could return to; because Bets would be there. Without that comfortable assurance this would have been just another voyage into exile. But as it was I could sit back and enjoy myself.

I find it odd now that it never once occurred to me that although I knew I could always count on a welcome from Bets, her husband might be less welcoming. So, freed from the dreary prospect of yet another period of exile that could, this time, possibly be permanent, I was free to enjoy to the full the experience of travelling in luxury on a 'slow boat to China'. And this time, thank heaven, I was not seasick, not for a single hour.

The *Conte Rosso* loafed across blue seas under cloudless skies, escorted by teams of dolphins and attended by the occasional sea bird. The seas we sailed on were still unpolluted, and the water so clear that every jellyfish or basking shark showed up as though it were embedded in glass. I was no stranger to sea voyages, and had on several occasions seen the white fountains thrown up by spouting whales. But I had never before seen them from so close; whole families of them. So very many that it does not seem possible that, in the years since then, those huge, harmless leviathans have become an endangered species, hunted to the verge of extinction.

For the first few days of the voyage we saw no sign of another ship, and no glimpses of land. Nothing but leagues of empty ocean rimmed by a seemingly endless horizon; until suddenly the empty world became sprinkled with islands. Hundreds of them. Tiny, romantic patches of dense greenery fringed by white beaches and encircled by opal-coloured lagoons, most of them apparently uninhabited and all of them, seen from the sea, unbelievably beautiful. I think now that they must have been either the Andamans or the Nicobar Islands, and I remember them as pure magic – the coral islands of story and legend. Once in the Straits of Malacca we saw more land and more ships, then another flurry of islands and we were docking at Singapore.

The *Conte Rosso* was to stay in Singapore for two days, and Tacklow had booked rooms for us at Raffles Hotel. We went there in rickshaws, which in those days outnumbered taxis by twenty to one, if not more, and I remember that the open sea was on our right for the whole way.

When we reached Raffles, it seemed a very big building in contrast to the small wooden shacks of the fisher-folk and shopkeepers that clustered along the left-hand side of our road. I remember too, very clearly, a young Chinese woman standing on the dock looking up at the faces of the passengers who lined the deck rails of the *Conte Rosso*, as they waited to disembark. She was wearing a plain white *cheong-sam* and black silk Chinese-style slippers, and she stays in my mind as one of the four most beautiful women I have ever seen.[*]

In those days the garden of Raffles Hotel ended in a large swimming-pool that lay between the green lawns and the open sea, and I remember being told a horror-story about it by one of the local inhabitants. Singapore had recently been badly battered by the tail-end of a hurricane that had sent huge waves crashing over the sea wall at the far side of the swimming-pool. One of them had carried with it a large shark, which found itself trapped in the pool once the storm had passed. Because of the damage to the trees and flower-beds and the endless debris to be cleared away, no one had gone near the pool for at least a week, and the shark had got hungrier and hungrier. And when at last the sun rose in a cloudless sky, the ravenous creature discovered that there was only one place where it could hide from the glare – in the black shadow thrown by the diving-boards. It was lying there when the first swimmer, a young woman off one of the tourist ships, came down for a pre-breakfast dip, and jumped in off the high diving-board straight into the jaws of the shark. 'She hadn't got a chance, poor girl,' said my informant with an eloquent shudder.

I don't know if that story was true, or merely invented to take the mickey out of me; if so, he had a very nasty imagination, for his horrifying tale gave me nightmares for months afterwards, and it was years before I stopped myself instinctively checking any shadow in a swimming-pool in case it harboured a hungry shark. The pool has vanished long ago, and with it all but the façade of the old Raffles Hotel, which now looks out on a mile or more of houses, roads and skyscrapers galore, where once there was open sea. None of the distinguished visitors who stayed there in Victorian and Edwardian days, and throughout the first two-thirds

---

[*] The other three (and this is despite the fact that I once met Marlene Dietrich!) were Indian: Sita of Kaputhala; an unknown Parsee lady seen one evening dancing in the crowded ballroom of Bombay's Taj Mahal Hotel; and a Kashmiri girl paddling a *shikarra* near the Dāl Gate.

of the twentieth century, would recognize much of the old Singapore.

The Governor, who was a friend of Tacklow's, sent an invitation to lunch and a car, and in the afternoon we were given a tour of the island and its famous and beautiful Botanical Gardens, which, in those days, no car except the Governor's was allowed to enter. I remember it as being green and scented – and full of shade and orchids and brightly coloured birds. Towards evening it rained, and I was told that this was a feature of Singapore's climate, that nearly every day ended with a tropical shower which not only saved people having to water their gardens, but made the evenings pleasantly cool.

The *Conte Rosso* sailed next day at sunset. And as the ship threaded its way out between the tiny islets that lie scattered round the harbour, we saw a graceful white steam-yacht coming in to anchor offshore in the lee of one of the islets, and were told by the pilot that it belonged to that world-famous clown of the silver screen, Charlie Chaplin, who was on a honeymoon cruise, following his marriage to the second (or was it third?) Mrs Chaplin, the beautiful Paulette Goddard. And instantly the quiet, opal-coloured evening became drenched with romance, and I thought with envy how heavenly it must be to marry the man of your dreams and be able to sail away with him to such enchanting places as this. Lucky, lucky Paulette; what wouldn't I give to be in her shoes! Provided, of course, that I could choose a different bridegroom. For at that time, having never seen the famous comic except on screen, I could only think of him as a funny little man in baggy trousers with an absurd moustache.

The weather changed as we turned northward into the South China Sea, and it was there that I saw my first water-spouts, thin, dark columns, very far away, racing across a slate-grey sea. Tacklow called us out on deck to see them and the Captain told us that they might look interesting enough from a distance, but could be lethal if they struck a ship broadside on. The wind driving them had not yet reached us (I would have been prone in my bunk if it had!) and the horizon was a jet-black line dividing the ink-dark sea from a long bar of almost white sky. Above this lay a dark pall of cloud that had the appearance of being held up by the pillars of the water-spouts. The whole enormous seascape looked like a steel engraving of one of Gustave Doré's illustrations to Dante's *Purgatory*. But though the wind was beginning to reach us in little whining gusts, I made no attempt to go below, for another water-spout was forming right in front of us.

It was the most uncanny thing I have ever seen. It began with that ominous pall of clouds turning darker and darker, and then beginning to sag down at one point towards the sea until it seemed that it must burst at any moment and empty its load of rainwater into the sea. Instead of which, it was sucking the sea up towards it. We saw the sea pucker up, as though drawn up by a gigantic suction-pump towards the cloud-bank above it, which by now had formed itself into a long funnel that was swirling round at a ferocious speed and drawing the sea remorselessly into it. Another few seconds and the two columns would have joined and gone racing away, sucking up more and more salt water as they went. But the wind had been too quick for it. The sinister, swirling funnel of clouds had barely touched when it hit them with what must have been the speed of an express train and blew them apart, and the great hill of water fell back into the sea with an enormous splash.

I'm glad I saw it. Even though the very thought of it still gives me a shiver down the spine, because both the grey, foam-flecked water that appeared to be lifting itself up and the black, groping funnel reaching down for it seemed to be alive and know what they were doing. That must have been the way the Red Sea looked when it lifted up and drew back to let the Israelites pass over – and when it fell back on the pursuing army of Egypt.

The *Conte Rosso* left the bad weather behind, and the skies were once again blue and cloudless by the time we reached Hong Kong, where we were met on the dock by one of Mother's sisters, Aunt Lilian, and her husband, Uncle David Evans-Thomas (at that time the manager of the local branch of the Hong Kong and Shanghai Bank), who drove us up to the Bank House on the Peak, and from there to lunch at the Repulse Bay Hotel.

Hong Kong, like Port Taufic on the Suez canal,* was one of the places that I fell in love with on sight. You have no idea how green and glittering and beautiful it was, back in the decade which was fated to end with the Second World War. There were few skyscrapers in those days and I remember (probably inaccurately) the Hong Kong and Shanghai Bank building as being much the tallest on the waterfront. There were sampans and sea-going Chinese junks among the ships reflected in the clear blue and green waters of the uncluttered harbour, and the hillsides that

* See *The Sun in the Morning*.

surrounded it were thick with flowering shrubs: yellow, red and coral-pink hibiscus and acres of heliotrope, that sweet-smelling plant that at one time used to grow in every cottage garden in England, and which the country-folk nicknamed 'cherry-pie'. The air was heavy with its scent – and full of butterflies, more brilliant than any I had seen in India, and so large that at first I thought they must be brightly coloured birds until their lilting flight betrayed them.

Our next stop was Shanghai, where, on a cold day, we parted with regret from the *Conte Rosso** and her friendly crew. Their next call was Japan, while ours was in the North China Treaty Port of Tientsin. The business of disembarkation took a great deal longer than we had expected, and Bets and I, after having our faces checked against our passport photographs, were left to our own devices for what seemed like hours, while our parents queued patiently to be interviewed by a number of Chinese port officials, explaining to the satisfaction of passport officers their reasons for wishing to enter China and how long they expected to stay, answering endless questions put to them by customs officials and health inspectors, and finally signing any number of papers. All this meant that I had plenty of time in which to take my first look at China proper. Frankly, I thought nothing of it.

I had not counted the Treaty Port of Hong Kong as 'China proper', because in those days it was still part of the British Empire, with the date on which it was due to be handed back to China so far in the future that it did not even occur to me that I might live to see it. But Shanghai, despite its impressive Western-style buildings and the fact that it was at that time a truly international city, was also unmistakably Chinese. The swarming crowds on the dockside, the coolies and dock-workers, the stevedores who were loading or unloading cargoes or coaling the ships and, almost without exception, the merchants and educated middle-class men and women who had come to greet or wave goodbye to passengers were Chinese, dressed as their nation had dressed for many centuries past, and would, all too soon, never dress again.

Looking down at them from the deck of the *Conte Rosso*, I did not realize that I was seeing the very last of that Old China, the fabled country which many of its citizens refer to as the 'Middle Kingdom', because to

---

* I hate to admit it, but a reader tells me that we sank the *Conte Rosso* in the Second World War. Not, I do hope, with our Captain and crew aboard.

them it occupies the centre of the world, and who had dressed in this self-same fashion when the British were living in caves and painting their bodies with woad. Had I known, I might have been less critical of the scene below me. And for the first time since we left Delhi, I was afraid. Deadly afraid that I was never going to see India again, doomed to spend the rest of my life in this chilly, colourless country whose people spoke a language that had no alphabet but only picture-symbols – thousands of them, a different one for each word.

It was all very well for Tacklow, who acquired languages as other people collect stamps or matchboxes, and for Mother, who had been born in China and had spoken the language from her babyhood – as I had spoken Hindustani. But I could not see myself at my age learning a new and very complicated language. Besides, I didn't want to, because I had no intention of staying in this country for longer than I could help.

Perhaps if the sun had been shining I would have taken a kinder view of Shanghai. But the day was grey and lowering, and a chilly wind was sweeping along the decks and singing through the funnel stays. And ominously, in the far distance beyond and behind the crowded rooftops that stretched to the horizon, the grey of the overcast sky was smudged here and there with darker stains of smoke that rose up sluggishly into the cold air and were, had I but known it, a grim reminder that below them lay the ruins of what had once been the overcrowded Chinese workers' suburb of Chapei, which was still burning.

Barely two months before, and without warning, the Japanese had attacked it, and, as I was to learn later, on the night when the attack was launched the firing had brought the Westerners in the International Settlements, who were streaming out of theatres and cinemas, crowding into the streets in evening dress to see what was going on, and staying there to watch. They were quite confident that because they were foreigners and this was nothing to do with them, no one would harm them.

That story of an interested crowd watching without realizing it the death of Shanghai as an International City and the birth pangs of the Second World War reminded me of a tale about the early days of the American Civil War, when the crinolined ladies of a Southern city were so confident of victory that they put on their prettiest bonnets, took their parasols and picnic baskets, and drove out to watch the progress of a decisive battle – which the South lost. It took the obliteration of Chapei to show the West that the Japanese would stop at nothing.

Standing on the deck of the *Conte Rosso*, and looking at those smoke-stains on the sky, all I thought was that there must be a house on fire somewhere out there. It never occurred to me to ask questions. It was just another dreary smudge on a dreary view, and I missed the colour of the Indian crowds. Here the only colour was the blue of the picture on willow-pattern plates, which I learned was the cheapest of dyes: indigo. This vegetable dye had been used for centuries and made the fortunes of successive generations of indigo planters until some intelligent inventor came up with a synthetic dye of the same colour, with the added bonus that it did not fade. Whereupon the indigo planters all went broke. Almost every working man or woman I could see from my vantage point on the top deck was wearing clothes that had been dyed willow-pattern blue with indigo, in every shade of that colour. The new clothes were dark blue, while the less new, down to worn-to-rags raiment that was a pale dingy grey-blue, rang all the changes in between.

The more affluent middle class wore sober street-wear in black or slate grey – long coats with high collars fastening with elaborately designed loops and toggles over slightly longer skirts that were slit at one side. The outfit was completed by thick-soled shoes of black silk, and topped by a small round cap with a button on top. Many of the older men sported long, thin mustachios and a long narrow beard; exactly as they do in the pictures and paintings of grey-haired family elders in bygone China.

There were a good many alarming incidents taking place in China at that time, but I was soon to discover that not only Shanghai but the world in general had chosen to refer to the most serious of them – the Japanese takeover of Manchuria and the recent bombing and total destruction of Chapei – as 'the China Incident' and refused to take it seriously. The trouble was that Shanghai considered itself to be unique among the cities of the world, in that it was truly 'international'. This was because back in the nineteenth century the Chinese had been pressured into granting settlements or 'concessions' of land to the merchants and traders of a large number of foreign countries – among them Japan. The Japanese settlement of Hondew lay on the far side of Garden Bridge, and its market was said to be the largest in Asia, while its population had swollen to such proportions that it was nicknamed 'Little Tokyo'.

China in the spring of 1932 had got itself into a terrible mess, and I still cannot understand how my darling father could have decided to move himself, his wife and his two daughters (neither of whom could speak or understand a word of Chinese) to that war-torn and disaster-prone country, with the intention of spending the rest of his life there. I suppose the Rajputana episode had hit him so badly that he wanted to get shot of India and everyone in it. And he had obviously been remembering China as it was in the old days, when the twentieth century was young and there was still an Empress in the Forbidden City and a Son of Heaven on the Dragon Throne . . .

A time when he, a bachelor Captain in the 21st Punjabis,* had not only fallen in love with the country and its people but lost his heart to a girl whom he had first glimpsed on the platform of Tientsin's railway station, had subsequently tracked down and married, and with whom he had spent an unforgettably romantic honeymoon in the little fishing village of Pei-tai-ho on the shores of the Yellow Sea.

All his memories of that lost China were happy ones, and I have come to believe that he thought of it as Tennyson's King Arthur thought of 'the island valley of Avalon'. 'Where falls not hail, or rain, or any snow, Nor ever wind blows loudly', a safe and pleasant refuge where he could rest and, like Arthur, 'heal me of my grievous wound'. Because for someone like Tacklow the wound had indeed been grievous, and it was a measure of just how bad it had been that he should have returned to the China of the 1930s in the middle of what was casually called 'the China Incident' without realizing how enormously the country had changed in the past thirty years.

---

* A British Indian Army regiment that had been drafted out to North China to help clear up the havoc created by the Boxer Rising (see *The Sun in the Morning*).

Chapter 2

~❧⊙❧~

The usual contingent of Mother's Bryson relations – on this occasion two of her brothers, Arnold and Ken, and their wives – were to collect us off the ship. And since Ken was Mother's twin, he had insisted that we should be his guests during our stay in Shanghai. So it was with him that we finally left the ship and drove away from the docks.

I don't know what sort of house I had expected Uncle Ken to live in. Something on the lines of a bungalow in Old Delhi perhaps? A house with whitewashed walls and wide verandahs, overhung with purple and scarlet bougainvillaea and surrounded by a shady garden full of trees and flowers . . . In the event it turned out to be as disappointing as my first view of Shanghai. Here too there was no hint of Far-away Places and the Exotic Orient; one might just as well have been in the suburbs of any British 'New Town' complete with grey skies and a steady drizzle. My spirits fell even further. But China has always kept a card or two up her silken sleeve, and now she produced one . . .

Uncle Ken, incoherent with disappointment and apology, explained that his Joyce, who had always been delicate, had recently suffered a nervous breakdown and been strongly advised by her doctors to return to England to undergo special treatment in a nursing-home. She had already gone, leaving the housekeeping in a state of chaos. And since Ken's office would keep him too busy to entertain us during working hours, and without Joyce on the premises he did not trust his cook to be able to cope with us, we would be staying a mere two days under his roof, after which Aunt Peg and Uncle Alec would be taking over.

I cannot help suspecting that the prospect of having to put up no less than *four* of her in-laws, on top of chronic ill-health, had probably been the last straw for Aunt Joyce, for even having us for those two nights was obviously a strain on Ken's staff – though the twins clearly had a whale of a time discussing the old days and reminiscing about the friends of their youth. The next day must have been a Saturday, for in the morning, urged by Mother, Uncle Ken took us out shopping in Bubbling Well Road, where, in those days, all the best makers and embroiderers of women's underwear lived.

Mother and Bets had a field day here, on the excuse that Bets, now that she was officially engaged, should begin collecting her trousseau. Compared with the prices of today, those lovely garments were absurdly cheap. But I had little money to spare for fripperies, and in the end I settled for a single petticoat: a slip of soft, cream-coloured satin, woven from pure silk (China still scorned to use anything else) and decorated with an elaborate spatter of roses on insets of fine net. It was a work of art, and I still have it, sadly worn and frayed, but still too beautiful to throw away.

In contrast to the beauty of those silk-and-satin creations, Bubbling Well Road was quite as unalluring as the Shanghai docks, a crowded thoroughfare crammed with hurrying humanity in drab city suits and mackintoshes. The Chinese, wearing either black or indigo, outnumbered the foreigners by ten to one, as the rickshaws outnumbered the cars and buses. But half-way through the following day the clouds lifted and the sun came out. And by the next day I had changed my mind about China, and was willing to concede that there might even be something to be said for Shanghai.

It wasn't just the sunshine and a blue sky that made me change my mind, though possibly that helped. It was discovering that there was more to Shanghai than a disappointing number of English-suburban houses, the ugliness of the docks, and the unexpected drabness of Bubbling Well Road. It depended largely on which quarter of the city you lived in. For in those days most of the British and Americans, as well as a great many other foreigners trading with China, had their homes in the International Settlement, which in times of stress could be barricaded off from the Chinese sections of the city. The French, however, had obtained a separate concession of their own, and since you did not have to live in your own concession, Uncle Alec had been able to acquire a house in the French Concession.

Mother's family were, on average, a noticeably good-looking lot with the exception of Alec, who looked like a prize-fighter crossed with a bull-frog. He was, in fact, an extremely skilful and successful surgeon with a reputation that stood high among the rich Chinese as well as among his fellow *gweilos* ('foreign-devils', as they were still referred to by a majority of the citizens of the country). Aunt Peg, on the other hand, more than made up for her husband's lack of good looks, for she was the most attractive and elegant creature, and I suspect that their choice of a house and its stunning interior decoration had nothing to do with Alec's taste, and everything to do with hers. It was an old Chinese house, which she had subtly modernized; and though I was to see a great many more such during the next few years, this was the first one. And by far the most beautiful.

The house, as with the houses of all well-to-do Chinese of the old school, consisted of a series of one-room, single-storey quarters built around a paved courtyard. The graceful tiled and tip-tilted Tartar roofs extended over the verandahs and curved upward to show a profusion of carved and painted flowers and mythical gods and animals decorating the underside of the eaves. The rooms had doors and windows only on the side facing a courtyard, and the nearest courtyard was connected to the main house by a moon gate, a perfect circle cut in the courtyard wall. The entire complex, which surrounded three sides of a wide lawn, was protected by a high wall above which we could see tree-tops and the graceful roofs of other Chinese houses, and Peg had decorated the long main room – which would once have been either a reception room or a hall of ancestors – in the Chinese manner.

The furniture was of lacquer or carved blackwood, and the curtains and cushions were of heavy, cash-patterned Tribute silk.* The floor was of exquisitely inlaid and polished wood, strewn with old Chinese carpets, and the long room was dotted with wonderful examples of Chinese art, every one of which was a gem in its own right. It was easily the most beautiful room I have ever seen, and it goes to my heart to realize that the entire house, and with it those whose roofs showed above the surrounding wall, would almost certainly have been smashed into rubble by Japanese bombs in that attack on Shanghai during the Second World War. So much beauty destroyed. And so very many lives – among them Aunt Alice's husband, Howard Payne, the young man who had happened to see the seventeen-year-old Alice walking down the gangplank of a ship that had brought her, with my mother and grandmother, back to North

* See page 53.

14

China, and seeing her had said: 'That's the girl I'm going to marry!'*

No less than five – or was it six? – of Mother's family were held in the notorious Japanese prisoner-of-war camp in Shanghai. Poor Uncle Howard died there.

The only room in the Brysons' house that contained no trace of China, but was wholly twentieth-century European, was the master bedroom. It was pure Syrie Maugham,† and Bets and I were left gasping with admiration. We had seen photographs of this style of decoration in the glossier women's magazines, and knew that all-white rooms were very much the fashion. But we had never actually seen one before; probably because no one we knew well would have been able to afford the vast dry-cleaning bills.

Peg's bedroom was a revelation. One entire wall was covered in looking-glass which reflected a king-size double bed backed by graceful draperies and standing on a platform approached by three shallow steps. The floor was carpeted from wall to wall in plain deep-pile carpet of Chinese manufacture – possibly the only Chinese thing in the room – and there were white flower-vases full of lilies, filling the room with their scent. A final touch of charm and opulence was the enormous rug made from polar-bear skins that covered the steps leading up to the bed. Some years later, audiences in a London theatre watching a long-forgotten musical show entitled *Helen* were to gasp with admiration at a scene depicting the legendary Helen in an all-white bedroom. The set that earned this nightly tribute from London audiences was the work of that famous theatrical designer, Oliver Messel. But Peg had anticipated him.

Bets and I might be stunned by that bedroom, but Uncle Alec was less enthusiastic. He said it was OK for his decorative wife to wake up and see herself reflected in acres of looking-glass, but the sight of his own face, first thing every morning, never failed to give him a nasty shock: 'Talk of Beauty and the Beast!' grumbled Alec. 'One may be fully aware that one resembles the latter, but it doesn't help to have it rubbed in first thing in the morning – especially when one has gone to sleep after a late night on the tiles!'

---

* See *The Sun in the Morning*.

† A well-known English interior decorator of the time, ex-wife of the writer Somerset Maugham.

I couldn't help sympathizing with him. Uncle Alec cannot, at the best of times, have been shown to advantage in that setting. But Uncle Alec in pyjamas, waking up with a shocking hangover, unshaven and with bags under his eyes, must however have been no ordinary blot in those glamorous surroundings. He may only have been pushing out the boat for us, but the fact remains that during our stay in that lovely house we went out dancing and partying every night, and it soon became clear to me that my uncle's lack of good looks did not prevent him from being a wow with women and a very popular guest at parties. Our stay with him and Aunt Peg turned out to be one enjoyable party after another, interspersed with sight-seeing, and meeting such exotic wildfowl as Mussolini's daughter and her husband Count Ciano.

My clearest memory of that stay in Shanghai is of dining and dancing into the small hours in a series of fascinating nightclubs. Tacklow, no dancing man, would make his excuses and fade unobtrusively away fairly early on in the evening. Not so Uncle Alec! Alec was always among the last to leave, and I well remember an evening – or rather an early morning – at 'The Little Club' when, noticing the time and the fact that my uncle was on the top of his form, I remarked anxiously to the man I was dancing with that Alec would never be able to keep his appointment to operate on someone at six a.m. To which my partner replied that I obviously didn't know much about Alec. 'Your uncle,' he said, 'has the reputation of being a superb surgeon when sober, but an inspired genius when tight – ask the Chinese. Ask anyone!' I presume that verdict was correct, for it is certain that rich Chinese queued up for his services.

Tacklow had been interviewed by a variety of local journalists on the day we landed, and later we had all been photographed for one of Shanghai's magazines. The photographs, and another article, appeared on our first day at Aunt Peg's, and I was shaken to see in cold print that: 'Sir Cecil Kaye, one-time Head of the CID India, has arrived in Shanghai with the intention of retiring in China.' No 'ifs' or 'buts' about it. I could not believe that he could be serious. Not now, when only a few months before over 14,000 Chinese and Japanese had died at Chapei, while many times that number of wounded and homeless Chinese, who had fled for their lives into the countryside beyond, were being attacked and robbed by hordes of bandits – men of their own race. It was unbelievable.

Four photographs accompanied that ominous article, one of each of us. Unlike most newspaper photographs, these were very nice and we were charmed when the paper sent us each a couple of large complimentary copies of the set. I still have them.

In the mornings we went shopping with Peg (she shopped, we just looked and envied, for none of us could afford to buy the glittery, alluring things displayed in those wonderful Aladdin's Cave shops that lined the main streets of the city). But it was quite an experience just to look at the tempting objects on offer. Wonderful clothes from London, Paris and New York; furs and hats and shoes (there was a tale that the film star Mary Pickford bought all her shoes in Shanghai). Shops that sold jewels that would have graced a Queen; incredibly elegant shops that sold make-up and scents in fascinating bottles, and others that sold works of art and wonderfully illustrated and bound books.

After several hours of wandering and window shopping, Peg would take us to lunch in one of the city's splendid hotels that lined the Bund; and on one occasion we spent a sybaritic day at the races. On another we were taken out to see what memory has labelled as a meet of the 'Shanghai Hunt' – though that cannot be true, because first, there was no huntable animal in China (in India 'the Raj' used to hunt jackals), and second, it was late May, a time when the young crops would have been at their most vulnerable and the year well into the 'closed season'. I also don't remember seeing any hounds; only ponies and their *mafoos* (grooms) and a lot of chatty people in riding coats and hard hats milling around.

This was the first time I had seen 'China' ponies – or, to be accurate, 'Mongolian' ones, since they are imported from the grasslands of Mongolia. These miniature creatures from Central Asia look like shaggy nursery toys when they arrive, but when they have been clipped and groomed, and properly dieted, they look very presentable; and they are renowned for being tough, quick on their feet, and capable of carrying really heavy weights for long periods. They even made very passable polo ponies, despite the fact that the soles of their riders' boots were alarmingly close to the ground.

Seen for the first time, these sturdy little ponies seemed tiny. But it's surprising how soon one gets used to their size: less than two years later, when I saw a normal-sized racehorse in Hong Kong, it looked to me as large and as clumsy as a carthorse compared with the little 'China ponies' I had become accustomed to.

I had been enthralled by Singapore and Hong Kong; they were both places that I had taken an instant fancy to and felt that I would dearly like to stay in for a long while – two or three years, perhaps. Or even more. They were places where one could put down roots. Not so Shanghai. Although socially speaking I couldn't have had a better time, I always felt that I was a raw newcomer, a foreigner from a different world.

Back in what was then British India the social structure had been different: starting at the top with the Viceroy and his staff and moving down to Governors of Provinces. Next came members of the 'Heaven-born' – ICS (India Civil Service) – and the Foreign-and-Political, followed by the Army, the British Cavalry, British Infantry, Indian Infantry and Cavalry, and finally the merchants and traders, whom Anglo-India loftily called '*box-wallahs*'. There was no such pecking order in Shanghai. Here the *box-wallah* was King and the Shanghaiers behaved as though they were a breed apart – free citizens of some powerful city-state. It was this, I suppose, that had enabled the denizens of the International Settlement to stand out in the street in evening dress and watch with detached interest as Japanese marines attacked the Chinese suburb of Chapei. It was not their business. It still astonishes me to think that only a little while later, while ugly wisps of smoke could still be seen rising from the ruins of Chapei, I was lunching, dining, dancing and generally enjoying a terrific party in a city where the curtain had already gone up on the hideous overture to the Second World War – and where representatives of every nation that was to take part in it had been able to sit and watch the opening of hostilities from the stalls . . .

The protagonists were all there. The French and British, Americans, Japanese, Germans, Jews and Gentiles from every country in the world. Russians, too; hundreds and hundreds of Russians. For the late Great War-To-End-War had only been over for fourteen years, the Russian Revolution for fifteen. Hordes of 'White Russians' had fled for their lives. The westernized ones, who had money in foreign banks, made for Europe, while the rest turned eastward, trudging across Siberia to Vladivostok and, when that too fell to the Red Army, to Harbin in Manchuria – and eventually, to Tientsin and Shanghai.

Many died on that journey. But many survived, and one of the saddest sights of Shanghai during the early years of the Revolution was the sight of White Russians: tattered and barefoot men, begging from coolies or, if they were lucky, pulling rickshaws. By the time Tacklow brought us to Shanghai the Russians in that city were estimated to number more than 25,000 – they were the second largest group of foreign nationals, the first being the Japanese. And though still technically stateless, the White Russians had taken over the night-life of the city. Every dance hall had its quota of Russian 'hostesses', some as young as twelve or fourteen, some elderly and raddled, women who would partner anyone for a price, either for the duration of a dance or for the remainder of the night. You saw them everywhere, working as shop-girls, waitresses, hat-check girls, or in the chorus-lines of cabarets or floor-shows. Their men played in dance-bands and orchestras, sang, acted or put on performances of the ballet. There was more than one Russian theatre in the city and several Russian churches.

Many of the women claimed to be princesses, or the daughters of grand-dukes, and some of them may well have been. But in one respect their stories were chillingly similar: the horrors they had witnessed or endured at the hands of the Bolsheviks. The terrible hardships of escape and flight across endless, empty miles of some of the most hostile territory in the world, where the weakest – the old or the very young – had died from thirst or starvation, or merely from exhaustion. Many of these refugees were robbed and cheated by the wandering tribes of Central Asia and Mongolia, with the result that by the time they reached China – or Manchuria – they were penniless and forced to beg for food or for any work, however ill-paid or degrading.

Tacklow's intention had been to travel to Tientsin by the Shanghai Express. But he changed his mind when he learned that the train had recently been ambushed (and not for the first time) by night and in the middle of nowhere, probably by the private army of one of the self-styled Generalissimos who were rampaging around in those days, creating havoc wherever they went. The train had been stopped in a particularly desolate stretch of country, its passengers robbed of everything they possessed, and a good few rich Chinese taken captive and held for ransom. One or two people who had objected had been shot, and after that the rest of the passengers and crew had given no trouble.

We were told that one intrepid Consular lady, an Austrian or Italian Contessa as far as I remember, had not only had the sense to realize at once what had happened, but, acting with lightning speed, had tilted the entire contents of her well-stocked jewel-case into a brown silk head-scarf and, unseen in the darkness and confusion, had jumped down on to the track, hastily scratched a hole in the nearest bit of earth, buried the loot and scrambled back into her compartment. There she brushed the mud from her hands, filled the empty jewel-case with odds and ends of make-up and hair curlers, and put on a convincing act of being asleep when the raiders reached her compartment and proceeded to strip it of all her cash and belongings, together with any of the carriage fittings that were not actually nailed down.

And did the resourceful Contessa get her jewels back? Yes, she did indeed. But I imagine that the tale of how she nearly lost them may have had something to do with Tacklow's decision to finish our journey by sea.

We said goodbye to Shanghai with some regret, for thanks to Aunt Peg we had had a lot of fun there – and expected to have a lot more, for Peg had said: 'Once you get really settled into a house of your own, and begin to get used to living here, I hope you'll come down here and visit us whenever you feel like a change of air. We shall expect to see a lot of you.'

But we were never to see Shanghai again, or Peg and Alec either – though Mother did, when they were old and ill and living in England and the Shanghai they had known was about to become no more than a memory. A happy one for almost all of the ex-Shanghaiers, for in later years I never met one of them who did not say: 'It was a wonderful city to have lived in. We had such *fun*!'

Chapter 3

The voyage from Shanghai to Tientsin was not a long one: a few days at most. And there was nothing much to look at, because the ships in those days (and even more so now, I gather) feared piracy more than bad weather, and did not hug the coast. Our ship took us northward up the Yellow Sea to Tsing-tao, where we stopped briefly, and from there past Wei-hai-wei, still at that time a British Concession and headquarters of our China Fleet. On across the Gulf of Pe-chih-li to Ta-ku, where we waited for the tide before crossing the Ta-ku bar and sailing up the Wang-Pu river to Tientsin, which like Shanghai and Calcutta is a major port on a tidal river, and not directly on the sea.

We must have passed Wei-hai-wei in the dark, because I don't remember anything about it. But I do remember the scenery on the way up river, and the Ta-ku forts, which had been fired on in the days of the 'Old Buddha' Tse Shi, the last Empress of China, and created an international incident. They were to create another one in the future, but that was still a good many years ahead.

Contrasting our voyage up river to Calcutta with our present one up the Wang-Pu, I gave the present one no marks at all. For once again the sky was grey and lowering, and the clouds were spitting a thin drizzle that did nothing for the scenery. If this was China proper, I thought nothing of it. The land appeared to be harsh, flat and treeless, and land, houses and people together a study in grey and beige. I couldn't think how Tacklow could have fallen in love with it so many years ago when he came this way in a Victorian troopship. Bets and I leant side by side on the railings and stared at the view in mutual condemnation.

Tientsin was another Treaty Port in which, as in Shanghai, a variety of different nations had been granted Concessions. It turned out to be far less attractive than Shanghai (and I hadn't thought much of *that*). To begin with it was much more parochial, and there seemed to be none of the speed and excitement about it that had been so noticeable in Shanghai. Tientsin plodded. We were now in June, and it was summer, but even when it stopped raining and we were treated to patches of warm sunlight, the temperature was depressingly low and the central heating in all the houses was much too high.

We shivered outside and sweated indoors, and my memory of those first few days is muddled and chaotic. We met and made laborious conversation to a series of unfamiliar people: aunts, uncles and numerous cousins, none of whom, to my knowledge, we had ever met before. Our first few nights were spent with a Mr Isemonger, whose daughter had been a friend of ours in India. He had been Chief of Police in Peshawar in the days when Tacklow had been head of CID, and they were old friends. When his wife died and his daughter married, he decided to retire in North China – heaven only knows why!

Someone took us out to lunch at the Golf Club, where I was startled to see a large noticeboard in the hall which said: 'Players finding their ball in a coffin may remove it without penalty.' On demanding an explanation for what I took to be a macabre joke in distinctly bad taste, I was told that as a general rule the only uncultivated land in that part of China would be a disused graveyard – particularly if it had a few clumps of trees growing on it. If it were not so, the trees would almost certainly have been cut down for firewood or building material, and the land used for crops or hay. Only when a graveyard fell into disuse, either because of overcrowding or because the descendants of the dead had moved away or their line died out, leaving no one to tend the graves or remember the names of those who lay there, would the land be regarded as waste and left unused.

The Tientsin golf course was a case in point, and since the Chinese do not bury their elaborate wooden coffins deep in the ground, but place them in a shallow trench and cover them with earth on which they plant grass and flowers and seedling trees, centuries of wind and rain would have worn down each grassy hillock into little more than a low mound and rotted the wooden coffins within, exposing the bones of the long-forgotten occupants in a shallow depression that trapped many a golf-ball.

All I remember about Mr Isemonger's house is that it was as depressingly Edwardian-suburban in design as Uncle Ken's had been, that it was much too hot, and that there were several fantastic Japanese goldfish in a large glass bowl in the drawing-room. One of the goldfish was jet-black, and astonishingly like a miniature version of Mr Isemonger's little dog, a very small and equally jet-black Peke. The resemblance between the two was remarkable, and both appeared to be aware of it, for the little dog would get on to a chair from where he could press his nose to the glass, each quite obviously admiring the other. The only other memory I have of those first days in Tientsin is a tune.

Mr Isemonger had a wind-up gramophone and a stock of gramophone records, and the top one of the pile of records was new to us; neither the tune, nor the Astaire–Rogers film that it appeared in, had yet reached India, let alone any of the dance-bands in Shanghai. Bets, left alone in the house one morning, put the record on, and was so fascinated by it that she spent the next hour or so playing and re-playing it. It was still being played, for at least the twentieth time I gather, when the rest of us returned to the house. And Bets continued to play it whenever she had the chance. It was one of Cole Porter's best: the immortal 'Night and Day' which still surfaces frequently to this day; and whenever I hear it – even just the opening bars of it – I am back in Tientsin. Finding Bets so smitten with it, Mr Isemonger presented her with the record, so that the melody followed us to our next port of call, 'Ewo'* – the large and very comfortable house in which Mother's sister Dorothy, 'Aunt Dor', and her husband, Cameron Taylor, lived.

Here Bets and I were left for some days in the care of Aunt Dor. And fortunately for me, since I don't think I could have stood the non-stop 'Beat, beat, beat of the tom-tom', there was not only a gramophone in Aunt Dor's vast drawing-room, but an outsize grand piano plus piles of sheet music of the type that Victorians and Edwardians liked to bully their guests into singing after dinner as an alternative to playing whist or bridge. Among these were the 'Indian Love Lyrics' of one Adela Florence Nicolson, better known as 'Laurence Hope', set to music by someone who rejoiced in the name of Amy Woodford-Finden. I feel pretty sure that there can be few people of my age group who have not, at one time or another, heard some concert-circuit baritone or tenor warbling, 'Pale hands I loved beside the Shalimar.'

Mother having been the first of my 'China-side' grandparents' family

---

* The Chinese name for Jardine Matheson. Uncle 'Cam' (Cameron Taylor) was the representative of J M in Tientsin.

to marry and acquire a family, Bets and I were the oldest of the Bryson grandchildren, the rest of whom were still attending the Tientsin High School at a fairly junior level. (A later alumna of Tientsin High was to be that world-famous prima ballerina, Dame Margot Fonteyn.) Dor's lot – Mary, Ian, Alan and Robin Taylor – left for school after an early breakfast and did not reappear again until tea-time; and, since Uncle Cam spent most of his days in his office in the city, and Aunt Dor, who was addicted to Good Works, spent most of her days dealing with the wants and woes of others, Bets and I often found ourselves alone in the house (with the exception of four or five silent, soft-footed and unobtrusive Chinese servants who ran the place with the utmost efficiency).

I have never been able to play the piano, but Bets could, and did – once I succeeded in weaning her off 'Night and Day', which I did with the aid of Laurence Hope and Amy Woodford-Finden and the fact that we were both bitterly homesick for Kashmir. From then on the 'Beat, beat, beat of the tom-tom' gave way to 'Kingfisher blue, bird of the sunlight, who/Over the silent streams at will doth wander.'

We sang those songs solo or as duets, again and again, and even now if I hear one of them – as I very occasionally do on some Golden Oldie radio programme – it jerks me back into Aunt Dor's drawing-room in Tientsin. Although I have forgotten so many things that I should have remembered, I can still remember nearly all the words of those songs and the fear that was in my mind as I sang them, nagging at me that it might be years and years before I saw Kashmir or Delhi again. Because the reason that Bets and I had been left behind in Tientsin with Aunt Dor was because our parents had gone house-hunting in Peking.

Tacklow, as I have mentioned before, was not a particularly sociable type. He was a kind, quiet man who, while not exactly unsociable, far preferred to stay at home with a pipe and a good book than to go out partying – he left all that sort of thing to Mother, who adored it. But he must have done quite a bit of Making Friends and Influencing People when he was young, for he seemed to have the most unexpected friends in all parts of the world, few of whom he had laid eyes on since his careless youth, but all of whom had kept in touch with him ever since by letter. Now, once again, another friend of his youth turned up trumps.

This one too, like the senior member of the Suez Canal Company who had given us such an entertaining evening at Port Tewfic when we were on our way out to India several years previously,* was, I think, a Frenchman; though I could be wrong about that, because I never met him. But whatever his nationality he was plainly loaded, since he seemed to have houses in several different countries. On learning that Tacklow intended returning to China, he wrote to say that he happened to have a house in Peking that he hadn't made use of for several years and, if Tacklow liked, it was at his disposal for as long as he cared to live there. The house was furnished and in the charge of an efficient and thoroughly reliable resident *K'ai-mên-ti*,† who could be trusted to engage such house servants as would be needed, and Tacklow would be doing the absentee landlord a favour by seeing that the place was lived in again. Or words to that effect . . . *Well* –!

That letter had caught up with Tacklow when we reached Tientsin, so my parents left for Peking as soon as they could to see if this magnificent offer was going to prove an answer to their prayers, or a booby-trap that had to be politely but gratefully declined. What *sort* of house was it? Large, small, 'all-mod-con' or mid-Victorian plumbing? And where situated? Inside or outside the Tartar Wall, or somewhere out in the suburbs, and if so, how far out? Above all, if it had lain empty for a number of years, would it need a lot of expensive repairs before it could be lived in? These and several other questions would have to be answered before Tacklow could reply to that magnificent offer, and if for any reason it had to be turned down, some serious house-hunting would have to begin, which meant that my parents could be absent from Tientsin for some time.

They had intended from the first to buy or rent a house in Peking. But there had been no hurry about moving there until mid-autumn at the earliest, since Peking was intolerably hot during the summer. Moreover, the Bryson clan always spent their summer holidays in Pei-tai-ho, the little town on the shores of the Yellow Sea where Tacklow and Mother had spent their honeymoon in the early years of the century. The Grand-dadski ('the Dadski' for short) had a house on the beach in which, by tradition, his family would foregather in the hot weather, either *en masse* or in relays; they had already rented another one for us, further along the beach. The plan was that after a short stay in Tientsin to meet the family we would go straight to Pei-tai-ho, leaving all our heavy luggage in one

---

* See *The Sun in the Morning*.
† The 'Keeper of the Doors'. Or 'of the Gate', if you prefer.

of Uncle Cam's garages, and that once we were settled in there, Tacklow and Mother would leave on a house-hunting expedition to Peking while one of the Aunts could move in to keep an eye on Bets and me and help us cope with the servants who went with the house and who only spoke Chinese. This programme had now been abruptly altered, and our parents dumped us on Aunt Dor for an unspecified time and left at short notice for Peking.

We had expected them to be away for at least ten days. But in the event they were back in a fraction of that, though I still think of it as being an inordinately long time in which I did nothing but wander around that cold, empty drawing-room singing, to Bets's accompaniment: 'Pale hands, pink tipped like lotus buds that float on those cool waters where we used to dwell.' Oh, beautiful Kashmir! – what wouldn't I give to be back there! All the same, we made several good friends in Tientsin. Among them was Evelyn Young, who drew like a baby angel and who I was sure would one day make a name for herself with her enchanting sketches of Chinese children. Then there was a most attractive American girl called Florise* Chandless, and the two daughters of Colonel Hull, the commanding officer of the Queen's Regiment which was stationed at the time in Tientsin and would later move up to Peking.

Tientsin can't have been an ugly city, but I remember it as such. Red brick and mid-Victorian ugly. And in retrospect (though I know this too cannot be true), the short time that we spent there seems endless and I don't remember seeing anything old or picturesque. All I remember being shown were the few remaining late Victorian buildings that had been designed by the Dadski; the church that Tacklow and Mother had been married in; the platform of the Tientsin railway station where Tacklow had first seen Mother and fallen in love with her on sight, and the house in which she had been living when he proposed. Interesting, naturally, for family reasons, but apart from that we could just as easily have been in Camden Town or Clacton.

Then suddenly, Tacklow and Mother were back. They had not had to go house-hunting because the house they had been offered was, according to Tacklow, perfect; a single-storey house on the Jade Canal, adequately furnished and with a small garden; kept in apple-pie order by the elderly *K'ai-mên-ti* and his wife, who had agreed to choose a staff of servants

* She pronounced it 'Floor-ease'.

ready to receive us when we moved in at the summer's end. Mother confined herself to being reassuring about the plumbing and I visualized a modern European-style house in a row of similar houses.

With that problem settled, we left for Pei-tai-ho by train, and I took my first long look at China's countryside. I found it in general flat and featureless, dotted here and there with walled villages and the occasional clump of trees that denoted a graveyard. Watching the scenery trundle past the windows, I found it hard to believe that most of the land had once been covered with forest – and not *all* that long ago either. For Abbé Huc, one of the Jesuit missionaries who had worked in China, had complained bitterly, back in the early years of the nineteenth century, that nowhere in the world had the cutting down of trees been so devastating – or so stupidly short-sighted. Daniel Vare, writing in 1939, says that even then the last of the old virgin forest at Tung Ling was being cut down, leaving little more than a waste of tree-stumps, and that the whole of North China had been stripped of its trees so that already the sands of the Gobi Desert were beginning to creep inside the Great Wall. This, he pointed out, led inevitably to floods and drought and famine, which in turn led to civil war, revolution and anarchy. 'And all because they have cut down the trees!' I was told that even during my few short years in China the magnificent avenue of rare white pines at the temple of Lung-men-ssu in the Western Hills was chopped down by order of some self-styled 'General' whose private army of vandals were in sore need of fuel for warmth and cooking-fires, and for the construction of shelters during a hard winter.

You could see why they did it, for at several of the station platforms where we stopped there were troop-trains standing in the sidings – open trucks packed with bewildered young soldiers who had almost certainly been farm-lads or shop-assistants until caught by the press-gangs of one or other of the war lords and forced to serve in the ranks of his private army. Some of them were only boys, wearing uniforms that had obviously been intended for grown men. At one station a squad of some twenty or thirty of them, their faces drawn with exhaustion and their ill-fitting uniforms grey with the dust of the unmade roads, had collapsed on to the platform, sitting on the ground with their backs to the fence that surrounded it, their legs stretched out before them. I saw with horror that, although the uniforms looked new, their feet were shoeless and the rags and cardboard and newspaper that they had tied on to them with string had disintegrated into bloodstained fragments, the result, presumably, of days of marching and counter-marching across country as the fortunes of their particular 'General' rose and fell.

Those poor boys! I hadn't really taken in the fact that their country was in turmoil, or what civil war and anarchy were actually like, until I saw those exhausted ranks of young soldiers whose feet had been reduced to bloodstained pulp. The sight of them stays in my memory as an illustration of the cruelty and stupidity of war, and did nothing towards reconciling me to life in China. For it is one thing to read about such happenings, but quite another actually to witness them yourself.

Pei-tai-ho, when we reached it, was a relief. A small town, then little more than a village on the shores of the Gulf of Pe-chih-li, it was set on a sandy plain dotted with wind-blown pines, casuarina scrub and fields of Indian corn and *kao-liang* (sorghum millet) and protected from the sea by a line of Victorian-style villas, white-painted, clapboard houses with wide verandahs, standing on the landward side of a long, sandy beach that curved away to left and right towards distant hills and far-off mountains. At one of these houses we unloaded the Dadski and Aunt Dor and her offspring, before moving further on down the beach to the one that had been hired for us.

I still have the impression that there was nothing more to Pei-tai-ho than these houses, though a photograph of the place from the air shows that behind that sandy track and the casuarina scrub lay a not insignificant little Chinese town.

Our houses all faced out on to a long, sandy shore sloping downwards to the sea's edge, where it formed itself into several small bays, interspersed by outcrops of rock and long sweeping stretches of sand. To our left, looking seaward, the beach rose in a line of low cliffs that became higher to form a headland that was known as Lighthouse Point, on which the British Embassy had a holiday house, or rather, houses. Beyond this promontory, among a series of little bays, lay the Cathedral Rocks, and up on the East Cliffs stood the little cottage which, almost thirty years before, a Miss Winterbottom had lent to Mother and Tacklow for their honeymoon. Beyond that again the shore and the flat lands swept away in a wide bay to meet the mountains that lay along the eastern horizon, and the town of Shan-hai-kwan, where the eastward end of the Great Wall of China ends in the sea.

To the right of our house, apart from a few small caves, the shoreline stretched away westward, flat and featureless, to the foot of the Lotus Hills, pine clad, enchanting, and full of old temples and carved stone stelae erected to the memory of men and women long dead. The most charming of these were enormous tortoises carved in elaborate detail, supporting a tall slab on which characters giving the name and deeds of the departed were cut deep into the weather-worn stone.

The staff who went with the house consisted of a Number One Boy, a cook and an *amah*. They spoke 'Pidgin' – in other words Pidgin English – a fascinating language that had come to be the lingua franca of coastal China and can now be regarded as a language in its own right, since books have been written about it, and poems and songs* written in it. Tacklow and Mother could speak to them in their own tongue, and though neither Bets nor I ever got further with Chinese than a handful of phrases, we could just make out in Pidgin.

Still homesick for Kashmir, and missing Neil† far more than I had thought I would, I hadn't expected much of that first summer in North China. But, looking back on it, I don't remember a single day when the sun did not shine. The sea was almost on our doorstep and we more or less lived in it, bathing for half an hour or so before breakfast and again at intervals during the day. Two of the girls we had made friends with in Tientsin, Evelyn and 'Bobbie' (I don't think I ever heard Bobbie's real Christian name) were on their summer holidays in Pei-tai-ho, and the four of us used to spend long, lazy hours in a casuarina-shaded sandpit, discussing life and speculating about the future.

Evelyn and I were going to be artists (famous ones we hoped), while Bobbie, who was engaged to a young man in the Diplomatic Corps, already had a fairly shrewd idea of what lay ahead of her – as had Bets. Our American friend, Florise, paying a flying visit to Pei-tai-ho, joined our quartet for the duration of her stay. It is a sharp reminder of how greatly the pattern of behaviour has changed since then that Florise, who had been out the previous evening on what she called a 'blind date' (the term was new to us), after describing the events of the evening and speaking enthusiastically about the charms of the said date (a young

* See Leland's *Pidgin English Sing Song*.

† A handsome, high spirited and very endearing young man who had proposed to me at frequent intervals during the last Delhi 'Season'. See *Golden Afternoon*.

Englishman newly arrived in North China), ended up by admitting, regretfully, that she had completely failed to make a hit with him. Since this was something that I could not believe – Florise, as I have said before, being a notable charmer – I demanded to know how she could possibly know that? 'Well, he didn't even *try* to kiss me when we said goodnight,' said Florise indignantly.

Few people now alive can realize how shocked I was by this statement. 'But Florise, he'd only just *met* you!' I protested. 'Surely you don't expect a man to kiss you the very first time he takes you out? Englishmen don't.' 'Americans do!' retorted Florise. 'And so do the French – and the Italians!'

The unsophisticated British were evidently still clinging to a code of morals and behaviour that had died with the Great War and the arrival of the Roaring Twenties. It had never occurred to me that any young man whom I had met for the first time at a dinner party, and later that evening danced with, would attempt to kiss me when we said goodnight, however much I might have been attracted to him – or him to me!

Discussing the matter with Evelyn, Bobbie and Bets, we agreed that this was probably the pattern of the future, because anything that Americans did was sure before long to cross the Atlantic and be copied by Europe. Florise had merely shown us the shape of things to come. But we did not envy her. On the contrary, we felt sorry for her, because she missed all the fun – the thrill of meeting someone you were attracted to, and hoping that he might with luck feel the same about you. Of watching for the signs that he did; of seeing more and more of him, and then wondering if – when – he would kiss you.

'Courting' was, on average, a long-drawn-out affair and as fascinating as dancing a minuet or a pavane. For the 'Colonial' British still lived in a world that was at least a quarter of a century behind the times, and probably more, a world in which a kiss was still a serious thing, almost as binding as a proposal. A kiss still meant 'I love you', and was accepted as such. I suppose you could say that we were among the last generation to be 'courted'; and we wouldn't have changed it for anything. Fancy swapping all that thrill and expectation for a kiss taken and accepted as a matter of course after only an hour or two's acquaintance, and knowing perfectly well that every girl the man had previously fancied, however briefly, had also been kissed by him, and that it didn't mean a thing. I could only be grateful that I had been born when I was, and not into the heyday of the Thoroughly Modern Millies. They may have had more freedom, but we had more fun.

I had not imagined that we would have much fun in Pei-tai-ho, and had resigned myself to making the best of it. But in fact we had a wonderful summer – two wonderful summers, for by now I find that I cannot separate them in my mind, or remember if this or that happened during the first year, or the second. We seem to have done exactly the same things in both years: had one long party, with never a dull moment.

This was largely because as soon as the weather in Peking became uncomfortably hot, the British Ambassador with his daughters and his staff moved down to Pei-tai-ho. In consequence it had become the custom for a British warship of the China Fleet to visit Pei-tai-ho and 'show the flag'. Each ship on arrival would throw a cocktail party on board to which all the summer visitors were invited, and the Ambassador would reciprocate by entertaining the members of the Wardroom, and giving them the use of the Embassy tennis courts and bathing raft. In this way we came to know all the officers of each ship in turn.

Bets played tennis with them on the Embassy courts, and there were picnics to the Lotus Hills, and to Shan-hai-kwan and any number of normally inaccessible little coves, in one of the ships' boats. The only reason I know the order in which the ships came in is because Mother was a compulsive album keeper, and there is a photographic record of both summers. The first ship to pay a courtesy call during that first summer was HMS *Kent*, commanded by a Captain Drew who, together with his junior officers, added greatly to the gaiety of the various nationalities who were holidaying at Pei-tai-ho, while the sight of HMS *Kent* at anchor offshore gave the European contingent a welcome feeling of security.

That security was needed, for ever since 1911, when the Manchu dynasty had fallen and the last of its Emperors, young Pu-yi, had been deposed, all China, in particular the northerly territories, had been subjected to a series of lawless uprisings, instigated, as often as not, by some ambitious landowner who had hitherto owed allegiance to the throne but who now saw himself as the possible ruler of a province. The undisciplined armies raised by these Candidates-for-Power all too frequently degenerated into bandit hordes who ravaged the countryside, looting and burning. Only recently three British citizens, a girl, and two young men who had been out with her for a morning ride in the open country surrounding

31

Ching-wan-tao – one of the popular summer resorts of the northern Treaty Ports – had been kidnapped and held to ransom by a gang of hooligans, who had kept them chained to one another for the best part of a month.

As far as I remember, their fate was still in the balance when we arrived in Pei-tai-ho and, judging from the daily bulletins in every newspaper, at least half the English-speaking world was putting up prayers for their safety. Happily, these were answered, and later the girl, a pretty young thing by the name of 'Tinko' Pawley, wrote her account of the terrifying affair in a book entitled *My Bandit Hosts*.

If the kidnapping of young Tinko Pawley and her friends shed an unpleasant light on one side of the Chinese character, the present that Tacklow gave me on my birthday threw an equally bright light on another. It was a three-quarter-length kimono in dull, heavy-weight Chinese silk of a curious grey-blue colour. It was very plain, except for three Chinese 'good fortune' characters embroidered in pale grey silk: one near the bottom of each sleeve, and one on the back between the shoulder-blades. It fastened with matching grey silk cords and tassels and was lined with peach-coloured silk.

I had seen it hanging up in a little shop in the Bazaar, among a number of garish machine-made and pseudo-Chinese-style garments which, judging from the plethora of spangled dragons, phoenixes, birds and bats that crawled all over them, must have been intended for the tourist market. It stood out among that mess of tinsel and clashing colours like a Quaker girl in a line-up of bedizened cabaret dancers, and I pestered Tacklow into buying it for me. It was only when I had it in my hands that I discovered that every inch of the peach silk lining, even to the lining of those full Chinese sleeves, was hand-embroidered in a slightly paler shade of peach, with a design of birds and butterflies among branches of apple-blossom. No one but the Chinese would have taken the trouble to do that exquisite embroidery where it would never be seen, and only the wearer would know that it was there.

Chapter 4

There were two bathing rafts at Pei-tai-ho, complete with diving boards, one anchored off Lighthouse Point and more or less the property of the Ambassador and his guests, and the other in deep water off the little bay that was almost opposite our bungalow. This was the one that we used every day, and I was charmed to discover that it was the same one that Mother and her family and friends used to swim out to and dive from back in the early years of the century, and that Tacklow had presented them with a diving board.

Oddly enough, the next year, 1933, the *Peking and Tientsin Times* of 27 August printed a 'Thirty Years Ago' column, one paragraph of which read: 'We have seen some fine amateur photographs of the Pei-tai-ho Beach. Some of them showing remarkably graceful diving from the raft by a young lady expert. If all we hear to be true, the gentlemen will have to look to their honours in this respect.' And a month later, someone who had read that column had told on Mother, for another column of the same paper quoted the paragraph, and went on to say: 'This paragraph referred to Miss Daisy Bryson, and by an extraordinary coincidence she chanced to be at Pei-tai-ho, still diving from the raft on possibly the same beach, when this paragraph reappeared. The photograph reproduced on page eight, taken of Lady Kaye (as she is now) diving at Pei-tai-ho Beach this summer, shows that she is as graceful as ever in this exercise.'

As far as I remember, it was during our first summer at Pei-tai-ho that Edda Mussolini and her husband Galeazzo Ciano spent a holiday there. They were not there for long, and we saw very little of Edda. But her handsome husband could be seen daily, displaying his spectacular torso in the shade of a *pang** to an assortment of admiring young women of

* A beach shelter consisting of four poles supporting a square of matting – which was supposed to provide shade for those who needed it, but was in fact a meeting place for friends.

several different nationalities. We did not need to be told that the Count was a famous Casanova, because we had already seen him at work in Shanghai. He attracted women like wasps to jam. There was also a female of that species, the Countess of Carlisle, who matched him in glamour.

She, like the Count Ciano, was one of those glamorous creatures whom a future generation would nickname 'the Beautiful People', and on many a moonlit night you would see her floating down the beach with a rug on one arm and a Lieutenant-Commander on the other. I imagine she must have broken the hearts of at least half of the officers in the China Fleet. But romance, that summer, was not only confined to the celebrity fringe, for my parents were clearly enjoying a second honeymoon, and were charmed to discover how little Pei-tai-ho beach had changed. The bungalow that old Miss Winterbottom had lent them that first time looked exactly the same. So did the rocks that enclosed the little bay below it, where they used to bathe and laze and laugh together, and make plans for the future when the twentieth century was still in its hopeful infancy.

When the tide went out the long stretch of wet sand was still strewn with small, iridescent shells that Tacklow had never forgotten and which he now took to collecting, sorting them each evening into sizes and colours – pearl-pink and yellow and apricot, pale green, turquoise and lavender. I still have some of these shells, for he kept the best of them and had them made into spoons by a Peking silversmith: the smallest size for salt spoons, the next for coffee spoons, the next for teaspoons, and a few of the largest for sugar spoons. When I look at one now, I find it difficult to believe that these fragile things can actually be the same shells that were once, so very long ago, left by a receding tide on the shores of the Gulf of Pe-chih-li in North China, and picked up by darling Tacklow.

Mother spent much of her time sketching, and Bets, who also went in for landscape painting in watercolours, would often go with her. But although I too did a good bit of painting that summer, I hadn't yet become interested in landscape painting or found a style of my own and a medium that suited me. The only stab I had ever made at painting in oils had been over a year before, in Kashmir, when, inspired by the view from our houseboat, I had spent all the money I had made from the sale of some of my illustrations on oil-paints, brushes and turpentine, in order to try my hand.

The result was a very amateurish effort, totally lacking in either style or technique; one look at the finished painting was enough to convince me that oils were not my medium. Yet curiously enough, that amateur daub somehow managed to pin down the exact look and feel of the scene that faced me from the roof of our houseboat on that long-ago spring morning in Kashmir. For that reason I cherish it, and it hangs on the wall of my study, where I can see it as I write, a reminder of how beautiful that now war-torn and devastated valley once was.

After that initial failure I returned to my first love, illustration in watercolour, and painted such subjects as 'Undine', floating up through sun-spangled water, the Kashmiri Love Songs – 'Ashoo at Her Lattice', 'The Song of the Bride', and 'Kingfisher Blue' – together with various nursery rhymes: the lullabies, and the one about the 'King of Spain's daughter'. These sold well at art exhibitions; largely, I think, because the subjects chosen by amateur artists are nearly always landscape or flower-pieces – plus the occasional portrait. Illustrations, particularly nursery ones, were few and far between. So while Mother and Bets went sketching, and Tacklow accompanied them to carry Mother's gear and laze in the shade of the rocks nearby, I stayed behind in the wide, covered verandah that doubled as the sitting-room of our bungalow, and drew Madonnas and mermaids and the Spanish Infanta who, according to the nursery rhyme, 'came to visit me, and all for the sake of my little nut-tree'.

In spite of the fact that both Bets and I would much rather have been in Kashmir, the summer had been a very pleasant one for both of us, and I was beginning to feel more kindly towards the Chinese. I liked the three members of our staff and was captivated by the artistry of their nation. There were still astonishing examples of craftsmanship to be seen in the little shops of even such a small seaside resort as Pei-tai-ho, and one superlative one on the shore.

This last was a man who practised an ancient craft that I had never heard of before – and have never heard of since. He modelled tiny figurines out of a soft clay and carried the tools of his trade around with him in a light wooden frame which included a stool on which he could sit while he worked. Each figure was built on to and around one end of a slip of bamboo, not much more than six inches long and no thicker than a matchstick. He had an enormous repertoire of characters for you to choose from: court ladies with wonderful, elaborate headdresses, Emperors in their state robes, Manchu Bannermen, armed to the teeth, legendary heroes, heroines and villains, and innumerable gods and demons and goddesses.

To watch him at work was to know that you were in the presence of a master craftsman, and that here was the mind of China. The patience and application, the painstaking attention to minute detail, the beauty and the ferocity – the horrific, grimacing faces of the Demons and Guardians of the Gate – hideous monsters who brandished thunderbolts and blood-stained swords.

The tiny masterpieces cost so little. But money was always tight with us, and there were so many things that had to be paid for before I could think of spending even the smallest coin on something I didn't need. But watching was free, and I must have watched the making of scores of those enchanting trifles that summer, in the course of which, inevitably, I could not resist buying a few for myself. The paste of which they were made dried fairly quickly, and when dry had the appearance and feel of being carved from bone or ivory. But they were as fragile as bone china, and did not stand up well to the constant packing and unpacking to which they were subjected as we moved from one house or country to another. I have only the broken remains of one left, and no longer remember what character he represents; a Demon or a Guardian of the Gate? He is a scarlet-faced, scowling and ferocious little man with a white beard that positively curls with fury, and whose minute hand (broken, I fear) clutches an elaborate spear. The other arm is missing. But he retains his magnificent headdress and most of a wide, brightly-striped sash that he wore swathed about his hips.

I still have a clear mental image of that sash being made. The artist, having mixed a small supply of the modelling paste with several different colours, took a pinch of each and, having rolled each one separately into a tiny ball, placed them all into the palm of one hand, kneaded them together and rolled them out flat, as you would roll out a piece of pastry. And there, believe it or not, was a neatly striped piece of red, yellow, emerald green and white dough, exactly the right size to do duty as a sash. Those colours are still as bright as on the day it was made, and each stripe in the tiny sash is no wider than a strand of cotton. But alas, I feel sure that Mao and his murderous Red Guards will between them have put an end for ever to the men who practised that particular and fascinating craft. Certainly no one who had been forced to work as a farm labourer for three years would have been able to model those beautiful little objects, for the hands of the man who fashioned them with such skill and speed on Pei-tai-ho beach were not made for digging and ploughing and pulling up weeds.

In addition to her art, China was to provide me with two of those magic moments that I imagine all of us experience at least once in the course of our lives, and for which I have no explanation. I can only describe them as a brief span of time in which the ordinary suddenly becomes extraordinary, and we know, without a shadow of doubt, that this is something that will be stamped on our memory long after a host of far more important things have been smudged out and forgotten.

The first came one September evening when Bets and I had gone for a walk to Lighthouse Point and, having reached the high ground, sat down on a boulder to admire the view. In those days there were hardly any houses between the British Embassy buildings and the Cathedral Rocks which marked the far end of a long, shallow curve of beach. If there were any, they too were hidden by dips in the ground, and all around us was barren, uncultivated land patched with wind-blown scrub and grass.

To our left, beyond the Cathedral Rocks, the land sloped down and merged with a wide expanse of plain that stretched away to meet the mountains that hemmed it in on the north, and the small garrison town of Shan-hai-kwan where (according to the Chinese) the Great Wall of China begins, or alternatively (according to the Europeans) where it ends. And in contrast to the biscuit-brown country around us, every inch of the plain appeared to be cultivated. Fields and fields of *kao-liang* stretched across it like a pale blue carpet, dotted here and there with the occasional tree or a cluster of brown-tiled Chinese farmhouses. In front of and around us there was nothing but barren ground and the squat stump of the ancient, stone-built lighthouse, and I remember thinking how drab and uninspiring it was, and that I would never want to paint it. As the sun went down behind us, any colour there may have been before drained away and left the whole world looking depressingly dreary . . .

And then suddenly it was as if I was watching one of those transformation scenes that were an obligatory part of the pantomimes of my youth, when Cinderella's kitchen seems to quiver and melt and change before your eyes into the shimmering crystal caves where a host of dwarfs and fairies are busy making those glass slippers. A moment before I would have said that there wasn't a cloud in that Isabella-coloured sky. But as the daylight faded and the sky began to darken to a soft Adam green I realized that the whole expanse of the eastern sky had in fact been full of invisible threads of vapour, some no longer than the palm of my hand. The vanished sun was now catching them, turning them from gold and apricot to every possible shade of pink, until the whole sweep of the sky, and the satin-smooth sea that reflected it, glowed and shimmered like some fabulous fire-opal.

There was at no time any harshness in those colours, and as the hidden sun sank lower and lower and the duck-egg green of the sky darkened to jade and amethyst, it remained a picture in pastel and gold dust. We stayed where we were on the headland, watching while the colours flamed up and faded, and though I had in the past seen more spectacular sunsets and would, I was sure, see more of them in the future, I knew that this one was different. This one was special. One of those things that are 'marked with a white stone'.

The house lights of Shan-hai-kwan at the far end of the bay had begun to flower in the dusk before Bets and I tore ourselves away and made for home. And a few days later, having booked the house for next summer, we left Pei-tai-ho and set off for Peking.

Chapter 5

~※∂∨∂※~

Neither Tacklow nor Mother had told us much about the house in Peking. Only that it was a Chinese-style one, but not to be compared with Aunt Peg and Uncle Alec's lovely house in Shanghai. I can only suppose that, realizing that both their daughters took a poor view of China, they hoped to surprise us. They did.

We broke our journey at Tientsin, and after spending a night there we left for Peking, our train pulling out from the same platform on which, some thirty years previously, Tacklow – until then a confirmed bachelor – had caught sight of a pretty teenager kissing her father goodbye, and fallen in love on the spot.

Once again the countryside was not particularly interesting. The same fields of *kao-liang* and Indian corn, the same shortage of trees. A pagoda, a temple, narrow canals, walled clusters of farmhouses with their distinctive tiled roofs tip-tilted in the Chinese fashion, a sprinkling of fruit trees, willows, almond and walnut trees. And always, somewhere in the picture, a little man in a rush hat ploughing his fields with the aid of a lumbering water-buffalo. This, after my disappointment at finding that neither Shanghai nor Tientsin looked in the least like the China of my romantic imaginings, was distinctly encouraging. For one thing, it looked a lot more like the place Tacklow had tried to describe to me, the country that he had fallen in love with so long ago, even before he had laid eyes on Mother. And for another, it was exactly like one of those fascinating little landscapes, lightly sketched in monochrome on yellowed scrolls of silk by Chinese craftsmen using the minimum of lines to maximum effect. Those landscapes were actually there outside the windows of our railway-carriage, exactly as they appear on the scrolls. Perhaps after all we were not too late to see the fabulous China of history and legend before the West, we, the 'Outer Barbarians', succeeded in destroying it.

Peking was there at last. But oddly enough, I don't remember anything about our first sight of it, except that the station was much like any other station, and that the built-up area around it was as forgettable as the surroundings of most railway stations. Grimy and industrial. Our new Number-One-Boy, a relative of the *K'ai-mên-ti*, as were all the staff, was there to meet us, and in no time at all we found ourselves packed on to rickshaws and whisked off through the mazes of this most ancient of cities, Tacklow's leading and the rear one being brought up by the new Number-One-Boy's.

The first nip of cold weather had already been felt in Peking, and everywhere the trees were turning gold or red as if to match the colours of a city whose massive walls and gate-towers were every shade of red from rose-madder to scarlet, while the glazed roof-tiles throughout the enormous acreage of the Forbidden City glistened with the Imperial Yellow that in China is the prerogative of royalty. Most of the roads we passed along were dusty and full of potholes and, apart from a few reasonably tall European buildings, few of the Chinese houses seemed to be more than a single storey high; most were hidden behind high walls, so that all one could see of them were ridges of those grey or brown tiled roofs with their tip-tilted eaves, with here and there clusters of tree-tops that told of unseen gardens.

Tacklow had told us that our house had no name and was known only as No. 53 Pei-ho-yen. This had instantly made me visualize a solid row of Pont Street houses, all exactly alike, until he added that Pei-ho-yen meant 'the Jade Canal', which sounded much more romantic. I should have learned by now to make allowance for the Chinese love of bestowing wonderfully fanciful titles on almost everything within reach – 'The Black Dragon Pool', 'The Green Cloud Temple', 'The Gate of Quietude in Old Age', 'Hill of a Thousand Flowers', 'Pavilion of Great Happiness', and many, many others.

The Jade Canal, when we reached it, certainly lived up to its name. It was a long, narrow strip of water, crossed at intervals by enchanting humpbacked bridges and bordered on both sides by willow trees that leaned above their own reflections and turned the whole thing into a long, green tunnel. The water too was green, the darkest of jade greens. It also, unfortunately, possessed a good dark-green smell. Which was not surprising, since it turned out to be a main drain.

Fortunately for the success of the day, I had barely taken in this unpleasant fact when our cavalcade stopped at a gate in a long stretch of wall that ran parallel to the canal on one side of the dusty road. The gate was open, and outside it stood the *K'ai-mên-ti* and an assortment of Chinese servants, making welcoming noises. It seemed we had arrived. And suddenly the rest of the day became magic.

For this I shall always be grateful to Tacklow, who had known from the first that both Bets and I took a poor view of this move to China. But apart from our initial and instinctive wails of protest and woe, once we had taken in the fact that both he and Mother had set their hearts on it and were not going to change their minds, we had done our best not to spoil it for Tacklow by continuing to grizzle. Any further hostile criticism was to be kept strictly between the two of us, for we were both aware that he had – at considerable cost to himself – given us ample opportunity to meet and marry that legendary Mr Right whom the majority of girls of our class and generation were brought up to believe was waiting somewhere out in the great blue yonder to meet and marry us. If I had failed to do so, it was no fault of dear Tacklow's, and now that Bets was engaged, it was high time that the poor darling did what *he* wanted for a change.

Yet I should have known that I could not fool Tacklow by pretending to an interest in everything Chinese. He knew what I really felt about it and that was why he had purposely refrained from describing the house on the Jade Canal. With Mother's help he had allowed me to think that it wasn't much of a place: merely a comfortable house within walking distance of the Legation Quarter, and complete with all mod cons. Which had made me visualize something tediously suburban and much like Uncle Ken's house in Shanghai. I couldn't have been more wrong.

No. 53 Pei-ho-yen had once been part of the palace of a Manchu prince, and except for the addition of such things as Western baths and plumbing, it remained a purely Chinese house. The entrance to it was sunk back into the wall, forming a square porch, and on each side of it stood a stone 'lion'. These 'lion dogs' are not lions at all, but 'butterfly hounds' – stylized Pekinese dogs, creatures which have always been greatly prized by the Emperors of China because in spite of their small frame they are credited with having great hearts and great courage. Their effigies, carved in stone and on occasion cast in bronze and mounted on ornate pedestals, stand guard at the gates of every sizeable house in the city. One male and one female. At first sight they seem to be identical, each with its chrysanthemum plume of a tail curled over its back and its luxuriant ruff depicted as hundreds of tight, formalized curls, and each with a front paw holding down a ball. But if you look carefully at the ball you will see that one is just a ball, which represents the world, while the other, under the female's paw, is a rolled-up puppy.

There is a charming story in Peking that tells of two pairs of stone lions who, in the course of their construction in the studio of a sculptor in the city, became great friends, but were parted when, on completion, they were dispatched to houses in different parts of the city. This so upset them that they took to visiting each other by night. In time, though, they grew careless and made so much noise about it that they woke up the residents, who rushed out one night, banging gongs and tin pans, to drive them away. The two male lions fled, but the two females with their puppies leapt up on to the vacant pedestals – where they remain to this day. And that, it is said, is why one house in Peking is guarded by a pair of male lions and the other by two females.

There must be thousands of these pairs of guardian lion dogs in Peking, and they come in all sizes. Some, in the Forbidden City and the Lama Temple for instance, are bronze and immense. Ours were of stone, and small, and our front door, the 'To-and-from-the-World-Gate', was not impressive. But it opened into a courtyard the sides of which were the rooms where the *K'ai-mên-ti* and his family lived, and in the centre of which stood a Spirit Gate. This enchanting feature owes its existence to the fact that Chinese evil spirits – most conveniently – can only walk in a straight line. So just in case the residents, or any person visiting the house, should have been followed in by one or more of these ill-disposed *djinns*, the prudent householder installs a second gate, facing the entrance and permanently locked, which since it does not extend beyond the gateposts each side of it allows anyone coming in to walk round it and into the inner courtyards, but forces any evil spirit one might have picked up in the course of shopping or visiting friends to beat a retreat.

The door of our Spirit Gate was of green lacquer, faded by the years to a pale shade of its original turquoise green. The base and steps were of weather-worn marble, while the uprights and roof ends were lacquer red, and the tiles, like those on the rest of the roofs, were Imperial Yellow, denoting the fact that it had belonged to a member of the royal line. The ends of the wooden beams had once been coloured, and it must have been a flamboyant sight when the house was new. I preferred it the way it was, worn and faded by the centuries and totally charming. The whole courtyard had once been lacquered in red, and in place of glass in the windows there was oiled paper, which let in light but preserved privacy and, unlike glass, is not a conductor of heat or cold, so that it helped keep the rooms behind a lot warmer in winter, and slightly cooler in summer.

The house, like all Chinese houses, consisted of a series of courtyards, the sides of which were rooms that faced into the open courtyards. The first courtyard, where the Spirit Gate stood, was a small one, and led by way of three or four stone steps to a door that gave on to a open corridor surrounded by blank walls, in one of which was the entrance to the first courtyard proper. Here again a small pair of stone lion-dogs stood guard on either side of the top of the steps that led through the ornamental gateway. The rooms on each side of this courtyard were guest-rooms, and the one that faced you as you came through the second gate was a single long room that filled the whole side of the open courtyard.

This was the dining-room, the most beautiful room in the house. The furniture in it was blackwood and black lacquer, and set in one of the two end walls was a huge clock which, we were told, was the oldest clock in China. It was of European manufacture, supposed to have been brought to Peking by a Jesuit priest as a gift to some bygone Emperor from a King of France. It was not a particularly beautiful object, though it was in its way a work of art. Its roman numerals were black, each on a separate small shield of white enamel, inlaid on a larger shield of elaborately worked bronze in a circular frame of black lacquer. The bronze shield was almost certainly a Chinese addition, because it was covered with a beautifully worked design of chrysanthemum flowers in the Chinese manner, and I imagine that the white enamel shields, the hands and all the mechanism were brought into the country separately, and set on the bronze background at a later date. What was astonishing was that it still worked!

The dining-table was a marvel of lacquerwork; so mirror-smooth that at first sight I would have sworn it was just that – a long slab of black looking-glass that was reflecting the few pieces of silver placed on it and the gold and red of the Chinese lanterns hanging above. The walls, both here and in the drawing-room, were covered with ordinary close-woven sacking which provided a marvellous background for the decorative openwork panels of carved blackwood that overlaid it, and complemented the spidery elegance of the lacquerwork chairs, the gorgeous jewel colours of the enormous *cloisonné* vases that stood one at each end of the sideboard, and a thin, worn carpet on which a pair of dragons writhed in fiery gold against a background of faded yellow. Whenever I look at the photographs that Mother took of that fabulous house, I think, 'Oh, if *only* colour photography had been invented by then!'

The rooms surrounding the next courtyard were, on either side, our bedrooms (Bets's and mine to the left, Mother's and Tacklow's to the right), while the far side of the courtyard was taken up by the reception room, where the original occupant had received visitors, and the drawing-room. There was one more courtyard: the garden courtyard, which may once have lived up to its name, but which had been sadly neglected. It consisted of a square of overgrown grass that showed signs of being hastily and very roughly chopped down, probably with a kitchen knife, and a single almond tree, now yellow-leaved in autumn, but a delight in spring. This courtyard was reached by way of a small passage in the extreme corner of the bedroom-and-reception courtyard, and included a gardener's shed and a tiny greenhouse in which our Chinese gardener performed miracles of horticulture, right through the coldest of cold weather and despite the terrible Peking dust-storms and the scorching summers.

The *en suite* master bedroom boasted a large nineteen-twenties European-style double bed, draped in dull gold satin. But the beds in both Bets's bedroom and mine were proper Chinese *kangs*: hollow oblongs, roughly four feet high and five across, built of mud bricks plastered over, and with a small hole in one side through which sticks and live charcoal could be thrust in to make a fire during the winter months. A thick mattress would be laid on top, and this, together with several padded quilts (plus pillows in place of the wooden neck-rests that the original owners would have used), made warm and wonderfully comfortable beds.

The most spectacular room was the reception room, which like the dining-room was panelled and decorated in lacquer. Red lacquer this time, the proper, classic red. It may sound gaudy but was in fact beautiful. Here once again (as throughout the entire house) the windows were covered by a delicate fretwork of carved red lacquer, and against the far wall, directly opposite the french windows by which one entered the Hall of Welcome, was a wonderful lacquer screen, against which stood a magnificent red lacquer throne on which, I presume, the master of the house used to sit in state to receive his guests.

Chinese characters in gold leaf decorated the walls, and about the only thing that wasn't red or gold was the polished wooden floor, on which, when our heavy luggage had been unpacked, we laid Tacklow's tiger-skin, an object that greatly impressed the servants.

At one end of the reception hall, partitioned from the rest by carved and lacquered archways, was a small reading room furnished with a couple of bookcases and a round table and four chairs, also of carved lacquer. And it was here on the wall that Tacklow hung the *Kossu* scroll that he had bought for a modest sum from a corporal who had served in the French contingent of the International Brigade that had marched to the relief of the Europeans besieged in the British Residency in Peking during the grim days of the Boxer Rising.

Having lifted the siege and restored order in the city and the countryside around it, the International Brigade had got down to some serious looting, and there was no doubt that the *Kossu* scroll had been filched from the home of some local mandarin – not, I would have said, a very high-ranking one, for the scroll is not by any means a 'showpiece'.

Kossu, one of the great works of art of China, is a very fine tapestry and in the best examples of the work every single colour that appears on it, however small, is woven into it. But in this scroll, though each of the main pieces is woven, the detail, such as the pattern of the flowers, stars and bats-of-happiness on the dress, are only painted and not woven. Still, it is a very attractive example of Chinese art, and never before had it shown to such advantage as it did here. The lacquerwork provided a perfect setting for it. I knew that in bringing it back to Peking we had brought it back to the city it had been stolen from and I used to wonder sometimes if, by some curious quirk of fate, this could be the same house?

Yet even if our scroll had not returned to the same house from which it had been snatched well over a quarter of a century earlier, it had certainly returned to a place where it was appreciated, for a few weeks after we had settled in, when we were beginning to feel at home, Tacklow, awakening early one morning and remembering that he had left something he needed in the reading room, went in search of it, to discover our entire Chinese staff down on their knees, knocking their foreheads on the floor in the deepest of *kowtows* before the scroll.

Becoming aware of 'the Master's' presence, they shuffled backwards a pace or two, still kneeling, before rising unhurriedly to murmur a polite greeting and back out of the room, leaving the Number-One-Boy, who had ushered them out, apologizing for having disturbed the Master. The Master assured him that he had not been in the least disturbed, and had only come into that room by chance, but he would be interested to know what the servants had been doing. At which the Number-One-Boy looked faintly surprised and replied that they had only been paying their respects to the Old Buddha. Did the Master not *know* that the scroll was a portrait of her, posing in the dress and character of a Goddess?

No: Tacklow had not known; though he later admitted that he ought to have done, for just as the Dragon is the sign of the Emperor, so is the Phoenix that of the Empress. And the lady depicted on the scroll is not only attended by a young acolyte, but also by an admiring phoenix.

The scroll was one of possibly dozens of contemporary *Kossu* portraits of Tzu Hsi, Dowager Empress of China, who in her old age had become known to her admiring subjects by the honorary title of *Lao Fo Yeh*, 'the Old Buddha', and whose extraordinary life story I have already touched on in the first volume of my autobiography. She was the last of the Old Guard, in that she represented a tradition and an Imperial Empire in the same way that Queen Victoria had done. However, I doubt if you could have found a handful of the latter's subjects genuflecting before a picture of her, a quarter of a century after her death.

Chapter 6

More than half a century has scurried past since the morning on which Bets and I set out on foot for our first conducted tour of the streets and *hutungs** of Peking. So I hope I can be forgiven for having only the sketchiest recollections of the two men who did the conducting. All I can remember is that both our escorts were connected with the British Legation, one of them middle-aged and the other young, and both were tall and thin and wore spectacles. But I still have a clear picture of what we saw. And an even clearer one of what we smelt that morning. Perhaps Mao and his Little Red Books managed later to clean up the Tartar City, but in those days the smells were truly horrific and like nothing I had ever come across before. India could come up with some startling odours, as could parts of the Middle East and some of the slums in Naples. But they fade into insignificance in comparison with the stink here. We learned early the exact location of the really fierce ones, and kept a large folded handkerchief, soaked in eau-de-Cologne, handy (or in winter, a fur muff) so that we could bury our noses in them as we approached or passed. The gesture became automatic.

Chinese houses were, in general, spectacularly clean. But their ideas of sanitation remained archaic, and there appeared to be no such thing as main drainage. One merely dug a large pit outside the walls of one's domain and threw everything into that, presumably scooping it out from time to time when the garden – if any – needed a dressing of manure. The network of narrow *hutungs* was the worst, for here the inhabitants merely cut a long communal open drain down the centre of the lane, and let it go at that. The main roads were a good deal more salubrious, being straight and wide and spanned at intervals by graceful wooden *P'ai Lous* – Memorial Arches that, all over China, are erected to the memory of

* Alleyways.

men or women of note, but which in Peking are more likely to be put up because they are decorative. Every *P'ai Lou* had its own name, and one learned to find one's way, or pinpoint a particular shop or district, by asking to be directed to (or if in a rickshaw taken to), let's say, the Tung Tan P'ai Lou – the East Single Arch. Some of the *P'ai Lous* boasted as many as four arches, but I'm afraid all memory of their names has vanished; together with the little – the *very* little – Chinese I managed to acquire in the course of the two years we spent in that country. No one could forget the Tung Tan P'ai Lou, could they? Or the Ing-guo-fu, which means the British Legation.

Peking turned out to be a repeat of the Kashmir experience; my early impressions of both having been deeply disappointing, largely because I saw them for the first time when they were not looking their best. But just as Kashmir had grown on me until I ended up thinking it was the most beautiful place in the world, Peking grew on me – though never to the same extent. Yet now, looking back on those days, I remember the charm of that strange, incredibly ancient city that was in fact several cities, one within the other, each one surrounded by its own massive wall, topped with gate-towers and crammed with temples and palaces, lakes, gardens and pagodas and a rabbit-warren of houses. In the outer, southern one, 'the Chinese city', lay the 'Altar of Heaven' and its attendant temples of Heaven and Rain, while on the north the adjoining Tartar City contained at its centre the walled and moated Forbidden City, further protected by the walls of the surrounding Imperial City. The whole thing reminded me strongly of those intricately carved ivory globes that turn out to be nests of them, one within the other.

On that first exploratory walk, however, I don't remember seeing anything in the way of temples or palaces, only streets and smelly *hutungs*, and the tiled roofs of innumerable houses, few of them more than a single storey high and all of them packed together like anchovies in a tin. The people, as everywhere, wore the dress of their country. I don't remember seeing a single Chinese person wearing European clothes, though I did notice, and deplored, a regrettable tendency among the citizens towards topping the loose, high-collared jacket and pantaloons of China with European headgear – a peaked golfing cap or, more often, a Homburg hat. It seemed a pity.

There was little traffic, and what there was consisted of rickshaws and carts, some of the latter drawn by ponies, but more often than not by coolies. There were hardly any cars, and very few tall buildings. So few, in fact, that when I think of Peking I always see it as an ancient parchment map of a neat, low-lying gold-brown city, blotched with lakes and densely criss-crossed with lines, some thick but most of them spider-web-thin, with the only tall things the graceful bell-towers and gate-towers and the great white Buddhist *Dagoba* which tops the little hill that dominates the Pei-hai – the North Sea, which is the largest of Peking's lakes.

From the top of the massive Tartar Wall you can see the Imperial City spread out like a *Kossu* carpet at your feet; a carpet laid down on a plain that stretches away for some twenty-five miles, to end at the foot of the beautiful, tree-clad Western Hills. In my day the circumference of the 'City of Northern Peace' was said to be just under fifteen English miles, for it still ended at the outer walls, whose gates were closed and barred at night, and though there were farmhouses, temples and a few small villages scattered around it on the plain, the land was mostly under cultivation and if you could have seen Peking from the air – as many people do nowadays – you would understand why I think of it as being a map.

The only tall buildings were the European-style hotels and some of the buildings in the Legation Quarter, itself yet another walled city tucked inside the walls of the Chinese city on the south and the Imperial City on the north. Or that's what it looks like on my exceedingly outdated map. Nowadays, any amount of European-style high-rise concrete horrors have apparently been built at the cost of pulling down and smashing centuries-old temples and historic buildings.

Peking turned out to be a very social place, and my impression of our first months there is a succession of parties. Embassy parties, where dinner was followed by games, the kind where each guest is provided with a pencil and a small block of paper and expected to pair up with one or more of the fellow guests (depending on whether it was a 'team' affair or couples) and answer exhaustingly erudite questions, solve sophisticated puzzles or, on one occasion, identify by smell the contents of rows of little glass cups, each of which contained a wad of cotton-wool soaked in some scented or smelly substance. I wasn't too bad at that one. But oh, how I hated those games!

To begin with, I cannot and never have been able to spell, and I did not relish giving a public demonstration of this failing, or of my deplorably

49

sketchy education. Although my nose was always glued to a book or drawing-board, I seldom if ever read a newspaper; so my knowledge of contemporary history and politics was nil, and my heart used to sink and my brain turn to a lump of cold suet-pudding whenever I saw those dreaded pencils and bits of paper being distributed at some party.

The British, I was thankful to discover, were the only ones addicted to this type of parlour game. I can't remember any of the other nationalities making their guests entertain themselves in this particular fashion. I suppose they made allowances for the fact that any party was likely to contain a certain number of dim 'foreigners'. This too was another cause of mingled embarrassment and regret to me, for in those days the diplomatic language was, and had been for centuries, French. And since every sizeable party in Peking was likely to include anything up to twenty-three different nationalities, everyone spoke French as a matter of course. Everyone, that is, except Mother, Bets and myself.

Bets – who has a good musical ear and was the last to leave school – still retained enough schoolgirl French to be able to scrape along. But I had thankfully forgotten the little – the *very* little – that our useless (English) French mistress had managed to drum into my head. How could I have guessed that before many years had passed I would wind up in Peking of all places, a cosmopolitan city if ever there was one, where everyone spoke at least *some* French?

What with one thing and another, I have seldom felt so uneducated and so plain *stupid* as I did during those first few months in Peking.

Chapter 7

~⚔⚔⚔~

Peking was full of foreigners. Legations to the left of us, legations to the right of us! Consulates galore. Ambassadors by the dozen. All with their attendant staffs and legation guards, wives, families and language-students. Not forgetting businessmen, artists, writers, doctors, dentists and missionaries. There was also a surprising number of expatriates, men and women who had visited Peking on some package tour to the Far East and, having fallen in love with the place, had on reaching home sold their belongings and rushed back to Peking to buy a Chinese house, learn the language, and settle there, if not for life, then at least for part of each year. And all of them threw parties.

I had thought of life in Delhi as a whirl of gaiety, but compared with the social merry-go-round of Peking it was staid. There was always dancing at one or other of the hotels, the Hotel de Pekin, the Wagons-Lit or the Nord, as well as the French Club or the Peking Club. The legations gave balls and dinners and luncheon parties, and there were frequent picnics and expeditions to the Western Hills, and days at the racecourse out at Pa-ma-Chung. And for newcomers such as ourselves, there was sight-seeing. Endless sight-seeing.

For the majority of the foreigners in Peking the city and all its sights had become familiar, and they had come to take it for granted. But to us it was all new and enthralling and I can never be sufficiently grateful to God for allowing me to see it before all the glamour was lost in a tidal wave of war and the West's idea of progress. There had been changes, of course. Many of them. The Legation Quarter was one, a fifth walled city inside the old four-walled city that was Peking. But so much of that old one was still there, and I never ceased to stare at it all, fascinated.

The Chinese babies who played in the streets, flying paper kites or chasing brightly coloured balls, still wore a one-piece blue cotton garment on the lines of the overalls worn by workmen in factories, from which the lower back had been removed, so that although from the front they appeared covered from neck to ankle, from the back a small pinky-beige bottom was on display – thereby eliminating the need for such things as diapers, nappy-pins and potty training.

The vendors of hot food who pushed their barrows through the narrow streets still served their wares to the public in enchanting green crackle-ware bowls with a throwaway pair of bamboo chopsticks on top. In season, the most popular street-food consisted of locusts dipped in a bright red sauce and deep-fried. They looked revolting – like a huge heap of red spiders – and though I was assured that they tasted delicious I could never bring myself to try one.

There were many stores where one could buy tea, but one sold nothing else. It was on the left-hand side of a wide street (I think the Hatamên) in the Tartar City; a small, dark shop whose walls were lined with shelves that held rows and rows of metal, wood and porcelain containers full of different varieties of tea. The proprietor and his assistant looked as though they had stepped off an ancient scroll, and I was told that this was one of the few remaining shops in which an older generation of customers still paid for their purchases in pure silver, shaved off a 'shoe' of that metal and weighed against the tea in a pair of scales. The 'shoes' were so named because heated raw silver was poured into ingots roughly the shape of a woman's shoe – one small enough to fit those terribly deformed feet known as 'golden lilies'.

This appalling fashion, which predated the Manchus by several centuries, was still the norm among the upper classes in my grandmother's day. It consisted of binding the feet of a girl-child with narrow cotton bandages, in order to draw the heel and the great toe as near together as possible. The process began as soon as the child was six years old, the bandages being removed and tighter ones applied approximately every two weeks, and the whole agonizing business taking two or three years. According to my grandmother Isabella Bryson,* three inches was the correct length of the fashionable shoes in which Chinese ladies toddled and limped, supporting themselves on a child's shoulder or a strong staff. She added that the question that guests at a Chinese wedding asked about the bride was not 'Is she good, clever or beautiful?' but 'What is the size of her foot?'

* *Child Life in Chinese Homes* by Mrs Bryson. Isabella gives a detailed description and two illustrations of this peculiar and appallingly painful fashion.

Apparently there were still old ladies who tottered about on 'golden lily' feet, though very few young ones, for the fashion had been frowned upon by the Old Empress, who early on in her reign had issued an edict forbidding any small-footed woman to enter the Imperial Palace. Yet one could still, if one wished, buy a pair of second-hand 'golden lily' shoes. These tiny shoes were made of satin, covered with silk and most beautifully embroidered with birds, bats and flowers and graceful abstract dragons, and were tied on with ribbons.

There were a great many relics and customs belonging to an Imperial past still to be found in Peking. The Jade Market, for instance, which was open on only one day of every month. On another day, for only two hours in the early morning and held in one of the small side courtyards of the Imperial City, there was a sale of Tribute silk. If you arrived too late the door would be shut, and for nothing or nobody would it be opened. And if you had not allowed yourself enough time in which to decide on a particular purchase you would be arbitrarily hustled out in mid-transaction.

I only went once to the Jade Market. Tacklow took me, just to see it. It was well worth seeing, but of course we could not possibly afford the jade on offer. This was bought by the real connoisseurs and collectors. 'Jewel-jade', the bright and intensely green stones, fetched the highest prices. In the end, having saved up for at least a year, Tacklow bought a pair of drop earrings in a second-grade jade and a necklace of mauve jade for Mother. The mauve jade is rare, though not to be compared with the true jewel-jade. But I didn't think much of it. It was a pale greyish mauve, flecked with small splashes of brown.

The Tribute silk was more my cup of tea, and Bets and I attended those sales as often as we could, even if we were penniless, because it was so well worth looking at.

Many of the Provinces used to pay part of the Imperial Tribute in kind rather than in cash, and a large part of this tribute was paid in silk – handwoven silk that was used for the robes of the Emperor and his Empresses, his concubines and various members of the court. The Empire had fallen in the autumn of 1911, and China had been declared a Republic. But though ever since then successive governments had looted the treasures and the tribute that had been collected by the occupants of the Dragon Throne, there were still enough left to be sold off in the monthly sales. Among them the Tribute silk . . .

This fabulous material was being sold at a price that even we could have afforded – if it hadn't been for a maddening, unexplained and typically Chinese rule that laid down that the silk could only be sold by the bolt, or as an already cut piece, never by the yard. If you wanted to buy, you must take whatever remained of the bolt. Bets was lucky, for having lost her heart to some heavy, cash-patterned satin, it turned out to be a piece that had been intended for a wide-sleeved, floor-length coat. The traditional 'cash-pattern' that had been woven into it – a decorative circle roughly the size of a soup plate – was placed so as to ensure that the pattern would match when the pieces were sewn together. I think Bets got it for the equivalent of two pounds.

I was not so fortunate, for anything I yearned for invariably turned out to be part of a sixty-yard bolt at the very least, and I still remember one such bolt of heavy, dull-surfaced very pale blue silk, decorated with a cash-pattern in glinting silver. It was fabulous stuff, but its length put it way out of my reach. Mother struck lucky with a small length of plum-coloured satin, shadow-patterned with wisteria, which she had made into a short coat and wore until it fell to pieces.

For those who had the money, Peking was still a Tom-Tiddler's-Ground of treasures that dated back to its Imperial past. But we, worse luck, were not among them. We had to count every cent. The trouble was that I yearned to buy almost everything I saw, and began by buying beautiful junk whenever I could. When at last I got my eye in, and I began to appreciate the truly good things as opposed to the junk, I had spent my little all. So I ended up buying nothing more, something I now regret because compared with what one can buy these days, even the junkiest Peking-junk was an enchanting piece of art. I am sorry that I didn't settle for second-best while I had the chance!

Even China's third- or fourth-best could be charming, and all three of us ended up acquiring several exquisite mementoes of her Imperial days, almost by accident. The coat sleeves of the three-piece pyjama-style outfits that we ordered from a Peking tailor were finished off with beautifully embroidered satin sleeve-bands, nearly all of which included the famous 'Peking stitch' which, I had been told, was becoming (some said it already had become) a lost art. When I commented on this, and congratulated the tailor on his skill, he shook his head regretfully and disclaimed all responsibility. He could not, he said, lay claim to such workmanship, or spare the time in which to do it. It was cheaper to buy the sleeve-bands, of which there were still very many for sale. He himself had laid in a large store of them, and he suggested that if we liked we could choose our own. Which we did – from a whole pile of them! He must have had hundreds of them, and when we asked him where they came from, he told us that they were the work of the Emperor's concubines.

All those poor, pretty creatures – most of whom would never attract the Emperor's attention – numbered embroidery among the lady-like skills they had been so painstakingly taught, using that skill to fill their endless, idle hours in producing exquisite sleeve-bands for their own and the court ladies' robes!

Looking back on the China years, I see Peking in a series of disconnected pictures. One is of stopping by the roadside to watch a Chinese funeral or a wedding procession go past. These were such every-day sights to the citizens that they hardly turned their heads to see one pass. But it was one that I never tired of, even though in a city like Peking there were so many of them. Presumably the riches and the social status of the family had a lot to do with the size of these processions. But even quite humble ones were celebrated in a colourful manner, and all appeared to be joyful occasions, since to display grief at the death of an adult is to suggest that the dead have not 'filled the years of their life wisely'.

It is (or was) customary for those who could afford it to have the coffin stored in the nearest temple until the arrival of whatever date the priests declared to be the most auspicious for its burial. I gathered that if the corpse were that of some really rich person the auspicious date could often be months if not years ahead, because temples charged a fee for storing the coffins. One result of this (besides enriching the priests, of course) was that by the time the day of burial arrived the family's grief would have had time to subside, and the only sign of mourning would be the white clothing worn by the chief mourners – white being the East's sign of mourning and red the colour of rejoicing.

The coffin-bearers, as well as those who followed behind, some carrying a portrait of the deceased in an open palanquin and others who played on drums and flutes or threw up handfuls of paper money cut from sheets of gold and silver paper, wore green tunics and trousers, the tunics emblazoned on the back and breast with a single scarlet cash-pattern.

The weddings looked much the same, except that the bearers of the bride's palanquin and all the rest of the 'hired help' wore red and gold in place of green and scarlet, and carried decorative branches of paper flowers and similar gaudy ornaments – and that, what with drums, firecrackers and flutes, the procession was twice as noisy. I had always enjoyed watching Indian wedding processions go by in the Month of Marriages in India. But those were a jumble of different hues and a glitter of tinsel, and lacked the organized use of colour that China stage-managed so effectively.

Having begun by thinking the country and its people were depressingly drab, and Peking a maze of slums, a closer acquaintance with that city, and in particular my first sight of the Lama Temple on a brilliant autumn day, made me hunt out my pencils and sketchbooks and start painting again. As for Mother, she went wild about it, and a paintbrush was seldom out of her hand.

Various artistically minded members of the city's expatriate community had got together to form an art school, and Mother, Bets and I wasted no time in joining it. The only thing I remember about it was that although there was no difficulty in finding a model to sit for the life class in costume, no local woman, not even the poorest Chinese vagrant, could be persuaded to pose in the nude. The Japanese, however, were not so prudish, and we eventually acquired several charming young models who took turns in posing for the life class, demonstrating, in doing so, why the average Western woman cannot get away with wearing a kimono and obi, while almost any Japanese looks enchanting in them.

It is all a matter of legs and bosom. All our little models had near-perfect Botticelli-Venus figures as far as their neat little bottoms. But all of them had short legs which showed up when they were standing or lying, but were not noticeable when they were sitting down. The bulky obi sits beautifully on those small, perfect breasts, while the straight line of the folded kimono, falling from the lower edge of the obi to the ankle, gives the small elegant figures – and the stout ones too! – an illusion of height.

Our time in the art class produced an unexpected bonus in the form of a request from the Peking Institute of Fine Arts that Mother, Bets and I should join forces and give an exhibition of our paintings at their gallery. So we did, with great success. The *Peking Chronicle* gave us a terrific write-up, and the exhibition was a near sell-out – largely due to a second column in the *Chronicle* which began: 'The public is reminded that this is the last day in which the pictures of Lady Kaye and her two daughters may be seen. The Gallery of the Institute of Fine Arts has been filled with visitors the entire week.' It had too. We did very well out of it. And so did the Institute. I still have a letter from them that Mother pasted into her current photograph album, along with cuttings from the *Chronicle*. The letter is headed by the name and address of the Institute printed in English and Chinese and is signed by a Lilian Wang, who was either the 'Hon. Sec.' or the President of the Committee – I don't remember which. It ends: 'Really you had the greatest success of any exhibition I have ever staged, and FACE is what the Institute has gotten!'

I was charmed to find that our efforts had paid off so well, for we could certainly do with the money, and it was even more gratifying to hear that the Institute had acquired 'face' on our account, since we had already discovered that 'face' is one of the most important things in China. To 'lose face' is about the worst thing that can happen to a member of the Celestial Kingdom, while to gain it is, for all of them, 'a consummation devoutly to be wished'. We lost two sets of excellent house-servants in rapid succession entirely on account of this invaluable commodity.

The first was a result of Mother's first dinner party, which she gave early that winter. It was a rather formal one, consisting mostly of people from the legations, and one old friend of Tacklow's, the Swedish explorer Sven Hedin.

The party was, as far as I can remember, a great success, and the food was wonderful – Chinese cooks being among the best in the world. Everything, in fact, went like clockwork until the moment when (the entire party being safely back in the drawing-room) the Number-One-Boy brought in the coffee tray and Mother poured out the first cup . . . only to discover that the coffee-pot contained something that looked like slightly dirty water. Mother, considerably taken aback, directed one anguished glance at the Number-One-Boy, but received no help there. His assistant, Number-Two, merely looked interested. Mother lifted an eloquent eyebrow and flicked a dismissive finger, and the inscrutable one, translating this correctly, whisked the tray, himself and Number-Two out of the room with considerable speed.

If anyone noticed this brief episode, they didn't show it. And since the last of the guests did not leave until well after midnight (always the sign of a successful party), the subject of the coffee that wasn't did not come up until the following morning, when Mother asked the Number-One-Boy for an explanation. The Number-One-Boy offered the most profuse apologies. It was all most regrettable, and there were not enough words in the language to express the shame and sorrow that he and the cook, and in fact the entire staff, had felt at bringing such shame upon the *Tai-tai*;* and in front of such important guests. He and the staff were entirely responsible, and no *shadow* of blame rested on the *Tai-tai*. 'I know that,' agreed Mother impatiently, 'but how did it happen?' Well, it was this way, explained the Number-One-Boy . . .

Only when the time came for sending in the coffee tray was it discovered that there wasn't any coffee. The only coffee in the place was a cupful or so left over from breakfast, so it was decided to use that, by the simple method of filling up the unemptied coffee pot with boiling water, and hoping that it would pass muster. Sadly, it had not . . .

Mother said that she understood their dilemma, but in that case it would have been better to skip the coffee. Such a thing must never happen again. The Number-One-Boy repeated his apologies, and that, one would have thought, was that. But no sooner was breakfast eaten and cleared away the next morning than the entire staff, overcoated and carrying its collective luggage, lined up in the courtyard and, having once again expressed its collective sorrow, announced that it was leaving.

Tacklow, hastily summoned to deal with the crisis, inquired what the trouble was, and Number-One, speaking for all of them, explained that since they had caused the *Tai-tai* to lose so much face on the previous night in the presence of her foreign guests, their own loss of face was so great that they could no longer work for her, and since they were all to some degree related, they all bore a share of the disgrace. When Mother tried to talk them out of it, saying that the episode of the coffee, though unfortunate, was not all that bad and she didn't mind losing face, the Number-One-Boy was plainly horrified, and replied tartly that she *should* mind! Nothing persuaded them, and the entire lot swept out, no doubt feeling that they were well out of working for someone so deficient in proper feeling.

The next Loss-of-Face-Disaster arose from an even slighter cause. We were expecting a visitor who would, on his arrival in a few days' time, be occupying the guest room in the second courtyard, and orders had been given for everything to be ready for him, the bedding aired and the room swept and garnished. This had been done, and a day or two before his arrival Tacklow, thinking that his friend would probably like a bit of light reading matter, collected a few books and a magazine or two and took

* Mistress, Lady of the House.

58

them round to put on the guest-room writing desk. Unfortunately, he had chosen the wrong time of day for his mission; it was the hour of the siesta, when all who are at liberty to do so treat themselves to a nap. And there, treating himself to one – comfortably disposed and snoring gently on the guest-room bed – was the new (or newish) Number-One-Boy.

Tacklow always swore that he had recognized the danger immediately and had done his best to retreat before the sleeper awoke. However, it was not to be, for, trying to tiptoe out backwards, he tripped on the edge of the carpet and dropped one of the books. Well, I don't have to tell you what happened then. Within an hour our entire staff were lined up in their going-away clothes and explaining, through a second Number-One-Boy, why the squad could no longer remain in a house in which their senior member had lost practically his entire allowance of face. And that since they were all related (which this time I didn't believe for a minute – I think it was team spirit), they must all leave. And leave they did.

It was no good Mother being cross with her 'China-side' relations and muttering darkly that 'They might have *warned* me!' No amount of warnings could have prevented either of those débâcles. It was just China.

Mother got no sympathy from her family, all of whom, I imagine, had stubbed their toes on this type of situation time without number. But it has to be said that apart from such quirks, the servants were to be valued above rubies, and the life of a foreigner who possessed a well-trained and industrious *amah*, a competent Number-One-Boy and a really good cook could truthfully be likened to a bed of roses.

Chapter 8

~ﾈﾒﾒﾎﾈﾒ~

Winter crept up on us almost without warning. One day Peking was ablaze with the red and yellow and gold of autumn, and the next it was misty with the smoke of the countless bonfires of fallen leaves that flamed or smouldered throughout the walled cities, and there was ice on every patch and puddle of water in Peking, so that one had to be careful not to slip and fall when out walking.

But though the leaves and the chrysanthemums had gone, the colours were still there in the Imperial yellow of the roof-tiles, the blood-red of the walls and the scarlet and blue and green of the *P'ai Lous*. And now the thin silk robes and small, button-topped caps of the old gentlemen who used to come out each evening to give their pet singing-birds an airing – each little bird tethered to its owner by a long length of the finest silk thread, which enabled it to fly around as though it were free, and be wound in again like a hooked fish on a line – were exchanged for long padded and quilted coats and (if the cold was particularly intense) fur-lined caps with ear pieces that tied under the chin. Every child became a small rotund object, wrapped in a well-worn padded coat and quilted bootees, while the beggars, many of them White Russians who could not even afford that much cover, wrapped themselves in tattered newspapers under their rags, and smothered their poor, blue-and-red chilblained feet in more of the same, kept on by bits of string.

Then one night the real winter, the 'Great Snow', fell silently upon the city, and we woke to a glittering world in which every stick and stone was frilled with frost, and our Jade Canal frozen solid: a long sheet of ice bordered on both sides by the silver lace of the leafless willows that overhung it. We learned then what a winter in North China is like. The Pei-hai had turned itself overnight into an immense skating rink, and it looked as though all Peking had taken the day off to skate on the canals and lakes of the Forbidden City. 'Make the most of it,' said the old China-hands. 'You won't be able to do this for long!'

I thought they meant that the icy spell would soon end in a thaw – we had already heard that the sea had frozen for three miles out from Chin-wang-tao. But it was not so. A day or two later the sky turned a dull yellowish-grey at midday, and the wind began to whine viciously through the delicate carvings and along the verandahs of the painted pavilions, pagodas and palaces, as one of Peking's infamous dust-storms swept through the city.

Rajputana had accustomed me to dust-storms. But this was not dust as I knew it. This was the sand of the great Gobi Desert, which bit and stung as it filled the air with tiny sharp-edged particles that laid a thin, gritty blanket over every surface in the city, including, of course, the ice. There were no more skaters to be seen on the Pei-hai or the canals, and although there must have been periods when the grit sank a little way into the ice so that the surface was temporarily smooth again, they never lasted long, for the wind seemed always to blow in from the Gobi, and the dust-storms were many.

Not that it worried the foreign population much, for the members of the Peking Club had learned long ago how to deal with this, and no sooner had 'Come Winter' set in than the entire space taken up during the greater part of the year by tennis courts was flooded, and protected from the winds by a vast canvas enclosure so closely fitted that only the occasional draught managed to creep in. The result was an admirable rink. But oh, was it cold! It might have been a giant freezer, and about twenty minutes was the longest I ever lasted on it. By the end of that my feet were like solid blocks of ice, and the bitter temperature outside felt almost warm by contrast – though that must have been imagination, for there were days when even the canvas was not proof against the worst of the dust-storms, and the rink would be unusable for a day or two while the surface melted just enough to let the dust sink before it froze again.

Later during that same winter, while driving along the canal road to Pa-Ta-Ch'u to watch a point-to-point, we passed a part of the canal where gangs of coolies were cutting out the ice in large chunks, which they wrapped in coarse sacking before carrying it up to the road and stacking it into a number of carts that were waiting for them. We stopped for a moment or two to watch, and I asked our driver, a friend of Tacklow's who was something to do with the British Embassy, what they were doing that for. He replied casually that the ice they were collecting would be stored in deep pits to be used for cooling all forms of cold food and drinks in the summer. And when I exclaimed in horror that all the drains of the city ran into the canal, he laughed and admitted that was so, adding cheerfully that what made it worse was the fact that the high ground overlooking the place where they were cutting the ice happened to be the Criminals' Graveyard, which drained into that part of the canal. *Ugh!* I may say that I never touched any iced fruit or drink during the rest of the time that I was in North China.

The point-to-points across the open country and the racecourse at Pa-Ta-Ch'u were a popular form of amusement throughout the winter, and despite the fact that anything to do with horses bores me rigid, I would always accept an invitation to attend them, merely because '*tout* Peking' turned out for them: the foreign contingent to participate or watch, and the indigenous to bet. Lacking the courage to admit to my unfashionable dislike, I would roll myself up like a sausage in winter woollies and spend hours out in the freezing (and totally uninteresting) countryside – clutching a muff. My nose and toes blue with cold, my teeth gritted together to prevent them from chattering, I pretended an interest in watching relays of tough little ponies from Outer Mongolia scuttling over the banks and ditches and artificial jumps with what seemed to me hulking, oversized riders on their backs. Looking back on those hours of self-inflicted purgatory, I can't think how I can have been so wimpish. But since the winter point-to-points were as much a part of expatriate life in Peking as the dust-storms, they deserve a mention. Especially as I wrote them down, most unjustly, as another black mark against life in China.

The plus marks were the art classes and some of the more exotic parties. There was the one given by a rich and flamboyant character who had fallen in love with Peking on a visit to China, and had bought himself a beautiful Chinese house. I remember the rooms in some detail because I thought they were simply wonderful. The walls of one of them had been papered with the large, square sheets of gold or silver paper that one could buy in Peking. The paper used here was dull gold and the thin lines formed by gold edge-to-edge squares made a lovely pattern on the walls and a wonderful background to the carvings and other Chinese *objets d'art* that stood against them.

Another room had a pair of oval-topped niches in the wall, one each side of the door as far as I can remember. And in each niche stood a carved and gold-lacquered wooden vase bearing something that looked very like the stylized flower and leaves of a full-blown artichoke, such as one often sees in Chinese temples decorating the altar tables where the incense bowls and offerings stand before Kwan-yin, the Goddess of Mercy, and her celestial attendants. The vases stood on circular stands that turned out to be a pair of ordinary wooden kitchen sieves covered on the upper or mesh side with oiled paper, and each hiding an electric light bulb which, when switched on, lit the vases from below and gave them the enchanting effect of being made of Lalique glass.

I hadn't seen anything prettier in years, and from then on I hunted through the junk shops of Peking, hoping against hope to find another pair. But though I saw plenty of them in the temples, I came across none that were for sale; until at long last, grubbing around in a shop full of assorted rubbish in one of the villages near a temple in the Western Hills, Mother came across a rather battered specimen, and bought it for me. I still have it, though I can't think how it managed to survive. Sadly, in its travels, it has lost at least two of its branches of leaves, and though I meant, for years, to give it a sieve to stand on, so that I could light it from below and see if it would look like Lalique glass for me, I never did.

I can only remember attending one party in that fabulous house, and since my memory for names has always been hopelessly bad, I am only guessing when I say that I think our host was Harold Acton. But the high spot of the evening's entertainment was definitely memorable. The guests, about twenty in all, were seated in a ring against the drawing-room walls, some on chairs and sofas and the remainder on the floor, and all the lights were turned out except for a dim one that enabled the host to turn on a gramophone record of 'L'Après-midi d'un Faune'. As soon as the music started a single spotlight was switched on, to disclose, in the empty centre of the room, a young man curled up pretending to be sound asleep and (apart from a few blotches of brown paint here and there) apparently starkers.

We had barely taken in the fact that he appeared to have no clothes on when at the bidding of the music he began to wake up and we saw that the lower third of him, that is from his buttocks downwards, was covered by a furry and extremely skimpy pair of tights, and that we were

in for an imitation of Nijinsky dancing the young satyr in 'L'Après-midi'
. . . I don't know what anyone who had seen Nijinsky dance the faun
would have felt about that earnest young man writhing about in the
almost-nude to the strains of Stravinsky played on a gramophone. But
the whole performance struck me as hysterically funny, and I nearly burst
a lung trying not to laugh.

As someone coming from India, where holy places and different religious
beliefs yearly give rise to riots, bloodshed and general uproar in one part
or another of that priest-ridden country, the Chinese attitude towards the
gods struck me as astonishing – and admirable. Temples abounded; it
would have been hard to throw a brick in any direction without hitting
one. And they all seemed to be well attended by devout believers. There
were as many gods and as many festivals here as there were in India –
and as many priests: but those one came across seemed a remarkably
gentle and tolerant lot, and I was fascinated by the fact that any foreigner
who had the means to do so could rent one of the temples as a week-end
cottage. Or a full-time one if he wished. The larger and more important
temples in the Hsi Shan – the Western Hills that fringe the amphitheatre
of mountains which encircle Peking to the north and west – are really
monasteries, and temples such as T'an-chê-ssu and Chieh-t'ai-ssu (whose
kindly and much respected Abbot was well known to the foreign contingent in Peking) kept rooms that were at the disposal of any visitors
wishing to stay overnight, but could not be reserved for a season as the
smaller and less important ones were.

The first time I ever spent a night in one of the latter was when we
were invited to spend the weekend with Colonel and Mrs Hull and their
two daughters. The Hulls had rented a small temple out on the plain,
and nearer to the city than to the hills. And since the temple was only a
small one and accommodation was strictly limited, Bets and I were asked
if we would mind sharing the girls' bedroom. This, I was fascinated to
discover, turned out to be the 'Goddery' itself. And here once again the
goddess was dear Kwan-yin, the Mother-figure that all religions seem to
have revered since the beginning of Time, the Goddess of Mercy, of
whom it is said that 'there is no sweeter story told' than that having
reached the gates of Paradise, she turned back – because she heard a baby
crying.

Carved from wood and lacquered in gold, she sat enthroned, flanked by her attendants and backed by a panelled and lacquered screen that ran the length of the room, as did the altar in front of her, a long narrow table bearing the incense bowls and vases of temple flowers, also carved from wood and lacquered in gold.

The windows were criss-crossed with thin red lacquer in geometrical designs, as in all Chinese buildings, and in place of glass there was the usual oiled paper. Our four beds were set up in a row facing the row of Heavenly Ones, and there was a moon that night: a full moon that shone from a frosty, cloudless and, in those days, unpolluted sky so brightly that, as on the lakes of Kashmir, one could have read a newspaper by its light.

I'm not sure what woke me, the moonlight or a sound. Or both. I woke up suddenly, and there, moving noiselessly in front of the gods, was a white-robed figure. Talk about your heart jumping into your throat –! Mine almost jumped out of my mouth, and for a crazy moment I was sure that this time I really *was* seeing a ghost instead of just hearing one.* The ghost, perhaps, of some devout Chinese who had taken exception to the Goddery being used as a spare bedroom by foreign devils. Well, it wasn't of course. It was one of the Hull girls who had woken with a bad toothache and, slipping out of bed in her nightie, had tiptoed out in search of her mother who would know what to do about it. She had put about ten years on my life in the process.

Some time during the early weeks of the winter I had acquired what my grandparents would have termed a '*beau*' and the twentieth century had taken to calling a 'boyfriend'. John was a language student attached to the British Legation, and in his company and that of his fellow students, among whom we made many friends, Bets and I attended a seemingly endless round of Peking parties, went shopping, explored the Forbidden City and were taken on numerous expeditions to the Summer Palace, the Jade Fountain Pagoda and the Black Dragon Pool. We spent hours wandering around the Temple and the Altar of Heaven, and the little, blue-tiled temple that was then known as the Temple of Rain, but in the modern tourist guidebooks is called the Temple of Agriculture, which may sound more brisk and forward-looking, but is not nearly so romantic.

One paid a small fee to enter those parts of the Forbidden City which

* See Chapter 11 of *The Sun in the Morning*.

were open to the public, and though the sum was a very modest one I was always surprised to find how few people took advantage of it. Judging from occasional press photographs, that is no longer true and you can hardly move for the crowds of comrades and conducted tourists who swarm through the city in their thousands. But it was not so in the early years of the thirties, and one of the charms of the Forbidden City was that I often felt that there was no one there except myself and the ghosts of a tremendous past. Certainly no one ever bothered us as we strolled through the vast deserted rooms with their acres of dusty floors and locked cabinets which presumably contained the treasures of the great days that were gone. Those that were still on display were inadequately guarded, and I remember walking along a narrow, only partly roofed passageway between two halls, and coming across a fabulous oval block of jade that had been hollowed out to form something that could have been a baby's bath-tub. The outer sides of this were elaborately and most beautifully carved into a panorama of woods and trees and winding paths, temples and pagodas, barns and houses, all peopled by groups of little figures – village folk hoeing in their fields or herding their animals, and rich folk jogging past on horseback, escorting their women who were carried in palanquins . . .

The whole staggering work of art was standing on a brick plinth which brought it up to just below eye-level, and it was protected – if you could call it that – by a rusty piece of chicken-wire that covered the whole. Inside this fantastic tub, along with an accumulation of dust and dead flies and the odd sparrow's feather, there was a somewhat grubby visiting card, on which someone had scribbled in Chinese, English and French, 'Empress's Jade Flower-bowl'.

Mother used to sketch a lot in the Forbidden City; it was one of the few places where she could sit down on her sketching stool, put up her easel and get down to it without immediately attracting a horde of children and passers-by who would crowd around, breathe down the back of her neck and ask endless questions. It was one of the advantages of that entrance fee. Unfortunately, I have only one sketch left out of all the many she painted in the Pei-hai, and that is unfinished.

I liked going sight-seeing with Tacklow best, because he had actually seen the Forbidden City when there was still an Emperor of China and a Dowager Empress, the Old Buddha herself, living there, surrounded and waited upon by innumerable courtiers and concubines, eunuchs and servants. And just as he had done when I was a small girl in Delhi, and he had made the history of its Seven Cities and its great and violent past come alive for me as we drove back from Okhla by moonlight from picnics among the ruins, so now did his tales of the rise and fall of the Manchus and the fantastic and often gruesome things that had happened within the walls of the Forbidden City, during his own lifetime, people for me the empty halls and gardens and palaces with the throngs of gorgeously dressed aristocrats and their servants, hangers-on and hordes of scheming eunuchs who had once lived and died here.

There were endless tales and legends that I would never have heard if Tacklow had not told me them. One was the story of the Chung Lou, the Bell Tower, built some time in the thirteenth century. Another was the legend of the Lonely Pagoda. There were so many pagodas in and around Peking and scattered among the Western Hills that I don't remember now which one the Lonely Pagoda was. Nor do I remember which of the many temples was the one that told fortunes, except that it was in one of the maze of *hutungs* in the Tartar City, not far from the Temple of the Polar Star, and that one of the language students took me there, presumably John.

The Temple was small and dark and full of smoke and the scent of joss-sticks, and the 'fortunes' were engraved on long slips of bamboo stacked in a large bronze jar on the altar in front of the gold-lacquered gods. A second bronze jar stood at the opposite end of the altar, and between the two was a large oblong bowl, also bronze, full of the ashes of innumerable joss-sticks. There were also bowls of temple flowers, lotus buds and flowers, seed pods and leaves, each on its own long stalk and all of them exquisitely carved out of wood and lacquered in gold.

The left-hand bowl was full of joss-sticks, and I was told to take one and, having lit it, to add it to the small forest of smoking sticks of incense that worshippers had stuck into the bowl full of ashes; then to draw out one of the slivers of bamboo at random and hand it to the priest, who would read the characters engraved on it. I did so, and the old man peered at it incuriously and then wagged his head and smiled widely, as did every other Chinese in the room – several of the women reaching out to touch me, as though some of my good luck would rub off on them. For it seemed that I had drawn the equivalent of a winning lottery ticket. According to my fortune-stick, I was to have *seven sons*! The women looked at me enviously and the men made approving noises, and having tipped the priest we left on a wave of congratulations and good will . . . Far from having seven sons, I finished up with two daughters.

There is so much that I remember about our time in Peking: so many stories. So many fascinating festivals – quite as many as in India, if not more – festivals like the 'Feast of Lanterns', and the one dedicated to the Kitchen God. Then there is the sweet, unearthly sound that is part of life in China, and that is caused by the charming habit of fastening little bamboo flutes under the wings of their pigeons which, when the birds take flight, fill the air with strange airy music. An *embarras de richesses* of gracious, centuries-old temples, gateways and palaces makes it impossible to choose one rather than another, though I suppose if I had to, I would choose the Lama Temple. Yet I am not even sure of that when I remember Fa-hai-ssu, which was one of the least important of the many temples and monasteries among the Western Hills, and had been rented as a holiday and weekend retreat by some of the British Embassy language students. Or, strangely enough, one very new building: a hospital built by the Rockefeller Institute, which I would not dream of including if Bets and I had not happened to walk past it late one evening, on our way back from visiting someone in Hatamên Street.

The exterior of the white-walled hospital had been built in the style of the country, with green-blue tiled roofs, tip-tilted in the Chinese fashion, and stone lanterns on the top of the gateposts flanking the walled courtyard. There were lilac trees in bloom in the courtyard, for it was spring, and the air was sweet with their scent. With sunset the lights in the stone lanterns had been turned on, and glowed apricot in the dusk. I remember Bets and me stopping simultaneously, and standing in the road to stare – and to sniff the scent of lilacs.

The sky behind the blue-tiled roofs was still tinged with the sunset and, seen through the branches of blossom, the twentieth-century building looked like something out of a Chinese fairy story illustrated by Edmund Dulac. I number it among the 'white stones' – those brief glimpses of something you know you will never forget. Nor have either of us ever forgotten it, though it was by no means the only time I had seen the hospital. An American friend who was on the staff there had taken us round the maternity wing and I had been impressed by the size of the long, airy, glass-walled ward where the newborn babies lay, and enchanted by its occupants, who were without exception the most adorable things you ever laid eyes on. Not red and crumpled, but beautiful pink and ivory dolls with long silky-black eyelashes and short black hair cut in a fringe.

If the sight of that hospital in the dusk is the only 'something new' in the list of memorable things that remind me of the China days, then the oldest has to be the Great Wall. This too we saw in the springtime, when all the almond trees were a spangle of pink blossom against the bare brown hills. We had been invited to join a party of friends to visit the Wall, and went part of the way by train and part by car. There were fourteen of us in the party including the Number-One-Boy of someone from the Embassy. Some of us did the last leg on the back of local donkeys, and we must have spent two or possibly three nights away from home.

Except for the almond blossom, the bare hillsides were still brown from the winter, with only touches of green where later on, if the rains did not fail, there would be new grass, and the Wall (which I am told has now been tidied up and re-pointed) looked as old as Time, older by far than the Pyramids. It took your breath away.

We are told that it is the only man-made object that is visible from the moon, and I don't doubt it. But what is really amazing about it is the fact that it was made by human hands, long before men had learned to harness steam and fashion engines of iron and steel to do the hard work for them. The men who built it made no attempt to take the easiest line, but just went straight ahead, up one side and down the other of every hill they met, so that from any high point of the Great Wall you can see it snaking ahead and behind you, climbing the steepest slopes and crowning the crests, to dip downward on the far side and up again. For mile after mile after mile . . . There is something terrifying about it, because it seems to epitomize all the ruthlessness and indifference to human suffering of those who ordered it to be built, and the terrible cost in lives of the thousands of slave-labourers who died in the making.

Historians say that work began on the Wall long before the birth of Christ, with the object of keeping the Mongol hordes out of China. And judging from what we saw of it – even after the passage of so many centuries and the depredation of men who used it as a quarry – when it was new it could have prevented even a mouse from invading Chinese soil. Nothing that one reads about it gives one an impression of its size or its height. Or its massiveness.

At least ten armed men could have walked along it abreast, and every quarter of a mile or so there is a block-house built above an archway in which there were once two massive doors, one leading into Chinese and the other into enemy territory.

Except where the block-houses stood, with quarters for the garrison and rooms for the officers in charge, the space between the inner and outer walls had been filled with rubble from the off-cuts of the great stones of which the walls are made; and this, together with earth and rubbish and anything else that came to hand, apparently settled down with the passing of the centuries into a solid filling that is far tougher than concrete. For when, in the 1930s, Japan invaded North China, her troops attempted to breach the Wall not far above where it ends in the sea at Chin-wang-tao. They were said to have used enough high explosives to sink the Acropolis and blow up Hong Kong. But when the dust and debris of the explosion settled, all it had done was to knock a small dent in the Wall. They didn't try again.

Chapter 9

In the spring of 1933, my brother Bill took advantage of a popular offer by one of the eastern shipping lines of a round trip from Calcutta to Yokohama and back, stopping briefly at Penang, Singapore, Hong Kong, Shanghai and Tokyo and returning by the same route. I imagine the line must have consisted of cargo-ships, for though comfortable, it was far from luxurious; while the price, which was not much above £20 for the round trip and included all meals, was within reach of even the most impecunious of young subalterns.

Since the offer, which was a flat rate for the trip, allowed passengers to do more or less what they liked within the terms of the prospectus, Bill elected to leave the ship at Shanghai and catch the Shanghai Express from there to Peking. By cutting the Japan bit out of his schedule, he could have a good ten days with us before returning by train to Shanghai and picking up the ship there on its return journey.

He had a marvellous holiday, seeing all the sights, which included the Great Wall and the Ming Tombs. These have a long avenue of outsize marble guardians set in pairs, facing each other on either side of the wide dusty track that leads across a flat, treeless plain edged by a distant fringe of low hills, where the funerary temples and the tombs of the Emperors lie. We took him picnicking to the Summer Palace and the Jade Fountain Pagoda, and to lunch with friends who had rented temples among the Western Hills. People lent him ponies on which he went riding at Pa-Ta-Ch'u, and he dined and danced on the roof-top ballroom of the Peking Hotel and, being Bill, fell madly in love with Florise Chandless, our pretty American friend who was up in Peking from Tientsin for a short holiday.

He was fascinated by our Chinese house, and our Chinese staff were charmed by the 'Young Master'. (They took a poor view of daughters: particularly unmarried ones, for this is a country in which one of the terms for describing a woman is 'the mean one of the inner rooms'; and neither Bets nor myself had as yet justified our existence by producing a grandson for 'the Master'.) Tacklow's stock went up considerably when they realized that there was a 'Young Master' in the offing, though Bill's first day in No. 53 Pei-ho-yen led to some confusion.

Last thing at night, before locking up, the Number-One-Boy inquired of Bill what he would like for breakfast. When Bill wanted to know what there was on offer, the Number-One-Boy said grandly: 'Everything,' and then added a few suggestions, among them prawns. Now Bill was very partial to prawns, so he nominated them, and was surprised when Number-One-Boy inquired how many Young Master would like. Young Master said: 'Oh . . . er . . . I don't know. About a dozen, I suppose? Not much more.' 'A *dozen*?' gasped Number-One, plainly awestruck. 'Well . . . er . . . yes. That ought to be enough,' agreed Bill. Number-One retreated – probably to talk things over with the cook, for it hadn't occurred to any of us to explain to Bill, or the Number-One-Boy either, that in England a prawn is merely one up on a shrimp, while in China a prawn is its freshwater cousin, a really large one at that. Next morning, while the rest of his family was dealing with eggs and bacon, the Number-One-Boy appeared, looking anxious, with an outsize dish on which, when he removed the cover, were displayed on a bed of rice and water-cress three outsize crayfish, each one a meal in itself. The Number-One-Boy apologized on behalf of the cook and explained that although the kitchen boy had left early for the market, others had been before him and he had been unable to acquire a dozen prawns. These were the only three that were left. Mother, petrified for fear that we had landed ourselves in yet *another* walkout on the grounds of 'face', frowned us down when we began to shriek with laughter, and hastily assured Number-One-Boy that three would do admirably, and that the Young Master would not make the same mistake again. Young Master didn't, though as far as I remember he chose prawns – or rather *a* prawn – for breakfast every day for the rest of his stay.

China's festivals, like India's, peppered the country's calendar, and seemed, if nothing else, to provide the populace with endless excuses for taking a holiday. What's more, the majority of the holidays appeared to last for several days (the Chinese New Year being a case in point). Most, if not all of them, involved feasting and fireworks, dressing in traditional clothes and parading through the streets. Each change of season is celebrated by a festival. The Chinese New Year comes first, and is followed by 'Welcome to Spring', the 'Feast of Lanterns', 'Get up Insects' (variously translated as 'Wake up Insects' or, more charmingly, 'Excited Insects'). Then comes the 'Corn Rain', the 'Beginning of Summer', the 'Dragon Boat Festival', 'Sprouting Seeds', the 'Feast of Heavenly Gifts', the 'Beginning of Autumn', 'Autumn Divided in the Middle' or 'Harvest Moon'; 'White Dew', the 'Frost's Descent', 'Come Winter', 'Little Cold' and 'Great Snow'. And that was only a few of the calendar ones! There were any number of others, because weddings, funerals, births, deaths and kite-flying all merited colourful processions and pageantry. A walk through the streets of Peking invariably included a free and fascinating show.

I never could make up my mind at which season of the year the city looked its best. The red and yellow of autumn, with its 'mists and mellow fruitfulness' and the harvest moon shimmering on the acres and acres of Imperial yellow tiles that roof the Forbidden City, and with it our little house by the Jade Canal, turning the man-made lakes and water-ways of Peking into liquid silver. Or 'Come Winter', 'Little Cold' and 'Great Snow' – when the lakes and canals turned to solid ice under a carpet of snow, and every tree looked as though it had been fashioned from crystal and diamonds, and every house wore a six-inch-deep white duvet on its tip-tilted Tartar roof – and every guardian lion dog a cosy cap and shawl of snow. Or in springtime, when the dour, dark days of February, with its bitter winds and the sudden lashing storms of rain and sleet, have washed away the snow and helped to thaw the canals, although this unleashed the appalling stench of the city, including, alas, that of the Jade Canal, which ever since the time of 'Frost's Descent' had been sealed in by ice (a circumstance that had not prevented the local citizens from continuing to use it as a main drain for the disposal of sewage and every form of household waste from cabbage stalks to fish-heads and a dead cat or two).

The reappearance of the Peking smells was the only drawback attached to 'Welcome to Spring'. And fortunately, these were almost eliminated by the scent of blossoming fruit trees, lilacs and magnolias and all the flowers of spring. For several weeks at the end of winter, the *hutungs* and houses in the poorer quarters of the city looked as muddy and dour and dun-coloured as a huddle of toadstools, and while the cold lingered, so did innumerable dirty patches of snow, coated with the dust of the Gobi Desert and pitted with dark holes from rain or melting icicles. Any stranger

73

visiting Peking for the first time would have written it off – as I had once written off Srinagar – as a grubby and hideous town, with nothing to be said in its favour. Yet that same stranger, arriving a week or so later, would have found a city scented with flowers and spangled with blossom. Almond and apricot, pear, peach and cherry, plum and apple-blossom, each took over in turn. The dust and the dirty snow patches were washed away by the spring rains and the whole place looked as though it had been through some supernatural car-wash.

But if it was difficult to decide at which season Peking looked its best, there was never any doubt as to which was the worst. Summer was plain horrid. India had accustomed me to the drawbacks of hot weather, but at least her people knew how to deal with soaring temperatures. Here there were no high-ceilinged rooms, thick walls and wide verandahs, and the courtyard system ensured that there was no question of a draught. Chinese houses were designed to keep one warm in winter, and to heck with summer: you can't have both.

The only attempt at keeping the place cool was to shade the entire courtyard with an outsize *pang*. These sunscreens certainly prevented the courtyards from turning into furnace-hot sun-traps. But they also helped to keep air out of the place, and anyone who could afford to do so made for the coast or the Western Hills. There the period between 'Welcome Spring' and 'Great Heat' was one of the pleasantest times of year, and we were lucky enough to spend several weekends as guests in Fa-hai-ssu, a temple in the Western Hills, part of which had for years been rented for the summer months by members of the British Embassy.

Fa-hai-ssu was only a small temple, and not important enough to be listed in the official booklet on 'The Temples and Monasteries of the Western Hills'. I can't think why, since to my mind it was one of the most attractive. We would drive out along a tortuous and very bumpy unmade road for miles, and on reaching the foothills, leave our cars in a small village and walk for the last part of the trip up a stony track through the trees until we reached the temple.

The hillside on which it stood was clothed with stunted fir and pine and small oak trees. One entered the temple up a flight of stone steps flanked by four ancient pine trees, leading to a gate-house which housed a pair of ferocious 'Guardians of the Gate', one on each side of the entrance hall. These glaring-eyed, threatening and more than life-size figures were wonderfully modelled in clay and a mixture of mud and straw, and were works of peasant art. Brilliantly coloured and gilded, wearing elaborate clothes and brandishing daggers or thunderbolts, their faces contorted into expressions of furious rage, they defy evil spirits to enter the temple.

The larger temples – the monasteries – have several courtyards, each one reached by an entrance hall and a flight of steps. But Fa-hai-ssu had only two. The first was very small, leading up to the main one where, raised on a brick platform and reached by a few shallow stone steps, stands the sanctuary in which three great golden figures of Buddha, barely visible in the incense-scented gloom, sit enthroned on tattered red silk cushions behind the altar. We were to find that there were nearly always a few joss-sticks burning there, for the rules that permit the temples to be used as hostelries by all and sundry ensure that they are always open to anyone who wishes to enter them in order to pray or make offerings, consult the resident priest, or burn incense-sticks to the gods. There were nearly always worshippers from the village, as well as the occasional traveller, to be seen entering or leaving the sanctuary.

I was not particularly interested in the sanctuary and its gods, having seen a good many of them. But the trees made Fa-hai-ssu special: a pair of spectacular white pines that grew out of the flagged courtyard on either side of the steps that led up to the 'Goddery', and that together with an ancient and decorative pine tree shaded the courtyard and added the clean fragrance of pine needles to the musky scent of the smouldering joss-sticks burning day and night before the gods.

If you have never seen a white pine you cannot have any idea of how spectacular they are, and your instant reaction to them is that someone *must* have painted the trunks and branches with whitewash. They are not white as some varieties of poplar and silver birch are white. For one thing, their bark is much smoother. Mother painted endless pictures of Fa-hai-ssu, but unfortunately (though we did not think so at the time) they were always sold at once. Only two unfinished sketches of the temple survive: a charming one of the entrance, and one of the upper courtyard that might have turned out well when finished, but in its present state is too harshly coloured – as though she had slapped the paint on in a hurry, or else painted it from a photograph rather than from life. But I am deeply grateful to it, because this was before the age of colour photography, and without Mother's sketches I'm not too sure that I would have remembered how colourful Fa-hai-ssu was.

Mother's sketch confirms that the roofs of Fa-hai-ssu were tiled throughout in the golden yellow of royalty, and that its walls and doors and latticed window-frames must once have been scarlet, though the suns and rains of close on six centuries had turned them to the deep rose-red of dried rose petals. The legends illustrated under the eaves of those tilted Tartar roofs were as bright as ever, having escaped the sun, and, with the brilliant china-white of the pines and the contrasting darkness of the pine tree, the little temple was a treat to the eye, one of those places where one simply wants to 'stand and stare'. Or, if you are an artist, reach for a paintbrush.

To add to its charms, the tree-covered hillsides that rose steeply up behind it were the haunt of that most English of birds, the cuckoo. Bets and I liked to climb the hill behind the temple and, subsiding on to the warm, pine-needle-strewn grass where we could glimpse the glimmering golden roofs between the tree trunks below, listen to the cuckoos calling, as they call each spring in the woods and meadows of Shakespeare's Warwickshire and Kipling's Sussex.

There was only one serious drawback to staying in Fa-hai-ssu. We discovered it on our first visit there. It was Bobbie Aldington who alerted us, by yelling the roof off. That particular weekend party consisted of the Aldingtons – Bobbie and her husband Jeffrey – three student interpreters:* John, 'Mac' (Ian MacKenzie), Gordon Creighton (always known as 'Teddy Bear'), and us Kayes. Tacklow, Mother, Bets and I were guests, and the others our joint hosts from the Embassy. The resident priest – a gentle old monk who took to Tacklow on sight – occupied, together with one or two of his fellow monks, the rooms on the left-hand side of the courtyard, the remaining accommodation being divided by flimsy partitions into as many rooms as were needed for guests.

Mother and Tacklow had a room with a double *kang*, nearest to the monks; then came Bets and myself, next door to the Aldingtons, and beyond them the dining-room, the end wall of which was one side of the entrance to the courtyard. On the other side of that, a dormitory for the student interpreters and rooms for such servants as the party had brought with them. Temples hired out accommodation and basic furniture only. Everything else had to be provided by the guests.

---

* The words 'student interpreter' had once been mistranslated by a Chinese member of the Embassy as 'stupid interrupters'. It stuck. As did 'Teddy Bear'.

On our first night at Fa-hai-ssu, after we had eaten supper in the sketchily furnished dining-room by the light of a Petromax lamp, we retired to bed early, for it had been a long and tiring day. But barely ten or fifteen minutes after the last lamps had been put out and darkness had descended on the temple and its inmates, a torch flashed on in the next room – the partitions between room and room were of the flimsiest – and Bobbie started yelling at the top of her voice.

Instantly, candles, lanterns and torches flared, and chaps in assorted nightwear shot out of bed and into the courtyard, demanding vociferously to know what on earth was happening and who was being attacked and by what.

'It's only a scorpion!' shouted Jeffrey as the rescuers converged on his room. At this point I noticed that Bets, who had also leapt out of bed, was staring down in pop-eyed horror at something that was advancing in a purposeful manner across the carpetless floor. We too, it seemed, had acquired a scorpion, and a large one at that.

Bets's yell was at least as piercing as Bobbie's had been, and she was back on her bed in considerably less time than it had taken her to leave it. After which I don't think anyone got much sleep that night, for the place was *crawling* with scorpions. I hadn't realized before that these creatures, like cockroaches, like to rest by day and swan about in gangs by night. Or is it only Chinese scorpions that prefer the dark? If only the wretched creatures hadn't made such a *noise* about it, I don't expect we would ever have realized that there was so much as a solitary scorpion in the place, let alone whole families of them. But those flimsy partitions gave them away. The partitions were hardly more than screens made of lath and plaster, covered by stretched hessian which was then papered over, and if you tapped them with your fingernails they made a faintly hollow sound, like a drum. The scorpions, as they climbed up those papered surfaces, had made Bobbie reach for her torch and switch it on to see what was scraping away on the wall behind her bed, and the spotlight had fallen on not one, but two scorpions, squaring up either for a fight or for a bit of love-play, and making far too much noise about it. Her subsequent shrieks had put an end to a peaceful night for everybody.

There followed a tremendous scorpion-hunt, to the dismay of the resident priest who, aroused by the uproar, came pottering out clutching a lantern expecting, at the very least, to find a band of brigands attacking his temple. Discovering what all the fuss was about, he came out strongly on the side of his fellow residents (who as members of the 'Excited Insects' rate a special festival in China's list of celebrations of the seasons) pointing out that all we had to do was ignore the little creatures and they would do us no harm. Had any of us been hurt? No . . . ! ('*Yes!*' put in Bets, convinced that she would have been if she hadn't taken evasive action.) The priest was not impressed. In all his years in this temple, he insisted, he had never once been attacked by a scorpion, and that was because he had never threatened the poor insects. 'Ignore them and they will ignore you.' On which he retired happily to bed.

I don't remember how we coped with the situation after that. The quicker-footed and more aggressive members of the party had already managed to slay several of the Excited Insects with the aid of bedroom slippers, and corpses were thrown outside the courtyard in the hope that their relatives would not connect their passing with us, and avenge themselves. I can't believe that any of us got much sleep that night, for I well remember that as soon as the lights were put out the scratching of little claws on Chinese wallpaper started up again. But by then we had all made sure that our mosquito nets were well tucked in, and put our trust in that.

We certainly had no more alarms and excursions on that same score again, and apart from the Great Scorpion Scare I remember Fa-hai-ssu as a place that was little short of Paradise. It was also possessed of a hidden treasure that was not officially discovered for some years after our stay there, so Bets and I can confidently lay claim to being the first foreigners to lay eyes on it. It happened this way, during a subsequent visit there . . .

Finding myself disinclined to sleep on a hot and drowsy afternoon when everyone else, including the monks, was enjoying a siesta, I decided to take a closer look at the Sanctuary. Having provided myself with a few small coins for an offering, I set off to explore. There were seldom any worshippers at that hour of day, since those who were not at work were taking a nap, and I had the Goddery to myself. It seemed very dark and cold after the glare and heat of the courtyard. I left my offering in one of the bowls on the altar and, lighting a joss-stick from the stump of the only one still smouldering, I pushed it into the awesome pile of grey ash that filled the incense urn to the brim and gave evidence of the thousands upon thousands of joss-sticks burnt there for years past, probably as far back as the beginning of that century.

I had not realized before that there were so many gods in the sanctuary. But, as my eyes became used to the gloom, the place seemed to be full of them, for the three large figures behind the altar were flanked on either side of the room by a line of seated *lohans*,* some sitting cross-legged and others with their feet resting on the narrow lacquered table of offerings. Behind them, as behind the seated Buddhas – almost invisible under layers of dust and smoke from votive candles and smouldering incense-sticks – it was just possible to see that the walls were frescoed with Buddhist saints floating among stylized clouds, and to make out that the reredos behind the central altar ended a few feet short of the outside walls. Behind it must lie a narrow passage, presumably a repository of broken and discarded temple bric-à-brac.

Walking round to the far end, I found myself looking down a dark tunnel that would have been pitch-black but for the faint gleam of light from the far end, which was just enough to give me the impression that it had been used for years as a lumber-room – though not recently, for here the dust lay so thick underfoot that it felt like walking on an expensive pile carpet. The darkness, and the thought of those scorpions, made me beat a hasty retreat, and I returned at speed to the bedroom in order to collect reinforcements in the shape of Bets, a torch and a walking-stick. Thus armed, I went back to explore.

That passage cannot have been more than six or seven feet wide at most, and now that I had a torch we could see that there was a small door in the back wall – which was also the outer wall of the temple, a way of escape in a crisis perhaps. It did not look as though it had been opened for years – if ever – and I had been right in thinking that the passage had been used as a lumber-room, for the dust lay thick on an assortment of broken bric-à-brac that had been thrown down there. A long rickety table, no more than a narrow plank of wood supported by straight wooden legs, stood against the inner wall, and on it were several small, battered and broken house-altars, each with its image of a Buddha and, judging from the thickness of the dust that coated them, presumably put to one side to be mended before the fall of the Empire and forgotten in the subsequent Republican years.

Broken spirit-drums, tattered banners and odds and ends of carved wood that looked as though they were parts of temple ornaments lay

* Chinese saints.

79

piled against the wall, and among them the beam of my torch fell on a little wooden hand, severed at the wrist and lying palm upward and almost concealed by dust. I guessed that it was the right hand of Kuan-yin-pusa, the Goddess of Mercy, raised in blessing. The covering of red-gold lacquer was sadly worn and chipped, but what was left of it was still bright enough to shine in the torchlight, and I picked it up and searched among the discarded junk on the floor for its owner. But though there were plenty of broken images, one or two of them minus a thumb and many without any fingers, none was short of an entire hand, and it was only when we gave up rummaging among the broken bits of throw-outs on the floor and I straightened up and flashed my torch across the wall that we saw one of the most enchanting sights that we were to see in China . . .

The entire wall had been frescoed in minute detail and in a manner that was unlike anything that I had seen before, though it reminded me of something. I did not realize what, until many years later when I saw the original of Botticelli's *Primavera* at the Uffizi Gallery in Florence, and was instantly reminded of Fa-hai-ssu. It was the airiness, and all that detail, I suppose.

Like everything else in that short dark passage, and throughout the sanctuary, the murals were half hidden by a veil of cobwebs and layers of dust from decades of slow-burning incense-sticks, augmented by the dry earth of the hillsides, the sands of the Gobi Desert and the great plain of China. This was why we had not noticed them until I flashed the torch directly at them. And even then I doubt if we would have taken much notice if it had not been for the glint of a thin, raised line of something like gesso that had been covered with gold leaf and formed the outer rim of the halo behind the head of the goddess that I happened to shine my torch on.

Pure gold does not tarnish and, as I moved the light slowly along the wall, it glinted on other touches of gold and showed us that not only the haloes, but the elaborate jewellery, coronets and ornaments worn by the goddesses and their attendants (at least two of whom looked quite as fiercely masculine as the Guardians of the Gate!) were also picked out with gesso, so that they looked almost real and as if we could lift them off the wall.

Only when the battery of my torch began to run out did we tear ourselves away from our enthralling treasure-trove, and discover that we must have spent a lot more time gazing at it than we thought, for by the time we left the Goddery the sun was nearing the tree-tops and the rest of our party were collecting in the courtyard for tea.

Bets and I, incoherent with excitement and convinced that we had stumbled on the Find of the Century, poured out our story in the expectation that everyone else would fall over each other in their eagerness to see the wonders we had been describing. It was a distinct let-down to find that they were far more interested in tea, and that our World-Shaking Discovery was, for the moment, of far less importance than cucumber sandwiches, scones and the best Lapsang Souchong from the tea emporium on the Hatamên. And when that had been disposed of, a few villagers, the day's work finished, began to drift in to light their joss-sticks and say a prayer, so it was decided that we would have to wait until tomorrow before 'poking about' in the back of the sanctuary and go for an evening walk in the woods instead.

Mother was the only one who showed any interest in the murals next morning. The others took their torches and, having stirred up the dust by tramping to and fro in the passage and made everyone sneeze, said: 'Yes, very pretty, if only you could clean it up a bit' – which was considered inadvisable, because if one started to brush off the dust, the plaster would probably flake off the wall; it was surprising that it hadn't flaked off already. And that was that.

Tacklow questioned the old priest about the frescoes, but all he got was a shrug of the shoulders and the information that the pictures were very old – as old as the Temple. However, he did manage to open the door in the back wall and let in a bit of daylight, and this, augmented by two Petromax lamps and several torches, produced just enough light for Mother to take a photograph of part of the mural.

Finding our fellow weekenders so uninterested, we buttonholed everyone we knew as soon as we got back to Peking. But no one, not even Sven Hedin, showed any particular enthusiasm. *Everyone* knew that there were frescoes at Fa-hai-ssu – well, *almost* everyone! – and if they were anything special we could be quite sure that someone would have taken notice of it and left a record. We gave up. But I kept the little gold lacquered hand and I have it to this day. It sits on a carved ebony base among a few specially treasured mementoes.

Four years later, back in London and waiting to meet a friend in the Ladies' Drawing-Room of the Army and Navy Club in St James's Square, I picked up a copy of the *Illustrated London News*. Turning the pages without much interest, I came across a full-page spread, complete with photographs, headed 'Wonderful Discovery of Ming Frescoes. Rivals to Ajanta!' And there was a photograph of Fa-hai-ssu and the Goddery, and that marvel of a fresco! Plus a whole lot of stuff about it being painted in the fifteenth century, during the Ming Dynasty, and that it was almost perfectly preserved and 'believed to be unknown until now to either Chinese or European art lovers'. I resent that last bit. I really do . . . Bitterly!

There were times when I used to have qualms about that little wooden hand, and wonder if I ought not to send it back to Fa-hai-ssu. It was a purely superstitious feeling, since I knew perfectly well that if I did it would merely be thrown away as rubbish, as it had been before. Yet I continued to toy with the idea that one day I might go back to Fa-hai-ssu and hide it on the altar behind the Buddhas and let *them* look after it. Only when China declared for Communism did I cease to worry; and when, much later, Chairman Mao's Red Army stampeded across their homeland, smashing and destroying thousands of irreplaceable examples of their country's art, I felt relieved to think that the little hand was safely wrapped in a piece of Chinese silk at the back of my handkerchief and glove drawer.

Chapter 10

China was in deep trouble in those days, but though I was aware that this was so, I took no interest in the political situation. China had done nothing about Manchuria in 1931. There was a story that the only people to make a fuss about it had been the students in Peking's university, who had demanded that they be given arms with which to march against the Japanese, who had been besieging the northern border-town of Jehol for some months.

The tale went that after several days of student demonstrations and deafening howls of 'Give us arms! Give us arms!' the authorities gave in and doled out hundreds of rifles – many of which were probably relics from the previous century. When every student had received some form of firearm and the ammunition to go with it, the demonstrators made for the railway station in a body, and caught the next train for Shanghai!

That story may have been apocryphal. But since I heard it from so many people who claimed to have 'been there', I bet it was true. Particularly since at this time, when China was being sporadically ruled by a variety of self-proclaimed generals and temporary war lords, possession of any form of firearm would have greatly increased its owner's prestige: no one dared argue with an armed soldier in those days.

A similar tale is one that I really can vouch for, because I saw the final act of the incident myself, and though I can't, at this date, remember the year, it has to be in the autumn of either 1932 or 1933. Japan had laid siege to Jehol, a fortified autumn residence and imperial hunting lodge, north-east of Peking among the mountains beyond the Great Wall, which was held by a garrison numbering several thousand troops under the command of a top-ranking general. The siege had been dragging on for some time, and casualties among the Chinese soldiery mounted steadily. Report said that many were dying daily, not from enemy action but from cold, for they had been hurried up to the defence of Jehol in the late spring or early summer, when they would be wearing light, 'warm-weather' clothing. The bitter cold of the North China winter, with its icy winds that swept in from the freezing plateau of Central Asia, was, literally, killing off the inadequately clad garrison like flies, by lowering their resistance so drastically that the least touch of ill-health became impossible to fight off, and they crawled into their draughty, unheated barracks and died there.*

A call went out for fur-lined coats for the shivering army: 40,000 was the figure spoken of. Sufficient money to buy 40,000 fur coats, and the cost of their transport to Jehol, was raised in next to no time, and the Committee responsible for collecting them and sending them off by train from Peking for as far as the railway line went (and from there presumably in carts along the winding mountain roads) advertised their departure with a good many patriotic speeches and headlines in the press. A large crowd of citizens, pressmen and high-ranking officials turned up to see the show, and Tacklow, who read the Chinese papers as well as the *Peking and Tientsin Times*, took me along to the station to witness the send-off.

As far as the Chinese officials went it was very impressive. But when it came to the consignment of goods to 'our heroic defenders', it soon became apparent that no allowances had been made for the Chinese addiction to *kumshaw* – 'squeeze' – levied on any sum that passes through successive hands. China had subscribed more than enough money to provide all the help that was so sorely needed by its shivering, half-frozen troops, but had forgotten that the money must, of necessity, pass through the hands of a great many officials before it was converted into the necessary fur coats, boxed and ready for dispatch from Peking.

Corruption had always been rife at all levels in the Imperial Kingdom, particularly in royal circles – as witness the appropriation by the Empress of funds set aside for China's navy. (She spent them on building a marble boat, and a variety of pavilions at the Summer Palace.) It became worse under an unstable Republic, and since every single individual through whose hands that fur coat money passed kept a proportion of it, it is not surprising that the help that was sent off to Jehol consisted of *eighteen*† fur coats and a few dozen boxes of crackers . . .

---

* China was not alone in this sort of behaviour, for I was told that an entire British regiment was once sent to Tientsin in thin hot-weather dress, because someone in Whitehall thought Tientsin was in the Tropics.

† Or fourteen? I am not 100 per cent sure which. The crackers were probably the kind you threw, not those you pulled.

The men who were garrisoning Jehol were their fellow-countrymen, dying for something as easily avoidable as lack of warmth. And all because a line of greedy and corrupt officials could not keep their thievish paws out of the till.

A garden party was to provide me with another example of a Chinese vanishing-trick. The party was given by the Chinese members of Peking's Town Council, in honour of the Crown Prince of one of the Scandinavian countries. Because of the Japanese siege of Jehol it had been thought prudent to send the treasures of the Forbidden City for safe keeping in Shanghai, but the entire collection would be put on display for the benefit of the royal visitor before being packed and sent off under a strong guard to the south.

The foreign ministers and the senior members of their staffs, together with most of the foreign residents in Peking, were invited, among them Tacklow and Mother. When the day came round, however, Mother went down with a migraine and retired to bed with aspirins and an ice-pack in a darkened room, and Tacklow, who didn't like the idea of going alone, suggested that I substitute for her. After all, the invitation was for Sir Cecil and Lady Kaye, and none of the hosts was in the least likely to realize that I wasn't Mother, for there were a lot of young wives among the Consular staffs. So, thrilled to bits, I hastily scrambled into my garden-party outfit and went off with Tacklow to the Forbidden City.

The party was held in the garden of one of the palaces, and everyone who was anyone, Chinese or foreign, was there in their best. The Crown Prince was everything one thinks a Crown Prince should be, and we all sat around under the shade of ornamental pine trees at little tables. Everyone there looked forward to seeing the treasures because it was well known that only a very few, and those of a size that made them impossible to steal – such as the 'Empress's Jade Flower Bowl' – were on show to tourists. The prospect of seeing *all* the treasures was enthralling.

But when the time came, our hosts selected a mere handful of people: the Prince and one or two of his suite, some, but by no means all, of the ministers and secretaries, a wife or two – and Sir Cecil and Lady Kaye! I couldn't believe my luck. I *still* can't. This small party of people was taken through the Forbidden City into palaces that were shut to tourists, and shown such treasures as had survived the looting and anarchy of the years that had followed the fall of the Empire, all laid out on display in cabinets and tables and on shelves.

Carved jade and ivory and rose-quartz; lacquer and porcelain and wonderful embroidered wallhangings; *Kossu* scrolls and celadon vases; and case after case of curious objects such as the curved sceptres which were presented to the Emperor once a year by various nobles or delegates from different states, and were supposed to bring good fortune. No two of these beautiful, useless objects were quite alike, except in general outline, and all were works of art. I could have spent hours with my nose flattened against the glass of the cases in which they were displayed, and I still remember them with awe.

That evening, when the party was over and the guests had gone, the gates of the Forbidden City were locked and barred, and all approaches were sealed off for some considerable time while behind those closed doors skilled packers stowed away the fabulous, fragile treasures in the many wooden crates that had been recently made ready for them. They were taken under a strong guard to the railway station and dispatched, with every possible precaution, to Shanghai, where they arrived safely. Or rather the crates did. No one would admit to knowing what happened to the treasures: when the crates were opened they were found to contain nothing but bricks.

I was convinced that the treasures were gone for ever, scattered all over the globe in bits and pieces. But there was a TV film not so long ago that said flatly that the treasure was safe and sound in a strongly fortified and most elaborate museum in Taiwan, that breakaway island to which those Chinese who did not choose to follow Chairman Mao and his Communists retreated. What is more, the film showed us many of the Imperial Treasures, beautifully displayed. They can't *all* be there, but at least a good many of them obviously are. Well done to whoever did it!

According to the China-side grapevine, the only treasure to escape being sent south was the more than life-size effigy that gave its name to the Temple of the White Jade Buddha. And that was only because when the packers came to remove it, it was discovered that at some time during its career, some opportunistic Emperor, eunuch, or abbot (with the agreement of some or all of the monks) had had a copy of the effigy made in alabaster and substituted it for the original jade which, cut up and sold by the piece, would have been worth a fortune.

There are so many things I remember about the Peking days which make me think: 'I *must* put that in!' There was the Cat's Christmas party given by a girl called Nancy Caccia, whose husband was at the British Consulate. The Christmas tree was decked with bits of fish and other snacks popular with cats, and the floor strewn with saucers of milk. I hadn't laughed so much in years.

There were dinner parties given by Tacklow's Chinese friends. And a ghastly afternoon in the Peking Hotel, when Bets and I had been dragooned by some senior consulate lady into collecting money from an influx of tourists off an American tour ship. The tourists, to a man – and woman! – had had enough of being badgered for money, and treated us as though we were begging for *ourselves*: they *couldn't* have been ruder. Or nastier. After an hour of this, our collecting boxes were empty, Bets was in tears, and I was almost sick with rage. I'd no idea human beings could be so beastly and, in memory of that ghastly afternoon, I have never passed someone with a collecting box without putting a coin in it.

Then there was a fascinating four hours at a Chinese theatre, where the heroine, and all the female characters, were played by men. There was having my portrait painted by an excitable Russian with an unpronounceable name, who half-way through the sitting suddenly flung his brush to the floor and shouted at me: 'There is nozzings in your face. But, nozzing! It is only a pink and white egg!' and stormed out of the room.

John commissioned a portrait of me from another painter, Nancy Caccia (she of the Cat's Christmas party), and when it was finished he gave a dinner party in his rooms, with the only light a few candles on the dining-table and a single brilliant electric bulb trained on the portrait: *most* embarrassing. Years later, when I happened to be in Washington, I called at the British Embassy and asked to see Nancy (whose husband was the then British Ambassador). She couldn't have been nicer; but alas, she hadn't the *remotest* idea who I was, or that she had ever painted my portrait or asked me to her Cat's Christmas party (to which I certainly did not contribute a cat).

Chapter 11

~꒰꒱~

Considering that I was born among the foothills of the Himalayas and spent the largest part of my formative years within sight of what was then – and one could almost say still is – the Edge of Nowhere, since only a single unmade track led out of my hometown of Simla towards Tibet, I can't explain why living in China should have given me such a strong feeling of being stranded on the edge of the civilized world. After all, we were merely living on a different section of the same huge expanse of nowhere, with Tibet to the south-west instead of due west of us.

But there was something about North China that made me feel, from the day I arrived there to the day I left, as though I had come to the world's end, and that there was nothing at my back except hundreds and hundreds of miles of uninhabited desert and tundra, shale and snow and glaciers, with an icy wind from outer space forever blowing across it. Thinking about it, I imagine that this may have had something to do with the fact that in those days, when the Air Age had barely begun and letters and parcels came by sea – and took an unconscionably long time about it – I found myself losing touch with Neil. Although he wrote frequently and faithfully, I tended to forget what he or I had said in a previous letter, and often failed to reply to some question that had been put in a letter written a month previously.

Bets and WHP managed to keep up an uninterrupted flow of correspondence, and Bets said it was my own fault for settling for an 'understanding' instead of getting properly engaged. She admitted that if she hadn't been engaged she might well have begun to waver under the strain of a long separation. I replied that this was exactly why I had refused to tie myself down – because if Neil really was the right man for me, no amount of separation would make the slightest difference. But if it didn't stand the strain, well, too bad. It had been fun while it lasted, and now it had better fade quietly away – 'No tears, no fuss. Hooray for us!'

Our letters had become fewer, and at longer and longer intervals, until one day they just stopped, and I didn't even notice for several months. But I think now that it was probably the length of time it took to get a letter during those early days that was the main reason for that uncomfortable feeling that I had come to the end of the known world and that anything could happen here – anything!

No; I didn't trust China. It frightened me stiff, and I used to remember that famous pronouncement of Napoleon's, 'Let China sleep. He who awakens her will be sorry!' and to realize that it was my countrymen who were largely responsible for awakening her. All the same, I am grateful that I had the chance to see the last flicker of Imperial China, the Celestial Kingdom whose rulers had believed their country to be the centre of the world, and had done their best down the centuries to keep the Outer Barbarians from entering it, believing (rightly when one comes to think of it) that we were all no better than foreign devils who would do our best to plunder and destroy if the door was once opened to us. The Empire had fallen more than twenty years before I set foot in China, but the echoes of its past greatness were still there: the scent and the smell, the same customs and the same dress that had been worn down the centuries, almost unchanged. And, despite the Republic, a respect for the Blood Royal and the ceremonies of the past.

You could sense all that, and still see much of a world that would have been familiar to the Old Buddha, who had died in 1908, the year in which I was born, and been buried with extravagant honours in the Imperial tombs. The list of the treasures that were buried with her in her coffin reads like something out of a fairy tale. There were ropes of pearls about her neck and a chaplet of pearls on her head, a mattress embroidered with pearls and a coverlet strewn with loose pearls; a rope of pearls encircled her body eight times, and by her side were laid 108 gold, jade and carved gem Buddhas, and any number of jade carvings. The gaps were filled with scattered pearls and jewels, and above all that lay a network of pearls. Finally, as the lid of the coffin was about to be closed, one of the princesses added 'a fine jade ornament of eighteen Buddhas and another of eight galloping horses'. And that, and a lot more, was only in the coffin. Endless other treasures of lesser value were placed in the vault. It sounds like the burial of one of the great Pharoahs of Egypt, doesn't it? Yet it happened in this century. In my *own* lifetime – just!

Needless to say, when the Empire fell a few years later and the country began to disintegrate under alternate blows from opposing war lords, floods and famine, it was only a matter of time before a gang of unpaid and masterless troops raided the Imperial Tombs and tore open the coffin. Having looted everything of value they flung out the corpse of the Great Empress and scattered her bones in the park. I hope she haunted them!

With the end of spring the weather became unpleasantly hot, and all over Peking the *pangs* went up to protect the courtyards of Chinese-style houses from the glare of the summer sun. The shade they provided was very welcome, since without it we would have been driven indoors from sunrise to sunset, as we had been in Tonk. But it made the rooms very dark, and effectively reduced the flow of air – which may have been an advantage, for as the temperature rose, so did the malodorous fumes from the Jade Canal.

Considering how often this could hit us in the face when we stepped outside our To-and-from-the-World-Gate, I was frankly staggered by how effectively our high walls and curved, tent-shaped roofs protected us from it. Perhaps the depths of the overhang beneath the upward curve of those tiled roofs siphoned away the air above the canal at a certain level. I can only say that if it was due to some ancient Chinese trick of construction, it worked astonishingly well – and that all the same I was deeply grateful to exchange Peking for the cool, salty sea air of Pei-tai-ho.

The remainder of the summer was a repetition of the previous one: sailing picnics and parties with young naval officers off the ships that took it in turns to put in at Pei-tai-ho. There were expeditions to the temples in the Lotus Hills and the Great Wall and Chin-wang-tao, lazy afternoons under the shade of our *pang* on the sands of the small bay where the diving platform was anchored; and lunches and tea parties with the Grand-dadski and a variety of aunts, uncles and cousins at the Bryson house overlooking the bay.

I made several friends and collected one serious admirer among the Navy men. Roger was, as far as I remember, Number Two of a destroyer, and one of the nicest of men, the kind that parents take to on sight. Mine were no exception. Like Tacklow, he was a 'quiet' man, and also very much like him both in height and looks. I can't think why I did not fall in love with him, for if there is any truth in the theory that girls who dote on their fathers invariably choose husbands who are exactly like them, I ought to have done. Particularly as he was also a dear. Perhaps it was because my mind still held a picture of a tall, ugly-attractive man who laughed a lot and had come to my rescue at one of the most miserably embarrassing moments of my school years, and turned it into a triumph.*

The fact, as I learned later, that my unknown knight-errant was a famous actor, Sir Gerald du Maurier, added considerable glamour to the memory. Dear Roger, though a good-looking man, was only an inch or two taller than I was, and in no way spectacular. On the other hand, he was a Navy man, and from an early age I had thought highly of the Navy.

The uniform had a lot to do with it, and the fact that during my school years my reading had included several books of short stories by a retired naval officer who called himself 'Taffrail'. I used to think how romantic it would be married to a Navy man and go sailing all over the world to strange and glamorous ports, where one would never stay long enough to get bored. If I couldn't marry someone in one of the Indian Services – and Tacklow, who foresaw the Second World War very clearly, was always warning me that the Indian Empire would not survive it, so that like it or lump it I would have to leave that dearly loved country some day in the not too distant future – my second choice would be a husband in the Navy.

I'm afraid it was that uniform, and the glamour of Taffrail's stories, that attracted me to Roger more than anything about the man himself. But because of him, I had a wonderful summer in Pei-tai-ho.

I'm afraid Tacklow did not. He had wanted too much to come back to this little town where he had spent his honeymoon and been happier than he could ever have imagined. But I think it must be almost impossible to recreate something like that over thirty years later. And though he was still deeply in love with Mother, and always would be, I think she was a good deal less so with him, and was finding it difficult to behave as though she was still a deliriously happy nineteen-year-old bride on honeymoon.

They hadn't quarrelled, or at least I don't think so. But there was a faint trace of impatience in Mother's manner towards him, and Tacklow had lost the high spirits of the previous summer and seemed unnaturally subdued. He still spent a lot of time walking alone along the wet sands when the tide was going out, selecting shells of the right size and shape to add to his collection, while Mother would sit chatting with her brothers and sisters and the Dadski on the verandah of the Bryson house, and

* See Chapter 25 of *The Sun in the Morning*.

Bets and I would be partying with the Navy or discussing life in general with Bobbie Aldington and Evelyn Young in our secret sandpit a little way behind the beach houses.

I don't think Tacklow minded the lack of entertainment; he had never minded solitude. But I think he had hoped to have Mother more to himself when he planned this repeat performance of his idyllic honeymoon and, though it had worked the previous summer, it wasn't going to work again. Mother preferred, or pretended to prefer, the company of her kith and kin and endless Bryson-family gossiping (which must have bored him rigid – it certainly bored Bets and me); and the news, which was largely rumour, and unreliable, worried him. He was not having a happy summer.

The only other thing I remember about that second summer in Pei-tai-ho is that towards the end of it we had a sudden plague of ladybirds that flew in by the million from somewhere on the far side of the Gulf of Liao-tung in the direction of Port Arthur. It was disconcerting to wake up one morning and find the waves depositing layer after layer of scarlet, black-spotted bodies, the majority of them dead, in long red lines at the sea's edge. I like ladybirds, and I encourage them on to my roses. But I admit I didn't like to find them crawling all over me by the hundreds.

We left Pei-tai-ho earlier, I think, than we had meant to. Peking was still uncomfortably warm, but the *pangs* had come down from over the courtyards, since by now it was not hot enough for us to need them.

Tacklow had a habit of singing to himself: generally in the bath and usually a song from Gilbert and Sullivan. So I was not surprised when returning from some expedition or other one evening I found my darling parent strolling around the Reception Courtyard in the dusk, singing to himself. It was 'Ol' Man River', a song from *Show Boat*, and, pausing to listen in the shadow of the gate between the courtyards, I heard him repeat two of the lines almost under his breath, almost as if he were talking to himself. They were the lines about 'getting weary and sick of trying' and being 'tired of living but scared of dying'.

There was something personal about that repetition, and the way in which he had sung it, that disturbed me, and I ran down the steps into the courtyard and said, 'You sound very gloomy tonight, Tacklow darling! Couldn't we have something a bit more cheerful?' I had expected him to laugh, but he looked at me for at least half a minute – which is a very long time if you count it off to yourself in seconds – and then said without smiling, 'I don't feel cheerful. And anyway, it's true.' I didn't ask what was true, because I didn't dare. I was suddenly so scared that I couldn't say anything at all, and he turned and walked away into the house where the Number-One-Boy was switching on the lights.

We had guests to dinner that night and I remember that Tacklow seemed to be in excellent spirits and Mother was as cheerful as ever. Nothing wrong there, I thought; and when, the next day, Tacklow was his usual self I persuaded myself that he had merely been pulling my leg or else I had misunderstood him. I think now that that incident in the courtyard coincided with the day on which he had come, at last, to the painful conclusion that China was not, and never would be again, the enchanted and enchanting country in which he had found such unexpected happiness and romance in the early years of the century. He was not going to be able to settle down and spend the rest of his days there after all, for with China and Japan at daggers drawn it was going to be too dangerous a place in which to leave Daisy and the girls. The sooner they left it the better: he had been mad to bring them here in the first place!

Poor Tacklow. He had pinned such hopes on retiring in the one-time Celestial Kingdom, and on returning there with his Daisy. But the Celestial Kingdom had become a far from celestial Republic; and, worse, the second honeymoon had not proved to be an unqualified success. Mother, to whom Chinese had once been a second language, had forgotten most of it, and made no attempt to learn it again; she thought nothing of the social life of a foreigner in North China as compared to that of India and the Raj – and said so at frequent intervals. And now there was the threat from Japan. And with it an even darker threat: that of another World War . . .

Japan had been our ally in the war that had ended only fifteen years before. But if there should be another, whose side would she be on? Then there was Russia to be considered – Russia, whose agents were busily at work trying, with alarming success, to convert young China to what the West still thought of as 'Bolshevism'. And in Germany an ex-house-painter, one Adolf Hitler, who during the war (it was still 'the' war in those days) had served in the ranks of the German Army, had invented a party of the extreme right which had come to be known as the Nazis, and had already attracted the adherence of most of Italy under the leadership of a short, stout and bald-headed rabble-rouser by the name of Benito Mussolini.

Peking being full of foreign legations, most of whose languages Tacklow could speak, he had come to know and get on friendly terms with many of their consuls and staffs, as well as with a number of well-to-do Chinese. And what he learned in the course of many long 'off-the-record' conversations after small, men-only dinner-parties in Chinese homes or the Legation Quarters of a number of other foreign countries had reinforced his fear that Europe was moving nearer and nearer to the edge of a precipice that could only lead to another war.

The last one had ended to the accompaniment of hysterical scenes of rejoicing and innumerable solemn ceremonies at memorials to those who had fallen. Yet Tacklow had come to believe that we had learned nothing from the lessons it should have taught us, and that here we were again, advancing blindly towards the same cliff edge like lemmings. If the worst came to the worst and there was another war it was by no means certain that there would be the same allies. North China, with Japan having bombed Chapei and annexed Manchuria, menacing her borders, would be no safe place for his family, and the sooner he moved them elsewhere the better.

No wonder my poor darling parent was in such low spirits. The last thing he wanted to do was move house again; for in spite of the dangerously unstable conditions that prevailed in China, the mess and the muddle, the banditry and the blatant corruption, he was still fascinated by this country which, in spite of all he had seen and knew of it, he still saw through rose-coloured spectacles. The same rose-coloured ones through which he continued to see Mother. If it had not been for her, and the fact that he had never stopped being besottedly in love with her, I believe he would have stayed in China, in which case he would have ended up in a Japanese prisoner-of-war camp, like too many of Mother's friends and relations. So I suppose it was just as well that he didn't. And since Mother, Bets and I all wanted to go back to India, back to India we went, but by a slow and circuitous route.

With Japan cast as the villain of the piece, you would have thought that any father of a family would have avoided that country like the plague. Not so my darling Tacklow. If we had to move, then let us move to Japan. Not permanently, of course. Just for a time. Long enough to see something of the country and learn a little about its people. Anyway, he had always wanted to see Japan, and this was an ideal opportunity to do so . . .

Well, as it happened I too had wanted to see Japan. Not for 'always', but ever since my schooldays when Tacklow had given me a book by H. de Vere Stacpoole, an author who had made his name with a crashing best-seller called *The Blue Lagoon*. This one, also a best-seller, was a very short novel set in Japan in the early years of the twentieth century. It was entitled *The Crimson Azaleas*, and I suppose I must have been about fourteen at the time that I read it. When I handed it back to Tacklow I remember saying with the utmost fervour, 'I've *got* to see Japan one day. I've simply got to!' Tacklow laughed and said: 'Yes. That's the way it took me, too – I have got to go there myself one day.'

Once again there was the packing to be faced. But this time it was far less trouble than it had ever been before, for on the advice of China-side friends we hired a team of professionals to do the job for us. The result was a bit like watching a troupe of expert gymnasts at work. Mother, who rather prided herself on being a good packer, watched open-mouthed, and was betrayed into an unladylike shriek when, having urged a man who was wrapping up a much cherished cut-crystal bowl to be careful how he handled it, he finished turning it into a ball of dried grass and string, which he then flung across the room to demonstrate how well it would travel.* And how right he was. The team stowed all our breakable goods and chattels in barrels, not packing cases, and when, months later, they were unpacked in Delhi, nothing had suffered so much as a crack, let alone been broken.

Considering how China and the Chinese had scared me, and how reluctant I had been to go there, I was surprised to find how sad I was to see the last of Peking and that fabulous house on the Pei-ho-yen. I suppose it was because I knew that I was seeing the last flicker of the China that Tacklow had fallen in love with. Soon there would be nothing left of that world.

There was a round of farewell parties in Peking, and more of the same in Tientsin, where we stayed for a few days to say our goodbyes to all Mother's relations before embarking on the SS *Kaizan Maru* for Kobe.

* This is obviously a famous 'packer's' trick, for the writer Norah Wall saw it performed when she too was moving house in China.

And China, the country that I had known from the first I would never feel comfortable in, and whose people scared me stiff, forgave me for it and presented me with one last lovely parting present, something that has stayed with me always as another 'white stone' . . .

We had stayed on the open deck of the *Kaizan Maru* to see the last of the land, and by the time we crossed the Taku Bar and headed for the open sea, dusk had fallen and an apricot-coloured harvest moon, impossibly large in the dusty, golden-brown twilight, drifted slowly up out of the darkening sea. The sea, which only moments before had appeared to be as empty as the palm of my hand, was all at once full of ghostly silver shapes, as the strengthening light of the rising moon caught the lateen sails of the fishing fleet and laid a glimmering carpet across the waters of the Gulf of Pei-chih-li.

Years ago, when I was a very small girl, I had looked down at sunset from the then tree-covered slope of Bombay's Malabar Hill, and seen another fishing fleet sail out to meet the gathering night – its sails bright in the last rays of a sinking sun. It had seemed to me then, and still does, one of the most beautiful sights I had ever seen, and I have never forgotten it. Now China had repeated it for me. And again it seemed incredibly lovely, and, for some reason that I can't explain, more than a little sad.

❧ **2** ❧

Interlude: Japan

Chapter 12

~※※~

We were not alone on our trip to Japan. John and 'Teddy Bear' and 'George Blank' (another of the British Legation's 'stupid interruptors') had decided to join our party, and had wangled enough leave in order to do so. This proved to be a godsend, because although none of us spoke a word of Japanese, Tacklow and all three of the interpreters could write it – a curious anomaly that arose from the fact that the two languages, though totally different when spoken, are the same when written. I have no idea when, or how, this curious split came about, but I suspect that Japan had no written language for long after China had invented one, and that when their people at last decided that they must have one too, they couldn't be bothered to invent one – they merely appropriated the sign-writing of China, and that was that.

The weather was perfect and the sea so clear that you could see a dazzling variety of fishy life fathoms deep below the surface. Above them schools of porpoises accompanied us, leaping, diving and frolicking in the bow waves – and sometimes there would be a basking shark. And the islands . . . ! Oh, to be able to stop the ship and go ashore and spend a whole day on one. Oh, to *own* one, and have it all to yourself . . .

Coming from a family whose mother was second generation 'China-side', and whose father had lost his heart to that country many years ago, I had been familiar with Chinese and Japanese art from an early age. The houses of the Bryson aunts and uncles, and ours too, were full of Chinese or Japanese bowls, vases, willow-pattern plates and wall hangings. And now here I was, sailing past the real thing. Here were the very same islets that I had seen a hundred times painted on scrolls. And they were real. The artists had not exaggerated. They had painted exactly what they saw, no more and no less. And in this calm weather the tiny, rocky islands, carved into a hundred decorative shapes by centuries of wind and waves and topped by old, old pine trees, swept and bent sideways by the prevailing

99

gales, were duplicated for us by their reflections on a mirror-smooth sea.

Mother and Bets rushed down to their cabins to fetch their cameras, but as soon as they appeared on deck with them one of the ship's officers swept down upon them and, hissing politely, took them firmly into custody (the cameras; not Mother and Bets). It was forbidden, said the officer, to take photographs in Japanese waters. The same went for Mother's and Bets's sketchbooks. No photographs. No sketches. I went down to my cabin and took several photographs with my Box-Brownie and wondered why, when they were so fussy about visitors sketching or taking snapshots of their shoreline, they hadn't the sense to close or black out the portholes. Unfortunately, the snapshots turned out to be a total failure, for the little islands were too far away. Just small spots on a waste of sea.

Later on, when we cannot have been too far from Kobe, the *Kaizan Maru* slowed down almost to a stop as we approached a narrow strip of sea between an island on the right and an arm of the mainland to the left. A launch with several uniformed Japanese aboard came out to meet us, and a ladder was put down for them to come aboard. I presumed that they were were port officials, or from the pilot boat; and possibly some were. But two or three of them had come out to interview and meet my father. Tacklow, looking slightly surprised, was introduced to them by the Captain, after which they and Tacklow were ushered into the Captain's quarters, from where they did not reappear for some time.

I learned later that they knew almost everything there was to know about my dear parent – probably, since they are a thorough race, down to his taste in ties and the colour of his pyjamas. Tacklow had emerged wearing what I used to call his 'innocent as an oyster' expression when he and the reception committee came out on deck again just before we docked at Kobe, and they all appeared to be on excellent terms with each other. But after that – courtesy of the Japanese Government – we had an official guide attached to our party, presumably to keep an eye on us, because Tacklow said they were convinced that because he had been head of the CID he must have come to spy out the land – or something of the sort. The top Indian in the terrorist line, a dyed-in-the-wool anti-British Communist, one Subas Bose,* who had escaped jail by sliding out of India, some time back in the days of the First World War, had taken

* No relation to Subas Chandra Bose.

refuge in Japan where he had been welcomed with open arms. It was on his behalf that the reception committee had come aboard to interrogate Tacklow and find out what he was up to, and I can't think why they did this, since it was perfectly clear that they weren't prepared to believe for a moment that Tacklow had retired years ago. Even less that he no longer had any connection with (or interest in!) the Intelligence Service, but was merely visiting their islands as a tourist. Still, as long as it made them happy to think he was on some secret spying mission it was no skin off our collective noses, and we all found the official guide most useful in any number of ways. He not only spoke excellent English, but was a mine of information, while as for his effect on shop-keepers, it was electric: one look and a brief word from him, and inflated 'tourist prices' tumbled – he must have saved us quite a lot of money.

I had been wondering how to describe Japan, when memory came up with a phrase that had become something of a catchword in my family. It dated from the days when audiences queued to see the latest light opera by Gilbert and Sullivan at London's Savoy Theatre, and Tacklow, a dedicated Gilbert and Sullivan fan, had been taken to the opening night of *Ruddigore* by an elderly friend who was the music critic of one of London's newspapers. The old gentleman had not been favourably impressed by the opening acts and had said so in a series of audible asides. At last the score came up with the ditty that begins: 'There grew a little flower . . .' and this so caught his fancy that he kept on repeating, throughout: '*Sweetly* pretty! – *Sweetly* pretty!'

Well, that is how Japan struck me. It wasn't beautiful in the way that the Taj Mahal and the Dāl Lake at sunrise and sunset are beautiful, or that fishing fleet caught by the light of a rising moon. But it was sweetly pretty . . . Adorably so, at times. Yet I find that my memory of it is extraordinarily sketchy, and there are blanks I can't account for. Perhaps this was because none of us seem to have taken many photographs while we were there. Bets and Mother were both great ones for taking photographs and keeping albums, and though I was not (until the war years), our combined albums have taken the place of the diaries that none of us kept in those days, and I have found them invaluable.

There are endless snapshots taken in India and China, but the few taken in Japan are nearly all of groups. The only one we were allowed to take on the *Kaizan Maru* was a group of our party standing together in the bows, with a very small and far-away smudge on the sea behind us which I take to be one of the 'thousand islands'. I know that the ship stopped briefly at Nagasaki in order to discharge cargo and several passengers (and possibly take on more of both), because we had specially chosen a ship that took us via that port, instead of one that made straight for Yokohama. The reason for this was that the hero of *The Crimson Azaleas* had a Japanese house, 'The House of the Clouds', on a hilltop above Nagasaki. Yet I am quite sure that we didn't go ashore there; and what's more, I haven't the faintest recollection of laying eyes on the place.

Did we perhaps put in by night and leave again at daybreak? Or could the absence of any snapshots taken of Nagasaki have had something to do with the presence of our official guide? Were we again requested not to take any? If so I don't remember it. The only ban on our taking photographs or sketching was the one placed on us by the Captain of the *Kaizan Maru*, and the chances are that he was merely playing safe.

I remember a lot of train journeys. But not where we went or, specifically, what the country we passed through looked like – except that after China it looked very small and neat. A miniature country. One thing I do remember about it was that it lived up to all my expectations, which is quite something to be able to say of any land, even in those days.

We must have spent at least one night in a hotel at Kobe, because Tacklow wanted to see Nara. But though I remember Nara quite clearly, I have no recollection at all of where we stayed; or for how long. I think we went there by train. Looking at the map, it is quite a short journey. And we must have taken a boat for the last part of it, because I remember approaching it from the sea and admiring the huge red-lacquered *torii* (the graceful free-standing ceremonial gate that all over Japan marks the approach to a temple) which stands above its own reflection in the shallows off the coast of Nara Park. Perhaps I should say of this one that it 'used to stand'. For the park lies at no great distance from Kobe, and the epicentre of the latest earthquake to rack Japan was in a small island not so far from Kobe – which having been hit first by the quake was then destroyed by the resulting fireball caused by fractured gas and oil pipes. Judging from the appalling destruction that was caused in Kobe, it would be a near miracle if the charming park of Nara, with its tall cryptomeria trees, its lovely pagoda that stands near a lake screened by weeping willows, its avenues of stone lanterns, its *toriis* and temples and its herds of deer that are so tame – and so greedy – that they nudge you with their soft noses or (less pleasantly, if they are stags) with their horns, urging you to feed them with the biscuits that can be bought from stalls set up by vendors among the forest of tree-trunks, could possibly have survived.

We indulged the deer by buying little paper sacks full of biscuits, which was a mistake, for they immediately became more and more importunate and eventually had to be chased away. But biscuits were not the only thing for sale on the stalls. There were the usual cheap souvenirs, most of which appeared to be made in Birmingham, but among the junk were a few little painted Japanese figures, most beautifully and very simply carved out of wood; men and women and mikados, only a few inches high. Bets and I bought two each – they were not cheap! – and we have them still. They are our luck-pieces, and have travelled everywhere with us.

We all went shopping in every place we visited, and if we'd had the money to spend, we'd have spent every cent of it and returned from Japan stony broke. So it's just as well we hadn't got too much available, for the Japanese shops were irresistible. Most of my savings had vanished in Bead Street and Flower Street in Peking's Chinese City. What was left went on two magnificent Japanese obis, one of pale green satin with a woven design of yellow and white chrysanthemums, each petal, and the darker green leaves, edged with bright gold, and the other a day-time obi of dull orange silk, also patterned with chrysanthemums in several shades of orange, with a single flower picked out in gold thread.

I had hoped to buy myself a kimono or an obi patterned with sprays of fruit blossom, but here I came up against a Japanese custom which still fascinates me, and which I imagine is unique. In all the shops we visited in Kobe, Osaka and Tokyo, Nikko and Yokohama, and a couple of other towns whose names I can't remember, not a shop had anything patterned with blossom. Why? Because it was autumn, of course! Blossom is for the spring, and no one would be so out-of-date as to wear it in the autumn. What's more, they didn't. Only after I had discovered this fascinating Japanese quirk did I notice that not a kimono or an obi did I see with a blossom-pattern – either worn or on a shelf – during our entire visit. 'Come back in the spring,' they urged, 'and you will find hundreds of them – thousands. But at this time of year they have all been put away in store until then.'

The prettiest things in Nara – or indeed in all Japan – were the children, and next to them the women. For, thank heavens, the vast majority still wore their national dress. I can't remember seeing a single child togged up in European clothes, while the sight of a woman in them was so rare that you turned round to stare. Their men, alas, were beginning to imitate the West; still not to any great extent, though, as in China, far too many of them had taken to ruining the effect of their traditional dress by topping it with a felt Homburg or a straw boater. Or even an occasional bowler hat.

No one could have visited Japan in the days before the Second World War without being impressed by the charm and the sheer numbers of the children. One got the impression that they outnumbered the adults by roughly fifty to one, and every one of them was a miniature version of its elders in the matter of dress: the boys in dark-coloured kimonos and the girls in paler and brighter ones, complete with obis that tied at the back in a large bow into which the younger ones frequently tucked a doll in emulation of their mothers, who carry their babies in this manner. Even the older girls learnt early to carry a younger sister or brother on their backs, and one often saw a child who could not have been much more than six years old carrying a tiny baby on her back, tucked into her obi.

Since no one in Japan wore shoes when indoors, the almost universal footwear consisted of *tabis* – thick white socks with a single toe on which, outside the house, they wore *gaetas*, flat wooden clogs held on by a string that passed between the big toe, and lifted the wearer free of mud or puddles. The clatter of these clogs was the most familiar of all the sounds in Japan. It provided a backdrop to every day, and a Japanese woman or child, setting out to go shopping, visiting or to school, was a delightful sight: swathed in a wide-sleeved kimono with an obi that tied in an enormous bow at her back, her hair pulled up smoothly and held in place with several huge pins, perched up on her black-lacquered *gaetas* and carrying, either against the sun or the rain, a bright coloured oiled paper umbrella. They were in themselves sufficiently decorative to make the dullest street a treat to the eye.

Looking back over the last seventy years or so, the only countries to have escaped the craze for dressing up as Americans or Europeans are the Asian ones. Their women have continued to wear their own dress: saris, shalwar-kameez and the shador, which doesn't seem to have inhibited them in the matter of work, or made them look any less charming. I presume, though, that Japanese women will soon have altered in shape to suit modern clothes. After all, Western ones have done it often enough. After the opulent curves of the early Georgians, we turned ourselves into string-beans when the Directoire fashions came in, went back with Victoria to waists and crinolines, developed busts and bottoms when bustles became the fashion, and with the advent of the First World War abandoned tight lacing, let ourselves spread, and were once again string-beans with, this time, cropped hair and skirts above the knee in the Roaring Twenties. If we can do it, so can Japan. But it's a pity, and I'm glad I saw them while they were still different — and enchanting to look at.

Chapter 13

꧁꧂

One of the things that we had to see while in Japan was their sacred mountain, Fujiyama. And we saw it from a train in 'the early, pearly morning', rising above a belt of mist into a sky of duck-egg green, and looking as if it had just been painted on a huge canvas by a master artist and lit by an expert in theatrical lighting. I am told that 'Fuji-san' stands only 14,000 feet above sea level, which compared with peaks in the Himalayas makes it of little account. But like Kashmir's Nanga Parbat, there is no other high peak anywhere near it, which gives it an illusion of being a great deal higher than it actually is.

Standing alone against a cloudless sky, Fujiyama lives up to everything you have ever read or been told about it. But it is so exactly like the thousands of postcards, paintings and photographs that you will find in every souvenir shop throughout the land, that when you first see it you cannot believe that what you are looking at is the real thing and not an enormous poster. I thought for years that there could be nothing like it anywhere else in the world; until almost half a century later I saw, from a room on the thirtieth floor or so of a hotel in Washington State an almost exact replica of it in the evening sky, far away beyond the intervening city. And for a ridiculous moment I tried to visualize how near we were on the atlas to Japan.

That replica, I learned, was Mt St Helens. But Fuji-san is still unequalled, for not long afterwards Mt St Helens erupted, levelling miles of forest in every direction and blowing a large part of its top off, so that it no longer bears any resemblance to the larger and world-famous volcano on the far side of the Pacific.

The only thing I remember about Osaka is the castle, which like the one in *Lays of Ancient Rome* looked as though it had been 'piled by the hands of giants/For godlike kings of old', and was probably capable of withstanding any number of earthquakes. There were any number of temples, all with charming gardens and cloisters for the monks, and dozens of tea houses, where you were waited on by pretty girls in delightful kimonos and enormous obis patterned with autumn leaves, chrysanthemums and night-birds, who served you on their knees (the girls, not the birds), each folded double until their noses touched the matting. The only trouble was that you too were expected to sit on the floor and keep your feet out of the way; which is an art that I suspect has to be learnt young. We were none of us very good at it, except Bets, who had always been able to cross her feet behind her head – and could probably still do so if she hadn't, in her old age and a careless moment, fallen off the Aga and broken her hip. But that, as Kipling was fond of saying, is another story.

Leaving the coast behind us, we moved inland to Tokyo and spent a few nights at the Imperial, which must, at that time, have been one of the most famous hotels in the world. And, I would have said, one of the ugliest. But then it had not been built to look pretty. It had been specifically designed by America's most innovative architect, Frank Lloyd Wright, to stand up to a major earthquake. And it had done so.

Lloyd Wright used the idea of a raft on which the building would float, and where it would ride the tremors of a quake as a laden raft would ride a rough sea. He also built it with many different materials, all of which would give to the movement instead of standing rigid and cracking with the strain. And it worked. It looked as if it had been built of bits and bobs of anything that came to hand, including lots of what was probably pumice stone since it is porous and excessively hard and so light that it floats. The general effect was like the Witch's House in *Hansel and Gretel*. It all looked madly edible. It also looked like a trap, and was.

Nothing in that hotel looked like it was supposed to look. Handles of drawers or doors were flat-faced squares, oblongs, triangles or other geometrical shapes. Lamps and basins were hidden in the walls, and only sprang out provided you pressed down the right oblong, or pushed up that black and orange thingamebob on the left. ('No, that's not right, try sliding sideways . . . Oops! — sorry! Well, how was I to know that it would bring a mosquito net down on your head? You're lucky it wasn't the shower! Does anyone know where the electric light switch is? Or what it looks like? Or where the room service bells are – or the telephone? *Help!* I'm locked in! *Help!*')

Well, I suppose that is somewhat exaggerated. But not much, I assure you. What you needed to do – provided anyone had warned you, which of course no one had – was to pinpoint the door you had just been ushered in by, and then make sure of its position in relation to the window and the balcony, and the doors into the dressing-room and the bathroom. For if you didn't (and Bets and I didn't), the minute the bellhop vanished, you were lost. Because nothing looked in the least like a door, and if you weren't careful you'd push or pull something, or shove it to the left when you should have shoved it to the right, and suddenly find that you had blacked out the windows and/or turned on the fire alarm.

The rest of that unique building was on the same lines. It had come through an earthquake tremor as a boat rides out rough weather, and should have been kept as a monument, if nothing else. But it was pulled down or perhaps fell victim to some bombing raid in the Second World War. I felt sad when I heard that the gallant old Gingerbread Palace had died the death.

Bets and I had been used from our earliest years to travelling on train journeys that necessitated spending a night or two in a railway carriage. But though we were familiar (via films) with American-style 'sleeping-cars', we had never seen one until we visited Japan, and I came to the conclusion that although the Americans may have invented them, they were obviously *made* for the Japanese and were never likely to catch on where the prudish and self-conscious British were concerned.

All that crawling into coffin-like, curtained upper berths in which you were expected to undress and wriggle into a nightdress or pyjamas. This after (or before, take your choice) washing in a two-by-four communal lavatory-cum-washroom at the far end of a corridor full of scurrying Europeans bundled in dressing-gowns and laden with sponge bags, plus scores of blithely uninhibited and totally naked Japanese of both sexes, who have never considered that there is anything particularly interesting or attractive in the naked body, and happily dress and undress in the aisle without bothering to go through all those bashful contortions behind the inadequate curtains of a pint-sized bunk.

As an ex-art student, accustomed to drawing the nude, I was not as startled by this lavish display of nudity as my elders and betters – in particular, a party of elderly globe-trotters from the English Midlands, who were obviously speechless from shock and doing their best not to look, an exercise that proved impossible, since there was a naked bod wherever they turned their horrified gaze. The poor things could only sidle past, shielding their eyes with one hand, and bolting for cover into their berths like startled rabbits.

The Japanese children, dressed or undressed, were adorable. One of these cherubic creatures, however, got a black mark from the foreign contingent in the sleeper. The little blighter woke up at far too early an hour, and having nagged its mother into dressing it and letting it loose, armed itself with a toy drum and scampered up and down the aisle between the curtained ranks of sleeping-berths, banging on the drum and shouting war-cries.

One could hear and feel the stir and rustle of numerous sleepers prematurely roused from their slumbers and hoping that the brat's owners would take the necessary steps to shut up their darling. But no such luck.

For Tacklow and myself, the high spot of our visit to Japan was Nikko. Nikko was where the author of *The Crimson Azaleas* began his story. He made it sound so attractive that Tacklow and I can have been only two among thousands of readers who had made a vow to try and visit it some day. One day . . .

Well, for two of us that day had actually arrived. And having just said that Japan had lived up to all my expectations, it sounds a bit silly to say, 'Except in the case of Nikko.' But that was true. And for a rather foolish reason. The fact was that not all that long after I had read Stacpoole's novel, I came across an article on Nikko which was lavishly illustrated with really beautiful photographs. Since these were in tones of black, white and grey, I imagined those elaborate carvings to be in wood and stone, and my reaction to the first sight of that brilliant colour and blaze of gold was shock. I thought it was cheap and garish.

It took me some time to get rid of my original idea of the Nikko tombs and realize that the builders and the artists who were responsible for it knew exactly what they were doing. For the entire complex – gateways, reception halls, courtyards, pavilions and tombs – stands on the side of a steep hill among a forest of cryptomeria trees (huge dark green pines that shut out the sky), rhododendrons, camellias, wild cherry and innumerable azaleas . . . It must look wonderful in the spring. But once the flowering trees have shed their petals and the forest returns to sombre green, the whole complex of the tombs would have been lost among the shadowed ranks had it not been for their colour. As it was, the vermilion and gold

– and, strangely enough, the dense, glittering black of the lacquered roof-tiles on a five-storeyed pagoda – seemed to be heightened by the sombreness of the surrounding forest.

'Nikko the beautiful, where the Shoguns sleep' is like an exquisite piece of jewellery. The detail, and the delicacy and charm, are beyond praise. The Three Wise Monkeys made their first appearance here – the ones who 'see no evil, hear no evil and speak no evil'. There is also a rather boring cat, which looks as though it was modelled on the Cheshire Cat in *Alice in Wonderland*.

There are scores of carved lanterns, some stone and others bronze, the stone ones green with moss and the bronze ones green with age, and enormous bronze incense burners and dragons and storks, each one a masterpiece. The mausoleums stand on terraces on the steep hillside, each with its own fantastically decorated gateway and courtyard, and reached by stone steps cut out of the mountainside. When you think you have reached the last one you find there is one more still. A very modest one this time, but I only just made it. If anyone had told me before I started up that there were *two hundred* steps to go before this one, I would have given it a miss. I never was much good at heights. The other members of our party simply bounded up, and when I finally got to the top and collapsed, panting, Tacklow, very unkindly, murmured the lines of a nonsense poem that he kept for this sort of occasion:

> *There was an old man who said 'What*
> *A remarkably beautiful spot!*
> *Now really this view is too good to be true.*
> *I had rather have seen it, than not.'*

Well, yes: I suppose so.

The little town of Nikko, which has sprung up near the tombs and their attendant complex of buildings, lies in a narrow valley through which the main road from Nikko to Lake Chuzenje winds upward through steep-sided gorges, thick with trees and laced with waterfalls that pour down in veils of silver over huge moss-grown rocks to join the narrow rushing torrent that runs along one side of the road. Nowadays, I am told, there is a railway through the gorges. But we were lucky enough to be able to drive up to Chuzenje, taking our time about it and stopping half-way at a little tea-house high above the road to refresh ourselves with tea and cakes.

There was a local fair being held on the shores of the lake, where we stopped to wander among little booths kept by women wearing entrancing kimonos, and bought paper fans and matchboxes full of tiny coloured discs, no bigger than a fingernail, that took Bets and me straight back to our childhood in Simla. We hadn't seen them since then. But when we were small we used to buy them from a Japanese shop on the Mall. You dropped one of these little discs on to the surface of water, and lo and behold, after a moment or two it began to unwind, until suddenly, like magic, there was a pink-tinted lotus complete with lotus leaves, stem and buds lying on the water!

It was wonderful to find them again after so many years. The stallholder's children gathered around to watch and applaud, enjoying the water-toys as much as we did. Almost all the women carried a baby on their backs, solemn, adorable little cherubs who never seemed to cry. One of the mothers – using Teddy Bear armed with a pencil and block as an interpreter – asked Bets if she saw nothing she wanted to buy, and Bets replied: 'Yes, I do. How much do you want for the baby?' – an enormously popular answer that produced a roar of laughter from every stallholder within earshot, and was even a success with our official guide, not the jolliest of humans.

Having loafed round much of Japan and fallen in love with it, we were sorry that we had not arranged to stay there longer. But since we had arranged to spend two or three weeks in Hong Kong with Aunt Lil and Uncle David – whose guest-rooms were seldom if ever empty – before boarding a ship that would take us via Penang to Calcutta, we could not extend our stay in Japan by so much as a day.

After a final orgy of sight-seeing and shopping in Yokohama, where whom should we meet but the First Officer of the Nageem Bagh Navy, Mike Aylesford,* of all people, we were seen on board for a last party by Mike and our escort of 'stupid interruptors' (who were returning to China by a different ship) and given a moving goodbye from the official guide – who actually seemed desolated to see the last of us; in particular of 'Honourable Sir Kay', for whom he had obviously developed an enormous admiration. He assured Tacklow that our company had given him immense enjoyment and the best time of his life, and we parted in a haze of compliments, and with sincere regrets, since we had all become quite fond of him.

* See *Golden Afternoon*.

Chapter 14

~ᴥ~

This time the ship we sailed on was owned by some European line (presumably British, if the nationality of her Captain and First Officer was anything to go by). But since we sailed on an evening tide, we were once again to pass through most of the Inland Sea and the Thousand Islands by night. Watching our friends wave goodbye as we drew away from the docks, I did not realize that I was among the privileged number of foreign tourists who had seen Japan when that country still looked, in many ways, like a scene from *The Mikado* or *Madame Butterfly*.

Our voyage to Hong Kong was a peaceful interlude after that orgy of sight-seeing in Japan. The sea was as smooth as glass and the skies were cloudless, and we lay around in the shade of an awning or leant on the deck rails to watch the many different kinds of sea-creatures that floated past us – the same squadrons of jellyfish of every colour, size and description; the same flying fish, porpoises, and Portuguese men-of-war; and, fathoms down, the same vast silvery shoals of unidentified fish, glimmering and flashing in those clear blue-green depths.

It was a halcyon period, made the more memorable by the fact that it was accompanied throughout by its own theme song. Our Wireless Officer liked to broadcast the more popular seventy-eights on the tannoy throughout the day. His favourite record, which he played at least once or twice an hour, was a world-wide best-seller at that time, 'Parlez-moi d'amour', sung by Lucian Boyer, a French *chanteuse* as famous in her day as the 'Little Sparrow' would be a decade or two later: 'Parlez-moi d'amour, et dites-moi des choses bien tendres' . . . 'Speak to me of love – repeat to me tender things . . .'

That charming melody and enchanting, husky voice accompanied us all through those lazy days down the Pacific coast of Japan to the East China Sea, past a peaceful island called Okinawa – a name that meant nothing to us in those days – and on through the Straits of Formosa to

Hong Kong. It met us again in the ballrooms of Hong Kong's hotels: 'Parlez-moi toujours, mon coeur n'est pas las de l'entendre' . . .

Uncle David was still at that time Number One in the Hong Kong and Shanghai Bank, and we had a wonderful time as house guests of him and Aunt Lil in the Bank House on the Peak. The China Fleet was in dock, and we already knew most of the officers because the ships that had called in at Pei-tai-ho one by one were now all collected here in the naval dockyards, and busy throwing parties in the intervals of playing Navy war-games and steaming off on manoeuvres.

Tacklow was immediately scooped in by the Admiral and taken off for several days on one of the exercises, and Mother was taken under the wing of an old family friend, one 'Tam' Pierce, who had entertained us when we stopped at Hong Kong on our way out. Old Mr Pierce, who appeared to be President of the consortium that ran the racecourse, had a box there, and threw large parties for all the race-meetings, either there or at his magnificent house. There seemed to be no one he did not know or who did not know him, in all of China; and he saw to it that Mother had a splendid time while she was there.

Looking back on those days, it seems to me as if the inhabitants knew that time was running out for them, and were having one last, glorious fling. There were race-meetings and polo matches, dinners and dances, bathing and lunch-partying at the Repulse Bay Hotel – which at that time was still the only building on that lovely curve of beach. There were sailing parties and picnic parties among the sweet-scented scrub that covered the hills surrounding the bay, and every night, on returning after midnight from dancing somewhere or other, the first thing you did was take off your shoes and throw them into the hot-room; followed by your evening dress, which you hung up on a rail that stretched from one side of the room to the other. This was because although the weather might be delightfully warm, in the dark hours or the early morning mists would descend on the Peak; and unless you remembered to stash away shoes and anything made of leather (and, to be on the safe side, your best dresses and hats) you would find them coated with mildew by morning. A hot-room was an essential part of living for a dweller on the Peak, for there was a rainy season (which we fortunately missed) when they lived in the clouds and never saw the harbour or the hills of China for weeks on end.

We would breakfast every morning in the terraced garden of the Bank

House, looking out across the harbour, with the naval dockyard far below us; if you dropped a cherry-stone over the balustrade at the edge of the terrace, the chances are that it would land in the dockyard.

It was a lovely house with a heavenly view, and I believe it is one of the few that date back to the last days of the nineteenth century and is still standing; it certainly was in the 1980s when my publishers included it in a publicity tour of Australia and the Far East. Old 'Tam' Pierce's beautiful house had been looted and destroyed by the Japanese, and Tam himself had died fighting them in defence of that indefensible outpost of a now vanished Empire.

Mike Aylesford, having almost missed us in Japan, had decided to follow us to Hong Kong. It was good to see him; and better still to discover that we could greet and embrace and laugh together with the affection of dear friends, and without a hint of regret for anything more. We had a great deal of fun together, and while we were about it did not forget to send telegrams of loyal greeting to the Captain, Bosun and one or two senior members of the Nageem Bagh Navy. Roger, too, was in port with his ship; and since he usually formed one of the party at dinner dances at the Hong Kong Hotel, or bathing picnics at Repulse Bay, we made him an Honorary Member of the NBN. Able Seaman 1st class.

All in all, it was a splendid interval, and we came to the conclusion that this was largely because, if one lived on the Peak as a lot of people did, all parties and dances had to stop by 11.45 p.m. at the latest. For that was when the dance-bands closed down, because the last train on the little Peak Railway stopped at midnight on the dot, and if you failed to catch it you must walk home or get a taxi. And taxis were not only in short supply in those balmy days, but very expensive. So with one eye on the clock, the dancers and merry-makers would invariably end up racing through the streets to catch the last train.

This meant that every party finished while you were still enjoying it to the hilt and wishing it would go on for ever, which probably accounts for the impression I have that those few weeks in Hong Kong equalled the most marvellous non-stop party of a lifetime. Masses of lovely men, an enchanting house with a marvellous view and run like clockwork by lots of wonderful silent-footed Chinese servants (you couldn't put a scarf or handkerchief down for one minute without finding it whipped away to be washed and ironed and returned to you, within seconds, in pristine condition, by an enchanting little *amah*). And a garden full of flowers high

Below: Myself and Bets on the SS *Conte Rosso* en route for China.

Above: Shanghai. This is a proof copy of the portrait of the Kaye family selected for reproduction in a Shanghai magazine. I sent one of the finished copies to my brother Bill, who was serving as a gunner in Razmak on India's North West Frontier, and his response was a plea to me not to come to Razmak. *Brothers!*

Above: A family group on the steps of Aunt Peg and Uncle Alec Bryson's fabulous Chinese house in the French Concession of Shanghai. *Clockwise:* Roy and Rhoda Wells (he was her second husband, following the death of Uncle Tom), Tacklow, me, Uncle Alec, with Bets and Aunt Peg sitting on the steps.

Left: Tientsin. The twins and their father meet again. Mother and her twin, Uncle Ken, with the Grand-dadski.

Below: Pei-tai-ho. My parents where they used to sit to watch the sun go down in 1905, on their honeymoon.

Below: Aunt Norah with some of her mission children.

Above: My mother doing a swallow dive off the bathing raft at Pei-tai-ho. By an odd coincidence the *Peking and Tientsin Times* of that week carried an almost identical picture of her in their 'Thirty Years Ago' column, without realizing that the duplicate photograph someone had sent in was the same diver, thirty years on.

Above: Our house in Pei-tai-ho, with Bets, Florise and Mother on the garden wall.

Right: Peking. The Jade Canal which, in those days, I grieve to say, was little more than a main drain, however pretty it might look with its willows and camel-back bridges. It was at its best in winter, when it and the trees were white and glittering. The wall of our house is on the far left.

Below: Our Number-One-Boy (the gentleman in the white coat) seeing Mother off in a rickshaw in front of the 'To-and-from-the-World Gate' of our house on the Jade Canal. Bets says she is standing next to him. I thought it was me, but I think she is right.

Below: Our K'ai-mên-ti – the Keeper of the Gate – standing by the Spirit Gate in our outer courtyard. The Spirit Gate prevents any evil spirit entering, for the gates are permanently locked but open at both ends so that people can go round. But since Chinese evil spirits can only walk in a straight line (and presumably turn around), they retire, baffled.

Above: Tacklow hung the Kossu scroll of the last Empress of China on the wall of this red lacquer reading-room in our house.

Left: This is the little Japanese girl who used to pose for the Peking Art Society's 'life classes'. I am interested to discover that Bets's sketchbook (in which there are several different sketches of her) confirms that those tiny feet are not just bad drawing on my part.

Below left: A party of us arriving at the Great Wall. *Left to right:* Tacklow, Derek Calthorp, John, me, Bill, Mrs Tuson, Bets and Elizabeth Wilkinson. This looks like the same train that was in use in 1904 when one compares it with the photograph below right.

Below right: Mother in 1904, probably in the same train.

Below: The white pines in the courtyard of Fa Hai Ssu, the temple in the Western Hills that was rented by the British Legation.

Above right: Mother's photograph, taken by lamp- and torch-light, of part of the wonderful frescoes on the inner wall behind the gods, at Fa Hai Ssu. The frescoes were not 'discovered' until nearly five years later, when they were acclaimed as 'A Chinese rival of Ajunta – or Florence: a Ming Fresco Discovery' (*ILN*, 27 February 1937).

Above: Japan. The Imperial Hotel at Tokyo, where we stayed for a few days.

Right: A snapshot taken by me of a road in Tokyo. Not a 'dressed as a foreigner' within sight. Japan was still wearing its age-old, beautiful dress. Only a single child wears a hideous European hat.

Left: A stop at a wayside café on the road to Lake Chuzengi. *Left to right:* the Japanese owner, Teddybear, our 'accompanist', who seems to be really enjoying himself, Tacklow (ditto), John, myself, Bets and the unknown addition to the party, whose name we can't remember, and Mac, who took the picture.

Right: Hong Kong. The Peak in 1932. So much of this mountainside is now smothered in skyscrapers.

Below: Bill, Bets, self and Joanie Richardson (*née* Lamb) with dogs in Gulmarg.

Above: Kitten. She really was a honey-pot.

Right: Another picnic at Gulmarg thirty years later, near the remains of the Moons' house. Mother, myself and Bets.

Below: Srinagar. Bets on her wedding day surrounded by her bridesmaids; I am on her left. Bets had her dress made up from yards and yards of pearl-white silk she had bought in Peking. Ours were the colour of the pale mauve alpine primulas we had seen in the early spring at Gulmarg.

Right: Srinagar. Myself in the drawing-room of the
Kashmir Residency. The outfit was designed by myself
and made up (including the hat) by our verandah *darzi.*
Shoes by the little Chinese shoemaker in Srinagar bazaar.
Who needs *haute couture?*

Below: Christmas Day 1934 at our ghat at the Residency on
the Jehlum. *Left to right:* Tacklow, Mother, our first cousin
Dick Hamblyn, me and Bill.

Below: This is one of my paintings of the
Dal Lake and surrounding mountains at
Srinagar.

Left: A snap taken by Mother while on a sketching trip in Kashmir with the Resident and his wife (Colonel and Mrs Lang, Joanie's parents).

Right: Tacklow holding his beloved Lizel Kaz, his half-Siamese cat – the only Kaye cat that was not called Chips.

Above: Tacklow by the Jehlum River with Angelina Sugar-peas and Lizel Kaz. This was the last photograph ever taken of my darling father.

Right: Tacklow's grave overlooking the Kalka–Simla road. He loved this view and these hills.

up on a hillside overgrown by bushes of hibiscus and heliotrope, looking out above the harbour towards the miles of fields and open country, towards the green acres of the golf-course at Fan-Ling and the wooded hills of China.

Only once during our stay did we wake to a sky dark with threatening clouds and a high wind that roared in from the South China Sea, making the junks and the small boats furl their sails and huddle together along the shore in tossing confusion, and sweeping the wide stretch of the harbour free of all but the largest ships. Aunt Lil's Chinese staff had already made sure that every door and window was secured against the gale, the more vulnerable ones being reinforced with shutters. Uncle David pointed out a tall flagstaff, and told me that the balloon that had been hoisted to the top of it could be seen by every boat in the harbour and almost every building in the port, and that it was a signal that warned sailor and citizen alike of the approach of a typhoon.

According to Uncle David, it was only when a black balloon was hoisted that everyone knew what they were *really* in for, and took cover – and prayed hard. During the course of the morning the balloon's colour went from bad to worse, but stopped short of the black. Much to my disappointment, I regret to say, since if the typhoon *had* hit us, there would inevitably have been casualties among the Chinese who lived in the *dhows* – there always were, I was told. But I still hankered to see what it would be like to be caught by a typhoon, for even when the last-but-one signal went up, the spectacle was pretty exciting. Trees, branches, leaves, palms, flowers and roof-tiles, anything that hadn't been nailed down or otherwise secured, whirled through the air, while the sea below us was a wild white froth of flying foam that almost obliterated the packed mass of tossing junks anchored in the harbour. The rain lashed down like steel bullets, driven by a wind that screeched past with the din of a hundred trains blowing their warning whistles, and the noise was so deafening that you almost couldn't hear yourself think. What on earth must it be like to be caught out at sea in this sort of weather?

Fortunately for us, the typhoon missed us, though not by very much, and a day or two later the sun was shining down from a cloudless sky. You would never have believed that there had been anything more than a passing rainstorm.

Tacklow and I went for an evening stroll on the Peak on one of our last evenings, and as we were returning to the Bank House, he suddenly said to me – breaking a long interval of silence during which we had been admiring the sunset and sniffing the lovely scent of heliotrope and hibiscus and new-washed greenstuff – 'Why won't you marry Roger, Moll? I think he'd make you a very good husband.'

The question was so unexpected that I tried to laugh it off and make a joke of it. I said: 'But darling, he's such a little man.'

'Speaking as another little man,' said Tacklow severely, 'I resent that! And don't beg the question. You'd make an excellent Navy wife. You like moving around and seeing new countries and strange places, and you don't mind living in rented rooms and boarding houses. Besides, he's a reliable type; a good man. I like him.'

'So do I,' I said. 'But I don't love him. I wish I did.'

'So do I,' sighed Tacklow – and changed the subject.

Poor Tacklow. I only realized later what a weight it would have taken off his mind if he could have seen both his daughters safely married to men he liked and considered reliable. China, that charmed country that he had looked back on with such affection, had proved to be a sad disappointment. He had been forced to leave it and, worse still, to return to India, to see his younger daughter married to a man of whom he knew next to nothing, and at the same time try to find a job for himself that would allow him to remain in that country until his elder daughter found a husband for herself, or proved that she really could make a reasonably good living with her paintbrush. It must have seemed a bleak outlook for him.

Mike threw a terrific farewell party for us at the Majestic Hotel, and we sailed next day for Calcutta, stopping briefly at Singapore, and for a night and the best part of two days at Penang. There we spent most of our time at one of the most beautiful beaches I have ever seen, a small secluded horseshoe of white sand, shaded by coconut palms and bushes of scarlet hibiscus, and sheltered by a high, thickly wooded hill. There was no one else there but ourselves, a few birds and any number of butterflies. The sea was like silk and here too it was clear as crystal. Enormous sea-worn rocks formed a natural breakwater on each side of the beach, and it was one of the most perfect spots you can imagine.

I had an old friend in Calcutta, one I had made while I was staying in Simla with the Birdwoods.* He was theatre-mad and had written several

* See *Golden Afternoon*.

short one-act comedies in which Judy and I had appeared. When not on leave, he was head of the Customs Department, with headquarters in Calcutta; he sent down one of his young men to get our luggage off in time to catch the mail train.

I had imagined that with the help of one of the Customs Department we could sail through the barriers. But I had reckoned without my darling Tacklow. The trouble was that Mother, enchanted by the charm and cheapness of the trinkets and pretty things for sale in Peking's Chinese City – particularly in Flower Street and Bead Street – had had what she regarded as a brainwave. She had decided to spend her picture-money on buying a large selection of this enchanting junk, to see if she could set up shop with it in one room of the house we had rented for the cold weather in Old Delhi.

Thrilled by the prospect of making her fortune, she had acquired enough baubles, bangles and beads and other pretties to fill several outsize packing cases. And I, foreseeing hours wasted sitting about under the hot tin roofs of the Customs shed while ham-handed *coolie-log* undid the careful work of expert Chinese packers, had written to Charles (can't remember what his surname was!) enclosing details of all the junk, plus the prices paid, and inquiring if he could see to it that we did not have to have the stuff unpacked, because no way – *no* way – could it be repacked properly. We ourselves couldn't do it! Charles had risen to the occasion and the young man he had sent down to the docks to help us couldn't have been more helpful. He had gone through the lists and noted that this type of goods was not listed as dutiable, nor were there any of the proscribed items on the list that Customs officers hand to you in large type, and reel off if you don't seem to have taken it in.

The Customs officers, by this time exhausted by going through doubtful luggage and no doubt longing to get shot of the whole ship-load so that they could get a coffee-break, were preparing to chalk an 'OK' hieroglyphic on all those packing-cases of Mother's, when Tacklow suddenly drove up to the fact that this nice man who had met us in the Customs shed and been so helpful was not merely a boyfriend of Moll's, but a representative of the Head of Customs and Excise in Calcutta, and as such was apparently engaged in pulling illegal strings on our behalf. Up with this he *would* not put!

I think I have mentioned elsewhere that my darling Pa had a horror of the slightest dishonesty. 'Word of an Englishman' and all that. All very laudable. But it could, at times, be irritating, and this was one of them . . .

Tacklow had noticed that among the things that had to be declared was silk. Presumably in quantity, since clothing – even Bets's lovely trousseau underwear, and the wonderful dress-lengths of Tribute silk – had been glanced at and replaced with a total lack of interest. Even Tacklow seemed to think that things like Mother's scanties and his silk ties need not come under the heading of 'Silk' with a capital S. But when he discovered that the packing cases, on the word of this stranger from the Customs HQ, had been passed without being opened, he recalled that among the objects in them were at least a dozen four-sided hanging lampshades of carved blackwood, each panel being removable so that they packed flat and every panel (at a guess, probably four inches by seven inches) of stretched silk painted with designs of birds or sprays of flowers.

My parent, who ought to have known better, tried to explain this to the overworked Indian official who was dealing with our stuff, and merely succeeded in muddling the unfortunate man, who obviously had no idea what kind of silk the Sahib was going on about, and in the end demanded to be shown it. This meant opening a packing case – the wrong one of course. By the time a sample lantern was finally unearthed, the floor a sea of tissue paper and straw, and the silly little squares of silk with their flight of painted storks or whatever declared 'not dutiable', everyone was thoroughly out of temper, and the young man from Head Office said crossly: 'Why on earth did you bother to get me down here to help you get the boxes through Customs? You must have known what your father is like! Is he *always* like this?'

I said, 'Unfortunately, yes,' and apologized for getting the young man out of bed for nothing. It was all my fault really. I ought to have explained that I had written to Charles about the packing cases. As it was, I had only managed to give Tacklow the impression that I was pulling rank in order to put a fast one over the Customs! Oh dear –!

William Henry, Bets's fiancé, had been on the dock to meet us, and Bets says that Mother hissed in her ear that if she, Bets, found that she had changed her mind about him, she (Mother!) would get her out of it somehow. I think WHP must have felt much the same, for he had brought a squad of friends with him to break the ice and make conversation. However, fortunately we knew most of them, so all went well. They took us out to Tollygunge for lunch and saw us off on the Night Mail that evening.

It was heavenly to be back again in India. It was, and always is, like coming home. The familiar smells and sounds; the sights and the faces; the fireflies dancing in the canebreaks as darkness fell, and the yellow dawn sky reflecting itself between the little white water-lilies that spangle the ditches alongside the track. There were the familiar names of stations, telling us we had left Bengal and Bihar behind us and were clattering northward across the United Provinces to Delhi. Benares and Allahabad, Cawnpore and Agra, and so many more in between; all of them familiar since childhood. I remembered a story of Kipling's called 'William the Conqueror' in which an engaged Anglo-Indian girl is on the train to Lucknow, where she will be spending Christmas and getting married: 'the large open names of the home towns were good to listen to. Umballa, Ludianah, Phillour, Jullundur, they rang like the coming marriage bells in her ears.' We too would be spending Christmas in Delhi, and I wondered if the familiar names of the towns that we were passing through were sounding wedding-bells to Bets? She and William Henry were still a little stiff with each other, which was not surprising after nearly two years of separation.

Kadera and Mahdoo* were waiting on the platform to garland us when the train pulled into Delhi Central in the late afternoon, and we received an affecting welcome. But it was nothing like the one that awaited Mother when we arrived at 8b Atul Rahman Lane, Old Delhi, the whitewashed bungalow that Tacklow had arranged to rent for the season. Our monkey, Angie – 'Angelina Sugar-peas' – who doted on Mother and had not seen her for what, to a monkey, must have amounted to a lifetime, had been sitting on the ground at the foot of the pole on which Kadera had set up her house in the waste ground behind the bungalow, and she stood up on her hind legs at the sight of a stranger as Mother rounded the house. Then – even though the distance between them was all of two hundred yards – she gave a shriek of joy and, racing forward to the limit of her chain, leapt up and down screaming and yelling with excitement, and, when Mother reached her, leapt into her arms and clung to her, both arms tight round her neck in a strangling embrace, crooning and hugging her, rubbing her cheek against Mother's, which was wet with tears. I think

---

* Kadera was our bearer and Mahdoo our cook. See *Golden Afternoon*.

we all shed a few. Tacklow denied that he had, but he and Kadera and old Mahdoo did a lot of nose-blowing.

I knew from past experience that elephants do not forget. But I didn't know that monkeys didn't either. Kadera said that he and Mahdoo had both told her that Mother was coming back, but that she hadn't seemed to take much interest, and they were both as touched as we were at this funny little animal's faithfulness and devotion.

❧ 3 ❧

On a Clear Day . . .

Chapter 15

That season was almost as much fun as our last one in Delhi had been. It was wonderful to find that so many of my old friends were still around: 'Aud' Wrench in particular. She and I and a few others were co-opted to decorate the IDG* ballroom for Christmas as a medieval hall. Bets and I contributed several vast tapestries, using the technique that I had invented when Judy Birdwood and I did the scenery for *Faust* in Simla.†

We bought yards and yards of coarse sacking in the bazaar and got the *darzi* to sew it together in enormous squares, which we spread on the dry ground and painted with typical tapestry scenes: stylized trees and forests and castles, hunting parties with hounds in pursuit of deer, and elegant medieval ladies in flowery robes and tall, pointed headdresses. When finished, there was only one place high and wide enough to try them out on, and that was the flat roof of our bungalow. So we lugged them up there, anchored them with heavy stones, and poured bucketfuls of dirty paint water over them. Once again, it worked splendidly, particularly when they were hung on the walls of the ballroom; though I would have said that that huge, Georgian-style room was the last place in the world to try to convert into a baronial hall – somewhere between AD 1100 and 1200.

One of the first things that Mother did after settling into the house and making it look comfortable and charming and, unmistakably, *her* house was to set aside a room for all the Chinese bric-à-brac. And, having opened all those packing cases and arranged the contents to their best advantage, pin up, with the permission of the IDG and Old Delhi Club Committees, a small handwritten notice advertising the fact that they were for sale between such-and-such an hour on the following days.

* Imperial Delhi Gymkhana Club.
† See *Golden Afternoon*.

The result exceeded her wildest expectations, and if only she or Tacklow had possessed a grain of hard-headed business sense she could probably have made a small fortune during the next few years. For her stock sold at what seemed like bargain prices to Delhi; though on the advice of some more commercially minded friends like Buckie, she charged three or four times what she had paid for them, plus the packing and carriage. But it was December and Christmas was looming, and people in search of pretty and inexpensive presents descended on the bungalow like locusts, so that before she knew where she was, she had sold the lot – with one exception. Tacklow's contribution to her shop were the little spoons made out of the shells he had collected on Pei-tai-ho beach. A few of these were the only things that remained unsold when the shop was compelled to close down because there was nothing left to sell!

If Mother had been a businesswoman she would have made some arrangement for more of everything to be sent to Delhi. But she never even thought of doing so, and, though delighted by the run-away success of her shop, couldn't be bothered to follow it up. To do so, she argued, would give her no time for painting; and she was doing rather well with her sketches.

I wasn't doing badly with my pictures either. I sold a series of them to the *Illustrated Times of India*, plus most of the handful that I showed at a successful exhibition that Mother gave at Maidens' Hotel.

I saw a lot less of Bets during that season, for she spent most of the time that William Henry was not in his office in his company. They dined and danced together, played tennis and golf, picnicked and went to the 'flicks' (which was the thirties name for the cinema). Their wedding date had been arranged long ago, and they did not change it. But now that William Henry would not have to waste half his leave in travelling out alone to Peking (and the rest of it getting back to Delhi via a passenger steamer to Calcutta, in what could easily have been bad weather) they were to be married in Kashmir and spend their honeymoon in that idyllic spot, the Lolab Valley.

The season ended as usual with the Bachelors' Ball at the Old Delhi Club. And as the mercury in the thermometer that hung in our verandah began to rise ominously, and dust-devils danced like whirling dervishes across the 'badlands' on either side of the road to Karnel, we left for Kashmir. Kadera, Mahdoo and Angie with their respective luggage, plus some of ours, went by the Frontier Express to Rawalpindi, and from there by bus to Srinagar, Mother driving her family up in the car. We arrived to find our boat waiting for us at the Dāl Gate with Kadera's party already on board, together with a crew of four men armed with long poles, who pushed out the boat, there and then, to our old *ghat** at Chota Nageem.†

It had been wonderful to be back again in Delhi. But it was even better to be back in Kashmir. It was as if I had been away for several years instead of only two, and I remember the bliss of smelling again the special scent that all houseboats have, an incense compounded of lake water and water-weeds, the pinewood of which the boats are made and the smoke from the wood-burning stoves that are the only form of heating during the long winters when all the valley is deep in snow. The *manji* and his family had dressed in their best to greet us; his lovely wife 'Ashoo',† whom I had painted so often, had put on all her silver jewellery in honour of the occasion; and there on the bank to welcome us back was old Ahamdoo Siraj. It was wonderful to be back. The men whom the *manji* had hired to take the houseboat out to Chota Nageem – which is an arm of the larger and deeper Lake Nageem – poled us along the beautiful, familiar waterways and when, just before sundown, we reached our old mooring under the giant chenar, we found our little island white with wild cherry blossom and the young grass full of the little red and white striped tulips that are such a feature of Kashmir in springtime. I could have wept from sheer happiness.

We had managed to get our original houseboat, the 'Sunflower', back that year, and Tacklow acquired a cat, not by the usual method of the cat adopting Tacklow, but deliberately, from choice. He had wanted a Siamese cat ever since he had seen a pair of them that belonged to one of the keepers at London's zoo, and heard tales about their behaviour. This was long before Siamese cats began to turn up by the thousand in England. And now he had the offer of a half-Siamese one from a couple of women living in a houseboat on the Jhelum, who owned a pair of them. Both females.

---

* Mooring.

† A lake a few miles outside Srinagar, normally spelt 'Nagim', but always pronounced 'Nageem'. So I have used 'geem' instead of 'gim'.

‡ I can't remember her real name, but I had painted her for 'Ashoo at Her Lattice' and always thought of her as 'Ashoo'.

They had meant to find a tom and breed from them, but as anyone who knows anything about these cats will be aware, they are almost impossible to live with when on heat. And there was no proper husband available for them in Kashmir. Their immodest yowls called up every tomcat within miles of their owners' boat, and the noise got too much for the proprietors, who, after a third sleepless night and a pailful of complaints from the neighbours, lost all patience with them and let them out. The cats spent a happy night on the tiles and returned smug and satisfied. And pregnant of course. Husbands unknown.

The two ladies told Tacklow that there was always a chance that one kitten from a mixed mating (but only one) would be a proper Siamese, and that he should have it, as they could not keep it themselves. When the time came for the kittens' arrival, the ladies sent for Tacklow in case he would like to be present. He would, and he told me that he wouldn't have missed it for a fortune. Nor would he have believed it if he hadn't seen it . . .

The cats were sisters, but one was much larger than the other, and the kittens began arriving at almost the same minute. It was, he said, practically a dead heat. The big cat produced four kittens, and called it a day. But the little cat continued to have them, and when she got to five, and it was clear that there were more on the way, her owners had a brainwave and, removing the next one the moment it was born, gave it to the big cat, who accepted it happily, licked off the neat sac of membrane that kittens arrive in, ate the afterbirth and cleaned the kitten up, licking it all over from nose to tail, and got it started sucking with the others.

The little cat went on giving birth, and ended up with seven of them in her basket. None in either litter took after their mothers. They were all unmistakably Kashmiri Alley-Cat, except one, which though coal-black all over, showed signs of being sleek-furred instead of furry.

About half an hour later, when all was clean and tidy and all the kittens were sucking away peacefully, the little cat took a closer look at her lot, and quite plainly, according to Tacklow, counted them and found she was missing one. 'One, *two, three, four, five, six, seven* – where's the eighth? I know there were eight!' Whereupon she left her basket, stalked across the room to her sister's, looked that lot over, slapped the big cat across the nose with her paw, and, picking up one of the kittens – presumably the right one – carried it back in triumph to her own basket.

Tacklow was enthralled: 'I *must* have one of her kittens,' he said, 'and don't let anyone ever tell you that cats can't count!' He waited until they were a bit older, and then chose the all-black one, because its mother could count, and because it was Siamese in everything but colour. Shape, fur, tail, ears and eyes – turquoise blue slant eyes like its mother's. This was the only 'Kaye cat' that was not called 'Chips'. Tacklow called it the 'Lizel Kaz', which was Kaye language for Little Cat, and he adored it. The adoration was mutual, for the Lizel Kaz followed him everywhere, went for long walks with him and sat on his desk when he was writing. She came when he whistled, growled over bones, and fetched sticks or balls that were thrown for her, just like a dog. She also became a bosom friend of Angelina's. The two of them would share Angie's hut – the Kaz purring while Angie picked over her short, sleek fur, monkey-fashion, in search of fleas.

Mother did a lot of sketching that spring and summer, and Bets and I did a good many of our combined portraits – Bets drawing the sitter and I colouring them in with coloured pencils. They were rather effective; and certainly original. Something between a pastel portrait and a miniature on ivory. We only had one dissatisfied customer, who threw the finished portrait at us and flounced out in a rage. She was a rich globe-trotting widow of uncertain age, who had obviously been good looking in her youth and become pathologically vain.

Apart from this poor woman, who had to be written off as a dead loss, we did rather well financially with our new-style portraits; but ended up having to move our houseboat, bag, baggage and Angie, back to the Moons' ghat on the river, to cut down on the to-ing and fro-ing.

Bets had bought the material for her wedding dress in Peking, yards and yards of pearl-white Chinese satin. And within a day or two after our arrival in Kashmir she had decided on the colour, and I the design, of her bridesmaids' dresses. This had been the result of remembering our first ever visit to Gulmarg. I was never again to see Gulmarg in the early spring while snow still lay thick on the Outer Circular Road and between the pine trees in the surrounding forest. But I never forgot the sight of acres of pale mauve alpine primulas spread out by the hundred thousand on the short cropped winter grass of the *marg*. Nor had Bets forgotten them. On taking a look into the future, she had said confidently: 'That's the colour I'm going to have for my bridesmaids.' And she did. This was the year that a dress material known, somewhat inelegantly, as 'elephant crêpe' appeared upon the fashion scene, and among the various patterns of materials that Bets sent for to Calcutta, to Whiteaway and Laidlows or the Army and Navy Stores, there was an exact match of the lilac-mauve of the primulas.

I designed those bridesmaids' dresses, and their hats, in that crêpe, and a nice, plump lady called Mrs Cliffe, who was a whizz of a dressmaker, made the lot, including Bets's wedding dress. The pale yellow centres of the primulas were echoed by a primrose-yellow rose on the bridesmaids' hats and matching yellow roses on the muffs that they carried, while the pale emerald-green of the primulas' stalks and leaves was repeated in the long velvet ribbons on the muffs.

The wedding was set for the first of September, and the Resident and his wife, Colonel and Mrs Lang, not only lent us the Residency for the Reception, but the Residency *ghat* as well, the latter from 20 August until as long as we liked in September, so that we could be nearer the centre of activity. Bruce* and Edna Bakewell, who had always been particular friends of ours, had offered Bets the loan of the forest hut in the Lolab Valley for her honeymoon, and had been disappointed to hear that the wedding would take place in North China. But now that we were all back in India, they renewed the offer, which was gratefully accepted.

Our brother Bill was to be best man, and the line-up of ushers included Tony Sanger, who had captained the British Polo team to America, Bruce Bakewell, Ken Hadow and Gerry Lloyd our local Lloyds Bank manager, while the five bridesmaids, starting with me, were Joan-Mary Weir, Ray Lawrence, Connie Tallon and a charming American girl, Ora Otis Worden, who was spending the summer as a house-guest of Ken Hadow's wife, Peggy. William Henry and Bill arrived up on leave during the last few days of August. Mr Lang had put the best guest-room in the Residency at our disposal for Bets to dress in, and as the weather was set fair it was decided to hold the reception under the chenars on the Residency lawn. Everything, in fact, seemed in place for a really lovely wedding. And then, a mere two days before the balloon went up, the bridegroom elected to throw a spanner in the works.

I had acquired a cracking headache after spending an afternoon choosing flowers to pick for decorating the church on the following day, and as the day had been very hot I asked for my bed to be carried up to the flat top of the houseboat, and therefore missed witnessing the fireworks.

* Forest Officer. See *Golden Afternoon*.

The first I knew of it was when Bets rushed up the stairs that led up out of the pantry, and collapsed on my bed in floods of tears. It took me some time to find out what had happened, because unlike Tacklow I had never had any doubts about Bets's chosen chap. If she thought William Henry was the man of her dreams, well, it was all right with me and the fact that he wasn't my cup of tea was neither here nor there. I'd forgotten that Tacklow had been worried. But Tacklow was right.

I mopped up Bets, who appeared to be in a mild state of shock, and finally sorted out the trouble. The wedding was on Saturday, and tomorrow we would be spending the afternoon cutting the flowers we needed for decorating the church, and stowing them in buckets of water in the vestry, together with all the vases and containers and chicken-wire, etc. etc. that the flower arrangers would need on Saturday morning. It was unlikely that the Vicar would have much of a congregation for Evensong, and Mother suggested that we might all – five Kayes and the bridegroom – attend, to ask for a final blessing on Bets and William Henry. At which he announced that he had no intention whatever of letting himself be 'bounced' into going to church; now or ever.

I gathered that this had been received with the dropped jaws and pop-eyed silence of shock. Not so much for its content as for the extreme rudeness with which it was said. Mother had eventually said uncertainly: 'But you've been to church with us before – every Sunday when we were in Delhi.' To which WHP retorted that yes he had, and he might well do so again – if and when he happened to feel like it. But he wasn't going to be bounced into going, and he hoped that was quite clear.

Mother, to whom until now he had always been perfectly charming – and who had never been spoken to by anyone in that tone of voice before – quavered that she'd only meant . . . she only thought, 'that since it was Bets's last day as an unmarried girl, it would be nice if we all . . .' 'Well you can count me out!' said WHP. At which point Bets came rushing up to me. I don't know what my parents did; but knowing Mother I imagine she dissolved into tears and that Tacklow – who was as unaccustomed to rudeness as she was – was doing his best to smooth her down.

William Henry had apparently left the table and marched off on to the bund, and I don't know what evasive action Bill had taken. My memory of the occasion is confined to Bets's tearful account of the scene and of myself advising her to go downstairs and have it out with him, because if this was the way he was going to behave on the eve of the wedding, it did *not* augur well for her future. He'd certainly never shown us this side of himself before! 'And if he won't apologize to Mother for upsetting her so, I suggest you postpone the wedding until you've sorted it out!' (I *did* have a headache.)

Bets, aghast at the very idea, said how could she *possibly* do such a thing when everything was planned and ready, and she'd have to let everyone know, and return all the presents, and what about the band at the reception, and the food, and . . . I remember intervening tartly to ask her which was the most important to her – the rest of her life, or spending a few hours on the telephone warning a shoal of wedding guests that the festivities were off, and telling the caterers that their eats and drinks would not be needed. And, if it turned out to be permanent, returning the pile of presents (mostly tea and/or coffee trays as it turned out – a sad lack of liaison between guests). When Bets failed to rise to this, I said that if I changed my mind about marrying a man I had become engaged to, even if it was at the last vital minute before I had to say 'I do', I would drop my bouquet and run for the door, scandal or no scandal. For you have to remember that in the early thirties, marriage was still considered to be something you took on for life, though divorce was getting more and more common – or should I say 'easy'?

Bets's retort to this was a watery: 'Yes, I know *you* would. But I'm not you!'

She went downstairs and patched it up with him, and the wedding went forward as planned, Mother shedding more tears than are normally shed by the bride's mother and Tacklow looking resigned. Everyone else had a lovely party. The Kashmir Correspondent of one of the Raj 'dailies' (I don't remember which) said it was 'quite the prettiest wedding of the year'. The *Tatler* had a photograph of Mother, managing to look very elegant while sitting on the grass!

Chapter 16

~※※※~

There had been a depressing sense of emptiness after Bets left. A feeling of coming to the end, not only of a chapter, but of a whole book that has for a long while kept you interested, amused and entertained. From now on, for the rest of my life, nothing was ever going to be quite the same. I would see Bets again, of course. Often, I hoped. But not as a matter of right. She didn't belong to us any more, but to William Henry; and wherever fate or his firm sent him, there she would go.

Mother too felt flat and bereft and, owing to that behaviour from her son-in-law, torn with doubts and anxiety on Bets's account. Tacklow, I knew, must be equally worried, and I did my best to assure them – and incidentally, myself – that it could only have been the result of pre-wedding nerves and worry. After all, brides were known to be prone to attacks of what the Victorians called 'the vapours'. It was almost expected of them. Well, why not bridegrooms too? They had just as much reason for it (if not more), and William Henry had no one of his own family to support him. No wonder he was feeling nervous and on edge. He had never to my knowledge said or done a nasty thing before, he adored Bets and she was nuts about him, and the whole incident was nothing but a storm in an acorn-sized teacup, and should be brushed under the doormat instantly!

I think I convinced them (I certainly convinced myself). And since none of us felt like moving back to the Moons' *ghat*, or to our old one at Chota Nageem, we decided to try a change of scene, and had the houseboat poled downstream, roughly twelve miles below Srinagar, to a village called Shadipore, which stands at the meeting place of two rivers, the Sind and the Jhelum. Presumably on account of that joining (and the fact that the Urdu word for wedding happens to be *shadi*) the village was thought by the Kashmiris to be a particularly auspicious place in which to be married. But it was also a very paintable spot and one that Mother had always meant to visit. So this seemed a good time to do so.

It was the first time that I had taken a longish trip on a houseboat as opposed to being poled around the lake from one mooring to another. We drifted with the current down the Jhelum in charge of a steersman, ate lunch and tea on the way, and as dusk began to fall pulled into the bank and, having set up Angie's pole-house for her, took her for a walk along the towpath while the houseboat and cook-boat were moored for the night, returning to find everything *teek* and *accha* – or Indian ship-shape. We must have spent at least a week at Shadipore. Yet I never got used to the fact that all our belongings were with us. I kept on thinking: 'Oh, I *wish* I'd had the sense to bring this or that with me,' and then suddenly realizing that everything *was* with us. It was all there: carpets and furniture, books and painting materials – the lot, and I decided that this was the perfect way to travel: take your home with you.

Shadipore turned out to be eminently paintable, and we returned with the nucleus of an exhibition and, as far as I was concerned, a new way of sketching that was to stand me in very good stead in the years to come. Tacklow was unwittingly responsible, since just before we set off for Shadipore he had paid a visit to Lamberts the Chemist, who also sold painting paper, brushes and a variety of paints and pastels. He had gone in to buy some watercolour paper for Mother, and while browsing through a newly arrived stock of art materials his eye had been caught by a set of miniature pots of Winsor and Newton's poster paints, each one measuring no more than one-and-three-quarters of an inch across and barely two inches high (I have the only unfinished one left in front of me as I write: I kept it as a souvenir).

The set, comprising a dozen different colours and two 'student's' paintbrushes, came in a narrow oblong box and was obviously meant as a present for a child. But the cheerful little row of clear, bright colours in their tiny glass pots and white screw tops had caught Tacklow's fancy, and since it only cost two rupees eight annas – the equivalent of about twenty-five pence at present prices – he bought it for me. He knew that I was feeling flat and lost and loose-endish now that Bets had gone, and hoped that those silly little bottles might cheer me up a bit.

Darling Tacklow! Little did you guess what a financial windfall you gave me that day, and what a help it was going to be to me in the future. I was as fascinated by the miniature paints as he had been, and because they were so small, I tried them out by doing a tiny sketch on the back of an envelope, of the view from where we'd moored for the night. I hadn't realized then that the only one of the little pots of colour that would need constant replacing was the Process White. The others, small as they were, lasted for years; literally. And as I have said, one (the purple) has never run out.

I experimented with that set of paints on different coloured scraps of paper, and finally hit upon black as the most successful. I had cadged a page of a new and as yet unused photograph album from Mother and discovered that I could leave the paper untouched for the shadows, and also leave a very thin line of the black as an edging to almost everything else in the picture. This had the great advantage of preventing the colours from running into each other, which in turn speeded up the process, as I didn't have to wait for a colour to dry before adding the next one; the effect was formal and very decorative.

I painted any number of 'little pics' during the week we spent in Shadipore, and Mother produced at least half a dozen really nice watercolours, one of which I still have. I begged her to keep it as a memento of that time, and since she wasn't particularly pleased with it (the foreground on the right-hand bottom corner, and a most peculiar tree, are *not* her best work) she let me have it. It may not be all that well painted, but somehow it has hit off that view from the roof of the 'HB Sunflower' so well that I sometimes feel that I can almost smell the smoke of the cooking fires as it drifts up from the *dhungas** moored in a backwater on the Sind bank of the river, a little way upstream from the village.

Greatly daring, I submitted six of the 'little pics' done at Shadipore to the Art Society's Selection Committee for the Autumn Art Exhibition. Done on that black photograph-album paper, and all of them only a bit larger than my first trial effort on the back of an envelope – roughly six inches by four. The mounts were much larger, fourteen by ten, which showed them off beautifully. But I was still afraid that the Committee might think I was being frivolous. In the event they not only accepted them, but all six were sold on the first day and in the first ten minutes, and a good many people asked for copies. Triumph! I had hit on something that would pay for my bread-and-butter.

Tacklow had arranged to rent the Club *ghat* when we returned from Shadipore because he and Mother would be going away for a few weeks, taking Kadera with them, and they did not like the idea of leaving me on

* Country boats.

my own in an isolated *ghat*, in sole charge of Angie and the Lizel Kaz. It was not that they did not consider Mahdoo and the *manji* and his family sufficient as protectors, but I was a young unmarried woman, and as such must be particularly careful not to offend any of the Old-Cats Brigade. As an additional precaution against this, it had been arranged for a friend of mine, one 'Kitten' Critchly (she wasn't Critchly then, but I can't remember her maiden name) to be my guest on the 'Sunflower' until they returned.

Having settled into our new *ghat*, we drove out to the Lolab Valley to have lunch with the honeymoon couple, who seemed to be having an idyllic time in their forest bungalow, and had nothing to complain of except for one rousing interlude when a Cona coffee machine, one of the wedding presents that they had taken out with them, had suddenly blown up like a bomb, spattering coffee all over everything in the sitting-room. Fortunately, neither of them had been in the room at the time.

Bets seemed to be full of the joys of spring, and as William Henry didn't put a foot wrong, we returned to Srinagar feeling greatly reassured. The next day Tacklow, Mother and Kadera left for the South. They had both been secretive about the trip, and I didn't realize until the last moment that as soon as Tacklow reappeared in India, quite a number of semi-independent potentates had written to him offering him jobs in their states. But since the majority of these states were in Rajputana he had to refuse.

Now the ruler of one that was not in the 'Country of the Kings' had not only written, but sent one of his senior officials to discuss the matter with him. It was an alluring offer; but in a part of the sub-continent that Mother did not know, and Tacklow was not sure if she would like spending the next three or four years there. Or if he would either. While he was still hesitating, an invitation arrived for both of them to visit the state for ten days or so, which would give Tacklow a chance to become familiar with the problems involved, and Mother to see the house that she would be living in, if that offer was accepted.

My parents, who would normally have left me in charge of Kadera, had taken him with them in order that he too would see what the problems were and decide if he could cope with them. For unlike Tonk, which was a Muslim state, this one was Hindu. 'I can't accept unless your Mother and Kadera feel that they would be happy there,' said Tacklow. 'And Mahdoo says that Kadera speaks for him.' So off the three of them went while I resigned myself to a period of peace and dullness, playing gooseberry to Kitten, who was never without a suitor in tow. In fact, the following weeks turned out to be some of the most hectic that I can remember.

What with all the pre-wedding flap, followed by that spell in Shadipore, and one thing and another, I had, again, been too preoccupied with my own affairs to keep track of Kitten's. I now discovered that she had written off the young man who had been in hot pursuit when I had last been paying attention, and that he had been replaced in her affections by not one but *three* ardent suitors, all in the Indian Cavalry, though in different regiments, and all equally tall and charming. Her trouble at the moment was that she could not choose between them. I insisted on remaining strictly neutral and refused to advise.

Kitten was, when I first knew her, the most attractive creature: small and slim and green-eyed, with the most lovely red-gold hair, the sort of girl that chaps fall for on sight. The fact that the three she had acquired were all friends helped a lot; and since Kitten made it clear to them that wherever she went, I went too, I had a lot of fun, for I had met all three before and their manners were far too good to allow me to feel that I was the odd one out. Which would certainly have happened if there had been a single suitor. As it was, I was never allowed to feel *de trop*, and while Kitten was a house guest on the 'Sunflower', the days were filled with luncheons at Nedou's, picnics on the lakes or in a Mogul garden, expeditions to Vernarg, whose secret springs are the source of the Jhelum, and to the lovely little garden of Achabal that was planted by Shah Jehan and said to be his favourite among the Mogul gardens.

Some nights Mahdoo provided dinner for the five of us, but very rarely on dance nights, in other words every night but Sunday, for when there wasn't a dance in Nedou's Ballroom, there was one at the Srinagar Club, with the attraction of a 'gramophone hop' at the Nageem Bagh Club – an attractive option, since it entailed a half-hour *shikarra* trip by starlight or moonlight through the romantic waterways that link the Dāl Gate to the main lakes.

The *shikarra* rides presented a problem, for since none of the three boys would allow Kitten to be rowed *tête-à-tête* with only one of the others, she either had to go with me and one of her suitors, or with two of them while I went with the third. I got a lot of fun out of watching the manoeuvring of the boys, each of them keeping a wary eye on his friends for fear that one of them would outsmart the other and get her to himself. I lent an interested ear to all of them in turn, while they confided their hopes and fears to me, secure in the knowledge that Kitten was in the company of both the others. And because they were nice young men, and afraid that I might feel like the mother-of-all-gooseberries, and resent it, they put themselves out to be nice to me, so that although lacking a cavalier of my own, I was looked after and entertained royally.

By the end of her stay with me, my parents due to return 'any day now', not one of Kitten's three beaux had been able to get her alone (the other two always made sure of that!) and she herself had still not made up her mind which one she preferred. Asked for my advice for the umpteenth time, I said rather crossly that if she really was unable to choose between them, then she obviously wasn't in love with any of them. In which case I suggested that she kissed the boys goodbye and started again from scratch with somebody else . . .

On the other hand, if she was set on being cold-blooded about it, then why not play 'eeny-meeny-miney-mo' with them, or just toss a coin? Kitten said that I didn't understand, burst into tears and rushed out of the room. Well, she was right there. I didn't understand. But of one thing I was sure. The boys' leave was almost up, and they had already hired a car between them to take them down to Rawalpindi and the railway, and booked a table at Nedou's for a farewell dinner party and dance on their last but one night. One never knew when those dances would end until the band broke into 'J'attendrai'. That melody spelt 'Goodnight all, we're packing it in', and it had become a custom for couples with a sentimental interest in each other, if they were dancing together when the band launched into that tune, to make for the nearest door to the garden when it ended, instead of rejoining the members of their party on the stage or the sitting-out area around the ballroom floor.

I don't think Claud, Dick or Andrew had recalled this habit until the dancing began, but I was aware of their increasing anxiety as the evening wore on, for it was fairly obvious that whichever of the three happened to be dancing with Kitten when that tune began would whisk her away into the garden the moment that it ended. And though they continued to behave beautifully to me, and I danced every dance, they began to watch Kitten over my shoulder, and to lose the thread of any conversation. I was enthralled!

The floor was still cluttered with dancers and the time well past one o'clock when the band began that fateful melody. Kitten had been dancing with Dick, and they must have been near the door at the far end of the room, because we didn't see them leave. The band played 'God Save the King' and we all dutifully stood to attention. But when it stopped there was no sign of them; and though Claud and Andrew and I stayed on, talking and sipping our drinks long after the other dancers had dispersed and the big ballroom was empty except for ourselves and the hotel *khitmagars*, who were clearing away the usual debris of a dance night, they did not return. In the end, Claud took me home in a tonga, and came in and drank cups and cups of hot coffee (prepared by Mahdoo, who had been waiting up for me) and poured out all his woes. He seemed convinced (they all were) that the first one of them to get Kitten alone would be able to talk her into marrying him. I attempted to comfort the out-smarted suitor, but without much success, and finally, at about three o'clock, managed to persuade him to leave. Kitten returned shortly afterwards with the information that she was engaged to Dick, and I said: 'Oh, good-o,' and went back to sleep.

She told me next morning that he was the only man in the world for her, and that she couldn't understand why she hadn't realized it before; she must have been mad not to know it at once, and she was deliriously happy.

The boys left for their respective regiments; my parents returned from South India and received the usual delirious welcome from Angelina and the Lizel Kaz. Kitten left for Delhi, where Dick had arranged for some friends of his to put her up, and I received a distracted letter from her telling me that Dick had been sent off on some military business and had asked his brother to meet her at Delhi and look after her until he could get back to Delhi himself. 'But, oh Moll, I'm in such a muddle,' wrote Kitten. 'I don't know what to do. What would you do if you were me?'

It took me some time to sort out what she was in a muddle about, but in the course of several more distracted letters it became clear that Dick and his brother were twins. Well, we all knew that, and it had been mentioned to her again and again, but what with being too busy playing 'eeny-meeny-miney-mo' with her three suitors she hadn't bothered to pay much attention to it. The trouble was that they were very nearly identical twins. When I say 'very nearly', I mean that when they were together one could tell at once which was which. But if one of them walked into a room alone I never had the least idea which one it was. Kitten hadn't given the 'twins' angle a thought, and stepping off the train on to Delhi station platform, she had seen what she supposed to be Dick, who must have wriggled out of his Army chore after all, and had flung herself into his arms with cries of joy. Only to discover that she was embracing the wrong brother.

'The awful thing about it is that he's better looking than Dick,' wrote Kitten. 'And I *know* you won't understand, you never do, but what would *you* do if you'd just fallen madly in love with a man, and hadn't seen him for a week or two, and then met him again, and thought he was even better and handsomer and nicer than you'd thought, and having hugged and kissed him, found that it wasn't him at all, but his twin brother! What *would* you do? It isn't fair –!'

Well, I see her point. That's a *very* tricky one. The trouble was, of course, that Gerald *was* better looking and nicer than Dick, and she hadn't really had the time as yet to get to know Dick really well. If she'd met the two together, or Gerald first, there is no doubt at all which she would have gone after. I don't know how they sorted it out between them, but I was told by several chums who were at their wedding (which I missed by being incarcerated at the time in the Islington Isolation Hospital for Infectious Diseases, having acquired two kinds of measles, German and common-or-garden, at the same time) that Kitten looked ravishing in her wedding dress, but when she came up the aisle to where the groom and his twin, the best man, awaited her, no one was quite sure until the last possible moment which one she would marry.

She sent me her wedding bouquet, a lovely mixture of lilies and white orchids that sent the nurses in the hospital into raptures; the matron told me that normally the only time they saw that sort of bouquet was in connection with a funeral. But a bride's bouquet! – that really was something *romantic*. I handed it on to the Sisters' sitting-room. The marriage seems to have been a success.

Tacklow had finally decided to take the job that had been offered to him, provided it was cleared with the F and P. Mother had approved of the house and been charmed by the royal women, one of whom, with attendant ladies of the *zennana*, came up to Srinagar with her husband for a 'Princes' Polo Week' hosted by HH of Kashmir. Mother and I were both invited to a *purdah*-party, a women-only tea party in the upper room of one of HH's guest-houses, and I have never in my life seen so many truly beautiful women in one room. They were truly dazzling; even the older ones. Their saris were of the kind that were woven in Benares only for the wives and daughters of India's princely houses or, very occasionally, for the women-folk of her millionaires. But never for lesser mortals. Their jewels had been re-cut in Amsterdam and re-designed in Paris, and their shoes were made in Italy. And apart from their outstanding beauty and charm, on which no price could have been set, each one, as she stood there, must have been worth at least a million sterling, which in present terms would be thirty to forty million.

It was a privilege to see them; and we shall never see their like again. For after Independence and Partition, when the Princes were abolished and their revenues were subject to punitive taxes, it became too dangerous to flaunt fabulous jewels, since to own great riches brought the tax gatherers down. The legendary jewels of the 'Kings' went into hiding, and though men must still know where they are it is possible that in time their hiding places may be forgotten and they will lie hidden for centuries.

Chapter 17

You would have thought that the location of Tacklow's new job, and the identity of his employer, would have been of sufficient importance to me to ensure that I remembered all about it. After all, I too would be making my home there for the next three years, and that alone must have been a matter of considerable interest to me. Instead, there is a complete blank in my mind concerning that job, what it was, where it was, with whom it was.

The blank remains to this day. I remember them coming back and Kitten leaving; and I must have received the impression that all had gone well and the future looked rosy. Because if it were not so, I feel sure that I would have remembered that. I certainly remember a feeling of aimlessness and of being at a loose end without Bets around to talk things over with; and of flatness and nothing-to-do, without Kitten and her adorers to fill every minute of the day with interest and amusement. Now, with both Bets and Kitten gone, my days would have been dull indeed if it had not been for that box of miniature poster paints. I fell back on them for my entertainment and worked hard at improving the technique.

Mother and I went out painting almost every day, sometimes in a *shikarra* and sometimes in the car. We were never short of subjects, for there were pictures wherever one looked, and Kashmir spoiled me for ever for sketching in the West, particularly in the land that all Anglo-Indians invariably referred to as 'home'.

Srinagar began to fill up again for the brief autumn season, as up in Gulmarg the nights became too chilly and frost glittered on the *marg* every morning. One by one the huts emptied as their occupants left for the warmer temperatures in the valley below, leaving the *chowkidars* to roll up carpets, mattresses and curtains and stow them away among the shrouded furniture stacked for greater protection in one of the innermost rooms, before locking the doors and boarding every window with stout wooden shutters that would not be taken down until the following spring.

In the valley the willows and poplars, walnuts, chestnuts and fruit trees began to change colour, and high up on the side of the Takt-i-Suliman a single chenar tree that had somehow managed to take root and survive on what was then a completely barren slope signalled the coming of the cold weather by turning a brilliant scarlet. And one by one the holiday-makers began to leave for British India and the plains.

Houseboats, hotels and guest-houses emptied, and I started on a round of visits, spending a few days and nights with kind friends with whom I had danced and acted in a number of charity cabaret shows during the past year, and who in the kindness of their hearts decided that I must be cheered up and entertained to keep me from moping over the departure of my sister from the fold. It was very sweet of them and much appreciated, since it was also in a way a goodbye from the Punjab: the people I would meet down south would be different from the ones I had known in the north.

Tacklow was due to take up his new appointment at the end of October, which was one of the best times of year on the plains. September could be not only hot with the left-over heat-waves and dust-storms of the summer months, but intolerably damp and muggy from the remnants of the monsoon. The cold weather proper started at the beginning of November.

Bets's birthday being on 13 October, we used to celebrate the occasion by a picnic up to Gulmarg, returning to Srinagar in time to dine and dance at Nedou's that evening, festivities which also served to mark, for us, the end of the Kashmir season. After that all hot-weather visitors got down to packing up, paying their bills and saying goodbye to friends, many of whom would be leaving for widely separated sections of the map and whom we would therefore not see again until the hot weather drove them up to the hills once more. I would certainly have returned to the 'Sunflower' in time to help deal with this last stage of the annual sarabande, so I can only suppose that the letter cancelling Tacklow's job must have arrived while I was away and that they had had time to get used to it, and to accept it, and saw no point in writing to tell me about it, let alone sending for me.

If they could have got out of telling me about it, I am sure that they would have done so. But there was no way of hiding it, since all the plans for our removal from Kashmir, our stop-over in New Delhi to see Bets and her husband, and all the arrangements for the long journey south, had to be cancelled. Until we could make alternative ones we would have to retain the 'Sunflower' and its crew and stay where we were.

It was Tacklow who told me what had happened. I don't think he trusted Mother not to get too upset about it again. She had been so angry. He had received a most regretful and apologetic letter from the Diwan of his would-be employer, who was obviously deeply embarrassed by having to write it, to say that when (as was customary among the princely states) the Foreign and Political Department had been informed of the employment of Sir Cecil Kaye, they had been 'advised' against it on the grounds that Sir Cecil was *persona non grata* among the Department, and 'regarded as a trouble-maker' – *Tacklow*. Of all people! 'It's like being black-balled from my Club,' said Tacklow bitterly, 'and never being able to enter it again.'

The head of the state which had wished to employ him could, of course, have ignored the 'advice' and insisted on taking him on. Some most undesirable characters had, in the past, been employed by princes who had been strongly advised by the Government not to touch them with a bargepole, yet had insisted on their right to do so. Such appointments had frequently led to scandal and disaster and to the Department saying 'We *told* you so, didn't we!' And even when they didn't, a refusal to take advice went down in the books as a black mark, and was something to be avoided.

Nonetheless, there was a strong hint in the Diwan's letter that if Tacklow desired it, His Highness was prepared to tell the F and P to jump in the lake, and go ahead with employing him; and, speaking for myself, I was so furious that I was all for that. But I might have known that Tacklow wouldn't dream of agreeing – because to do so would only mean trouble for the state in the future. Besides, he simply did not know how to do nasty, sneaky, underhand things, any more than he knew how to tell lies.

He had been badly hit by the Tonk débâcle, so badly that he had wanted to have no more to do with India and its lies and intrigues, and had escaped from it to the China of his happiest memories. There had been no resting place there, and no option but to return to India, for his son was there and his wife and daughters couldn't wait to get back there – Bets to be married and Moll because she regarded it as home, and his darling Daisy because it was the country to which he had brought her as a teenage bride over a quarter of a century ago.

The pressure to return had been too great. But so had the expenses. The visit to Japan. A winter season in Delhi. Bets's trousseau and her wedding. It had all cost a good deal more than he had budgeted for, and if there was one thing that Tacklow was scared of it was getting into debt. He had had no desire to take another job, however well paid, in an Indian state. Not after the horrors of that last one. But when the offer came he could not afford to turn it down. And now this death blow . . .

I suppose he should have realized that in the Government of India the Departments stuck together in the manner of the mafiosi. According to Mother, there had been quite a lot of dismay when Tacklow, a soldier by profession, had been appointed Director of Central Intelligence – a post which until then had always been one of the plum jobs of the 'Heaven-born'. Mother had once told me that some of them 'hadn't liked it at all' and had been 'excessively catty about it' – their wives, I presume (though when it comes to cattiness no one can be as catty as a tom cat) – but that 'fortunately', that sort of thing 'slid off Tacklow's back and he never even noticed it'. He had *had* to notice it in Tonk because his nose had been rubbed in it. And he was noticing this time! Both of them were. The only thing I remember with painful clarity is how angry Mother was and how *old* Tacklow looked . . . how frighteningly old.

Everything had been discussed and decided upon while I was still away. I wasn't asked to give my views on my parents' future, or my own. This time Tacklow was going to do what he wanted to do. He had been a roving correspondent for the *Near East and India* ever since he had left England in the autumn of 1927, and now he had cabled them to ask if he could take over again as editor, a post that was due to fall vacant in a year's time. The reply being 'yes', he had written to book passages for Mother, himself and me on a passenger ship sailing from Bombay on the last day of March. Mother had already written off to a number of her special friends, asking if she could come and stay with them for a week or ten days, because Tacklow planned to stay with his sister, Aunt Molly, up with whom she would not put, while they went house-hunting. Since I was no fonder of Aunt Molly than Mother was, I also made arrangements to stay with friends until such a time as my parents found a house they liked and could afford. And in the meantime I went on what I thought was going to be a last, lovely spree in Kashmir.

There being no longer any reason for giving up the boat, we kept it on, moored at the Club *ghat*; and Mother and I went out painting every day, with a view to giving a last exhibition of our work in Delhi when the time came to pack up and leave for good. The valley put on its best party-dress for us and blazed with red and gold, and my brother Bill and my cousin Dick Hamblyn came up together to spend a short leave on the 'Sunflower'.

Aud Wrench had invited me to stay with her for Christmas. And now, since her father, Sir Evelyn, was due to retire in the spring and her family too would be sailing home at the end of the season, they invited me to come down again to Delhi ahead of my family, and spend ten days with them so that I could join in all the goodbye parties that they were planning. Bets, too, was in Delhi in a minute 'married-quarter' that had no room for guests, so she could not put me up. But we saw a good deal of each other during that Christmas visit to the Wrenches, and again when I came down at the end of February.

Tacklow and Mother were going to spend a few days in Old Delhi with a long-time friend of theirs, an Indian doctor who, years later, I used as the model for Gobind Dass, Kaka-ji's doctor in *The Far Pavilions*. He had a lovely house in Old Delhi, one of the old nineteenth-century bungalows, and I think he must have been the man who lent us the house in Gupkar Road in which we stayed when we first came up to Kashmir in that dismal March of 1927. He had been a friend and neighbour of my parents when Tacklow was the Director of Central Intelligence, and he and my parents had houses in Rajpore Road.

Bets drove me over from the Wrenches' house in New Delhi to meet them, and I was shocked to see how tired and depressed they both seemed, and that Mother's eyes were red as though she had been crying. I put that down to tiredness and the long, dusty journey down from the Grand Trunk Road from Lahore, which was their last stopping place. But it wasn't that. It was Angelina Sugar-peas . . .

They had both realized that they could not take Angie to England with them. There were no quarantine restrictions in those days, but they could not expect friends in England, or hotels either, to put up with a monkey – and an extremely destructive one too! – as a house guest. Nor was there any chance of their coming back again, as they had come back from China. For one thing, they couldn't afford to. And Mahdoo and Kadera had both been found well-paid jobs in which they felt happy and comfortable, but their new employers would not take on Kadera plus Angie.

Tacklow had arranged to take the Lizel Kaz to England with him. But Mother could not possibly take Angie. In the end Tacklow had made a special journey down to Lahore earlier that winter, in order to discuss the matter with the sympathetic head of the Lahore Zoo, who out of the kindness of his heart eventually agreed to accept Angie and do his best to make her happy. It was good of him, since brown monkeys are as common as locusts throughout the sub-continent and the last thing any zoo wanted was yet *another* of them. Tacklow had been so grateful that he had made the zoo a donation of a thousand rupees (which he could ill afford) in Angie's name.

Mother had taken a lot of comfort from the fact that Angie would have others of her own kind to play with, and when the time came for them to leave Kashmir, Angie spent most of the long journey sitting on Mother's lap, both paws on the wheel, pretending that she was driving, only retiring to Kadera on the back seat for the occasional nap. Mahdoo, as usual, had gone down ahead of them by bus and train to Delhi, to keep an eye on the heavy luggage, and Kaz travelled on Tacklow's knee.

The boss of the Lahore Zoo had been there to meet them, and be introduced to Angie so that she would know he was a friend and must not on *any* account be bitten, and she sat on his knee, sniffed at his coat and tweaked his ear-lobes, and decided that he was OK.

He took them to see the new addition that had been attached to the monkey cage, in which she would spend a few days, making the acquaintance of the other monkeys through the wire in case they might attack the stranger. Once they got used to her and she to them, she would be allowed to join the group, and with luck she would mate with the dominant male and have a baby to fuss over and keep her occupied and happy. Mother had taken her into the cage and let her look at it all, and touch noses with an inquisitive monkey in the main cage, and all seemed to be going well until Mother tried to leave. Angie leapt on her and hung on to her like a limpet, and it took a long time before she could be detached to let Mother get outside the cage. It was painfully clear that she knew she was being abandoned. She had leapt and howled and shrieked, clutching at the bars and trying to squeeze out between them – pushing her skinny little arms out and begging Mother to rescue her. Tacklow said it was a most harrowing performance, and in the end, he said: 'I had to *drag* your Mother away – she was in floods of tears.'

They were staying the night at Faletti's Hotel, so that they could pay another visit to the zoo the next day to see how Angie was settling in and make her feel that they were still around. But it had been a grave mistake. They had both expected her to greet them with rapture. But instinct had told her that this time she was being left for good, and monkeys can be horribly human. She was sitting on the ground staring out between the bars, and when she saw them she turned her back on them quite deliberately and refused to look at them or speak to them. She knew. Kadera, telling me about it, said, 'She knew that this was not like the last time. That this time the Lady-Sahib would never come back.'

Apparently they stayed there for quite a time, trying to persuade Angie to speak to them or look at them. But it was no good. They had sentenced her to prison for life, and she knew it. And when they gave up and left, they were all in tears. Tacklow said that it would probably have been far kinder to have a vet put her down, but that the 'zoo man' had been so *sure* that once she got friendly with the other monkeys, and could be allowed to have the run of the big cage with its trees and shrubs, she would enjoy life among her own kind and get herself a husband. Sadly, the zoo man was wrong. Angie went on hunger strike and starved herself to death.

A few days later Bets rang me up around breakfast time to say that Mother had rung her to say that Tacklow had just had a mild heart-attack and would she get in touch with me at once, and both of us come round as soon as we could. He and Kaz had been taking their customary pre-*chota-hazri* stroll in the garden and he was still in his dressing-gown, when he suddenly doubled up and collapsed on the lawn. Fortunately both the doctor and Kadera were on the verandah at the time, and seeing him fall they ran out and carried him back to bed, and the doctor, who must have been only too familiar with heart-attacks, had given him something that had brought him round. But he would have to stay in bed for some days, and he must be kept quite quiet if he was going to be fit enough for the train journey to Bombay.

It didn't sound too terrifying, and by the time Bets had dropped William Henry at his office, picked me up at the Wrenches' and brought us to the *Hakim-Sahib*'s house in Old Delhi, my heart had stopped flopping and twitching like a newly-caught trout, and I was almost able to breathe properly again. We found Tacklow sitting propped up on pillows in his bed, looking a bit pallid, but otherwise in fairly good shape, and were reassured to see the doctor sitting on the edge of the bed, issuing instructions to Mother about what she was to give him, and when, and how often and so on . . .

He had, he told us, phoned the Walker Hospital on the Ridge, who were sending along a nurse to keep an eye on the invalid for the next few days, 'just in case', and he would make arrangements for a night-nurse to take over from the day one. At which both my parents had protested, insisting that he wasn't nearly ill enough to warrant the valuable time of two nurses, and Mother, who like most women who had lived through the 1914–18 war had taken a course of nursing under the Red Cross, protested that she could do anything that needed to be done for Cecil; the doctor only had to tell her. The doctor, however, stuck to his guns, and a nurse duly turned up, though there didn't seem to be much for her to do.

For the next few days I spent most of my time in or near Tacklow's room, Bets fetching me from the Wrenches' every morning and taking me back every night. I didn't know anything about heart-attacks, and nor did Mother. But it worried me that Tacklow should insist on finishing an article he had been writing for the *Near East and India*. We did try to stop him, but he insisted that it must be done in time to catch the next mail boat, and seemed so upset at the prospect of missing it that even the doctor agreed that he had better be allowed to do it. So he sat propped up in bed with the ceiling fan sweeping round above him, and wrote and wrote, with Kaz lying curled up against him, occasionally making a dab at the moving pencil with one black paw.

I had cancelled all my daytime engagements, including one that Aud had arranged long ago, to drive over with a party of friends to Meerut to watch the final of the Inter-Regimental Polo Tournament. This was something Aud had avoided doing for several seasons past, because the last time she went she had seen Tony Greenaway, the young cavalry officer to whom she had only recently become engaged, killed on the polo-ground by a ball that struck him between the eyes. But one cannot wear the willow for ever; and since she and her family would shortly be leaving India for good, she had decided to take this last chance of seeing some of the best and most exciting polo in India, and made up another goodbye party of her friends, which included myself and about half-a-dozen others.

Tacklow had known about it well before he had had that heart-attack, and I hoped that he would forget. But he hadn't; and when, on inquiring, he learned this was one of the invitations I had cancelled, he put his foot down and insisted it be kept. He would, he said, have liked to have seen the finals himself, but since he couldn't, I must describe it for him. In the end I agreed, provided the doctor gave me the OK. Though in the event I very nearly cancelled it, and I shall always regret that I didn't.

One hot, still afternoon, when he had finished that article at last, and Bets had driven Mother to the Post Office with it because they wanted to be absolutely certain that it had the proper stamps on it and see that it went off safely; when the doctor was on duty in the hospital and the day-nurse was sound asleep on a cot on the back of the verandah, and Tacklow and I had the house to ourselves except for Kaz, who had tucked herself under Tacklow's chin and was purring gently, Tacklow suddenly said: 'This is the end of the road for me, Moll. I'm finished – my number's up.'

I don't remember what we had been talking about – nothing of much importance. But there had been a pause in the conversation, and without any warning at all, he suddenly came out with that terrifying sentence. It was as if he had thrown a great lump of rock into a quiet pool, and I couldn't speak. I've never been so frightened in my life. I'd been frightened in Peking when he came out with that verse from *Show Boat* – about being tired of living and afraid of dying. But this was pure terror and I was Lot's wife freezing into a pillar of salt, or one of Polydectes' guests turning into stone at the sight of Medusa's head.

Tacklow said: 'I've tried to warn your Mother . . . to make it a little easier for her. But she doesn't understand. It only upsets her . . .'

And because I was terrified, I leapt from terror into anger; it was a sort of escape from fear, I suppose. I remember shouting at him: 'Don't be so silly! You've only had a mild heart-attack, and you're getting on fine. You oughtn't to scare the daylights out of us by saying such stupid things! I'm not surprised Mother's upset!'

'She's no mathematician,' said Tacklow. And when I asked what on earth mathematics had to do with it, he said he'd worked it all out years ago: the ages at which four or five generations of his family in the direct line had died. 'That's why I know that my time is up,' he said.

Why, I wonder, should one find an escape from fear in anger? I couldn't *breathe* because I was so frightened. I wanted to throw my arms round him and hold him tight and beg him not to leave me because I could not cope with life without him. Instead I merely lost my temper, and if he had lost his we'd have had a blazing row. But then Tacklow wasn't that sort of person; he had always been a quiet man and now he only looked at me a little sadly as I flung a lot of angry words at him before running out of the room to bring up my lunch behind the bougainvillaea bushes in the garden. After which I didn't have a chance to see him alone and apologize, for by the time I was fit to be seen again, Mother and Bets had come back, and then Kadera arrived with the tea-tray and everything steadied down a bit.

The day-nurse reappeared, and when the doctor came back and seemed pleased with Tacklow's condition, I felt enormously reassured. Nothing really bad could happen to him while he had a doctor and a nurse all to himself, and when I said goodnight to him that evening I hugged him very tightly in a silent apology, and he said: 'Poor Mouse! Don't worry darling – I could have got my sums wrong. Have a nice time in Meerut, and you can tell me all about it when you get back.' And then Bets drove me back to New Delhi and dropped me off at the Wrenches' house. I know now why he invented that nonsense about mathematics. Because he didn't want me to blame anyone.* Darling Tacklow . . .

I rang Mother early next morning to find out how he was doing, and she put me on to the doctor, and since both reports were reassuring, I went off with Aud's party to Meerut to watch the finals of the Inter-Regimentals. I don't remember anything about them, except that there was a good game and we were all invited by mutual friends in the teams to have drinks in the Club afterwards; and that the celebrations went on until they turned into a supper party, so that by the time we got back to New Delhi it was far too late to call in at the doctor's house, or even ring up, as that would only have woken everyone in it.

Anyway, I knew that if Tacklow's condition had worsened, Bets would have contacted me in Meerut; and if she missed me there, a message would certainly have been left for me at the Wrenches'. Comforted by the absence of either, and tired out by the doings of the day and the two long and dusty drives to Meerut and back, I fell into bed and must have been asleep almost before my head reached the pillow – only to be awakened in the small hours of the morning by the headlights of a car flaring on my window and my brother-in-law's voice shouting my name.

I knew at once that this was disaster. It was like a knife being driven

* He knew very well whom I would blame, and hoped to stop me getting into trouble.

into one's chest. A terrible physical pain. I didn't seem to be able to think, and I remember tearing at my mosquito net in senseless panic, because I couldn't free myself from it, and when I did, I raced around my room like a rat in a trap, trying to find the door, while all the time those blazing headlights lit up the room and a man's voice kept shouting 'Moll! Mollie! Moll –!' I don't know how I managed to get out of the house, but the next thing I remember is that I was sitting huddled up on the back seat of the car and someone – Bets I suppose – had made me put on a dressing-gown over my nightdress and slippers on my feet, and that William Henry was breaking the speed-limit through the dark, empty streets.

Tacklow had had a second heart-attack, and this one had not been mild. It had been so bad that either the doctor or the night-nurse had rung William Henry's number and told him to bring his wife and her sister along as quickly as possible. Bets kept on saying: 'Hurry! Hurry!' while I just sat there and prayed and prayed; probably making all sorts of wild promises if God would only . . . only . . . Well, most of us have done this or will do it at one time or another, and too many have turned their backs on God because He hasn't granted them what, in most cases, would have to be a miracle.

I can't remember what promises I made in return for Tacklow being allowed to live into his eighties – he was only sixty-six, not even man's promised span of 'three-score and ten' – but I think if it had been granted I would have kept them. I kept at least one: from that night until this one, I have never once neglected to say my prayers, except when I have been ill enough to be sedated and unaware of time. Nor have I ever failed to say 'goodnight' to Tacklow, just in *case* he may be allowed to keep an occasional eye on me. I like to think that he may be allowed to do that; and I have always been certain that if anyone can get me through the Pearly Gates, it will be Tacklow.

I was still praying desperately when the car reached the gates of the doctor's house and I saw that they were shut, and jumped out and opened them enough to get through, and ran up the drive. There were no street lamps in that quiet road, but the bungalow was brightly lit. There were lights on in every room and I raced up the drive and made straight for Tacklow's room. There was no one else in it. Just Tacklow, lying on his back with his eyes shut, as I had seen him so often during the last few days, and I checked, looking at him, unwilling to wake him and thinking,

'Oh, thank God, he's still alive.' I tiptoed forward and bent down and kissed him. And only then knew, with an agonizing shock, that he was dead. That it wasn't Tacklow lying there any more.

Tacklow had gone, and this was just the old overcoat to which he had once compared his body when, for some forgotten reason, a party of us had embarked on a macabre discussion as to where, if we had the choice, would we prefer to be buried? When the question came round to Tacklow, he had replied that personally, he couldn't care less where he was buried, since he would regard his body as an old overcoat that had done him good service and could now be discarded as too worn and shabby for further use. Why should he care what happened to it? 'But if you *had* to choose?' insisted one of the party. Tacklow thought for a moment and then said that if he died in England, he would like to be buried in the churchyard at Sandy near Tetworth,* the house that his grandparents used to live in, and where he had spent many of his school holidays. But since it was far more likely that he would die in India, the place he would choose was a little British cemetery at Sanour, overlooking the Kalkar-Simla road and the cantonment of Dugshai,† the first hill station to which he was sent when he arrived in India as a teenage 'Griffen'.

If I had only kissed him on the forehead or the top of his head, or his hand, it would not have been so bad. But I had kissed him on his lips, and their total slackness and lack of warmth or response spelt death in a way nothing else could have done. I have never forgotten the feel of it, and nothing else in my life has ever been as bad as that was.

Someone was crying in the next room, and I realized that it must be Mother and that I ought to go to her. The next-door room seemed over-bright, and she was sitting at a table in the middle of it in an attitude of utter despair, her head on her outstretched arms and her beautiful hair all loose and tangled, spread out across her arms and the table-top. She was still dressed, as I was, in a thin cotton nightdress and kimono, and when I put my arms around her and hugged her, she lifted her head. Her face was so puffed up and smudgy with crying that it was almost unrecognizable, and I don't think she can have had the least idea who I was, because her eyes were too red and swollen to see out of, and tears were pouring helplessly out of them in an unstoppable stream, soaking

* See *The Sun in the Morning*.
† See above note.

the front of a kimono that Tacklow had bought her barely a year ago. I tried to say something comforting, but I was too badly in need of comfort myself, and all that Mother could whisper between sobs was, 'What's to become of me? What's to become of me?'

What indeed? She had only been in her sixteenth year when Tacklow had seen her on the platform of the Tientsin railway station and fallen instantly and forever in love with her. He had spoilt and petted and cherished her, treating her as though she was still that attractive tomboyish 'Gibson-Girl' with whom he had fallen in love in North China, and she had about as much idea of looking after herself as a goldfish. Tacklow had done everything for her. She hadn't known, until her first voyage home alone in 1919, how to write out or cash a cheque, because he had always paid all the bills and dealt with any household problems. And now she was on her own, with no one to do the sums for her or cope with things like rates and taxes, or teach her how to make ends meet on a drastically reduced widow's pension.

The doctor and the night-nurse were both in the room with her, watching her with the silent sympathy of those who are only too used to death, and Bets took over comforting her with a good deal more success than I had had – she had always been Mother's darling – while William Henry dealt with things like telegrams and announcements to the Press and, presumably, to Bill. Bets and the night-nurse managed to get Mother into her bed, which had been moved into another room after Tacklow's first heart-attack, and the doctor gave her an injection of something to help her sleep. When at last that worked, Bets and I went back to Tacklow and I carefully cut off a curl of his grey hair – one of the two that we used to twist into a pair of little horns, one each side of his head, in imitation of a cartoon character called 'Pop' who bore a marked resemblance to Tacklow. I kept that little curl for years, despite being told by Kadera, and later by several of my Indian friends, that to keep the hair of a dead person is not a good thing to do, for it ties them to the earth, which is something they may not desire.

Many years later, during a scrambled house-move, some unknown 'helper' opened the tiny silver *paan* box that Devika* had given me as a parting present when I left India for an English boarding school, and mistaking the little grey wisps inside it for padding intended to protect

* See *The Sun in the Morning*.

something small and valuable that was no longer there, shook them out and threw them away.

I don't remember crying; all that came later. But even now, after all these years, I cannot think of Tacklow's death, or talk or write of it, without crying. At the time I must have been too numbed by shock for tears, which was just as well, as both Mother and Bets were being torn to pieces by them, and *someone* had to be able to speak and answer questions. It was the doctor who asked me where we wanted Tacklow to be buried and reminded me that it must be some time today, because the weather was getting too hot to allow for delay. Well, I'd always known that those who died in this country must be buried within twenty-four hours. But this was *Tacklow* we were talking about . . .

A brand new cemetery had been opened in New Delhi, said the doctor, but he presumed that we would prefer to bury Sir Cecil in the Old Delhi one just behind Curzon House; the one in which General Sir John Nicholson of Mutiny fame had been buried.

Yes, I remembered it. That peaceful, tree-shaded, flower-filled spot, full of birds and squirrels and butterflies, where Bets and I used to play when we were small children; climbing over the wall in defiance of Punj-Ayah, whose muslin saris did not permit her to scramble over rough stone walls. But there was the hot weather to be considered; and I also remembered Tacklow reciting part of Kipling's *Ballad of Burial*, which begins: 'If down here I chance to die' and goes on to beg his friends to take his body to the hills for burial, because he could not endure the thought of the hot weather and the September rains 'Yearly till the Judgement Day' . . .

No. Stupid as it sounds, I could not let him be buried in the plains. But those lines of verse had reminded me of something else: that long-ago conversation about 'Where would you be buried if you *had* to choose?' Tacklow had mentioned the little British cemetery at Sanour – if he should die in India. Well, Sanour was not all that far from Delhi, and we could get there in a matter of hours.

'There will not be time,' said the doctor sadly, 'for there are rules about such matters. You would have to get permission from the local authorities – in this case, I presume, the Governors of the Lawrence School in Sanour. And to get that permission would take days, not hours: you know what red-tape is like in this country! It would take too long, and we cannot wait.'

Yes, I knew all about red-tape. But I also thought I knew how to get that permission in record time. As soon as the sun was up I rang Viceroy House and asked if I could speak personally to the Viceroy, emphasizing that it was urgent. The ADC who answered the phone, sounding scandalized, said no, I couldn't, not at that hour of the morning; but that if it was really urgent, I could leave a message and he would see that it reached His Excellency as soon as it was convenient. I told him that I couldn't wait as long as that. My father had died during the night and I would like to speak to His Excellency at once. The ADC said: 'Sir Cecil *dead*? Good God! Look, I *am* sorry. How ghastly for you,' and told me to hang on while he got hold of the Viceroy. A minute later Lord Willingdon was on the phone.

He *couldn't* have been nicer. He told me to give his deepest sympathy to Mother and the family, and that he quite understood about wanting my father buried in Sanour and not left behind in the plains, and that he would see to all that and I wasn't to worry about any of the arrangements; he would get his people to see to everything and someone would be ringing up about it in an hour or two.

Someone, I don't remember who, rang up and spoke to the doctor less than half an hour later, and we didn't have to do anything, except to get dressed, and to see that Mother was dressed and ready for the drive up to Sanour when the cars came to fetch us. The undertakers came to take Tacklow away and we kissed him goodnight and au revoir, and then they were gone, taking him with them in a makeshift hearse that left about an hour ahead of us. I don't remember much about the drive up to Sanour except that there were several cars in addition to the one we travelled in, and I only learned later that both Willingdons had sent 'representatives' and flowers, and that a surprising number of the men who had served under him when he was Director of Central Intelligence, mostly Indian, had taken the time off to attend.

I do remember how hot it was. There isn't a great deal of shade on the road that leads from Delhi to Kalka and the foothills of the Himalayas, across miles of baking, almost treeless plains which in those days looked as flat as a pancake (and where, of all places, Independent India chose to celebrate her freedom by wasting *crores** and *crores* of rupees on building yet another grandiose capital city, which she named Chandigore, and which must be one of the hottest places in the Punjab).

* Crore = 10 million rupees.

It was, as ever, good to feel the air turn cool and freshen as we reached the fringes of the foothills and the road began to climb. At last we left the bare hillsides and the candelabra cactus behind us, and were among pine trees, with Dugshai below us and the hill resort of Kausauli stretching along a ridge above and to our left, and Sanour, and the boys' school that Sir Henry Lawrence founded long before the Mutiny, among the pinewoods to our right. We left the cars at the school, and led by the Headmaster – who was in Orders and presumably took the service – walked in single file down the narrow, overgrown track that led to a seldom used and almost forgotten cemetery where, in the days when Victoria was Empress of India, the young Tacklow had chosen to sit and study, because 'it was such a peaceful place, and because the view from it must be among the most beautiful in India' . . .

We hadn't reached it when Bets stopped and clutched at Mother's arm, turned an alarming shade of pale grey and proceeded to faint. I can still see quite clearly in my mind's eye the few yards of road where she did so. It must have been on a particularly steep strip of hillside, because here there was a portion of low stone wall along its outer edge, which Bets had tried to sit on when she felt that she was about to pass out. Fortunately she didn't manage it, because had she leant backwards I don't know where she would have ended up; probably several hundred yards below and a hospital case. As it was, that faint of hers proved a godsend, for it gave Mother something else to think of.

She had been in a state of shock from the moment she came out of a drug-induced sleep that had lasted well into the morning. She didn't seem to know what Bets and I were doing, or take in what we were saying, and we might have been dressing a life-sized doll. Nor did she say a word during that long drive. She just sat between us staring at nothing and saying nothing. But when Bets clutched at her and flaked out she came out of her daze and behaved as any ordinary parent would have done, demanding brandy, keeping Bets's head down between her knees, and generally fussing over her; and when Bets came round (which was almost immediately) and refused flatly to be escorted back to the schoolhouse to lie down and recover, Mother half led, half carried her the rest of the way, made her sit down on a tree stump beside her and was so preoccupied with the state of Bets's health that she got through the subsequent procedures without breaking down or, I suspect, taking in what was going on. Which was plenty . . .

Because of the delay caused by Bets's faint, the coffin and its bearers had arrived some little time before us, and instead of just putting it down while they waited, they lowered it into the newly dug grave whose measurements had been telephoned to Sanour earlier that morning. Nothing wrong about that, except that they had laid it down so that it faced towards the steep pine-forested hillside behind it instead of towards the wonderful view that lay spread out before us.

I took one look at it and said: 'I'm very sorry, but you've got him facing the wrong way. Would you be very kind and turn him round, please?' But here the two *coolie-log* who had dug the grave came to life. They didn't speak any English, but they understood sign language and I had, as usual, been using my hands as I explained what I wanted done, and now they both protested loudly that it couldn't be done. The grave had been dug to fit the size of the coffin, and it would not fit the other way. 'In that case,' I said, 'just take it out and widen the other end so that it *does* fit. It's quite simple.'

No one else thought it was simple – with the exception of Mother and Bets who were paying no attention because Bets was still feeling groggy and Mother was worried about her. Whoever it was who took the service gave me a lecture on the un-Christian folly of thinking that the spirit of my 'dear departed father' would care about which way his 'mortal remains faced'. I told him that I couldn't agree with him more. But that *I* cared. I wanted to feel that we had left him lying in that particular place, facing that particular view – *not* with his back turned to it. And that I was prepared to stay here until it was done, however long it took!

In the end, and very crossly, they pulled the coffin out and we all sat there on the grass while the diggers widened the grave at the narrow end, and when the coffin was replaced facing the right way, the service went ahead. When it was over and the grave filled in, we went back to the cars. Leaving him on that tree-clad ridge among the foothills of the Himalayas, from where, on a clear day, you can see forever . . . *and ever* . . .

Later on, I designed a stone to mark the spot. A solid chunk of plain grey granite, cut in a flat-topped curve that is exactly the right height and width to make it an inviting seat; in the hope that an occasional pupil from the school, or some rare visitor taking a stroll along the hillside, may sit down to rest there and look out at the same view that Tacklow loved, and be as charmed by it as he was. His name and a couple of dates are carved on the face of the curve, and the only decoration is a pair of stylized daisies, one on each side. He would have liked that.

I have never seen it myself, but one of the Indian actors who appeared in the film version of *The Far Pavilions* told me that his son was a pupil at the Sanour School, and knew the stone seat. And later he took some very good photographs of it and sent me copies. Since then several tourists have done the same, and a few years ago a fan who was touring in the Simla Hills made a special visit to Sanour, and wrote to tell me that my father must have been almost the last, if not the last, person to be buried there, but that his stone still stands unchanged except for the golden circles of lichen here and there on the sides, and that standing on the exact centre of the grave was a single enormous fir-cone.

She had brought the fir-cone away with her because she 'thought I might like it'. Would I! The dear woman sent it to me; and my younger daughter, who has an antique shop, found me a charming stand complete with glass dome, under which it now stands in a place of honour in the corner cupboard of my drawing-room, looking exactly as though it was a wonderful piece of carving by some Chinese master-craftsman.

The days immediately following Tacklow's death were some of the worst I have ever had to endure. I needed him so terribly. I needed his advice and his criticism and his support and understanding, and the knowledge that he would always give me a straight answer, even though it might be a dusty one. I had always known that I needed him in my corner. That was why I had prayed every night that I might be happily married, and, hopefully, the mother of several children before he died, so that I might be at least partially insulated from the pain of losing him. And now he had gone. I hadn't been able to cry that first day, because Mother was crying so dreadfully and there were so many things that needed to be done. I couldn't let myself cry, not at that time, or for a day or two afterwards, because there were things that *had* to be decided, and Mother couldn't cope at all. In the end Bets and I, and presumably Bill, decided to go ahead with the programme that Tacklow had mapped out for us, exactly as if he had been with us.

Mother and I would go back to England, and spend the first six months staying with the various friends and relatives who would be expecting us, and take it from there. But first we must get through the remaining days before the one on which we were booked to leave for Bombay. I don't think there can have been many of them, but they were made hideous by Lizel Kaz. We had none of us had the time to spare for Kaz on that first day, but when we came back from Sanour in the evening, Kadera told us that Kaz had been yowling all day, and refusing to eat or drink. I don't think we took this seriously to begin with, but as the days went by and Kaz continued to search the bungalow and gardens for Tacklow, yowling piteously all the while and getting thinner and thinner, the situation became very tricky. Kaz would only drink if we gave her something that still smelt of Tacklow, and then she would purr and knead it with her paws, and take a sip or two. But she would not eat, and her search for Tacklow became too harrowing for words. In the end we called in a vet, one who specialized in cats and was crazy about Siamese ones. He volunteered to take her home with him for a few days to get her away from the bungalow. But nothing worked. It was Angie all over again; the vet said she was dying of starvation and the kindest thing that we could do was to put her down. The last time I saw Kaz she was nothing but bones inside a black fur sack, but when I kissed her on her nose she purred a little. Poor Kaz. And poor Mother. Poor me!

Chapter 18

~×⌒×~

In the end it was Mike who helped me the most during those nightmare last days in Delhi. I don't know what he was doing in India again, and I hadn't even known he was there. But he had been somewhere down south when he heard the news of Tacklow's death on a radio news bulletin, and he took the next train to Delhi and, walking unannounced into the Wrenches' house, abducted me in a hired car. There was a full moon that week, and he drove me to the Purana Khila, the Old Fort, and, leaving the car by the main gate, walked me off to the Sher Mandal – the library where a Mogul Emperor, Humayun, had killed himself falling down its steep and narrow stairway. Mike plonked me down on the steps that led up to it and said, 'Aud says that you don't cry, and that it's not healthy. Come on, Midshipmite, tell me all about it. What happened?'

So I told him; and when I got to the worst part – how I'd been angry with Tacklow because he'd scared me rigid, and had gone off to Meerut without saying I was sorry, and never seen him alive again, I began to cry. And found that I could not stop. Mike sat with me for a time and then got up and went off to walk across the grassy spaces – in those days there was nothing within the ruined outer walls of the Purana Khila except the Sher Mandal and the beautiful Mosque of Shere Shah. I was still sitting there in the moonlight, dripping like a leaking tap, when he came back a good half hour later. But the pressure was off. Temporarily, at least. Mike was a real friend in those black days, and I shall always be grateful to him. He saw to it that I shouldn't have more than a modicum of time to myself, and Bets and Bill did the same for Mother. I only remember one other night during that time. It was early morning rather than night and the sleeping pills I had been given didn't work, so in the end I got up and went out into the Wrenches' garden to try and tire myself by walking up and down in the moonlight.

I remember how piercingly sweet the night-flowering stocks and the

*Rat-ki-Rani** smelt, and how I couldn't stop crying; not because I would soon be leaving India with little or no prospect of ever getting back again, but because there was a single dreary sentence that kept on repeating itself in my brain with the maddening persistence of a frog croaking from the edge of a pond: 'When I am an old woman, if anyone asks me about my father I shall have to say: "He died when I was still only a girl in my twenties . . ."'

That seemed to me then, and still does, the saddest thing that anyone could say. Because it meant that he left me just when I needed him most. When I was adrift in an uncharted sea and badly in need of a pilot. I must have walked the moon down because in the end it dawned on me that the garden had become very dark and the sky in the east was growing paler every minute, and that tears were still pouring down my face and had soaked the front of my nightdress. And suddenly I stopped thinking of Tacklow and began to wonder where on earth one's tears came from. I seemed to have an inexhaustible supply of them, but from where? How was it possible to keep on and *on* producing this mysterious salt water, hour after hour, without the supply giving out? It was the sort of ridiculous question that Tacklow could probably have answered off the bat. How was I going to get through my youth without him? How was I going to get through the rest of my life without him? There was so much of it left. All the rest of my twenties, my thirties and forties; marriage, mother-hood and middle age, all without him. 'My father died when I was a girl in my twenties . . .' I suppose I must have managed an hour of sleep in the end, but not until the sun came up.

I don't remember anything at all between then and a day just before the ship that we went home on reached England, when I noticed with a sense of shock that Mother's hair had a broad streak of white in it that hadn't been there when we left Bombay. I hadn't known that one's hair could go white quite so quickly. Though I would see it all too often during the years of the Second World War, it shook me badly because it was the first time. And because I hadn't believed it could happen.

Another result of Tacklow's death was that I began to have nightmares. I have always dreamt a lot. But few of my dreams had been bad ones. These were bad, and to make matters worse, they were always the same dream, identical in every detail . . .

* Queen of the Night.

Tacklow and I were alone in an empty Dâk bungalow in the jungle, and it was beginning to grow dark, for the sun had just set and dusk was closing in. We stood side by side on the verandah, listening to the noise of peacocks and jungle-cocks saluting the approach of night. Somewhere not too far away a Karkar deer would bark its alarm call, and Tacklow would say, 'I think we'd better light a few lamps and start shutting the doors. This is tiger country.' We would walk along the verandah to the lamp room and collect and light a couple of kerosene lamps, and turning into the first of the empty rooms, all of which connected with each other, begin to close and bolt the doors. 'You close this half and I'll close the other,' Tacklow would say, and he would turn away and go out of the room and I would see the small glow of his hurricane-lamp fade until it was lost.

As it did so, the wick of my own hurricane-lamp would flare up and go out, leaving me in the dusk; and in the same moment I would hear, quite clearly in the silence, the soft *pad, pad, pad* of paws on the matting of the long verandah outside. My heart would seem to leap into my throat and choke me, and I would hear behind me a sound that I took to be Tacklow coming back, and turning round quickly, see a tiger standing in the open doorway, staring at me. At which point the horrid noise that a sleeper in the grip of nightmare makes when they try to scream would wake me, and I would find myself in bed, shuddering and sweating with terror and still struggling to scream.

The dream never varied by an inch, and it recurred again and again, generally when I was feeling particularly dispirited and things were not going right for me. I came to know that Dâk bungalow so well that when, years later, I needed a slightly sinister one for *Shadow of the Moon*, I used the one in my nightmares, though by that time those scary dreams were a thing of the past.

Our first few months in England stay in my head as a confused jumble of other people's houses, Mother in floods of tears, that terrifying, recurrent nightmare, and having to live out of suitcases, because the detailed arrangements that my parents had made with relatives and close friends during the past winter meant that more than half-a-dozen house-holds were expecting us to spend at least a month if not more with them. You have to remember that middle-class England, though badly shaken by the after-effects of the Great War, was still to a large extent living the life of Riley and – secure in the possession of a considerably reduced but still adequate domestic staff – still thought nothing of inviting their friends and relations for visits lasting from a fortnight to a few months.

The object of our lengthy visits was, or had been before Tacklow died, to let us go house-hunting at leisure instead of being rushed into buying a house – any house – for the sake of having a roof over our heads. Tacklow had wanted a little house in which he could settle down and spend the rest of his life peacefully, cataloguing Ferrarie's stamp collection, raising cabbages and watching his beloved Daisy grow old gracefully. But it had to be the right house, and he had intended to take his time about finding it.

Now, however, all thoughts of acquiring a house had to be put aside until Mother came to terms with widowhood, and I was deeply grateful that we had somewhere to stay for the remainder of that year. This, I thought, should give both of us plenty of time to plan for the future and adjust to life without Tacklow. But I soon learned that Mother was unable to do anything of the sort.

Instead of being able to stay in one place for several weeks (most of our visits had been planned for months), the most we managed were a few days. And I feel sure that all our kind hosts must have been unspeakably relieved to see us leave, for there are limits to how many times you can say to a grief-stricken friend or relative, 'Oh my dear, I am *so* sorry for you; I *do* so sympathize – it must be *terrible* for you; if only I could do something to help! . . .'

Mother's friends ran out of sympathetic repetitions in fairly quick time, because all she would do was collapse into the nearest armchair or sofa and cry. I don't think she heard a word of what they said to her. She would just sit there, staring ahead of her, with tears streaming down her face, hour after hour. Once again I was reduced to wondering where, in one's anatomy, one *keeps* this apparently bottomless well of misery, and what happens to it when one *isn't* crying? – or hasn't cried for ages?

Occasionally, some warm-hearted sympathizer would end up losing their cool and tick her off, urging her to pull herself together and telling her how *horrified* Cecil would be if he could see her going to pieces in this spineless manner. But nothing worked. Mother merely told them that they 'didn't understand', and went on weeping. Then after a day or two she would decide that she would feel much better once she was with Alice or Josie, or whichever friend or relative we were booked to stay with next. And before I knew it she had stopped crying for long enough to arrange a move over the telephone and pack her suitcases, and we were off, three weeks prematurely, to stay with Jessie or whomever, where, I regret to say, the same scenario was invariably repeated.

I can't think how she managed it without losing a whole row of dear friends for keeps, and can only suppose that they were so relieved to see the back of us that it outweighed the annoyance of having all their own plans upset and their hospitality rejected. But they stuck by her, and it was at this point in her life that she acquired a habit that was to madden Bets and me (who bore the brunt of it) and cause endless inconvenience, and occasionally great offence, to her friends and acquaintances. After the briefest of stays, she would take a scunner against whatever place she happened to be in, and having convinced herself that she would be much happier somewhere else, she would pack and move on. Only to regret, after a few days, that she had come there, and (now that it was too late to go back) begin to appreciate the charms and advantages of the place she had just left.

Poor Mother! From the time of Tacklow's death to the end of her days, she would always think that she could escape from unhappiness or insecurity, or whatever it was that she was forever trying to escape from, if only she could move on somewhere else. And only when she had done so, and could not go back, did she discover that the grass she had failed to appreciate while she was standing on it was far greener and more attractive than what she had exchanged it for.

Never ever again would she appreciate anything while she had it. Only after she had lost it. For she had become like the dog in Aesop's *Fables* who, standing by a river with a juicy bone in his jaws, dropped and lost it, because he thought the reflection of that bone in the water made it look a lot larger than the one between his teeth. He had grabbed at the shadow and lost the substance.

❊ 4 ❊

Digs in London

❊❊❊❊

Chapter 19

The extent to which Tacklow's death was going to change my life was painfully underlined on an evening at Pembury in Kent, where I was staying with my schoolfriend Helen, at her parents' home, the Manor House. It was just before sundown, and I was in the dining-room, helping Helen to lay the table for supper, when she suddenly said: 'Isn't it your birthday today, Tish?'*

And it was! I remember the knowledge hitting me as though someone had punched me in the stomach, followed by the horrid sinking feeling you get when one of those over-swift office lifts drops you down twenty storeys non-stop to the ground floor.

I didn't let go of whatever it was I was holding – side plates I think – but I very nearly did. I had known Tacklow's death meant the end of an era. But only with my mind. Not fully yet with my heart. Now it came home to me with the force of a knock-down blow. It was my birthday . . . and I hadn't even remembered it!

We'd always made so much of birthdays. Present-giving at breakfast. A birthday tea-party to which all one's special friends were invited. A birthday cake with candles on it and when we grew older a dinner party and a dance. And I hadn't even remembered! We weren't a family any more, now Tacklow had gone and Bets was married, Bill was somewhere on the North West Frontier and Mother a widow. I was on my own. It was one of the blacker and drabber patches in my life, and it was around about this time that Roger turned up again.

He couldn't have picked a worse time to look me up, and I don't think he had any idea of how much hung on our first meeting 'on home soil', so to speak. We had met briefly in Bombay, where Mother and I happened

---

* We had been known collectively as 'Pish and Tush' in our schooldays, but both of us answered impartially to 'Tish', 'Tishy' or 'Tishwig'.

to be staying at the same hotel as he was, all three of us homeward bound, though on different ships. Mother must have given him the Manor House as my only fairly safe address.

Roger was returning to England on leave and would be staying with his mother, who lived in a suburb of London, and he had written to ask if he could call at the Keelans' and take me out to lunch: a scheme that Helen was all in favour of, as she was deeply involved with the local church fête, which included lunches and teas among their day-long money-raising activities. (Tish scented another customer!) So Roger was duly invited down to collect me at the house and eventually stand me lunch in the grounds of the Vicarage, and be lured into buying home-made cakes, second-hand books, or assorted jumble off the stalls managed by the ladies of the village.

Helen and her mother, who were both stallholders at this yearly shindig, would have left long before Roger arrived. 'So you will have him all to yourself for at least an hour,' said Helen's mother – a keen match-maker who thought it was high time I was married, and had said so at frequent intervals ever since I had unwisely told her that Tacklow had approved of Roger. As for myself, I was in a thoroughly mixed up and miserable state of mind, and I have never before, or since, felt so totally lost. I was on my own now in uncharted waters, and Mother was proving useless as a source of either comfort or support, for she too was hopelessly adrift, and I knew that I would have to look after her – because there was no one else to do so. We would both have to learn how to make ends meet, and oh, how I wished that Tacklow had taught us something about balancing the books!

Mother had always known that our means were modest, and now that Tacklow had gone, his pension and salary had gone with him, and Mother was left to manage on a widow's pension of less than four hundred pounds a year (of which ninety-four pounds – or was it ninety-three? – was accounted for by the addition of something called 'The Royal Warrant' that was given in recognition of sterling work during the First World War – or something of the sort). As for my own princely pension as an unmarried daughter, it was one pound five shillings a week. And lucky to get it! (If Tacklow had been in the British Army instead of the British-Indian one, I would have got nothing.) There was no 'Cradle to Grave' stuff in those days!

The mere problems of how to manage on our pensions in what was, to me, almost a foreign country were worrying enough without Mother's uninhibited grief and continual moves at short notice, and I would have given almost anything for 'someone to watch over me' – someone on to whom I could unload a share of the problems and woes that had been piling up on me and who would provide a shoulder to cry on. I don't remember seriously considering Roger as a candidate for the post in the days immediately before his arrival in Pembury, but I suppose I must have done, because I know that I took a lot of trouble with my hair and my dress and my lipstick (Pond's Kiss-Proof – and it *was*, too!). And that I borrowed some of Helen's lavender water and went down to wait in the drawing-room with my heart beating a good deal faster than usual. The Keelans' maid, who had not yet left for the church fête, let him in, and I went out to meet him in the hall.

Dear Roger. His guardian angel must have been taking good care of him that day, because if he had grabbed me in his arms and kissed me, I would have clung to him like a bit of fly-paper and, mentally and most thankfully unloading all my woes and worries on to him, kissed him back warmly. And a month or two later I would probably have married him and made him unhappy ever after, for I wasn't the sort of girl he should have married at all. He deserved something a lot better than a wife who had married him as an escape from sorrow and the problems of penury. And his guardian angel must have known it, for when I ran out into the hall we were both suddenly overcome with shyness, which Roger covered up by starting to struggle out of the greatcoat he was wearing. There were raindrops on it, I remember. (One could have bet on that, since you must have noticed that the Devil, who has a warped sense of humour, does his best to ensure that any outdoor festivity on behalf of the church should be rained on.)

Getting himself out of that greatcoat gave Roger an excuse for getting his greetings over without having to accompany them with any demonstration which he was afraid I might not welcome. And by the time he had got it off, I had decided that he had done it on purpose for exactly that reason, for fear I might want to embrace him when he was no longer in love with me and had, in fact, found someone else. So in the end we didn't even shake hands, but were terribly bright and chatty.

It wasn't a good day. I took him over to the grounds where the fête was being held, and after I had introduced him to Helen and her parents, we had the sort of lunch one would expect in a tent at a church bazaar, and spent the rest of the day doing our duty by buying things we didn't want at a variety of stalls, or guessing the weight of large plum cakes – correct guess wins the cake – and similar games of chance. The rain must have stopped early on, since I took Roger for a stroll around the Manor House gardens and the orchards, and presumably told him all about Mother and our present situation, and was brought up to date with his news – it seems he had been posted to HMS *Excellent*, that bit of land in or near Portsmouth that is a Navy enclave and pretends it's a ship.

When, eventually, the Keelans returned looking eager and interested, and obviously expecting to be told the glad news of an engagement, Roger hastily presented me with all the junk he had bought and, taking his courage in both hands, pulled me towards him, gave me a brief kiss, and fled.

The kiss told me, if nothing else, that he hadn't found anyone else. But it came too late. If he had done that in the beginning, I am fairly certain that we would have skipped lunch and the fête as well, and spent the rest of the day with our arms about each other, either on the drawing-room sofa, or strolling arm in arm along the garden paths, making plans for the future. And I am fairly certain that I would have married him. But fortunately for both of us he had started off the day on the wrong foot, and stayed there, uncomfortably and immovably. And by the time he left I knew that if I married him it would be for the meanest of reasons. A meal ticket. Which would not only be cheating, but would put me under a lifetime's obligation to him, because if you marry for love and things go wrong, well it's probably fifty-fifty anyway. But to marry someone for escape or convenience, or a meal ticket, or merely for 'someone to watch over me', and it doesn't work out – well that's going to be your fault. Because it should be your part of the bargain to *make* it work.

An afternoon spent making polite conversation to Roger made it quite clear to me that I couldn't possibly pretend that he was the man I had been waiting for, the 'Some day he'll come along, the man I love' – the one-and-only that all the romantic books and songs tell you is out there somewhere, waiting for you to come his way . . . Oh, dear, what a lot of heartaches and disappointment those songs and stories are responsible for!

It is odd to think that there are times when one's whole life can be altered by a seemingly trivial incident, and I sometimes used to wonder what it might have been like if Roger had caught hold of me and kissed me instead of talking. Very different, I imagine. For one thing, I would not have been a writer, since it would not have occurred to me to try. I had hoped to be an illustrator of children's books, a second Arthur Rackham, or Edmund Dulac – and though I'm afraid I would never have been half as good, I might have made it on a much lower level. But a writer, never. The only reason I tried that was because although it was possible in those days to live on one pound five shillings* a week (and many people managed on much less), it was not all that easy. For a start, the tools of one's trade had to be bought and paid for. And one has to eat. If Roger had kissed me as though he meant it when we met, I would not have needed to worry about finding the money for the next week's rent or a shilling for that insatiable gas-meter. Odd, when you come to think of it.

Helen's parents, whom ever since my schooldays I had called 'Uncle Pat' and 'Auntie Winnie' (in the tedious Victorian tradition that all grown-ups were 'uncles and aunties'), had taken to Roger on sight, and were gravely disappointed by the outcome of his visit. In fact Auntie Winnie took the opportunity to read Helen and me a stern lecture on the conceit and stupidity of heedless girls who played fast and loose with the affections of their suitors, and thoughtlessly rejected eligible proposals that might never come their way again. Such young women, warned Auntie Winnie, were heading straight for that dreaded end of all hopes – 'the Shelf'. And Helen and I were both consigned to the doghouse, since Helen had disappointed her mother by continuing to turn down a devoted suitor, one Jack Glubb; known to fame as 'Glubb Pasha' – or 'Father of the Little Chin' – to his devoted Arab Legions. It used to amuse me to see the great man – a second, if considerably less romantic, Lawrence of Arabia, whose word at that time was law throughout most of Jordan – behaving like a wet doormat for the sake of a girl who kept turning him down.

I owe a lot to Helen and her parents, for they let me treat the Manor House as my home and set aside a room for me there, an enchanting little attic room reached by a steep winding stairway, with a window looking out across Pembury Green. It had probably housed at least three

* Five shillings was the equivalent of twenty-five pence today.

housemaids in the days of whichever Hanoverian George was on the throne when it was built (at a guess, George II) but since I was used to living in a houseboat it seemed fairly commodious to me, and Auntie Winnie allowed me to leave a lot of my luggage and various bits and pieces there. Helen's house was the one bit of stability I found in England in those days, and it was here, on another and much later occasion on a spring morning, sitting under an apple-tree in blossom in the Manor House orchard and doodling in pencil in an old school rough notebook, that I started to write a fairy story called *The Ordinary Princess*.

It turned out to be one of those rare and enchanting occasions when your brain and hand take over and write the story for you, and it was only to happen to me on one other occasion, many years later. But this time the story wrote itself for me in a single day, and with hardly any corrections. My hand could hardly keep up with the story that my brain – or possibly Amy, the Ordinary Princess – was telling me. I didn't do anything with that story for years, though now and again I used to do a few pencil sketches of the characters, and once I wasted an entire day making a doll's-house-size mock-up of what the story would look like as an illustrated book. But I didn't do anything with that either for years. It got put away and forgotten.

Mother continued to be a problem, and I decided that it was high time we ceased to burden our friends and rented a house or flat of our own. Mother had always been good with houses. She was a born home-maker, and it was a family joke that even during brief stops for a night at some Dâk bungalow she would produce a bed 'throw' and a few knick-knacks, and always a vase of flowers and her silver-backed brushes and comb, plus a few framed photographs, so that in no time at all the room was Mother's, and no one else's. Remembering this, and the series of bungalows, houseboats and houses in the hills on which she had put her own unmistakable stamp, I started to house-hunt in earnest. Not for a permanent home, but for a base from which we could scout around for one.

Mother had been staying for a couple of weeks with a friend from the old days, also widowed. She was the mother of a friend of mine from the Delhi days, Liz Glascock, a one-time member of the 'gang'. I had visited Mother there in order to meet Liz again, and been much taken with the little village of Yateley, near Camberley, where they lived. Mrs Glascock told me about a small house nearby that was to let furnished, and said that it would suit us down to the ground, and that it would be lovely to have 'Daisy living so close'. I thought so too. Liz's mother was a cosy old darling, and it would do mine a lot of good to be anchored for a while instead of moving restlessly and at short notice from one friend's house to the next, in a vain attempt to escape from unhappiness.

Mother liked the house and, even more, the idea of living so close to an old friend who knew all the 'Raj women' that she knew. So we hired it for a provisional six months and moved in, plus 'Shao-de',* the Siamese kitten that a friend had given her 'because they were such good company'. Shao-de, which is Chinese for 'small piece', was certainly that, and I was optimistic enough to believe that the worst was now over, and that I could start by looking for a job, while Mother took over doing the housework and cooking – she had become a very good cook during our time at 'Three Trees', the house we had rented unfurnished and that Tacklow had hoped to buy one day when he had retired from India Service in the early twenties.

Among the 'furniture and effects' in our furnished house were several cookery books, and I can't tell you how relieved I was when I saw her take them down and flip through them. But the relief was premature. She merely put them back and never looked at them again and, since we could not possibly afford a 'daily', if I hadn't taken over the cooking and cleaning we would have lived in squalor and existed on a diet of baked beans and biscuits and anything else that was cheap and came out of a tin.

It was only then that it dawned on me that for the past quarter of a century, Mother had been playing the role of home-maker solely for the benefit of an admiring audience of one – Tacklow. Now that he had gone, she 'couldn't give a damn'. What's more, she wouldn't even *try*. Once I had taken that in, I realized that we had made a fatal mistake in bringing her to England.

We ought to have taken her straight back to Kashmir and kept on Kadera and Mahdoo to look after her. And that night I sent an SOS off to Bill, beseeching him to ask for 'compassionate' leave to come back to England to collect her. India was the only place in which she could live comfortably on her pension and really feel at home. Besides, she would have both him and Bets there, as well as loads of old friends, both Indian and British. Best of all, she would be able to supplement her pension by

* The Chinese spell that 'Shao-di', but pronounce it '*Shao*-dee'.

selling her sketches, which would help pay for Mahdoo and Kadera and a small car. As for me, I would be able to set about supporting myself, which I hadn't been able to do while I had Mother on my hands in a perpetual pond of tears and despair. Bill cabled his agreement, and when I broke the news to Mother she cheered up wonderfully and 'couldn't think why we' (Bill and I!) 'hadn't thought of it before!'

I remember discussing the situation with Mike who, bless him – may he inherit one of those many mansions in Paradise – turned up on our doorstep one afternoon and, leaving Shao-de to look after Mother, drove me to London, gave me dinner at the Berkeley where he had rooms, and told me that he was in the doghouse with the manager and the staff because he had brought back a couple of wolf cubs that had been a gift from the head-man of a village somewhere in the Pamirs, where he had been on trek.

The cubs had had to spend a few months* at the zoo before he was allowed to take them away, and he had driven up with them to the front entrance of the Berkeley and said to the doorman, who had opened the door for him, 'Watch out for the back seat, I've got a couple of wolves in there!' The doorman smiled tolerantly, thinking it was a joke, and got the fright of his life when he found it wasn't. In the end Mike was reluctantly given permission to take them through the hall (where the mere sight of them cleared the place of the usual crowd of cocktail-drinking customers in a matter of seconds) and down to the cellars, in one of which they were locked up for the night.

Apparently the creatures were now parked in a special wired-off section of the park at Mike's ancestral home, Packington. He said the staff of the Berkeley had not been amused. I don't wonder.

We sat talking for so long that we missed a good half of the musical comedy he had booked us in for – *Balalaika* I think – and finished up in a nightclub somewhere in Regent Street called the Slip-in, one of several such clubs owned by a lady affectionately known to the gilded youth of her day as 'Ma Merrick'. It was the first time I had ever driven through London in the small hours when the streets were empty, and so quiet that you could hear the footsteps of the 'Bobbies' – London's policemen – on the beat, the *miaow* of a prowling cat and the racket (it seemed no less) of the car and the occasional home-going taxi.

---

* Quarantine.

The silent city fascinated me, and later when I was living alone in a London 'bed-sit', one of my favourite amusements when I could not sleep was to walk through the London streets after midnight, admiring those shop-windows that remained lit up all night. For some reason it always gave me a feeling of belonging. That I belonged to London, and that it belonged to me. It was *my* city. That was in the thirties, which still seem only a little way behind me. Sadly, few women of any age would dare to stroll alone through the midnight streets of any city in these 'peaceful' post-war days.

It must have been getting on for about four o'clock when we neared Camberley, and Mike said, 'Don't let's go back to the house. Let's go to Portsmouth – there's a chap I know there who has a small hotel near the front; you can see the sea from it. He won't mind giving us an early breakfast. What do you say?' What I said was 'No', because if Mother found I was still missing when she woke up, she'd have a stroke. 'Nuts,' said Mike – or words to that effect. 'We'll write her a note and push it through that slot in the front door, and tell her we'll ring her later to say we're OK and when we'll be back.'

So we did; and oh! how well I remember that part of the drive . . . how beautiful England looked on a clear, dewy morning with the sun still below the horizon but the whole world bright with the dawn and as empty as the palm of my hand. No dual-carriageways or roundabouts, and many of the towns that have by now become cities were villages then. Everything was so green – miles and miles of woodlands, fields, commons and meadows, and hedges full of wild roses – and always a cuckoo calling.

The staff of the hotel were barely awake, but its proprietor, an ex-Navy type, came out in his pyjamas and we were given an excellent breakfast, sitting in the glassed-in verandah and looking out at the Channel, watching the ships go by. Mike rang Mother around eight o'clock, and I remember we made an unsuccessful attempt to pay an unofficial call on Andy and the Bosun.* The night out with Mike, and that drive through sleeping London and through the dawn-lit countryside to Portsmouth and the Channel, still stay in my memory as a bright splash of colour in an otherwise grey and unhappy period, full of regrets. As does a visit we paid to Packington, not long before Bill's arrival. Mike drove down to spend another night with us, and on the following day he drove us up to Packington to spend a few days with him.

* Andy and Enid Anderson: Captain and Bosun of the Nageem Bagh Navy. See *Golden Afternoon*.

It was quite a long drive from Yateley, and I believe that the nearest town to the estate was Coventry. Packington was one of the weirdest houses I have ever been in. It was a huge Georgian pile that strongly suggested *The Fall of the House of Usher*, for it gave the impression (correctly as it happened) of being neglected for too many years. It must once have had wonderful gardens, but they had been shockingly uncared for and had become overgrown and run to seed. As for the vast park in which it stood, the entire space seemed to have been smitten by some disease. And that too was correct. The disease was called 'rabbits'.

Wherever one looked, the ground was humped and bumped and riddled with the burrows of rabbits, so many of them that when one walked out in it, the whole park seemed to surge up and run away, as if the ground itself was alive. You've no idea how gruesome the effect of scores of rabbits bolting into their warrens can be. Every inch of grass appeared to have been nibbled off short, and the entire place was patched with earth scratched out of the rabbit-riddled ground. The house itself was equally neglected, except for one end of it, which the brothers Adam had fiddled about with, adding their familiar touch of pillars painted to look like marble to a large entrance hall, in which there was a beautiful curving Regency staircase that swept up the wall and appeared to be attached to it only by gravity and mathematics.

Even Mike confessed to feeling nervous about it on occasions – when he was about half-way up, and looked down at the hall below. I don't blame him. I never felt 100 per cent safe on it myself. The sets of guest-rooms on that end of the house were modern and very attractive, but the majority of the rooms in the rest of the house were dusty and tattered. Apparently Mike's grandmother (a formidable Victorian beauty and girlfriend of the future Edward VII) had, when her son, Mike's father, was killed and her husband died, refused to retire to the Dower House as expected, but had dug herself with firmness into Packington and metaphorically drawn up the drawbridge and sat it out in the big house, allowing it to decay around her until she died.

We spent a lot of time exploring layers of empty rooms, when not punting around on the lake – or was it lakes? There was an enormous shuttered and never-used drawing-room that must have been redecorated (presumably in the heyday of Grandma, and towards the end of Victoria's reign) by Messrs Wedgwood. A mistake, I thought. The whole thing was a riot of Wedgwood blue plaques showing scantily clad gods and goddesses.

There was also a State bedroom somewhere in that maze of upper rooms, the chief feature of which was the vast and imposing four-poster bed. I remember walking round it, and thinking that even a feather-duster and a pot of glue would have been a help.

Somewhere well below the house lay a huge cellar, complete with enormous beer barrels that must have been built *in situ*, since they could not possibly have been man-handled there. These were scribbled all over with the signatures of distinguished guests, only one of which has stuck in my memory: poor Czar Nicholas, who had been murdered less than a decade earlier in a cellar in Ekaterinburg. I remember touching it with a kind of horror; because it suddenly made him *real*.

The wolves inhabited a nature reserve of their own in a large wired-in enclosure in the Park, not far from the house. The surrounding fence must have been fifteen to twenty feet high (it seems that wolves excel as high-jumpers) and turned inward in a line of spikes along the top. The fence surrounded a pinewood and (well underground) a disused ice-house in which they had made their den. Mother wouldn't go near the place, for the very idea of timber-wolves being kept as pets revolted her. But on the day after our arrival Mike asked casually if I'd like to meet his wolves, and as the very casualness of the voice in which he put the question made me 'think nothing of it' I said yes. He fetched a key and together we strolled off to the wolf-pen.

I must say that they looked pretty scary as they slunk through the pine-trunks of the wood, like the illustrations of wolves in one of Ernest Thompson-Seton's animal stories, and I wasn't surprised at the precautions that had been taken to see that they didn't get out. I hoped that they couldn't dig as well as they could jump, and was interested to find that there were two locked sections to the entrance. Mike unlocked the outer door of a short, wired-in approach corridor and, having locked it behind him, walked down to the end of it to unlock one at the far end. 'Just a precaution in case they make a sudden dash for freedom,' said Mike as he ushered me through the second gate and locked that one too behind us.

The wolves shot out of the shadows of the wood like a couple of grey torpedoes fired by an enemy submarine, and, ignoring Mike, came straight for me, nearly knocking me over as they jumped up at me, smelling me all over and finally giving me a few slavering licks. I accepted their exuberant welcome with pleasure, patting them and scratching them behind their ears, and interested to find how coarse their thick coats were when they looked so fluffy. Having given me the once-over, they turned their attention to Mike, fawning on him, putting their paws on his shoulders and lavishing loving kisses on him, and obviously trying to persuade him to play 'Chase-me-Charlie' with them.

I suppose we must have spent the best part of half an hour in there walking through their wood, while they gambolled beside us. They sobered up and became slightly hostile when Mike showed me the mouth of a dark, sloping tunnel that led down into the heart of a tall hillock that rose between the tree trunks over the spot where the ice-pit had been dug more than a century ago. 'They're a bit possessive about the ice-pit,' explained Mike. 'Probably because they regard it as home.' We left them to it, and only when both doors were locked and bolted behind us and we started walking back to the house, did Mike say: 'Well done, Number One. Nice work! I *knew* you could do it.'

'Do what?' I inquired.

'Meet the chaps,' said Mike airily. 'Do you know that you are the very first person to go in there that hasn't beaten a hasty retreat? My gamekeeper has made a hell of a fuss about going in there, ever since they tried to take a bite out of him. They don't like strangers.'

I could have killed him! – and I said so in no uncertain terms. If I'd had any idea that those creatures had attacked other people who had been introduced to them, nothing would have induced me to go inside that cage, let alone pat those creatures' heads and make a fuss of them. 'Of course you wouldn't. Don't be silly!' retorted Mike impatiently. 'Because you'd have been scared, and the chaps would have known it. As it was, just because I gave you the impression that they were safe as houses, they welcomed you in with open paws! Now that they've accepted you, you'll be able to go in whenever you like.' I replied suitably to that suggestion and didn't go near them again. They had a nasty habit of sitting on top of their hillock with their noses straight up to the sky, howling most mournfully at first light every morning and last light at night. It was a most haunting sound, a real 'call of the wild' in the depths of the English countryside.

Bill duly turned up to fetch Mother, and I seized the opportunity to go up to London and see Mrs Goulden, a one-time teacher at McMunn's Studio where I (and incidentally the three girls who made a great name for themselves* as theatrical designers in the thirties and who are still remembered as being among the greatest in their craft) studied when I first left school. Mrs Goulden, who was never known as anything but 'MG' to the generations of students who passed through her hands, was the only person I could think of who might give me sound advice as to what to do with myself in the commercial art world. And I was right. It was due to her that I was accepted into a group of artists who called themselves the Chelsea Illustrators.

Firms and people who wanted designs for book or magazine covers, illustrations for serial stories, fashion sketches, fairy stories, Christmas, birthday or anniversary cards – anything in the art line in fact – could (and did) submit their particular requirements to the Chelsea Illustrators. MG would let us know what was wanted, and one of us, or sometimes several of us, would take on the job if we thought it was in our line. The customers could do the choosing and a percentage of the price would always go to the group, to pay for such expenses as rent of the studio and heating and lighting bills etc. The rest went into the pocket of the successful artist. It was, for someone in my position, a lifeline, and I grabbed it with enormous relief and made many friends there. Two of them became lifelong ones: dear 'Fudge' Cosgrave, whose parents, like mine, were members of the Raj, and Temmy – Margaret Tempest, the illustrator of that famous series the *Little Grey Rabbit* books.

MG advised me to find myself a 'bed-sit' as near to the studio as I could, to save bus fares and to move into it as soon as Bill and Mother sailed. It was advice which I ought to have taken at once, if I'd had any sense. But when I returned to Yateley with the good news that evening, it was to discover that Mother had already been making inquiries about bed-sits in anticipation of this moment. Cull Brinton's new wife, 'Curly', who had been spending a few nights with us, had told her of a houseful of bed-sits in a Georgian square near Notting Hill, where her own daughter, a ballet-student studying under Marie Rambert at the Mercury Theatre in Notting Hill Gate, was already installed. Curly had given Mother the telephone number of the house and the name of the landlady, and Mother had rung up that very afternoon. Yes, there were still one or two vacancies in the house. We were to call and see it the very next day, and if we approved of it, I could move in at once . . .

* 'The Motleys', who were among the best stage designers of their time.

I didn't think much of the idea, as Notting Hill was nowhere near the Illustrators' studio in Park Walk, Chelsea. But Mother and Curly had got all that taped: there was a bus that I could catch at Notting Hill that would take me to Hyde Park Corner, where I could catch another one that would take me down King's Road and drop me at the King's Road end of Park Walk – all those bus fares! My heart sank. But Mother, wildly elated at the prospect of returning with her darling Bill to India (he had asked her to keep house for him in his new posting in Poona), had the bit between her teeth. So off to Notting Hill we had to go. And the moment I saw that square, I fell for it. It was the most beautiful bit of Georgian nonsense and as pretty as a picture. The church at the end of the square was exactly right for the design, and the central oblong of carefully mown grass that filled the square was edged with trees. The whole thing looked like a design by Motley for *Quality Street*, or something painted by that enchanting Dutch illustrator of nursery rhymes, Willebeck le Mair. I couldn't resist, and I took the room, even though it was going to cost me more than I could afford.

The room was on the ground floor, just behind Curly's daughter's, and its French windows faced on to a tidy little back garden. And on the same day that I saw Mother and Bill set sail for India – and oh, what *wouldn't* I have given to be leaving with them! – I moved into that ground-floor bed-sitting room. And found my gloomy, rock-bottom spirits surprisingly raised by a totally unexpected phone call.

The telephone in that house was in the hall, and when it rang it was customary for the nearest person to answer it and put the caller in touch with whomever he or she wanted to speak to. On this occasion it was our landlady who answered it and tapped on my door to say, 'It's for you, Miss Kaye.' Since I didn't think anyone as yet knew where I was, I picked up that phone in some surprise, and a voice at the other end said: 'You won't have any idea who this is!' But, inexplicably, I did. Why, I can't tell you, since it must have been a good eight years since I had last spoken to her. We had corresponded, of course, but not very frequently. Yet I knew at once, and without a second's hesitation said: 'Yes, I do. It's Bargie!'

And it was. My oldest friend, who appears frequently in *The Sun in the Morning*, the story of my childhood in Simla and Delhi and during my school days at The Lawn. Beautiful Marjorie Slater, now Marjorie Tancred, whose brother Guy had been my first beau when I was only four years old, and whom I had loved and admired for as long as I could remember. I don't know how she came to have my address and phone number, but it was one of those gorgeous flukes that brighten one's life and give existence a sudden, magical sparkle.

We talked and talked, and suddenly it was fun to be on my own and independent, no longer a member of the Fishing Fleet, but me – M. M. Kaye, setting out to make a career for herself with nothing but one pound five shillings a week and a paintbox. *Excelsior!*

Chapter 20

~ЖҳѵѻҲ~

When Mother and Bill set off for India, their plan had been that she should move into his Army quarters with him and take over the housekeeping, which, from Bill's description, was a shambles. The quarters in question were a bungalow in Poona, which he shared with another officer on the same course – Arthur Something-or-other, with whom Bill had discussed the idea and received enthusiastic agreement. Mother had suggested that she should pay her share of the expenses, but both young men had insisted that her housekeeping would more than pay for her keep.

On this happy understanding, Mother and Bill had set sail for Bombay. Having run short of money, their first call on landing there had been Grindlay's Bank, where Bill said there would be 'plenty of money' in his account, adding that Mother wouldn't need to draw on hers 'for ages'. He duly had a chat with one of the tellers and explained that he had just arrived an hour ago and would like to know how much he had in his account. The man departed, to return some minutes later with a small slip of paper which he slid across the counter, face down, to Bill. My dear brother, recounting the incident several years later, said: 'I flipped it up cheerfully, expecting a nice round sum, and there it was: "Rs: 1, annas 11". Gave me the shock of my life, I assure you. I don't know why I thought there would be quite a lot. I'd just forgotten how many cheques I'd signed. Worst moment of the year!'

Fortunately, mother and son both thought this was hilariously funny and laughed themselves into stitches over it, before taking the *tonga* on to Mother's bank, where Mother cashed a largish cheque to see them both through.

In the end she only spent a few days with Bill. Poona was still uncomfortably hot and she wanted to see Bets, who was in Ootacamund, staying in her mother-in-law's guest-house. As a result, Mother never did become Bill's housekeeper. For while she was away, Arthur Someone, the friend Bill was sharing the bungalow with, who had met a girl during his last home leave and subsequently become engaged to her by cable, confessed to Bill that he was in a 'hell of a hole'. Bill, supposing it to be financial, inquired for details, and was told that Joy, the fiancée, would be sailing on one of the next P & O boats for Bombay, complete with trousseau, bridal-gown, wedding-cake and a mountain of wedding presents, and was expecting him to arrange for the service, a reception and a honeymoon and, since she herself knew no one in India, someone to put her up for a night or two before the wedding.

'Well, what about it?' asked Bill, puzzled. 'You've known all that for months! And if you haven't coped with all the chores at this end, well, there's no tearing hurry, you've still got a good three weeks – bit more if she hasn't sailed yet. So what are you worrying about?'

'I don't want to marry her,' confessed Arthur.

'You don't want –? Good grief! Then why on earth did you get engaged to her?'

Apparently the silly ass had not known the girl for too long. They had met at a few parties on the Isle of Wight during his leave, and there had been a bit of hand-holding, a few kisses and sweet nothings in the rose garden, but nothing more than that. He had sailed without saying anything that might commit himself. But one day, sitting alone in the bungalow and feeling low and depressed and in want of someone to hold his hand and cherish him, he thought of Joy; a one-man-girl if ever there was one. A girl who would never let him down. And on the spur of the moment he sent off a cable asking her to marry him, and received a rapturous acceptance in reply.

There had been an exchange of letters, and Joy's parents had been distinctly difficult. But Joy had been well and truly spoiled as a little girl, and her elderly parents had always let her have her own way. So off she went, bag and baggage, to get married to a man she hardly knew, in a country about which she knew nothing, blissfully unaware that back in Poona the faithless Arthur had been wining and dining and falling hopelessly in love with a girl called Joan. And, as far as I can make out, doing nothing at all towards solving the problem that he had landed himself with.

Bill, on discovering that there was still time (though only just) to prevent the redundant fiancée from sailing, urged the instant dispatch of a cable calling the whole thing off, and was horrified to find that Arthur refused to do anything of the sort: 'No gentleman could ever, under any circumstances, break off an engagement. Only young ladies were allowed to do that.' He therefore proposed to let the unfortunate Joy embark for Bombay, in the fervent hope that she would fall in love with someone else during the voyage – this being something that occurred so frequently that the odds in favour of at least *one* eager fiancé hurrying down to the dockyard to greet his betrothed, only to find that she had changed her mind and was now engaged to marry someone else, were said to be around 75 to 2. 'And what if she doesn't?' demanded Bill.

Well, the answer to that one was simple: the 'gentleman' would have to behave so badly, and be so boorishly unkind, that she would have no alternative but to break off the engagement and creep home, lugging trunkfuls of wedding flummery, to explain to all her friends and relatives that she'd been jilted on the dock. Simple.

Believe it or not, Bill apparently saw nothing out of line in this appalling scenario. It was only when the girl arrived, looking radiant with happiness and expecting Arthur to catch her in his arms, only to be greeted with a curt 'Hello, Joy' and an immediate introduction to a strange young man – 'This is Bill Kaye who shares the bungalow with me. We're both on the same course. Bill, meet Joy Hutton' – that he realized the full horror of the situation.

Bill – confirmed by Joy's diary, read many years ago – gave a blow-by-blow account of the next few days. She was being put up by some friend of either Bill's or Arthur's, and I suppose she must have been told that the wedding could not be arranged immediately (presumably in order to allow 'plan B' plenty of time to work). There was a party on the night of her arrival, a dinner-dance at the Poona Club at which their guests included her supplanter, Joan. Joy imagined that Arthur had arranged it in her honour, and was stricken when he did not dance even one dance with her. There were several other women in the party, and he had danced once with each of them, and all the rest with Joan. Bill was horrified when he saw what was happening, and he says he tried to make it look as though Arthur would have asked her to dance if he, Bill, hadn't always cut in first. But I gather he was not very successful in this, which doesn't surprise me. He always was a rotten actor. Judging from that diary, Joy made a desperate attempt to persuade herself that Arthur was paralysed with shyness, and that it was this that was making him behave so badly;

all she had to do was to be patient and let it wear off. But it got more and more difficult to be patient . . .

Apart from Arthur's behaviour, she was stranded in a strange country where there was no one she could talk to and ask for advice. No one but Bill Kaye, who was being so kind and supportive. And who, incidentally, lacked the guts to tell her what was going on! (Bill says he *couldn't* do it. 'It was too cruel.') The dénouement came when a picnic that had been arranged by Arthur, consisting of himself, Joan, and Bill and Joy, ended up by being a twosome, because Arthur and Joan did not turn up. When it became plain they had no intention of doing so, Joy broke down and wept. This was too much for Bill, who did what anyone else would have done in the same circumstances; he put his arms round her and did his best to comfort her, petting and reassuring her, and begging her not to cry. At long last he blurted out that Arthur was only behaving like this to give her the chance of 'saving her face' by jilting him (noble fellow!) instead of him jilting her. I do *hope* this made her lose her temper with both those conceited young men, but apparently not, for Bill wound up by saying that if Arthur didn't want to marry her, would she please marry him instead?

Would she not! Arthur had not only proved himself to be a first-class rat, but had the face of one too, whereas my brother Bill was an outstandingly handsome young man and I have always considered that my sister-in-law – no raving beauty herself – was the luckiest young woman in India. True, she had been put through the mangle in the cruellest way during the last few days, but look at what she ended up with. A handsome, soft-hearted charmer instead of Arthur le Rat. On a par, I would have said, with winning a couple of million on the lottery, for though the way that Bill and his Joybell persisted throughout their lives in addressing each other as 'Beloved' used to irritate me somewhat, it says much for the success of their marriage.

Joy refused to accept Bill's proposal immediately, saying that she must be given time to think it over. But this was just eye-wash, as it was to Mother that she went for the intervening months before a proper wedding and honeymoon could be laid on, instead of a scrambled affair attended by half a dozen total strangers in a side room of the Club.

Mother had been in Kashmir painting in a houseboat on the Dāl Lake, and she first heard the news of Bill's engagement via a telegram that ended 'Letter follows'. She did not take the telegram very seriously, since

Bill was always falling in and out of love. But the lengthy letter that followed worried her a good deal, for this affair was different from all the others: he was making himself responsible for the girl, and if he should fall out of love with her as he had done with all the others, we were stuck with her. Nor did Mother like the idea of her darling boy marrying a girl who had come out to India to marry another man. The prospect horrified her, and I don't suppose that Bill, who was no letter writer and not exactly overburdened with intuition, had put Joy's case any too well. One has to admit that it does not make a very appealing story.

However, Mother had not only been brought up in a thoroughly Christian family, but she could refuse Bill nothing, so she agreed to put up Joy for a couple of months, until Bill had sorted out his end of the tangle. Joy came up to Srinagar, and one look at her was enough to convince Mother that here was no adventuress. And also that this girl was genuinely, and besottedly, in love with her Bill – which Mother thought was only natural. ('And so she should be!') Letters were exchanged between Mother and Joy's parents, and old Mrs Hutton invited me to stay at Oak Lawn, their home in the Isle of Wight, for a long weekend, where I was given the once-all-over and apparently passed with flying colours.

Oak Lawn was an enchanting house, surrounded by woods that ran down to the sea, and full of Victorian bric-à-brac that gave it a distinct suggestion of refusing to admit that it had left the nineteenth century, or that there was such a thing as the twentieth. As for Joy's parents, old Mr Hutton, who was easily old enough to be my grandfather, and lived a retired life among the book-lined walls of a musty and fascinating library, endeared himself to me for ever by presenting me with an 1896 edition of Seton Merriman's *In Kedar's Tents*, a much loved nineteenth-century novel given to me by Tacklow when I was at school, and which I had carelessly lost. Joy stayed with Mother on the houseboat for an unspecified time – two or three weeks I imagine – in the course of which her engagement to Bill was announced, and Bill put in for an exchange from the Gunners to the Supply and Transport Corps (rudely known as the 'Sausage and Tum-tum') because when it came to the crunch, he found that he could not afford to support a wife, let alone a future family, on a Gunner's pay. The S and T were a good deal better paid, and were also not moved about from pillar to post as the Gunners and most of the Army units were, no ordinary consideration. In mid-February Mother, whose friends were legion, sent out invitations in her name to 'the Marriage of Rosamund Gwendolen Joy Hutton with her son William, Royal Artillery' (Bill's application for a switch to the S and T obviously had not got through at that date) and they were married in New Delhi in the Church of the Redemption, with Bets as Matron of Honour.

Meanwhile, in London, I had to get up early in order to reach the studio by nine o'clock sharp: MG did not tolerate lateness. Besides, there were two buses to catch, as well as a preliminary walk (it was more often a run) from the house up a sloping street – the 'hill' of Notting Hill I suppose – to the bus stop at Notting Hill Gate. I was always afraid of arriving to see the bus I wanted pull away, because I knew that the next one might not be along for as much as ten minutes.

During the few months of that first autumn I used to see every day, as I hurried breathlessly up the crowded pavement, an elderly, grey-haired and very tall man with a nose like an eagle's beak, striding down the hill towards me as I scurried up it. His face was so familiar that I *knew* I knew him, and I decided that he must be a buddy of Tacklow's. But since I was always late and afraid of missing the bus, I was terrified that one day he'd stop me and ask about Tacklow or Mother, and make me late. So instead of cutting the poor man dead, I used to give him a nervous nod and a smile, indicative of a desire to stop and fill him in with the family news, but regret that I couldn't spare the time.

This went on for at least a month, until one day he did actually stop me. Late as usual, I had resigned myself to apologizing for not stopping to talk to him on previous mornings, and explaining why I hadn't, when he said: 'I'm sorry if I'm making you late for whatever it is you do, but I couldn't resist it any longer. You so obviously think I'm someone you know. *Do* tell me who it is?' Well, of course I couldn't for the life of me remember. And you know what –? He turned out to be George Arliss, an exceedingly famous film star in those days, who was over in England making a film about the Peninsular War, in which he played the Duke of Wellington. I have seldom felt such a chump. However, he couldn't have been nicer, and what really *was* surprising was that he *did* know Tacklow. They had attended the same prep school and were both nuts about cricket. I quite missed him when he went back to Hollywood.

I saw, and occasionally met, a lot of future celebrities through living near Notting Hill Gate. Peggy Ashcroft, looking exactly the same off-stage as she did on, was often to be seen shopping in Boots, though I never spoke to her. But nearly all the young men and women who were bed-sitting in the same house as I was, were, like Curly's daughter, hopeful ballet dancers trying their wings at the Mercury. Sometimes Marie Rambert let me sit in a corner of the practice-room and sketch them. I could never afford a seat for the lovely ballets that were written and danced in that minute theatre, but I used to stand at the back, squashed up against the wall, and watch them, entranced. I still think of them (as I do the Simla Theatre) as though they were danced on a stage the size of Drury Lane: *Cinderella* with the title part danced by beautiful Pearl Argyle, *The Haunted Ballroom*, *The Lady of Shalott*, *The Lilac Garden*. They were all magic to me.

So was a little second-hand jeweller's shop that I used to pass on my way up Notting Hill. There was a fabulous diamond ring in the window. A really beautiful thing, priced at eight pounds. When people talk rubbish to me nowadays as to the price of then-and-now being only 'relative' I remember that ring; and the fact that I knew, on an income of one pound five a week, that if I skimped and saved, it would not have been impossible for me to raise eight pounds. That ring now would be more like eighteen thousand, probably even more. I couldn't possibly afford it now. Any more than I could afford, then, a tin tub full of cut crystal chandelier drops – *hundreds* of them! – that I was offered in the Old Kent Road for one pound! 'Relative' my foot!

One of the things that continued to irritate me was the fact that in order to claim that £1 5s. a week Indian Army Pension, I had to clock in once a quarter to a certain section of, I think, Lloyds Bank, Pall Mall, to sign a piece of closely printed paper that included, among other things, my word of honour that I was not 'to my knowledge', married. I ask you! I was always tempted to write against that one, 'I'm afraid I can't quite remember what I was doing last Friday,' and see what they made of that.

Apart from George Arliss and the Ballet Club, only a few other things stand out in my memory of those days. Mike taking me to see the All Blacks play England. I had never seen rugby football played before, and I thought the whole business was Marx-Brothers-hilarious. I remember nearly crying with laughter, and Mike getting absolutely furious with me. He took his rugger seriously, and for two pins would have slapped me.

Sandy Napier, home on leave, took me to see the Grand National and I left the course a rich woman. Because the day was Mother's birthday, and since one of the lesser races had a horse running in it called 'The

Mum', I put five shillings on it (all I had!) and it romped home at something like twenty-to-one against. Sandy also rang up at short notice to ask me to join a star-studded party he was throwing at the Victoria Palace, where the auditorium was filled with candle-lit tables at which the clients dined and wined while a spectacular Folies-Bergère-style of show was performed on the stage, with intervals during which the stage was cleared so that the diners could go up there and dance. But the rules about evening dress were strict, and there was nothing in my scanty wardrobe that I had brought to my bed-sit that I could wear for such an occasion. Anything suitable was in the trunks I had left at the Manor House.

Since I was now rich, thanks to 'The Mum', I made for a large department store at the lower end of Oxford Street that was, in those days, a paradise for impecunious bed-sitters: Bourne & Hollingsworth of blessed memory. There I acquired, for the princely sum of £1 4s. 11¾d. (that last stood for three-farthings!) the prettiest evening dress – bar one (that too was another B & H!) – I have ever possessed. This one was a two-piece in grey 'elephant crêpe', and consisted of a cowl-neck, floor-length dress, cut on the cross, with a fingertip-length coat whose wide sleeves ended in a band of exactly matching grey 'foxalene' – a fake fur that looked exactly like dyed fox-fur. I wore it with a pair of diamanté earrings, bought from Woolworths for sixpence, and a somewhat elderly pair of shoes that I treated with a pot of silver paint, also from Woolworths. That outfit was not only a terrific success on its first appearance, but continued to be one for more than fifteen years. And when the 'foxalene' became tatty (which it did pretty quickly) I removed it and lined the cuffs with a wide band of silver sequins, also bought in the trimming department of dear B & H.

M G's words of wisdom on the subject of a bed-sit within walking distance of the studio had come home to me fairly soon. It had not taken me long to realize that I couldn't afford my present digs, let alone the bus fares to the King's Road and back. But in those days London teemed with digs of all descriptions, to suit every conceivable purse. There probably were bad or greedy landlords about. But if there were, there were not all that many, and the vast majority of landlords and landladies were a nice lot, renting out a room or two in their terraced houses to eke out their own modest incomes.

I found a large bed-sitting room on the second floor of a house in

Limerston Street, a mere two minutes' walk from the studio, and was immediately much better off than before, not only because the rent was far cheaper, but because there were no obligatory bus fares to pay. The solid rows of terraced houses in Limerston Street must have been built some time in the earlier half of Victoria's reign, for, believe it or not, the street was cobbled, and the houses had no bathrooms, and only a single lavatory. The original occupants had presumably stuck to the good old British practice of 'Friday night is bath-night', taking it in a tin tub in front of the kitchen fire. We twentieth-century bed-sitters either cadged one from a friend who lived in a house or a flat that boasted a bathroom (fortunately for me, I had several within strolling distance), or else we had one at the public baths. I never had to try those, but I believe they cost sixpence or, if one was fussy and prepared to pay a bit more, the same bath, accompanied by a rather flossier cake of soap, bath mat and towel.

My room overlooked the street, which, due to the cobbles, was mercifully free of traffic, with the exception of a milkcart which woke us up daily with its hellish clatter at the crack of dawn. Otherwise, the traffic was almost entirely pedestrian. The cobblestones were a feature which still fascinates me, since they are mentioned so often in Victorian novels. Not to mention 'pea-soupers' – those days of solid yellow fog in which you could barely see your hand in front of your face: I have to say I found them enthralling for the same reason. But they, and the cobbles, were already on their way out. No loss, I suppose. It was those cobbles, of course, that caused the daily milkcart and its load of bottles to jerk one out of sleep with the din of a clash of cymbals!

I paid nineteen shillings a week for bed-and-breakfast, and by arrangement with my landlady, dear Mrs King, another sixpence because I owned one of those 'new-fangled' objects, a portable radio that ran off the mains: Mrs King reckoned it probably used sixpence worth of electricity a week. The room was heated by a gas fire that had to be fed with a shilling in a slot. So did the little gas cooker that stood on the landing outside my door, on which I and my fellow bed-sitters could heat up canned soup, make toast and boil milk, and cook simple meals. A book of who had last fed it a shilling was attached by a nail on the wall.

We were forever running out of shillings, but fortunately, one of us – I think he had the room above me – had returned from a holiday abroad with a handful of small change that was exactly the size and weight of a shilling. This solved a pressing problem. Until the day the gas-man called, which was once a quarter. He was resigned to the problem and would sit on the top step of the stairs, sipping a mug of coffee or cocoa donated by one of us, while we sorted out who owed what and got together enough genuine shillings with which to pay him off.

It was while I was bed-sitting in Limerston Street that I made, inadvertently, one of the most profitable gestures of my life. I had returned to my room unexpectedly one morning, to find Mrs King sitting on the solitary chair in the hall in floods of tears. I thought at first that she must be ill, or that some disaster had overtaken the unseen gentleman always referred to simply as 'King', or their very pretty little schoolgirl daughter, the apple of their eye. But it was worse than that. I managed to get the story eventually, and this is what had happened.

Someone had rung the front door bell, and Mrs King, answering it, had been confronted by a nicely dressed lady armed with a collecting box. The lady ('And she *was* a lady,' insisted Mrs King, 'a *proper* lady') was collecting for some local charity, and she must have been tramping the streets for some time, for she appeared to be very tired. Mrs King urged her to wait while she fetched her purse and the lady sank down thankfully on the hall chair while Mrs King hurried down the stairs to the kitchen, and, returning with her bag, hunted out a modest contribution – sixpence or a shilling, for which the lady was most grateful. Rising to leave, she tottered slightly, and Mrs King, dropping her bag on to the hall table, leapt forward to support her. The lady apologized for being a nuisance, and wondered if Mrs King would add to her kindness by letting her have a drink of water. At which, pressing the visitor to sit down again, Mrs King ran back down the kitchen stairs to fetch and fill a glass, and carrying it up to the hall found that the lady had vanished, taking with her Mrs King's bag. The whole thing had been a well-thought-out and frequently successful confidence trick, that probably netted the thief a comfortable income. But to Mrs King it spelt disaster.

She had only just returned from the bank, or post office savings or whatever, with the cash she needed for the next week's household expenses, and now it had all gone, and what 'King' would say she dared not think. Her tears began to flow again at the very thought, and I imagined, from the depth of her woe and despair, that the sum she had been robbed of was alarmingly large. She kept on saying that *everything* was in her bag. Every penny! It was only on pressing her that she disclosed the extent of the damage. She had been robbed of five pounds, and as far as she was concerned it was the end of the world. I think it was only then that I realized for the first time how close to the edge of a yawning financial cliff thousands upon thousands of people have learned to live. And that I with my £1 5s. a week, which Tacklow had been paying for out of his scanty income ever since he joined the Army back in the previous century, was one of the lucky ones.

Well, as it happened, I had just sold a painting, a Christmas card design, to a firm called Raphael Tuck who used to do a lot of Christmas-cardery. What's more, I was on my way back from cashing the cheque, and I had the resulting fiver in my pocket. So I pressed it on dear Mrs King and said she was to regard it as an advance (or possibly belated) Christmas and/or birthday present.

Never, *ever* have I spent five pounds to better effect. If you think it was a trivial sum to me, you will be wrong, for we were in the days when the wage of a 'char', one of London's famous and invaluable scrubbing, cleaning and polishing women, had recently gone up to half-a-crown (i.e. two shillings and sixpence or twelve and a half pence today) an hour, amidst universal complaints about extortion and the threat of inflation. Five pounds was a lot of money, and the picture I had just flogged to Raphael Tuck and Co. represented a week's hard work. But it didn't mean to me what the loss of it had meant to hard-working, thrifty Mrs King and thousands like her. I still had my £1 5s. a week and I could manage on that (just!). Though I admit it was frequently a case of choosing between a cup of tea – after showing work to some clients such as the Medici Society, whose head office was just off Bond Street – or a bus back to King's Road. Because I couldn't afford both.

But after that, it wasn't a sacrifice on my part at all, for Mrs King looked after me like a devoted nanny. The breakfasts that went with the bed-and-breakfast rent had always been good. But now they were excellent, and Mrs King insisted on doing all my washing and ironing for free, as well as keeping my room like a new pin instead of the pigsty it had resembled before. My besetting sin had been untidiness, and she lectured me on this in vain. I remember hearing her complain on this head to my friend Fudge Cosgrave, who had called in with a packet of prospective work: '*Ooh*, that Miss Kaye! I've never had any of my young ones as untidy as she is. The worst time was when I found her frying pan in her bed!' (Fudge was always quoting that one at me, but I don't believe it for a moment. I *couldn't* have been that bad!)

It was also during my Limerston Street days that I took my first flight in an aeroplane, a small two-seater affair belonging to Tommy Richardson, a much admired childhood friend who has already figured in my account of an exhilarating school holiday spent with Aunt Lizzie in Bedford.* Having often thought how wonderful it would be to fly around those white, spectacular and apparently solid 'cloud capp'd towers, the gorgeous palaces' that on warm summer evenings stand heaped above the horizon, I jumped at the offer.

Well, they are a swizzle of course. As I ought to have realized. We went up on a marvellous evening when all the clouds were standing still against an immensity of blue. But the moment you tried to explore them, you found yourself in thick mist in which you couldn't see anything. Very disappointing.

Tommy had changed very little from the inventive gang-leader of our schooldays, and when the Second World War broke out he joined the Air Force, and died in a bomber that crashed over Germany. 'They shall grow not old, as we that are left grow old . . .' Dear Tommy!

* See *The Sun in the Morning*.

Chapter 21

It was Limerston Street that changed the whole direction of my life from art to writing. I could cope with the days, because I was kept busy working alongside the rest of the Chelsea Illustrators. But the evenings were long and very lonely, and in order not to sit and think of Tacklow and all that I had lost with his death, I joined a 'Tuppenny Library' at the end of the street.

Those libraries were wonderful institutions for the lonely and for those who did not wish to think, or remember. You paid a small deposit to register, and after that you paid tuppence,* which entitled you to take out as many books as you wanted, provided you returned them all within a week – or was it ten days? If you were late returning them there was a small fine.

The books that were stocked by the Tuppenny Libraries included love stories by the score, scads of whodunnits, of which those by Agatha Christie and E. M. Eberhardt were by far the best, and an almost weekly 'thriller' by a writer who turned them out like a sausage machine and called himself Edgar Wallace. That was about the level, and I would generally manage to get through one of them in a day. Nevertheless, it took a long time for my tuppence to drop, and I can remember the evening in which it happened as though it was literally yesterday.

I had just sold (for another fiver) a design for the cover of a sales catalogue in three colour-blocks, which included a good many figures and had given me a lot of trouble, and I had stopped at the little library on my way back to my bed-sit, handed over two pennies and (there was a weekend coming up) asked the girl behind the counter for six books, any books. I left the choice to her and, having collected them, plodded back up Limerston Street towards my gas fire and a cup of tea. It was

* Two old pennies.

raining, and I have seldom been more depressed, because I owed that five pounds, and didn't like being behind with the rent. My art was not proving good enough to keep me afloat, and I was beginning to lose faith in it.

I made myself a cup of tea, changed into pyjamas and a dressing-gown and settled down in front of that hissing gas-fire to read one of the six books. I ought to be able to remember its title and who wrote it, but I don't. I only remember getting as far as about Chapter Three, when at long last the latest of my tuppences dropped with a resounding clang.

It could not be possible, I told myself, to write worse than the author of this bit of drivel. No one could! And yet I was willing to bet that the author had been paid a good deal more money for perpetrating this slush than I had been for that catalogue cover! So, why not try writing one myself? Well, why not? Inspired, I fetched the block of the airmail-weight paper I used for writing to Bets and Mother and various friends in India, and roughed out the plot of a thriller-cum-romance, which I called *Six Bars and Seven*, and which very nearly wrote itself.

By the time I went to bed I had the whole thing worked out, and immediately after breakfast next morning I made for the nearest Woolworths, where I bought several ruled students' writing pads, half a dozen pencils, a few rubbers and a pencil sharpener. (Total outlay in those days around one shilling and fourpence, I reckon. Those pads used to sell at tuppence each and the sharpener was one penny.) From then on the book went slowly, because I still had work to do for the Chelsea Illustrators – and for myself – in order to pay the rent and keep eating. I couldn't just stop working at the studio and spend my time scribbling away at my story. But I used every spare bit of time I could snatch to get on with *Six Bars*.

Cull and Curly Brinton had invited me to spend my summer holidays at Croft House 'if I had nothing better to do'. I grabbed this wonderful offer, and spent day after sunny day lying in a hammock under the mulberry tree on the lawn, scribbling away at my book. I don't think it would ever have been finished but for the Brintons' kindness and, eventually, the help of Roger, and of Cull's chauffeur, Beddoes. I knew nothing whatever about cars, let alone their engines, and out of sheer ignorance had left a few blank lines in one section of my *Six Bars*, meaning to ask some motorist to fill it in for me. It was only when the first draft was finished and about to be typed by a kindly acquaintance who was studying at a secretarial school and had offered to type the MS for nothing, 'to keep in practice', that I found I had produced an impossible situation . . .

I had sent my Scotland Yard hero to an out-of-the-way inn in moorland country where, on arrival, he is startled to recognize the three villains of the piece (whom he has not seen for years and who have never seen him!), who are staying at the inn. Instantly deciding to stay there himself in order to find out what they are up to, he tries to book a room there, only to be told by the landlord that there are none vacant. Except for those already occupied, all the rest are closed for repainting, or some such excuse. Determined to stay, he pretends his car has broken down, so that he will *have* to stay. But he is spotted as a menace by the villains, who find the bit of his engine that he has surreptitiously removed in order to immobilize the car.

Knowing nothing about cars, I had been sure that this was something the experts could sort out with one hand tied behind their backs. In fact, I had produced an impossible situation. The villains are not mechanical experts, but they have arrived at the inn in a chauffeur-driven car, and their chauffeur, who *is*, examines the supposedly stalled car and cannot make out how it got there in the first place. But there *must* be something to give away the fact that the stalling of the car is deliberate. Well, *you* try it!

I took that infuriating problem to a flossy great shop that sold only the most expensive cars, and which I think is probably still there, in Piccadilly opposite the Ritz. No one knew a thing about me: I was just a scruffy art student who said she had written a book and would have to rewrite almost the whole thing again if this silly situation could not be solved. But those darling chaps took off their coats, spat on their hands, and took *endless* trouble to solve it for me. Hours of trouble. No good. 'Terribly sorry, but it can't be done!'

I tried all sorts of mechanically-minded car friends, and every time they were sure that they could come up with something. And every time they couldn't. I was faced with having to rewrite most of that ruddy book when Roger – an Engineer Commander in the Navy – came up with the solution I used. It had to be done on a car called an Alvis. Fortunately Bill Brinton, one of the Brinton cousins, happened to own an Alvis, and I was staying with the Brintons. Bill was *very* snooty about Roger's solution. Said it couldn't possibly work, and that if it was done to *his* car, he'd spot it at once: no one but an idiot, etc., etc . . .

Well, I had already explained the whole thing to Beddoes, and as Bill was staying to lunch, I asked Beddoes to try it out on Bill's Alvis and see what happened. It worked like a charm! Bill got crosser and crosser when he couldn't get his car to start, and only when he stormed indoors to ring for a taxi and a couple of mechanics did we tell him what we'd done. And he was *furious*. Fortunately, everyone else thought it was hilarious, and the crosser he got the more they laughed. Poor Bill! It took me ages to live that down as far as he was concerned. But the trick – although terribly far-fetched, as Roger had pointed out – did work, so I didn't have to rewrite that book after all.

I took the whole thing back to Limerston Street and had it typed by that angel of a girl, and sent it off to the publishers of the bit of total tripe that had decided me to try my hand at writing instead of art. And they took it!

If they hadn't I would never – hand-on-heart, *never* – have tried another publisher. I would have put it on the fire or into a trash-can and said, 'Back to the drawing-board, Mollie!' and that would have been that. Because I cannot say too often that apart from one brief episode when I can't have been more than ten years old, when Bargie and I decided to write a book about a haunted house that was going to make our fortunes, I do not remember having any serious leanings towards authorship. On the other hand, I felt pretty confident – until I tried it – that I could make a living as an illustrator. The switch was purely accidental. A single trashy novel, coming on the heels of a whole string of 'Tuppenny Library' novels, had convinced me that anyone who was even vaguely educated ought to be able to write one of them. And I was right. *Six Bars at Seven* was not only accepted, but paid for. More than fifty pounds, no less! I couldn't *believe* it. It was too good to be true. And was, of course. I'd neglected to read the small print, and only discovered much later that I had sold it outright.

But Fate was obviously pushing me towards a writing career, for at about the same time I noticed, while working away at the studio, a roll of typed paper lying on the floor beside Temmy's easel, and asked her what it was. She said it was the MS of the latest *Grey Rabbit* book, and I asked if I could read it and was told to go ahead. It didn't take long to read, and I remember handing it back and saying it was pretty good rubbish and I would have thought any chump could have written that kind of stuff. 'Oh you *do*, do you?' observed Temmy with a distinct trace of acid. 'Well, you go ahead and do it! Try it yourself; and if it's any good, I'll illustrate it for you! That's a promise.'

So once again I visited my local Woolworths, expended a few pence on a writing block and a small, flat notebook (one penny) and wrote a children's book about rabbits and field mice and similar country creatures, which I called *Potter Pinner Meadow* – a name that rose in my mind of its own accord, and that I honestly thought I had invented. But one day, at least a quarter of a century later, when being driven along a lane not far from Pembury in Kent, I saw it on the worn wooden notice-board of a farm and realized that I must have seen it during the days when Helen and I used to explore the country lanes around Pembury. Since then I have never been absolutely certain that something I have written, and been pleased with, is really original, or something I once read, or heard someone say. It worries me at times.

Potter Pinner Meadow got itself written in some rather peculiar places. I had to attend a surgery to be tested to see if too much sugar, if any, was being absorbed into my blood. I don't remember why this had to be done, but I was warned that I'd be there for several hours. This was because I was fed a large mug of – I think – glucose, after which I sat around for an hour, had a blood test taken, and drank another mug of glucose. And so on, for several hours. The verdict was OK; I *wasn't* absorbing sugar. But in intervals, I filled the time by writing *Potter Pinner*. In fact I very nearly finished it there, though not quite. The last few pages were written during an interval, standing up at the back of the Mercury Theatre where the Ballet Club were putting on a programme.

The story finished, I copied it out neatly in long-hand into the penny notebook, illustrated the cover with a little painting of a clump of primroses, the title and my name in poster colours, and took it round to Collins, who in those days hung out at No. 48 Pall Mall. And here luck took over. Billy Collins used to retire to his home at weekends, taking with him a selection of children's books to read to his own children. If they liked a book it would probably be published. If not, not.

Well, that Friday, I learned later, he was attending some cocktail party or other on his way home, and didn't want to lug along a lot of manuscripts. He called in to ask if they recommended any particular offering, and seeing my notebook on the secretary's table, said: 'What's that?' 'Oh, just some idiot who doesn't know that all MS have to be typed and double-spaced,' returned the secretary, picking up the notebook and dropping it into her waste-paper basket. W. Collins (realizing it would fit very easily into his pocket) retrieved it from the basket, pocketed it, and eventually read it to his young; who, bless their little cotton socks, liked it. A secretary rang the Chelsea Illustrators on Monday morning, and that afternoon Temmy and I set off to 48 Pall Mall. And that's how the *Potter Pinner* books saw the light of day.

There were five of them in all. And but for the war, there might have been more. Temmy illustrated them all for me, because she had a special talent, shared by the late great Beatrix Potter, for being able to draw, say, a rabbit, and put it in a dress and apron, and call it Mrs Someone, and it looked right. Whereas if I drew a rabbit, it was a rabbit; and that was that. I couldn't make them look anything else.

Temmy and I had a lot of fun with those books. Her brother, Frank, was the Commodore of the Harwich Yacht Club, and Temmy too was a sailing buff. She would often take me down to Ipswich for the weekend, where her family home was, to sail and sleep on the Tempest boat, which was moored at Pin Mill near that known-to-all-sailing-buffs inn, the Butt and Oyster. We would take the latest *Potter Pinner* with us, and work out each page during the train journey from London. The books were all written in Temmy's beautiful script, and as the illustrations were scattered across the pages, she would often demand that I write an extra word or two – or cut a sentence down to size – in order to fit the script round the pictures.

Years later, when the Second World War had been and gone, and Temmy was on one of her many successful lecture tours, she mentioned the way in which we had worked on those books page by page, sitting in the evening train to Ipswich. At the end of her lecture, she found a couple of elderly sisters waiting to speak to her. They had, they explained, been on the Ipswich train a few years before the outbreak of war, and been enormously intrigued by what the two fellow passengers in their carriage were doing which caused them to explode into laughter at frequent intervals. Now, listening to Temmy's talk, they had suddenly found this fascinating conundrum solved.

I have forgotten how much Collins paid me as an advance on the first of the series, but I know that together with the outright payment I got for *Six Bars at Seven*, I was suddenly in possession of the huge sum of £75! And this in a day and age when the *return* fare from London Docks to Bombay and back again, Tourist Class – three weeks either way with all meals included and no limit on how long one stayed at the end of an outward trip – was *forty pounds*! *£40!* Unbelievable nowadays, isn't it? I looked at my seventy-five-pound windfall and realized with incredulous joy that if I could make that kind of money by writing, then I could write anywhere. I didn't have to stay in London in a bed-sit in Limerston Street with the rain dripping dismally down on the cobblestones outside, when I could live a good deal cheaper on a houseboat on the Dāl Lake with lotus lilies looking in at my window. I was rich, I was rich, I was *rich*! Moreover, Fudge Cosgrave, the other lifelong friend I had made at the Chelsea Illustrators, had left before me. Her father, Sir William, had been appointed Chief Commissioner of the Andamans, and Fudge had given me a pressing invitation to spend the whole of the cold weather there. It was a chance not to be missed, and now – oh wonderful day! – I could afford to take it up.

Roger gave me a farewell party at the Hungaria, and Mike and Bargie and Sir Harold Snagge – the man she was to marry as soon as her divorce from the unsatisfactory Tancred was finalized – came down to Tilbury to see me off. I left England on a wet, cold, blustery day in early October, clutching under my arm a carbon copy of *Six Bars at Seven*, in case the publishers lost the top one before it appeared in print! I remember being scared stiff that some ill fate might befall it before it saw the light of day; the whole thing still seemed too good to be true.

Oddly enough, I don't remember anything at all about the ship or the voyage out, except that we ran into dense fog in the Bay of Biscay, and for the whole of one day we crawled forward into nothingness with our fog-horn howling like a demented sheep every few minutes, and being answered at intervals by the fog-horns of other ships (the Bay seemed to be full of them!) baying mournfully in reply. And the only reason I remember that is because I was afraid that if we collided with another ship in the fog, and had to take to the boats, I might lose my precious MS. I was so scared of that that I crammed the manuscript into my sponge bag,* in case it got damaged by salt water, and tied it on to myself – just in case! I blush to recall it.

Apart from that the entire voyage is a blank. I imagine I must have spent most of it with my feet at least ten inches above the deckplanks, metaphorically speaking, from sheer elation, for I was going home, and

---

* Plus a bathing cap!

I couldn't believe my luck. I was going to see my family again, and Kadera and Mahdoo, and any number of old friends, as well as all the loved and familiar places. I felt as if I had been away for years and years instead of only two, for so many things had happened since I had left India in that sad spring when Tacklow died. Among others, I had recently become an aunt, for Bets was now the mother of a baby son, Richard Henry Pardey, born in Srinagar, Kashmir, in the late summer of 1936. Since she and her baby, and Mother as well, had been spending the summer months in Simla as paying guests of a mutual friend, I intended to make Simla my first port of call, before setting off to join Fudge in the Andaman Islands.

Somebody must have met me and put me up for a day or two in Bombay, because I remember meeting one of the Burma-Shell people, whom I had known in Delhi, at the racecourse – one Sinclair, known to his friends as Sinbad – and telling him proudly that I had been able to come back under my own steam, because I had written a book that was shortly to be published. I rather expected to be congratulated on this success, but was firmly slapped down and snubbed when Sinbad asked what the book was about, and on being told, remarked loftily that anyone who had enough intelligence to get a book published ought to be above writing the sort of trashy rubbish that I had obviously gone in for. I have seldom had such a crushing put-down, and it remains like a sore patch in my memory to this day. Typical of Sinbad, said my friends consolingly. And it was, of course.

I caught the Frontier Mail to Delhi and travelled up across India with my nose pressed to the windowpane, revelling in every mile of the beloved land unrolling before my infatuated eyes. My companion in a two-berth *purdah* carriage (women only) was not, as I had hoped, some Indian lady on whom I could practise my Hindustani but a youngish Scots missionary, returning to a mission hospital in the hills after a holiday in Bombay. She may once have been dazzled by the charm of India, but if so, the gilt had worn off, and a too close association with the dark side of that great sub-continent had made her take a dim view of the country and its people. She could not understand how I could find anything to admire in the land that streamed endlessly past the windows of our carriage, and though plainly she was a kind-hearted and obviously dedicated do-gooder, she was not a particularly enlivening companion on a long train journey.

We parted at Delhi, where she retained her seat and I changed trains for the one that took me to Kalka in the company of a cosy old *pahareen*

– a hillwoman, bound for her home village somewhere beyond Kasauli – who thought my Hindustani was hysterically funny. Kalka is in the foothills of the Himalayas where the white, winding mountain road that leads to Simla begins, and I was decanted in the dawn on to a station platform that I had been familiar with ever since I first stepped down on to it at the ripe age of three. I took the rail-motor to Simla in preference to the much slower narrow-gauge railway in which I had always travelled before. This was on Mother's advice. She said it cost more but got there much quicker. I knew every inch of that road. Or thought I did. And as we passed Dugshai and saw the road veer away towards Sanour, I leaned out of the window to look up at a ridge that is high above both railway and road, where Tacklow lies buried, and felt like shouting out to him, 'I'm all right, darling. I'm back!' I didn't of course, but I expect he knew.

I don't think there was any part of the road, from the clumps of candelabra cactus on the bare lower hills, to the pines and deodar and rhododendron on the higher ones, and the villages and wayside shrines, that was unfamiliar to me. But I had forgotten the scents. There is a little yellow climbing rose that has the sweetest and most penetrating scent and which brings back the past as nothing else could – more even than the smell of pine needles and pine-cones. The rail-motor stopped, as the train always did, at Jatogue on the Simla side of the long and gritty Jatogue tunnel, for long enough for the passengers to alight and eat breakfast at the railway restaurant. And that too had not changed a whisker since I had eaten my first breakfast there back in the autumn of 1913. The restaurant used to make an odd form of scrambled egg that tasted exactly like the awful dried-egg concoctions that food-rationed Britons put up with during the Second World War. And I bet they still do!

Mother and Bets were on the Simla platform to meet me, and we were once more a family. I had come home again.

❧ 5 ❧

Islands in the Sun

❧❧❧❧

Chapter 22

~%⌀%~

I had brought two special parcels with me from England, in addition to that MS. One, for Mother, was a life-size head-to-waist portrait of Tacklow that Pedder, one of the Chelsea Illustrators, who was an excellent portrait painter, had painted from a photograph. Dear Pedder knew very well that I couldn't possibly afford the prices she got for her portraits, and she did that superlative one of Tacklow for *eight pounds* – which I imagine just about covered the canvas and the tubes of paint. The hours she spent on it were free, and altogether the whole thing cost me ten pounds, because Pedder couldn't invent the colouring of the uniform and medals, so I hired those, at a pound a time, from one of the theatrical and fancy-dress firms that dealt with this sort of thing.

Roger nobly sat for the portrait, dressed up in the ICS full-dress kit and orders, and the result could not have been better. I bought a large gilt frame for it at a junk shop on the Portobello Road for ten shillings (ah me, those were the days!). Mother took one look at it and burst into tears, and I was afraid that I had pushed her back into the ponds of woe that had made life so impossible for all her friends and relatives during the months after Tacklow died. But thank goodness, no. She thought the picture was a speaking likeness, which it was. And is. And for the rest of her life it accompanied her on all her travels. Nowadays it hangs in my hall, at the top of the stairs, and it is Tacklow standing there. As with Vermeer's *Head of a Girl*, if you smile at him he smiles back.

The other thing was a tablet to his memory, which was put up on the right-hand wall of Simla's Christ Church, the church in which both Bets and I were christened. I presume it is there still. I modelled it myself in clay, bought the bronze, and MG, who had a kiln in her back garden (her husband had been a well-known sculptor), cast it for me for nothing. They *were* a nice lot, those Chelsea Illustrators. I am eternally indebted to them.

Bets's first-born, a placid blue-eyed baby with a head covered in pale gold curls, only needed a pair of wings to be mistaken for one of the Heavenly Host, and was one of the best-tempered babies I have ever come across. He was uninterested in teddy-bears or rubber balls, and his two favourite things were an empty cigarette tin with a pebble in it, which made a fascinating rattle, and, of all things, a small enamel basin which gave him hours of amusement. He either sat in it – it just fitted his plump little behind – or turned it over and sat on it. And, when that palled, he used it as a *tabla*, an Indian hand-drum, or put it on his head where it looked like a First World War tin hat. He got hours of amusement out of those two everyday objects, both of which had to be put into his cot at night. I have often thought that it's a pity more mothers don't try the effect of similar things on their offspring, instead of wasting vast sums of money on coloured bricks and expensive woolly animals. He was an adorable baby, and grew up to design those hideous oil platforms that litter the North Sea.

I spent a month in Simla and then left for Calcutta, from where I was to set sail for the Andaman Islands to spend the rest of the cold weather with Fudge and her parents. I had booked a passage for myself on the SS *Maharajah,* the little steamer that was the only link between India and the Andamans, and which only called there once a month. I don't know who originally owned the Andamans, but someone must have done (it certainly was not India). Judging from the early nineteenth-century prints that I once saw, it was annexed in the usual high-handed manner by a British Admiral (or maybe he was only a Captain) in command of one or two Royal Navy ships. I got the impression from the prints, which included a lot of cotton-wool puffs coming out of the ships' guns, that they happened upon the islands by chance, fired on the few Andamanese who unwisely appeared on the beaches, and, when these ran away, sent a jolly-boat ashore to run up the Union Jack and announce that the islands were now a part of the British Empire. I know that the prints referred to the cotton-wool puffs as 'the battle of Port Blair'.

Having pinched the islands, the only thing we could find to do with them was to use those incredibly beautiful places as a penal settlement for convicted murderers who were considered to have had some excuse for their crime. (The ones who got 'life' instead of being hanged.) Much later, very much later and after my time, it was used, briefly, as a prison for political offenders. Much has been made of this last, to the detriment, naturally, of the Raj. The place has been made out to be a ghastly Devil's Island. In fact, it was anything but. The prison was a pink, star-shaped fort built of coral rag and surrounded by coconut palms, and the cells led off wide verandahs and were about the size of the average single room in a tourist hotel on the Costa-de-Whatsiz.

Prisoners were only kept here for a month, after which they were given a small plot of land and the instruments needed to farm it. The idea of the settlement was that it would eventually be colonized by the criminals (as was Australia!) and turned into flourishing tea-gardens, coffee plan- tations and saw-mills. Lifers were encouraged to bring their families out, at the Government's expense, and every able-bodied man or woman in the islands had a job. The servants in Government House, and in every other official's house, were all convicted murderers. And the only nuisance about that was that ever since a Governor's wife had been murdered by her cook, no European woman was allowed to go outside her house without an armed guard (an Indian policeman, or a *jawan*) walking behind them. The rule was made more irritating by the fact that anyone who ever met the murdered lady was convinced that she had asked for it, and richly deserved her sticky end. In fact a strong plea for clemency was put in on behalf of the wretched cook, who had to be hanged, since the law of the penal colony laid down that a lifer who committed a second murder automatically earned the death sentence.

My parents having been friends of the then incumbent of Government House, Calcutta, Mother had written to him to ask if he would see that I was met and put up for the night, and seen off safely on the SS *Maharajah*. So when the train fetched up in Calcutta, there, waiting for me on the platform, were no fewer than three charming ADCs, armed with a letter from His Excellency to say he deeply regretted that he had been called away on urgent business, but that 'the boys' would look after me and see me safely aboard.

Well, that was fine as far as I was concerned, and 'the boys' did me proud. They took me off to lunch at Firpos, whisked me out to bathe and to have tea at the Tollygunge Club, and having brought me back to change into evening dress, took me out to dine and dance at the Saturday Club.

I had imagined that they would add another couple of girls to the party that evening, but no. It was still just me and the chaps. And since they danced with me in turn, I danced every dance. It was also a very hot night

– Calcutta is always hot and muggy – and I had had an exceptionally energetic day. So that when my three ADCs, who took a dim view of the fact that in those days (and on the whole, in these too) I didn't drink any form of alcohol, suddenly produced, at a late hour of night, a long glass of something ice-cold and fizzy, full of slices of fruit and cucumber and lumps of lovely ice, I looked at it with some suspicion and said, probably crossly, that I'd already told them at least a dozen times that I wasn't being a prude about alcohol, I just did not *like* it.

'Oh, this isn't alcohol,' chorused those young so-and-so's. 'It's only Pimm's. You *must* have had a Pimm's before? It's only a sort of cup with a lot of lemonade and the juice of various fruits – that's all. You'll love it.'

I took a cautious sip, and they were right – I loved it. Just the thing for a hot night and with all that dancing. In the intervals between the next two dances I finished it, and when they asked me if I'd like another, I said I certainly would. By the time the band had packed it in and the dance was over, I had had at least three of those lethal drinks. Possibly four. I only remember that I had a wonderful evening, made more enjoyable by the envious looks I got from other and less popular girls, who couldn't understand why I should have *three* young men all to myself.

I arrived back at Government House in the best of spirits, and I remember mounting that long flight of marble stairs and looking down at those three young fiends who were standing in the hall below and staring rather anxiously up at me. I waved a cheerful hand, and one of them said a bit nervously: 'I think it would be a good idea if you took a couple of aspirins.'

'*Aspirins?* What on earth do I want aspirins for? I'm feeling fine!' I replied gaily. I fell into bed and was asleep almost before I could get my clothes off, but when I woke up, I wanted to die. I don't think I have ever felt so ghastly in my life, and if it hadn't been for the Government House *ayah*, who clucked over me in distress, managed to get me dressed and packed for me, I would never have caught that ship. The *ayah* helped me down those stairs, to where there were at least six if not nine ADCs waiting for me in the hall (their numbers seemed to double and treble and occasionally shrink into three), and I remember saying: 'You *beasts!* You horrid lousy little *rats* – don't you *dare* speak to me!!' They didn't. They got me down to the docks and helped me up the gangway and into my cabin, where I fell on to my berth and passed out cold.

*

The Andaman Islands are at the bottom of the Bay of Bengal, a long way off the coast of Burma and with very little between them and the Antarctic. The little *Maharajah*, chugging down those limitless wastes of sea, took a full three days to reach the only reasonable harbour in the Andamans – Port Blair.

Knocked out by that great-grandmother of all hangovers, I did not stir from my minute cabin, which fortunately contained all mod cons, for the entire three days of the voyage. Those horrid ADCs had obviously explained the situation to the Captain and the ship's doctor, for dry biscuits and various soothing drinks were delivered at intervals by a sympathetic little Goanese steward. But it was not until dawn on the third morning that I awoke without feeling that my head had been replaced by a red-hot cannonball, and that I was never going to eat or be able to see straight for the rest of my life.

I was aware that the ship was no longer moving, and I crawled out of my bunk and went out on to the deck, to find that we were at anchor in the middle of a wide harbour ringed by white sands, green hills and coconut palms, with, to seaward, a scattering of little coral islands that looked like a flight of brilliant blue-green butterflies taking wing across that enormous expanse of mirror-smooth ocean.

The nearest of these islands was a tiny affair, topped by a large sprawling two-storey house surrounded by flowering trees, with, lower down, glimpses of other roofs and gardens embedded in lush greenery. This island had a long jetty to which a single boat, obviously a ferry, was moored, and a small white-painted launch flying a Union Jack had just left it and was making its way towards us. 'That'll be the Government House launch,' said the Captain, appearing out of nowhere. 'They'll be coming to take you off. Hadn't you better get dressed?'

Well, yes, I'd better, for there, standing up in the prow of the rapidly approaching launch, was Fudge, waving her arms in a wild semaphore of welcome.

The next few months were among the happiest I have ever spent. There are few people who have the luck to live for weeks on end on a coral island, in great luxury, with nothing to do but laze and swim, paint and go fishing. To wake, morning after morning, to see sunlight dancing across the high, white walls of a huge, airy bedroom, as the palms and the gold-mohur trees, and the masses of flowering creepers in the garden swayed in a cool sea breeze. To hear the fluting and chattering of innumerable exotic birds and the lovely, monotonous music of the surf that washed the beaches of the little island. To stretch out one's arms under the mist of the mosquito net and think, 'Now what shall I do today?'

No wonder Tacklow's old friend, the one who had been Chief Commissioner of the Andamans many years ago, had managed to wangle extension after extension to a job that was looked upon by more ambitious members of the ICS and the F and P as a dead end. The old boy had fallen in love with the Andamans, and did not give a toot about trying to get himself moved to a grander post.

In point of fact, VIPs never included the Andamans in any of their tours, and so didn't know what they were missing. It had been tried once, when an undistinguished Viceroy by the name of Lord Mayo decided he'd like to take a look at the islands. The poor man became the only Viceroy ever to have been successfully assassinated. He was murdered by a Pathan 'trustee' – a lifer, who had managed to convince the local police that, apart from the fact that he had sliced the head off someone in his careless youth, there wasn't a blot on his character, and who had become one of the Viceroy's guards.

There is an interesting story attached to this. Lord Mayo had been spending the day at the hot-weather Government House on top of Mount Harriet – the highest point in the hillsides that overlook Port Blair. The party broke up rather too late in the evening, and it was dark by the time they reached the jetty at the foot of Mount Harriet, where a steam-launch waited to take the Viceregal party back across the bay to Ross – the little island that is crowned by Government House and is the administrative centre of Port Blair. The convict guard that lined the jetty had been given torches, and it was by the light of those torches that the Pathan tribesman who had been transported for a blood-feud murder (in his eyes a legitimate killing) leapt out of the darkness and stabbed Lord Mayo. The Viceroy fell from the jetty into the mud below, where he died in the arms of the young doctor who had been attached to the party as H.E.'s personal physician, and who had leapt down into the mud to do what he could for the dying man.

A blow by blow description of the incident – the torch light on the wet mud and the wetter blood, the panic and the turmoil – was given me by the son of that doctor, who in his turn had heard it described, in lurid detail, by his father. The doctor's son was General Sir Philip Christianson, Bart (plus a string of initials), a child of that doctor's old age. Poor Mayo, who had gone to the Andamans to try to better the administration of jails and penal settlements, was murdered on the evening of 24 January 1872. Well over a hundred years ago. 'Ah, did you once see Shelley plain?' – Well, almost. Fascinating isn't it?*

In the 1930s there were only about fifteen or sixteen Europeans on the Andamans (not counting a small detachment of British troops under the command of a junior captain, since these came and went and were not fixtures) – such as the Swedes who ran the saw-mill, and a couple of Scandinavians who had a coconut plantation, and so on. Unfortunately they all knew each other too well, with the result that the majority were not on speaking terms with each other. This made entertaining very difficult for poor Lady Cosgrave, who found it extremely tricky to plot out the place-names at Government House dinner parties without seating two implacable enemies side by side.

The house had been built in the nineteenth century at a time when the Raj was involved in hostilities with Burma. When the Empire builders had succeeded in grabbing Burma, they found themselves lumbered with an enormous number of Burmese prisoners of war, and no idea what to do with them, until some bright colonist had the brilliant idea of shipping the majority of them to the Andamans, where they would appear to have settled down very comfortably.

Among them were a good many members of King Thebaw's court: including a number of court artists and carvers. Why such persons should have been lumped together with prisoners of war I can't think, unless some artistically minded general thought they might be usefully employed tishing up Government House and the Club. Which they did most successfully. I only wish I could have seen their work before some tiresome Chief Commissioner's wife decided that the big drawing-room would look brighter and lighter if its walls and ceiling were smothered in white gloss-paint, thus almost obliterating the beautiful free-hand carvings that depicted hunting scenes, in which weird animals of every shape and description were pursued by men armed with spears or bows and arrows through the lush foliage of fantastic forests that could only have existed

* It is on record that an astrologer warned that the King of Delhi (i.e. the Viceroy) was dead five days before the news reached India.

in the artists' minds. It's a pity that woman wasn't bopped on the head by one or other of the convicts whose work she did her best to ruin.

Fortunately, there was a beautiful carved wooden screen between the dining-room and the upper hall of Government House, untouched by paint, and so skilfully done that both sides were perfect, the one that faced the dining-room being an accurate back-view of the one that faced the upper hall. The newel-post of the stairway that led up from the lower hall was carved into the likeness of some Burmese demon's head, and was always referred to as 'Hindenburg', and the club-house, which had been built so near the shore of the tiny island that in windy weather the spray would rattle against its windows with the sound of handfuls of pebbles hurled against the glass, possessed a double-sided screen that was even better than the one in Government House.

I thought the house with its wide, glassed-in verandahs and its wonderful views was near perfect. Yet I hated it. For if ever a house was haunted, that one was. And with reason. When you remember that every single one of the servants who worked in it was only there because he had murdered somebody, it would not be too surprising if the place harboured a few vengeful ghosts. And there were things that one could not explain about that house. It had only two doors on the first floor, the one that shut off the master-bedroom from the hall, and the one that shut off the main guest-room. My room, and Fudge's, had short swing doors of the type that one sees in bars. They did not lock, and lying in bed one could see the legs of anyone who passed as far as their knees.

Each bedroom had its own bathroom, plus proper doors for modesty's sake, and all the bathrooms could be reached from the outside by staircases leading down from them, at the foot of which, by night, a member of the Indian Police (recruited on the mainland, not from a jail!) stood guard under an arc-lamp, the lights being switched on every day at dusk, and turned off at dawn. Fudge's room and my own were connected by an open archway that had a curtain across it. And every room in the place had a big white ceiling fan that was hardly ever still, for the Andamans are not all that far off the equator.

The walls of Government House were not solid, but for some reason were hollow and pierced at intervals, on the inner side, by portholes. This encouraged bats, lizards, squirrels, wildcats, the wind and the odd owl or two to play around in the space between the double walls, and was responsible for the peculiar noises one heard in the night. It did not, however, explain the eyes that looked back at me from my mosquito-net whenever I woke at night. If they had remained in the same place they would not have worried me so. But they didn't. Sometimes they were at the top of the mosquito net at the foot of my bed, and sometimes on one or the other side. Sir William insisted that they must be made by some stray chink of the guard-light at the foot of my outside stairway, shining through a crack or reflecting off something. But though Fudge and I tried to track them down to their source we never succeeded in blotting them out. Our Indian doctor, Dr Choudrey, suggested that it was the result of some substance that was faintly phosphorescent, and had splashed on to the mosquito net. This seemed reasonable to me; if only the two pale oblongs of light had not moved. He could not come up with an explanation for that, but he did something better. He asked if they had done me any harm, or prevented me from sleeping. And when I said no, he said, 'Then why not believe that they are keeping a watch over you to see that you come to no harm? It could be true.'

So I did. And it stopped me worrying though it did not stop them watching me. Odd how one always thinks that something one can't understand or explain is frightening or nasty, instead of good. All the same, I never liked that house. I had the feeling that if I'd been a dog or a cat, my hair would have been permanently bristling.

I have told the story of how I came to write a 'whodunnit' about the islands in the foreword to a book called *Death in the Andamans*, so I won't tell it here again. But the hurricane that gave rise to it really happened, and it was an enthralling experience. It was not one that I would like to repeat though, since it was also terrifying. One minute we were in brilliant sunlight and driving as fast as we could make an ancient Ford car move, in an attempt to keep ahead of a great wall of blackness that had swept down on to the island and appeared to be chasing us. And the next second it had caught us, and we were being carried along with it as though we weighed no more than a dead leaf, by a shrieking gale and what seemed to be a tidal wave full of broken branches and other assorted debris.

I still don't know how we managed to make it to the jetty on Aberdeen, the only town in the islands, or how, or why, anyone in authority, let alone the skipper of the ferry, could have given the order to try and get it across to Ross. At a guess, it was probably because no one wanted to be stuck in a hurricane with the Chief Commissioner's daughter, in case she came to any harm. And in the event, we made it. Though I shall never know how, for we kept on being hurled back by a furious sea and alternately swept by that shrieking wind towards the harbour mouth and out to sea. I've never been so scared in my life. We all were. The crossing seemed to take hours, and we were all soaked to the skin by the time we crashed into the Ross jetty, and were able to scramble on to it and be taken up to Government House in the official wet-weather rickshaws.

To cap everything, it was Christmas Eve, and we were giving a dinner-party that night and another the next day. But only one or two guests who lived on Ross had managed to get aboard the ferry with us, and everyone else was stranded on Aberdeen for the duration. We were cut off from all communication with the outside world for the best part of a week, during which Fudge and I amused ourselves by inventing and perfecting the plot of a whodunnit, using the only characters who had remained on Ross during the storm. We needed something to entertain us, because the storm had ruined all of the planned Christmas festivities. We did manage, during a lull that proved to be only temporary, to struggle up to the little church and attend a Christmas service, at which the wind and the rain, and the roar and thunder of the sea, effectively drowned out the strains of 'Hark the Herald' and 'Away in a Manger' and made the spoken part of the service completely inaudible.

The thing that sticks in my mind most clearly is the sheer volume of noise that Mother Nature can produce when she puts her mind to it, and the feeling that not only the house, but Ross itself, was only a stuffed toy that was being picked up and shaken by the jaws of some giant puppy-dog, every time a particularly vicious blast of wind hit us. In the occasional lulls which fooled us into thinking it was all over, it would suddenly became quiet enough for us to hear the drips: *plink, tink, bonk, SPLOSH; splosh, bunk, tink, plink, plinkety-tink* – and on and on and on. Like a child playing a xylophone. For the hot days had dried out the house and left a myriad little chinks that the rain did not miss, and with the first 'plink', the Government House servants rushed into the breach with tin plates, pots and pans to catch the leaks.

In spite of mackintoshes, wellies, umbrellas and wet-weather rickshaws, we had all ended up soaked to the skin after our dash to the church and back on Christmas Day, and it was several days before we were able to leave the house and take a walk round the island. And several more before the jetty could be mended, and we were once again in possession of fresh milk and eggs, letters and telegrams and news of the outside world. Ross and Aberdeen, and the shores of Port Blair, had received a tremendous battering, and the sea was still doing its best to smash the enormous rocks that reared up on either side of the small sandy beach I could look down on from my bedroom window, and from where, in calm weather, Fudge and I would bathe. No one would have dared try bathing from it now, but we went down and clambered out on to the tallest rocks to watch the enormous hills of foam-streaked water that drove in from the open sea, rearing up higher and higher as they neared the island, and curling over and crashing down in a welter of foam and flying spindrift. It was a most awesome sight, and one which kept me riveted for hours.

I did a lot of painting in the Andamans. One in particular was a large picture of medieval carol-singers in the snow – 'Frost and carol, silver bell, high men, yeomen, sing Noel'. It took me days to finish, and it ended up on a Christmas card which I sold to one of the companies that specialized in such things.

Apart from the hurricane, the weather during the rest of the stay was idyllic. Day after blue-and-gold day. Nothing to do but bathe and laze and admire. The hurricane had ripped away the steel wire underwater fence that made a swimming-pool out of a section of sea between the jetty and the long, stone-built sea wall that protected the Club lawn, but no one noticed it. Not until Fudge and I resumed our habit of walking down the long drive to the gates of Government House, under an avenue of flowering gold-mohur trees, and from there down to the steep road that led past the guest house and eventually to the Club, where we would change into our swimsuits and spend the rest of the morning swimming and sunbathing.

I went in first, off the diving board, and was idly dog-paddling back when something like a red-hot whip lashed my bare thigh, and I yelled at the top of my voice and made for the ladder that was fixed to the wall. Fudge, who had been about to follow me into the pool, helped me up the last bit of the ladder, and we both turned and stared down into the clear, gently heaving pool. Fudge said, '*Wow!* – look there!' and pointed at something about the size of a bridge table made out of a square of black mackintosh that undulated across the sandy bottom of the pool below us and, slithering under the torn fence which was supposed to protect us from sharks, vanished into deep water. It was a 'devil-fish' that had taken refuge there in the storm. I had a sore thigh for several days.

Fudge and I used to bathe twice a day, except when we went deep-sea fishing: once in the morning and once at night. The night bathes were the best, because there was nearly always phosphorus in the water. Sometimes the whole sea would be milky-white with it. But the best times were when it only showed where the waves broke, since if you dived off the wall or off the diving board, the moment you hit the water you were outlined in fire. And when you climbed out again, diamonds by the millions dripped from your arms and your fingers. Those were magic nights.

I used to wonder why such ugly things as dugongs had been mistaken for mermaids. But walking down to the Club one morning Fudge and I both saw what we took to be one of the British troops bathing in the sea outside the stone wall, and breaking into a run we fled down the road, waving and shrieking at him to get back on the right side of the wire because there were plenty of sharks in the bay. I remember yelling: 'Get back! Sharks . . . *Sharks!*' and running as fast as I could. But all the silly ass did was to swim lazily away from us, further out into the bay. It was only when we tore across the lawn and out on to the sea wall that the rash bather turned to see what the fuss was about, and, deciding he didn't like the look of these shouting hooligans, withdrew in a dignified manner. It was a dugong, and I still can't explain why it looked so *exactly* like the upper half of a rather red and sunburnt swimmer. But it did. It never occurred to either Fudge or myself that it wasn't. Not until it turned upside down and you saw its arms were flippers and its bottom was grey, and it had fins.

We fished a lot in the Andamans. Sir William would lend us the Government House launch, the *Jarawa*, and we would go off down the coast and around the other islands. The method was quite simple. The seamen in charge would change gear and the *Jarawa* would stop loitering along the placid sea and, exploding into life, shoot off at speed, while the fishers would throw their baited hooks into the water and hope for the best. The first person to get a bite would yell 'Strike!' and at once the engine would stop and we would remain drifting while whoever had shouted played his or her fish.

Sometimes two or three people would get a bite at the same time and the lines would get tangled up like a bit of knitting. I remember one time when Fudge and I and the young Scotsman in charge of the police all got a bite at the same time. Shamus lost his after a few moments, and Fudge and I, having at last untangled ourselves, continued to play our fish, until suddenly Fudge said: 'Damn! I've lost mine. Go on, Moll, the field is yours and it looks like a big one.' It was indeed. But it wasn't a fish. It took me ages to reel it in, and when at last it gave up and I reeled it in to the side of the boat, it turned out to be a huge turtle! I was all for letting the poor fellow go, but the *Jarawa*'s crew were outraged. What, throw away good food? Was the Miss-Sahib *mad*? They hooked it in and killed it, and were all as pleased as punch at its capture. When that was out of the way, Fudge reeled in her line, and as it came nearer, she said: 'There seems to be something on it after all . . . When it stopped fighting so suddenly I thought it had broken free . . . But there is definitely something there and it's heavy.' It was indeed. Goodness knows what it would have weighed if it had been a whole fish. As it was, it was the head only. The head of a whopper of a fish that had been cut cleanly from its body, just behind the gills, by another and very much larger fish. A fish that must have had jaws like razors. Shark? Or possibly the grandfather of all barracudas.

We used to take parties of the soldiery out fishing sometimes, because they one and all hated being cooped up on Port Blair with sweet Fanny Adams to do. They got no kick out of bathing, sunbathing, or snorkelling, and their officers were kept busy inventing 'Exercises' to keep them occupied. But it was difficult. On one occasion, two private soldiers stole the company pay-chest and a fishing boat, and set out for what they imagined was the coast of Burma. They were scooped in, somewhat naturally, in double quick time. Their exasperated Company Commander asked them what on earth they were thinking of, did they *really* think they could get away with the pay-chest and live the life of Riley in Mandalay or Singapore, when there were thousands of miles of empty sea between them and the nearest coast? No, of *course* they didn't, said the culprits crossly. They only did it to stir things up a bit. And they explained what fun it had been, planning how they could swipe the pay-chest. They'd planned it down to the last detail and it had worked a treat! But neither of them even knew how to sail a boat, and they'd just wanted to see how far they could get. They'd had a lot of fun – and so, they hoped, had everyone else. The Captain, who'd had enough of the Andamans by then, let them off with a caution. (He said it had been the only enlivening happening during the hot weather months!)

For myself, with Fudge to gossip with, plenty of paints and paper, bathing, lazing, and picnicking, the islands were Paradise itself. There was one special place, Foster Bay, where we picnicked whenever we could borrow the *Jarawa*. It had the most beautiful beach, miles and miles of silver sand, backed by forests of coconut palms, padouk and bushes of wild lemon that smelt wonderful. These attracted hordes and hordes of butterflies – gorgeous butterflies as big as sparrows: some with black and gold wings, and others with pale blue 'window-panes'; enormous, swallow-tailed iridescent green ones; monarch butterflies by the score, and any number of common white ones patterned with red and yellow spots. We used to drop anchor as soon as the water grew too shallow to cope with the *Jarawa*'s hull, and, carrying all the picnic gear on our heads, wade the last fifty or sixty yards to the beach.

The beaches were all beautifully lonely, and deserted except for the occasional sea bird and any number of busy hermit crabs; all of them, it seemed, hurrying around in search of a slightly bigger flat, house or mansion than the one they were occupying at the moment. Just watching them moving in or out of their shells – and oh, how lovely some of those shells were! – gave me hours of amusement. But though the beaches might be deserted, there were always ships plying to and fro across that enormous expanse of sea. All of them – so they said – trawling for pearl-shell. And all of them Japanese. You wouldn't have thought it worth the while of so many ships to travel so many miles from their native shores in search of the pearl-shell from which they manufactured the small, gleaming buttons that fasten shirts and other European garments all over the world (buttons which in those days one could buy for sixpence a card of twelve, at any haberdashery anywhere). And you would be right of course.

Sir William, who kept a watchful eye on his fascinating kingdom, was suspicious of the numbers of Japanese ships that claimed to be fishing for such a very common commodity, and spent a lot of his time, paper, and ink in drawing the attention of the Government of India to this curious activity. He also mentioned the fact that among the shops that lined the single, short main street of Aberdeen there were no less than seven photographers, all of them Japanese-owned. This seemed a little excessive to say the least of it, considering that the convicts and their families were not likely to buy cameras and take expensive snapshots, which left only two possible customers per photographer's shop.

But the Government of India had far too many other things on its plate to pay the least attention to the numbers of Japanese who were taking an interest in the Andamans, and all they did about it was to decide to make use of the only flat bit of land in Port Blair, which until now had provided the residents with a golf-course, to make an aerodrome. This they did, but in such a leisurely manner that Sir William's term of office had ended and the Cosgraves and myself had left the islands quite some time before it was finished. But it was finished in time for the first plane to land upon it to be a Japanese fighter, when Japan took the islands, killed the inhabitants they had no use for, and tortured and finally beheaded the unfortunate Englishman who was the original of the man Fudge and I had decided to make the murderer in our whodunnit – because he was such a meek little man that no one could *possibly* suspect him of killing a fly!

And the pearl-shell fleet? Well, they had been prospecting for any suitable deep-water bays, however small, where cans of petrol could be hidden for the future refuelling of Japanese submarines. Ah well, 'those whom the Gods would destroy they first make mad'. And blind too, it would seem. *Seven photographers' shops!*

Among the other atrocities the Japanese committed on the islands was the wiping out of the Jarawas* – the only truly stone-age tribe left on earth. No one knows anything about them, because no one ever had the chance to study them. They lived in the almost impenetrable Andamans jungle, and they had no permanent lairs. They would pull down branches to serve as shelters, but that was as far as they went. When their temporary camping ground became too messy, they moved on and made another somewhere else. Their housekeeping was as simple as that. They wore no clothes, unless one can call a tiny square of coconut shell with its hairy fringe still attached worn in place of a fig-leaf by the women clothes. Not the men.

Both sexes used bows and arrows, the arrows being half a circle of coconut shell, its outer edge sharpened until you could have shaved with it. As they would seem to have done. They obviously did not know how

---

* I am obviously wrong there. I have just read a newspaper article which says there are still Jarawas on the Andamans. And they are still killers!

219

to make fire, or use metal, and would kill for both, raiding a forest camp and killing its sleeping inhabitants in order to steal a bucket or a *dekchi*,* or the glowing coals of some forest-guard's fire.

Mount Harriet, the highest point in the islands, was in Jarawa country, and we never went up there without a platoon of forest guards, who ringed the house for fear of an attack by the little people. And not long before I came there, the men of whatever regiment had provided the company of British troops stationed on Ross had tried to avenge a Jarawa killing by tracking down and attacking the group who had done the deed. A pure waste of time, as the Jarawas merely faded away into the jungle, and all the troops got were about fifty to sixty leeches apiece. (The jungle dripped with the beastly things!) They found and broke up one of the camping places, and actually caught a Jarawa, an elderly lady who was probably not spry enough to escape in time.

This little creature was taken back to Ross in triumph, and it was decided to treat her as though she were an honoured guest, so that she would be able to tell her people that 'the natives are friendly'. They kept her for about a week, I gather, giving her food that she didn't like, and taking her for a car drive out to Corbyn's Cove on the main island, which nearly scared her to death. Finally they took her back to the place where they had caught her, loaded her with gifts and, as a final gesture of goodwill gave her back her bow and arrow. This proved a great mistake, for the old lady, clutching her loot, scuttled away and, suddenly stopping, dropped all her presents, strung her bow and if she'd been a slightly better shot would have scored a bullseye on the Assistant Commissioner – it was touch and go. So much for teaching her what a kind, friendly lot we were!

Efforts had obviously been made before to catch a Jarawa and try to learn their language, because one day, when Sir William had allowed us to look through the Government House archives, Fudge and I came across a letter from some nineteenth-century official, complaining to the Commissioner that while he, the writer, had been dining out, 'that cad Tewson let my Jarawas out'. (As though they were rabbits, or white mice or something of the sort! – Fudge and I were fascinated.) The writer had apparently managed to catch a few, and had kept them shut up in his bungalow while he tried to make sense out of their language. He might

* Cooking-pot.

even have done so, and had already made a start when he was foiled by that possibly well-meaning 'cad Tewson'. And no one ever did learn it, because the Japanese, thinking that there were spies hiding out there in those jungles (there were too), bombed them very thoroughly.

Almost half a century later, at a drinks party held in the garden of a large house in Eastbourne on the Sussex coast, my hostess, towing a middle-aged stranger, crossed the lawn to where I was standing and said, 'I don't think you two have ever met before. May I introduce you to Mr Tewson . . .'

I had never come across anyone of that name either before or since the evening in Sir William's office on Ross, and I said without thinking: 'Good heavens! – that cad Tewson!' and started to laugh my head off. My hostess looked shocked to pieces and the wretched man looked terribly taken aback. But when I explained hastily why the phrase had jumped into my mind, he said: 'This is *fantastic* – that must have been my grandfather!' And it *was*. Or rather had been. I rang up Fudge that evening and we both laughed ourselves silly. Oh, how lucky we were to have lived on an unspoiled coral island.

✤ 6 ✤

GOLCONDA

The old name for Hyderabad

Chapter 23

~꙰꙰~

I left the Andamans in a worse condition than I was in when I arrived. Not, I hasten to say, the result of Pimm's No.1 this time, but because the islands had given me a vicious parting present in the form of an insect bite on my top lip. I got bitten at the very last moment, probably by something peculiar and nervous that had been lurking among the garlands of orchids that well-wishers had draped around my neck as parting presents.

Few people have penetrated very far into the Andaman forests, and all sorts of strange flowers and trees, insects and animals, could have been lurking there alongside those stone-age people the Jarawas. I didn't even see the insect that bit me. I only felt it, and yowled and slapped the place, thinking it was only a mosquito or a thorn among the flowers. But within seconds my lip had started to swell up, and by the time our little steamer upped anchor and was heading out of the harbour, with me hanging over the bows and waving wildly at Fudge and various friends in the launch and assorted sailing-ships around it, I could barely see them, or Ross; or Harriet either, because my entire face had swollen up into a rainbow-coloured suet pudding. I nearly had a fit when I saw my reflection in my cabin looking-glass. So did the Captain and the ship's doctor. They tried dabbing various disinfectants on to it, but nothing worked. In fact it got worse.

Three days later, having discovered that my eyes and forehead were comparatively unblotched, I landed at Calcutta wearing a very fetching yashmak (fashioned from a chiffon scarf that fortunately matched the dress I was wearing), and looking every inch like 'Olga Petloffski the Beautiful Spy'. It was the only thing I could do, and it was an *enormous* success. It is on record that gentlemen prefer blondes, but I soon discovered that they are also suckers for anything in a yashmak. Fortunately I have (or had) a fairly good pair of eyes, and this was instantly accepted by those who had not previously met me as evidence of other features to match. Yashmaked, I was credited with being a raving beauty, while underneath those layers of chiffon my face was an unholy mess.

This time the Governor himself (he had been a friend of Tacklow's) came down to meet me, accompanied by his private sec. HE* was fascinated by the yashmak. However, he refused to believe it was necessary – 'all this fuss about a mosquito bite that has gone bad on you!' – until back in Government House he sent for the Residency doctor who, prepared for a slightly unsightly red blotch (and also taking a lofty 'What's all this fuss about, young woman?' approach), took a hasty step backwards when I removed the yashmak, much as though I had unveiled a Dr Jekyll in the process of turning into Mr Hyde – either that or an advanced case of leprosy or the plague.

He rang up a colleague who was supposed to specialize in weird skin diseases, and the two of them wrangled over it for what seemed like hours. After this it was agreed that I could have all my meals by myself. They would have to be near-liquid ones because it was difficult to get anything into my mouth, since I could only ladle very soft things in at one corner. They also tried a variety of drugs and lotions (none of which did any good and most of the latter only stung), and finally wrote a joint letter explaining their views to the Residency doctor in Hyderabad, where I was heading to stay with Sandy, who had invited Mother and me to visit for a few weeks.

I only spent two nights in Calcutta, and those ADCs – only two of them, one had returned to his regiment and not yet been replaced – insisted on taking me out to a dance at the Saturday Club, solely on account of that yashmak which, as they prophesied, proved a spectacular success. Moving on to Hyderabad, Deccan (there is another Hyderabad in Sind), I found Mother and Sandy on the platform to meet me – Sandy established in a huge, white, two-storey house standing among lush flower gardens – and had my customary success with the yashmak. Believe it or not, that beastly Andamans-sting and/or bite took well over a month to subside, and I have a sad feeling that when I was eventually able to remove the yashmak I disappointed a lot of people who had obviously been expecting something like Greta Garbo or Marlene Dietrich to emerge from behind it.

* 'His Excellency'. The Viceroy, and all Governors, are Excellencies.

It was while I was in Hyderabad that Somerset Maugham and his secretary descended upon the State during one of that excellent but acidulated writer's many Eastern tours, and the Resident pushed him off on to Sandy to entertain him. I was enthralled to meet him, but disappointed to find him a sour and unfriendly old gentleman who stumped off fairly early to bed. It was after he had taken himself off that I told his secretary that I hadn't mentioned his books, because I thought the Great Man must be sick to death of people saying: 'Oh, Mr Maugham, I simply adored this or that book, and/or short story.' To which his secretary replied: 'You were wrong. It's the only thing he likes to talk about!'

So next morning we got on like a house on fire, and in the end I became brave enough to mention that I had just written a very light-hearted novel, but that I was afraid I would never make a writer. He asked why, in a distinctly bored voice, and I said because I wrote much too slowly and would stick for hours on end over a sentence that I couldn't get right, and though advised by any number of friends to leave it and press on, and come back and fix it later, I found myself totally unable to do so. I *had* to get it right before I could go on, and sometimes I got held up for hours on end.

The old boy peered at me over the top of his spectacles exactly like an elderly tortoise, and said: 'My dear young woman, that is the *only* thing I have heard you say that makes me think you may be a writer one day: *I* do that!' He also told me that Colette did it too, so I was enormously cheered. I asked him if it was true that the plots of all his stories were ones he had overheard or been told by people who had been involved in them in some way or another, and that they were all based on fact, and he replied that of course they were: 'Why should I cudgel my brains to invent stories when people keep giving me excellent real-life ones on a plate? If they ever stop handing me interesting stories I may have to start inventing. But not until then!'

He also gave me what he said was an invaluable tip: 'If a word is just what you want, don't try hunting for a similar one because you've already used that one several times. Even if you've used it six times in a row, if it's right, leave it.' I've tried following that advice, but it's no good. I hate repetition, and I fly to Roget for an alternative. Though I apologize to old Somerset's ghost whenever I do it!

*

Mother and I painted a lot in Hyderabad. I muralled two walls in the hall of Sandy's house, and met a lot of interesting people. Hyderabad was supposed to have the grandest Residency in all India, and was also one of the states that tourists visited because of the polo – there was hardly a day when some first-class polo-match was not being played there – and because of the legendary diamond mines of Golconda. The then Resident was not a social-minded man, so if he had to put passing VIPs up in the Residency (which was certainly the most lavish piece of showing-off to be met with in the days of the Raj – a palace, no less) he would send them over to Sandy to wine and dine them and arrange expeditions and picnics, and take them shopping. Among them that year we had Barbara Hutton, the Woolworth heiress, and her current husband, Count Reventlow. She wanted to go shopping for jewellery, so instead of taking her and her entourage to one of the glittering jewellers' shops in the flashiest and more Europeanized part of town, we took her down to the old city, where the *real* trade goes on in the houses of the jewel merchants.

Here we entered one of the tall Indian houses straight from a narrow, unpaved lane lined with similar houses, and climbed up innumerable stairs in the half light to a long, whitewashed room where there was no furniture at all, just thick druggets (or possibly carpets) covered with white cotton sheeting, on which the owner and a couple of assistants, also dressed in white, were seated cross-legged and smoking a hookah. They rose and bowed when we came in and then sat down again, gesturing us to do the same, which we did somewhat awkwardly – Barbara's high heels proving a distinct handicap in this kind of caper. Having got us all safely down on the floor, the owner clapped his hands and cups of coffee and various bits of this-and-that, *halwa* (sweetmeats) mostly, were produced and passed round. After an interval of polite social chit-chat the cups and dishes were removed and two more white-robed assistants appeared, carrying between them the type of cheap tin trunk that India used when it decided to travel and had more clobber than could be trusted to a bedding-roll. You could see them by the score on any railway platform all over the country, and they could, in those days, be bought for a few rupees.

A succession of these locked and unlovely objects was carried in and dumped on the white sheeting that covered the floor, and out of them, when the locks had been removed, an Ali-Baba's treasure of jewellery was lifted out and laid on the floor. This was the kind of jewellery that the average globe-trotter never sees, the kind that we had seen in the

Treasure House in Gwalior, incredible stuff: pearls the size of pigeon's eggs, carved emeralds, glittering rubies and enormous, table-cut diamonds. Sapphires, topazes and turquoises and a wonderful example of a fascinating jewel that I had only seen once before, in Peking, where I was told that they are so rare that their number is known, and that most of those had been in the Russian Crown Jewels: Alexandrites.

This was the first occasion on which I suddenly realized that great riches must be a terrible bore. Because I would have given almost anything to possess one of the magical works of the jeweller's craft that were being unwrapped and laid out one at a time on the cheap chudder-cloth in front of Barbara, yet she couldn't have cared less about them. She sat there on the floor, saying occasionally in a languid voice, 'That's pretty. I'll have that. And that one too. And that . . .' Just pointing a finger at the things that caught her fancy, knowing that she could, if she felt like it, buy the lot twenty times over. She couldn't have been less excited about them if they'd been two-cent trinkets in one of those souvenir shops in a seaside arcade, and I thought, 'You poor dear! What a bore life must be when there isn't anything you want that you can't have, and don't have to save up for.' Yes, I'd have changed places with her. Of course I would! But only long enough to buy that pearl and diamond and emerald flower-bracelet. She simply did not get a kick out of *anything*. And how could she?

Well, she did out of one thing. Sandy had made great friends with one of the nobles of Hyderabad, and since any friend of Sandy's was a friend of ours, Mother and I were soon privileged to become friends of his too. No one could possibly have done anything else, because he was one of the most attractive men I have ever met. He was an old man when I first met him, but when he was young he must have been devastating, and it can have surprised no one when the youthful daughter of the then Resident fell madly in love with him – and he with her. But though Christians are accepted by Muslims as 'Children of the Book', because the Koran acknowledges Christ to be among the prophets and contains the Christmas story, Sala Jung's family, who were too near the throne to get away with a mixed marriage, were horrified and refused their permission, backed by the then Nizam and the mullahs. The girl's father, equally horrified, also put his foot down and sent her back to England by the next available boat. The lovers had managed one last meeting, at which they promised each other that they would never marry anyone else. And they never did. Not so surprisingly from the girl's side of things, for Victorian damsels did a lot of 'going into a decline' because they couldn't have the man they wanted. But amazing for a Muslim royal. I suppose he had the odd concubine when he felt like it. But he kept that promise to the end of his life. And no, it was not Sala Jung whom Barbara fancied. It was one of his possessions.

He lived in a large and rather shabby palace in the city, which one felt he had lost interest in and was allowing to grow old gracefully around him. It was crammed with treasures, all of which could have done with a bit of dusting; huge oil paintings by Victorian artists covered the walls and wonderful Persian carpets covered the marble floors. He liked to give lunch parties on Sundays, and we were lucky enough to be asked to them fairly frequently. We thought it might interest Barbara and her Count to meet the old charmer and attend one of his famous lunches, so we asked him if we could bring her with us on the following weekend. Having told them a good deal about their host, we ought to have warned her that Sala's lunches were, as far as dress went, strictly informal. But we didn't even think of it and were very taken aback when we went to collect her and found her decked out like one of her own Woolworths jewellery counters.

I don't know why it is that too much glitter on anyone but the Queen – and then only on a State occasion! – always looks phoney. But it does. The Countess Reventlow must, that morning, have been worth several millions (billions in today's currency!) 'on the hoof'. It began with the hat, which was pinned to her hair with a couple of diamond hat-pins. Well, OK, but the hat was a small plate of multi-coloured artificial flowers, swathed in black net that had been liberally sprinkled with tiny sequins. The whole thing glittered. Worse, it topped a dress of multi-coloured, patterned crêpe-de-Chine, on which the late Czarina's pearls, a recent acquisition – or so we were told – gorgeous as they were, had somehow become artificial. Her earrings were in the shape of four-leaf clovers, each leaf a huge emerald and the centre a large diamond, and even her shoes glittered because they were made of shiny black patent leather. She was wearing a diamond ring that would have dwarfed Elizabeth Taylor's, as well as several simply gorgeous three-inch-wide 1920s-style diamond bracelets, and, to top all this splendour, in place of a bag she was carrying a platinum box about the size of one of the smaller paperback novels, the edge of which was paved with flat oblong diamonds, and on top of which were her initials in – I think – emeralds. As she walked out into the bright sunlight, the sun suddenly caught her and made her glitter all over as though she had been caught by a powerful spotlight. I think she must have dressed to impress a rich Indian royal. But she certainly made the rest of the party look as drab as sparrows on a wet day. Not a diamond among the lot of us. Or even a sequin!

Sala Jung may have become old and grey, but he had never lost his ability to charm, and in no time at all he had Barbara eating out of his hand. I'd never seen her look so alive and interested, and so charming herself. The lunch party was a great success, for the Count too was a charmer, and I am not surprised that she fell for him. All went well until we moved out to a flagged patio in the middle of the ground floor – the house, like many eastern houses, was built around an open square, and this one, like the majority of its fellows, had flowering creepers and brilliant sprays of bougainvillaea and jasmine growing in tubs in the patio, part of which was generally in sunlight.

Except during the monsoon, or the brief winter rains, coffee was always served in the patio, and Sandy having told Barbara about Sala's collection of daggers, she begged him to let her see them. A display of these daggers was apt to be a normal ending to those Sunday luncheons, because the collection was famous, and I must have seen them many times myself. But I never got tired of seeing them. No one could. They were wonderful. Once again, as in the jewel-merchant's house in the city, servants tottered out into the patio with a selection of cheap tin trunks, and having spread a large sheet over the marble paving stones, took out the daggers one by one, each in its own velvet-covered box. Each in turn was removed from its box and laid on the ground, and everyone 'ooh'd' and 'aah'd', and was allowed to handle the fabulous things.

The names of the previous owners read like a page from history and were even more fascinating than the weapons that centuries ago had been made for them and carried by them. Among them all, one in particular caught Barbara's eye, and she asked if she might handle it. It was a fairly short dagger and its curved hilt was made in the likeness of a parrot's head, the beak carved from a single ruby and the head from an enormous emerald. The eyes were rubies ringed by smaller jewels, either sapphires or diamonds, I don't remember which; maybe two rings, one of both. And a hole had been bored through the parrot's neck from which there hung a tassel of pearls. It was a beautifully made piece of jewellery, and,

I should imagine, a horribly effective weapon, for the steel of the blade, which was inlaid with patterns of gold, was as razor sharp as the day it was made. Sala warned Barbara to be careful she didn't cut herself as she eased it out of its green velvet diamond-studded sheath.

There were dozens of daggers, each one of them worth their weight in pearls or platinum, and each more dazzling than the last. But the one with the parrot-like head and the gleaming tassel of pearls had caught Barbara's fancy, and she kept on coming back to it. I think someone must have told her to be careful of how she admired the possessions of Eastern or Oriental potentates, because you could find yourself presented with the object of your admiration, and though it would be handed to you as a gift you were expected to give the donor something of equal value. She certainly went overboard about that parrot-headed dagger, bestowing only the most cursory of glances on the rest of the collection, and saying, 'Oh, yes, very pretty . . . But not a patch on this lovely thing – why, it might almost be a real bird! I'd give *anything* to own something like this! It's just about the most beautiful thing I've ever seen . . .' and so on and so on. Until our host suddenly took fright. He probably thought the young woman was going to back him into a horrid corner by asking him to sell it to her. Or give it to her! Neither of which he would have thought of doing. He gave a curt order to the servants, who whipped everything away at the speed of light. I should think that dagger was the only artifact that La Comtesse ever wanted that she didn't get.

Mother and I planned to spend the hot weather in Ootacamund, a part of India that I had never seen before. Bets had arranged to go up there to meet her mother-in-law and would be staying at Mrs Pardey's guest-house, and she suggested that Mother and I should do the same. So we had booked rooms for ourselves and arranged to drive there, via Bangalore and Mysore where Mother had old friends from the Delhi days. We should have left while the weather was still cool, but three accidents delayed us. The first was caused by Mother's Siamese cat, Shao-de. The second can also be laid at Shao-de's door, though it was hardly an accident, since Mother had arranged to mate her puss to a neighbour's tom, who was also a well-bred Siamese. With kittens on the way – and all of them 'bespoke' – we had to wait until they arrived and were old enough to travel.

It was during that waiting interval that I went out into the garden late one evening in the dusk to collect Shao-de, whom we did not allow out at night (too many jackals and pi-dogs around). Mother and Sandy had both gone out to some senior dinner party, Kadera was out on the town with Sandy's bearer, and I was more or less on my own in the house. Shao-de obediently gave herself up when called, stalking elegantly out from under a mass of bougainvillaea at the far end of the garden, and I picked her up and was carrying her back in my arms, cradling her like a baby, when a hyena that had probably been stalking her suddenly broke cover and galloped away across the lawn. Shao-de lashed out in a panic, trying to turn over, and one of her claws slashed across my left eye.

Normally, an eye's reaction is so swift that I would have closed it in time. But it was nearly dark, and by the time I got the cat and myself into the house I discovered that I was pouring blood all over the place. Realizing that my eyeball had been neatly slashed, I rang the Residency Surgeon as my best bet. He was out of course. So I rang the people Mother and Sandy were dining with, and they managed to ring the Residency Surgeon (who was not pleased!) and they all turned up, to find me with gore pouring down my face. It looked much worse than it was. The Res. doc. turned pale green at the sight and said it would have to be left until tomorrow morning, since he knew nothing about eye surgery. I would have to go to the hospital to sort out the damage. Fortunately, Mother had a couple of great friends, a doctor and his wife who were natives of Hyderabad. She managed to get them on the phone, but the doctor had two operations on his hands that night, and having told me what to do in the way of bandages, asked me to turn up at the City Hospital as early as I could on the following morning.

The City Hospital was enough to make a modern doctor or hospital nurse swoon with horror. It was a huge barrack-like Victorian structure that strongly suggested the hand of Florence Nightingale – high-ceilinged rooms and plenty of light and air. It was crammed with rows of low iron bedsteads in every room and along all the verandahs, each bed surrounded as with a swarm of flies by what appeared to be every member of the patient's family. For India does not approve of leaving its sick to the mercy of the doctors and nurses, let alone in peace and quiet. A horde of anxious relatives accompanies a sick or dying man, woman or child to the hospital, where they squat beside the bed (veiled, if female, against the glances of strange men) so that they can offer comfort and sympathy and, too frequently, sips and scraps of unsuitable food, and pat the hand or shoulder of the sufferer in a soothing manner. (I notice with interest that the idea of allowing relatives to attend the sick in our children's wards is catching on. India has been doing it for *years*.)

Sandy drove Mother and me to the hospital, where we were met by her old friend Dr Dutt and his begum, Carrie. (This was not her real name, but a nickname given to her long ago by some humorist when they were first married: 'Dutt and Carrie'. It had caught on, and I don't think any of their many British friends could have told you what her real name was.) Carrie had come to hold Mother's hand in case, when the bandaging job she had done under telephone instructions last night was removed, it turned out that I had lost the sight in one eye. However, luck was with me.

Shao-de's claw had slit the white but left the iris untouched, and Dr Dutt did a wonderful job on it. I watched enthralled through a small square, exactly the size of my eye, that had been cut out of the centre of the large sheet of rubber spread over me. My eye had been treated with a local anaesthetic, so that I couldn't feel anything. But I could see, enormously enlarged, what appeared to be a needle the size of a small flagpole stitching up the slit in my eye with a rope capable of holding a battleship. The whole thing took less than a few minutes from start to finish, and when, some days later, I was allowed to take off the dressing, I could see as well as ever. For a year or two I had a small red scar on that eye, which gradually faded to a faint yellow and then vanished. He was one heck of a good eye surgeon was Dr Dutt.

And not only an eye doctor, for some time before the eye incident Mother had begun to suffer from what she was told must be rheumatism. She had told the doctor about this, and he had said cheerfully, 'Oh, I can give you something for that,' and had given her something that I can only describe as being exactly like a single floret off a cauliflower. It was about the size of a thumbnail, and she was told that she must put it into a glass of fresh milk – it *had* to be fresh or it wouldn't work – every evening, and drink it first thing next morning. That was all. The thing fed on fresh milk and would, he warned her, grow. But since all she needed was a single floret, she could keep the latest one and either throw the rest away or give them to friends of hers who suffered from rheumatism. Mother followed his instructions and whatever it was (sounds like *dai* – yoghurt – to me, except the milk never thickened) it worked like a charm. And I have always believed that it was one.

*

Having recovered from the eye scare with no ill-effects, our departure for Bangalore was again delayed, this time because I developed a raging toothache. On being recommended to take myself off to a German dentist, newly arrived in Hyderabad and equipped with all the very latest and most expensive things in the way of dental gadgets and outfittery, I rashly clocked in as a patient, had my jaw X-rayed and was told that the nerve in my back tooth was causing the trouble and must be killed off. Well, I won't go into the subsequent agony; anyone who has had tooth trouble knows what it can be like. I practically had to be strapped down in the chair, and the result was an increase of agony and no relief. Eventually Herr Whatsiz said it wasn't a harassed nerve that was to blame, but an abscess, and the offending molar 'go she must'! And go she did. (I presume from this that German teeth are feminine?) But in the process of yanking out the wretched thing, the Herr Dentist managed to break my jaw, so thoroughly that splinters of bone kept on surfacing and having to be removed for years to come. But at this time the pain was so bad that I couldn't sleep, despite the endless painkillers and sleeping pills.

In the end the poor man himself came round and gave me a strong shot of morphine – which didn't work either, except to make me feel woolly. And just to round everything off we had a sudden dust-storm that blew up without warning, and a huge square bottle of scent, a birthday present from Roger and quite the most expensive and glamorous gift I have ever received, Elizabeth Arden's 'Blue Grass' (it was new then), was swept off my dressing-table by a curtain that suddenly streamed out on the wind. The floors in that house were all of stone or marble, and since that lavish bottle of scent landed on one corner, which snapped off neatly, not so much as a drop could be salvaged. The entire house reeked of 'Blue Grass' for days, and I remember weeping from sheer rage! And in the middle of this Shao-de's kittens arrived: eight of them, no less.

We discovered quite a long time later why that unfortunate dentist had made such a hash of my teeth and my jaw. Apparently he wasn't a dentist at all. He was either a German or a Polish Jew who could see only too clearly what was coming to his people, and knew that he could never escape to another country, *any* other country, with money. A dentist friend had advised him to put all the money he possessed into the most up-to-date equipment possible, which could let him (after studying the subject from the newest books) either set up as a dentist in a foreign country, or sell the equipment, for which there would always be a market. I don't remember the details of his story or how or why this sort of thing could be got out of Germany or Poland. But it explained a lot, and though at the time I have seldom felt more uncharitable towards anyone, when I heard his story I couldn't help hoping that in the end everything would work out for him, and that he would turn out to be one of the lucky ones. Poor fellow; what a jam he must have been in, to start practising before he was ready for it.

By this time, the hot weather was well and truly upon us. The temperature rose steadily, and at sundown each day the *bheesti** would splash water from his bulging *mussack* – the sheepskin that is filled at the well, and carried round the garden – no longer confining his attention to flower-beds and flower-pots, but plodding upstairs and, starting at the top, spraying water on the stone flagstones of the roof and the verandahs. As the cold water hit them, you could hear it hiss. Only when all that had been done (and it dried far too quickly) would he water the gravel paths, the lawns and the flower-beds, and the fresh, pungent scent of water on parched ground is one that no ex-member of the Raj will ever forget.

Mother and I would not normally have dreamed of setting out to drive several hundred miles on unmade roads across some of the barrenest stretches of the Deccan to the Nilgiri Hills and Ootacamund, at the height of the hot weather. But what with one thing and another, our departure had been so delayed that we decided to do the first leg of the journey by train to a small station, little more than a wayside stop, a night's journey from Hyderabad. From there Kadera and the luggage would stay on the train as far as Bangalore, while Mother and I and the cats would finish the journey by car (a Baby Austin known as 'the Beetle'). We had booked a two-berth sleeper for ourselves and the cats on the night train, and Sandy and about a dozen friends gave us a beautiful send-off, complete with goodbye garlands and gifts of fruit and *halwa* from the Hyderabadi contingent.

I don't think we slept much, because Shao-de and her kittens took a poor view of railway travel. And an even poorer one of having to use a scratch-box in a rattling, shaking, noisy carriage. They all took refuge

* Water-carrier.

236

under the lower berth, and refused to come out, so we left them to it. And when we surfaced in the early dawn they were all back in their travelling basket, looking very dusty, but otherwise O K. I can't remember the name of the station we disembarked at, though one would have expected it to be engraved on my memory in letters of blood. We arrived at it in the cool of the morning, a good half hour before sun-up, and discovered that it was indeed no more than a wayside halt. No sign of a village. In fact no sign of life beyond a station-master and a couple of rickety stalls in the shade of a neem tree, one of only three or four trees in an otherwise treeless landscape. The stallholder's stock consisted of a few packets of country-made cigarettes and matches, *paan* and some fly-blown *halwa*, and a selection of bottles containing highly coloured and certainly lukewarm soft drinks, some of them fizzy, and all guaranteed to inflict a severe attack of Delhi-belly on any unwary paleface unwise enough to sample them.

Quite a lot of passengers alighted from the train, but only, it appeared, for sanitary purposes or to stretch their legs, and Mother and I were the only ones not to scramble back again when the train moved on. Its guard and the station-master and his minions had helped offload the Beetle, and while this was being done Kadera produced *chuppattis*, hard-boiled eggs and mugs of hot coffee for us – apparently out of thin air – as was the custom in the old days. I never knew how Indian bearers managed to come up with these commodities at the drop of a hat, however unpromising the situation. But rain or shine, desert or jungle, they never failed one. Money could not buy such service, and we shall never see their like again.

The train, after uttering a few tentative hoots, got up steam and trundled off again, taking Kadera and our heavy luggage with it, while Mother and I, having reimbursed the station-master and his assistants for their help, checked that the cats were all present and correct, the hand luggage safely installed and the car's petrol, oil and water topped up, climbed in ourselves and were off into the great unknown. And a great unknown it turned out to be. I don't think I have ever come across such a treeless and desolate wasteland before, unless it was in the desert country of what in my day was called Arabia, and I hadn't been there yet! It reminded me of a particularly dreary bit of country that we had once driven through going to or coming from a shooting camp in the then empty country beyond New Delhi, and I remember Tacklow observing meditatively in Kaye-language: 'A dezolaze country, entirely inhabizez by goze.' This too was a 'dezolaze' country, and so far, there didn't seem to be so much as a single goat in sight.

Chapter 24

~୪Ἀ৪Ἀ~

The morning was still reasonably cool, and since the unmade road, though deep in dust, was comparatively free from faults and potholes, Mother thought that at this rate we would make better time than we expected. Especially as we seemed to have it to ourselves. Nothing moved on it for miles except the occasional dust devil. This might have been a good thing if the Beetle hadn't come to a grinding halt, bang in the middle of the road and after we had driven three or four miles at most. What's more, she would not budge.

We could not even persuade her to let us push her into the side of the road. Mother had taken a few lessons on car engines and she had become quite a good mechanic. But this was something she didn't understand at all, and she finally gave up tinkering with the engine and joined me under a solitary tree – the only one for miles as far as I could see – providentially growing near the edge of the road not far from where the car had stopped.

The morning was growing steadily hotter as the sun climbed slowly up a cloudless sky and when, after about twenty minutes, there was still no sign of traffic on the long, dusty ribbon of road that ran straight towards the horizon, and the land had begun to shimmer and dance in the heat, Mother announced that there was nothing for it but to walk back to the station, reasoning that the train would not have stopped unless there was a fair-sized village somewhere within range. And where there was a village there was always a bazaar, and every bazaar, however humble, boasted a shop that repaired bicycles and the occasional lorry, patched up burst tyres and employed a mechanic who knew enough about car engines to tell her what had gone wrong with hers. Better still, there was a telephone in the station-master's office, and she could ring up the garage in Hyderabad, where she and her car were known, and ask for advice.

I was not in favour of her setting off to walk several miles in that blazing heat, and we wasted some considerable time in wrangling about which of us should go and which should stay with the cats. But in the event neither of us had to walk, for Providence suddenly presented us with a *tonga*. The dust lay so thick on the road that we hadn't heard it approach, and the belt of dancing heat-haze – and the long dips in the road that it had helped to disguise – had hidden it from us until almost the last minute. Also, wonder of wonders, there were only three passengers in it instead of the normal round dozen (Bets and I once counted seventeen passengers in a single *tonga*). I believe the law lays down that the maximum load must not exceed four passengers in addition to the driver. But India has never paid the slightest attention to this type of law, which it regards as petty interference with the Liberty of the Individual. And although the RSPCA does its best on behalf of the unfortunate ponies that pull such vehicles, they fight a losing battle.

Finding its way impeded by a stationary car in the middle of the road, the *tonga* pulled up and Mother ran out, and having explained our predicament, begged the driver to take her to the station if his other passengers had no objection. They had none, and welcomed her aboard with enthusiasm, hospitably vacating the front seat next to the driver so that Mother need not be too squashed up among the passengers and their bulky luggage: '*Baitho, Mem-sahib, baitho! – bahut jugga hai.*'* Once aboard, the driver edged the *tonga* cautiously around the car and, as he flicked the pony with his whip and it broke into a smart trot, Mother leant out over the wheel and yelled, 'I've no idea when I'll be back – could be hours!' And on that somewhat pessimistic note the rescue party vanished into a cloud of dust, leaving me 'alone and palely loitering' in the middle of nowhere.

Looking back on that morning, I find it typical of the India-That-Was that it never crossed my mind, or Mother's either, that I could possibly come to any harm by being left stranded unarmed (and why would I need arms in friendly, kindly India?), alone except for the Siamese cats, in a totally strange part of the map. Not that my situation could occur nowadays, for a flood-tide of new villages and towns has already invaded those once 'Empty Quarters', and almost every road has become a river of traffic. Buses, lorries, cars, motor-bikes and bicycles by the million fighting it out with bullock-carts, *tongas* and such horse-drawn vehicles as remain.

* 'Sit, Mem-sahib, sit. There is plenty of room.'

Over seventy years before the day on which Mother had thankfully grabbed a lift off a passing *tonga* and left me in the wilderness, Edward Lear had been invited by the then Viceroy, Lord Northbrook, to visit India as his guest for a year, in return for 'one or two of his Indian landscapes'. Lear accepted and spent over a year there, living mostly in Dâk bungalows. Lear wrote that he regarded it as a 'semi-miracle' that 'even in such a remote locality – a sort of nowhere on the borders of India and Tibet' – they had not only been well fed and comfortable, but had never felt in any danger of being molested; though there 'was not a bolt on the doors'.

There weren't any in my day either. I wonder if there are now? Or if there are still any Dâk bungalows in existence? What *would* we have done without them?

As the shadows shrank and the heat increased, the interior of the little car, which had been standing in the blazing sun for well over an hour, began to get too hot for Shao-de, who put her head out of the near-side window and told me so in no uncertain terms. Well, there was nothing I could do except remove her basket from the back seat of the car and plonk it down in the shadiest spot I could find among the roots of the tree. Which I did. But unfortunately Shao-de thought nothing of the Great Outdoors. To her it was hostile territory, and she growled her disapproval; snatching up the nearest kitten by the scruff of its neck, she carried it back to the car and returned for another.

The next ten or fifteen minutes was occupied by a bad-tempered contest between Shao-de and myself, I returning the kittens to their basket and Shao-de snatching them away and putting them back in the car as fast as I replaced them. Shao-de won easily because she was prepared to keep it up indefinitely and I was not. Also she suddenly switched tactics, and started leaving the kittens under instead of in the Beetle, where the car itself provided a dense patch of shade, in addition to the ghost of a draught. I found this so sensible that I pushed the cat-basket under the Beetle and left her to collect the entire gang in it.

I had a lot of trouble with that cat. She was tediously coy about being watched while engaged in dealing with a call of nature, but there came a time when this would not be denied, and deserting her offspring she made for the shelter of the tree, which provided the only protection from aerial attack by a hungry kite or eagle, of whom there were always a few around.

Having taken an age to select a suitable spot, she scratched a hasty hole for herself above it. At which point she suddenly lowered her tail and, flattening her ears, began to growl in a menacing manner. It seemed she had spotted a couple of stray goats, and she wasn't going to get down to the job in hand with them watching!

She really was a maddening creature, and after about twenty minutes of this Victorian prudery I could gladly have slapped her. If it wasn't a goat it was a jackal or a crow, and once it was a solitary chinkara. But in the end nature proved too strong for her and she finally got the whole business over and returned to her kittens. About a couple of hours after that, though it felt like a hundred, Mother and the *tonga* returned, minus its original passengers, who had been dropped off at their destination, and accompanied instead by a rescue party consisting of a lorry and a number of interested helpers armed with ropes and planks and various DIY bits and pieces, headed by a little man wearing nothing but a loincloth – and how I envied him! – who Mother said was a mechanic whom she had 'found in the village'.

She seemed to be on excellent terms with the entire rescue party, and after the 'mechanic' had tried the gears and peered under the bonnet and conferred with Mother, she fished the cat-basket out from under the car (Shao-de growling and spitting the while) and asked the *tonga-wallah* to take it and me back to the station waiting-room, plus cats, picnic basket and as many pieces of luggage as we could cram into his *tonga*, in order to lighten the load on the car, which was being brought back to the village for the mechanic to have a good look at it. Mother meant to stay with the car and do any steering that might be necessary, but in the end, since the car refused to respond to anything, the rescue party managed to drag it up on to the lorry and get it back to the mechanic's shop in the bazaar.

'He says he thinks he might be able to do something about it,' said Mother, who from long experience (she had been one of the first women in India to drive a car) had developed a strong belief in the powers of India's wayside mechanics. She told me that she had telephoned her garage in Hyderabad, and the head mechanic had rung back to say that he was sure that it could only be the failure of a part known as a crown-wheel pinion. Since the car would not move without a replacement, they offered to put one on the night train, which stopped at our station at first light on the following morning – provided, of course, that there was someone available to do the job of fitting it in.

Right: Mike (*centre*) at his house, Packington; I'm on his left. I can't remember who the man on his right was – the owner of the dogs, I presume. I can't believe they were Mike's, not with those wolves around!

Above: Tommy Richardson, a hero of my childhood, with his plane which he kept at a flying club on the outskirts of London. He took me up in it to see the sunset clouds at 'close range' – a let-down. They were just mist! Tommy, like so many of the Few, died for his country in the war years. As did Mike.

Left: Margaret Tempest, the illustrator of the *Grey Rabbit* books, of her own *Pinky Mouse* books and my own *Potter Pinner* book. A dear friend.

Above: The Andamans. 'Fudge' – Rosemary Cosgrave, one of my best friends. She is sitting on the rocks in Forster Bay.

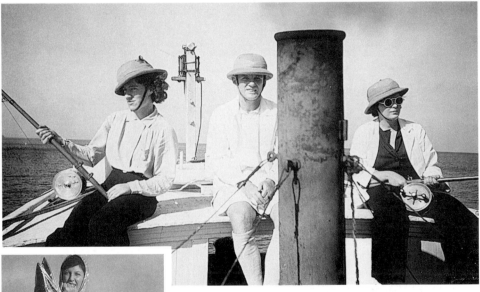

Above: Fishing from the Government House launch *Jarrawa.* Fudge, Denis, who was the head of the police in the islands, and me. I can't recall Denis's surname, but I do know that when the Second World War broke out and the Japanese occupied the islands he volunteered to be parachuted back into the jungle near Port Blair and collect information, armed with only a small radio. He should have had a VC for that.

Left: Me with my largest catch, a barracuda. (There were a lot of much larger things on offer.)

Above: Bill and Joy coming out of the cathedral in Delhi under an arch of swords.

Right: Myself in Calcutta.

Above: Mother and 'Bingle' Ingle in Ootycamund. I used to sing duets with Bingle in amateur shows, cabarets and such!

Right: I am now blonde as a result of a visit to Jess in Cawnpore.

Right: Jess and the hydrangeas from Government House at Naini Tal. Photographed, enlarged and hand-tinted by me. Pity you can't see it in colour!

Above: Bets's baby Richard was born in Srinagar. Here he is with Kadera.

Right: Mother by Hal Bevan Petman. Hal's portraits were usually in pastel, but this was in oils and is a lovely piece of work as well as an excellent likeness.

Left: My pink and silver bedroom in Khorramshah, showing the awful matting dado that covered the lower part of every wall in the house in order to hide the salt stains that leaked up from the ground.

Right: Calcutta. One of the six 'Cocktail Girls' that I painted for a fête in aid of raising funds for buying more Spitfires. I think this one was 'Angel's Kiss'; they fetched high prices when they were put up for auction.

Above: Delhi. Three WVS girls in an army prefab with a mural painted by me. The girl in the centre is Lorraine Graddiger, head of the WVS in Dera Dun and district. I am the one on her left. I can't remember who the other person was.

Above: A palace banquet at Karpurthla given by the Maharajah of Karpurthla. Mother is in the centre of the table, on the right of the Maharajah, who has a white carnation in his buttonhole.

Left: Sir Peter Clutterbuck, Director of Forests, sitting cross-legged on his own drive. Behind him, I am in the shadow, Cuckoo Wall, Lady Clutter and our friend Sandy.

Below: Bets in uniform. She joined the St John's Ambulance.

Above: Sheila Gascoigne and myself in our WVS outfits. Cheap and utilitarian, but hardly becoming!

Left: Gordon Watt of Queen Victoria's Own Corps of Guides.

Myself photographed by a friend, Sydney Ralli. We took photographs of each other in Bets's flat in Calcutta and this one was reproduced in a local weekly. It was that hat I think! She and I had a lot of fun taking Cecil Beaton style photographs in the flat. I had bought the silver fox with some of the money I got for the first book I ever wrote, *Six Bars at Seven*. It was Sydney's idea to turn the tail into a hat. The rest made a large floppy muff.

Goff Hamilton of the Queen Victoria's Own Corps of Guides. When on active service, British officers of the Frontier Force Regiments habitually wore the same headgear as their men in order to prevent becoming the favoured targets for enemy snipers.

Mother had said confidently that there was. And how right she was. She herself had never even *heard* of such a thing as a crown-wheel pinion, but as soon as she mentioned it to the mechanic he had said cheerfully that he'd got one of those! He had apparently acquired it from a car that had been in a collision with a lorry some years ago and had been so badly damaged that the wreckage had been abandoned as worthless.

It had proved anything but worthless to him, for he had towed it back to the village and learned a lot about engines by studying the wreck of that one. Its crown-wheel pinion had been practically undamaged, and he had wrapped it in an oiled cloth to preserve it from rust, and added it to a magpie hoard of bits-and-pieces that he thought might 'come in useful' some day. This one's day, he was convinced, had arrived, and he assured Mother that with a bit of tinkering he could make it fit.

Mother, after a good look at this unfamiliar bit of machinery for which her garage quoted a hefty figure from their spare-part catalogue, was not so sure. But feeling that she could always do with a spare, she told him to go ahead and try, and returned to the station waiting-room where the cats and I were sitting among our collective gubbins and trying to come to terms with the fact that we would have to spend the rest of the day and all the night here. At least I was. Shao-de was merely 'lounging round and sufferin''. And making a lot of noise about it too. She didn't approve of any of this, and I couldn't blame her, for though the temperature of the little waiting-room, with its windows closed and shuttered to keep in some of the cool air of the past night, was a degree or two below the grilling, blazing heat of the platform outside, once you got used to its illusion of shadowy coolness, you realized that it must be registering *well* over a hundred degrees, though it was not yet midday. Only six hours since we had set out in the cool, yellow dawn of our fatal drive. And now we were stuck here until another dawn! That good Samaritan, the station-master, donated a bucket of lukewarm water with the suggestion that it would cool down the room if we splashed a cupful or two on the stone-tiled floor. And it did, though only temporarily, since it dried in seconds.

To Shao-de it was a life-saver. She spread herself out on the damp stone, paws outstretched and looking exactly like a doll-sized tigerskin, and not only abandoned her kittens, but refused to let any of them near her. I took off the domed top of their travel basket to give them more air, and they crawled out of it and tried to converge on their mother for a drink. But whenever one of them touched her she got up and moved away; and in the end they gave up, and copied her by spreading themselves out as flat as they could, so that the floor appeared to be covered with little white tigerskins. 'If it gets any hotter than this,' said Mother, 'we shall lose the lot of them, and Shao-de as well – Oh dear!' 'And me too,' I said. I had removed my dress and was wearing nothing but pants and a bra so that I could dip the dress into the water bucket (which was getting dangerously low) and use it as a sponge to damp myself all over, which was heaven for about ten seconds. After that I was dry again, and hotter than ever.

We were wondering how on earth we were going to last out until the sun went down, when we heard a car drive into the station yard, and heard someone calling out: 'Mem-sahib! Mem-sahib!'

Mother shot out of the door, while I hastily put my dress on again. She was back after only about five minutes, breathless with excitement: 'Now listen,' she said, 'that's my car out there. He drove it here from the bazaar' (roughly a quarter of a mile) 'and he says he's sure it won't let me down. Now do we take a chance on his second-hand gadget not breaking down, and start off at once? Or would it be safer to wait until the other one gets here on the train tomorrow morning? I'm not going to cancel it because I don't know how long his one will hold out, and we may need a spare. But the station-master says he could always forward it on to Bangalore. What do you think?'

'Chance it and leave at once!' I said, reaching for the nearest piece of luggage. And we did. With the help of that wondrous mechanic, the station-master and assistant, and the *tonga-wallah* who was still around 'just in case', we got everything back into the car, the cats going in last. And having distributed largesse and shaken hands all round, we put up a short prayer and set off again in the blinding heat down the same shadeless, dusty stretch of road that we had driven along so gaily in the cool of the early morning.

Bad as the midday heat was, it was preferable to being shut up in that oven of a waiting-room, for the very fact that we were moving created a suggestion of a draught, and before we started we had rigged up a sort of tent around the cats, constructed out of towels that we kept damp, in the manner of kus-kus-tatties, so that the air blowing through it lowered the temperature quite considerably. So much so that Shao-de, who had refused to stay in the basket with her kittens and spread herself out along

244

the back seat, changed her mind and actually got back among them for long enough to allow them to take a reasonable drink off her. I had to wet our improvised kus-kus-tatties at shorter and shorter intervals, because they dried with the speed of lightning in that searing heat, and our water supply began to run out.

I can't remember passing any other traffic – motor-, bullock- or horse-drawn. Or any pedestrians either. But I suppose we must have done – unless the local population had enough sense to restrict its movements to the early morning and sundown – for I know that we drove through the occasional village where we replenished our water bottles and attracted the usual number of small children – the young of whatever race seem to be impervious to extremes of heat or cold. None of them had ever seen a Siamese cat before and they were enthralled by Shao-de and her kittens, asking in tones of awe, '*Yea kis kism ka janwa hai?*' – 'What kind of animal is that?'

It was a very long day, one of the longest I have ever spent. And every time we stopped we were scared to death that the car would not start again. But Providence and the genius of that mechanic never let us down and, though Mother eventually collected the parcel containing a brand new crown-wheel pinion, she never had to use it.

Chapter 25

꙳ⵣⵡⵣ꙳

As the road took us further south the traffic on it increased and there were more trees, mostly broomstick palms and not many of those. I took over the driving to let Mother get a bit of rest, and was relieved when she fell asleep for several hours. By the time she woke up the shadows had begun to lengthen and the heat had changed from intolerable to bearable. She consulted our road maps again and announced that we were never going to make it to Bangalore that day and must start looking out for a Dâk bungalow where we could spend the night.

This turned out to be easier said than done. We were so used to driving across and around the fertile and well-populated Punjab, where there always seemed to be a Dâk bungalow when needed, that we hadn't realized that in this barren patch of wilderness such things as Dâk bungalows might be few and far between. But so it was. We asked hopefully whenever we came to a village, and the answer was always that there was sure to be one at this or that small town – '*lakin bhoat dur hai*' – 'but that is very far'. Which was not much help. 'Oh, well, we must press on,' said Mother. And we did. Until with the swiftness that one never quite gets used to in the East, the vast rose-red globe that had been tormenting us all day, its size now enormously increased by the dust in the air, stood for a moment on the horizon line before sinking below it in a matter of minutes. And suddenly it was dark and the sky was full of stars. And once again we were stranded in the middle of nowhere with the prospect of spending the night in a small car and in the company of nine cats.

We had stopped to watch the sun go down, which in the plains is a sight that I never grew tired of, and we waited to see the sky put on its usual dazzling 'pantomime-transformation' scene. All that lavish gold and red and green, like some immense fire-opal. And when the curtain came down and the show was over Mother reluctantly switched on the headlights, and instantly everything beyond their range was black, and she started up the engine again and drove off hopefully in search of a Dâk bungalow.

Apparently there wasn't one in this particular strip of wilderness that included the borderlands of the Nizam's dominions and Madras, which was part of British India. I can't remember after all this time which one we were in now, but I do remember how hot the darkness was now that we had got used to it. I had been expecting the night air to be much cooler than the day, but it wasn't, not all that cooler anyway. It was as if the earth had been inhaling the oven-heat of the sun all day and was now exhaling it into the darkness. We had still found no Dâk bungalow, or any sign of human habitation, when around eight o'clock that night we saw lights ahead. Too bright to be made by anything but electricity, and too small a patch to be a village. Nearing it we realized with rapture that it was actually a modern petrol station in the wilderness, complete with pumps and a small brightly illuminated office and forecourt.

Better still, as we drew up in front of it, there was a large, family-sized car standing in the forecourt, its very British-looking owner, who had obviously been paying his bill in the office, just about to leave. Mother stuck her head out and hailed him, and he came over to us looking more than slightly surprised at finding a couple of dusty, crumpled and exhausted Englishwomen in such a place at this hour of night. Mother asked if he could direct us to the nearest Dâk bungalow, and when he said there wasn't one nearer than fifty miles, she said: 'Oh, *no* –!' in such a tone of despair that he asked her what on earth we were doing there, and on hearing a potted version of our saga, said we had better come back with him to his house for the night. It turned out that he knew Sandy, and was the local District Commissioner, or something of the sort, and he took Mother in his car and left me to follow in the Beetle. This was easy enough, for he left a trail of dust that could probably be seen for miles in daylight, and looked like the Biblical 'pillar of fire' in my headlights.

The house had probably been built in the early years of the previous century by some affluent member of the East India Company. It stood in an acre or two of what appeared to be totally barren and very stony ground, and depended on oil lamps for illumination, as we had done throughout Tonk State. The brilliant show of electricity that had impressed us at the petrol station did not extend to the house.

Our rescuer's wife had only been waiting for the return of her husband to sit down to supper, and though plainly taken aback by the arrival of unexpected house-guests, she rose nobly to the occasion and insisted on us sharing their meal while a room was prepared for us by the servants. This, she explained with many apologies, would have to be on a covered section of the roof, because there were no other rooms available at present. Mother assured her that we were not fussy, for we had been facing the prospect of spending the night in or under the car, and a *barra-durri* on a rooftop would be luxury.

We had left the car under the porch, and since Shao-de and her kittens made no sound, we left them alone until we had finished a light supper – all we needed was sleep, not food! – and when the bearer came down to announce that was all was '*te ah*', or Indian 'ready', we collected what little we would need for the night, and while Shao-de, who had abandoned the basket and been lying along the top of one of the suitcases, refused to move and was carried up by Mother, I followed with the kittens. It was only after climbing the first set of stairs and finding that the second set, which were much narrower and led up to the roof in a tight curve, were a bit difficult to negotiate with a large oval basket in my arms, that I put down the basket and decided to carry the kittens up two at a time in my hands. And picking up the first one I got a nasty shock. The tiny creature was dead.

Its minute and almost weightless body lay across my palm exactly as Shao-de had done on the stone floor of that railway waiting-room, like a miniature tigerskin rug, limp, boneless and completely devoid of any sign of life. I picked up another, and that one too hung like a tiny scrap of lifeless fur from my hand. There was no reaction from any of them, and I can still remember the feel of those limp and apparently boneless scraps of fur as I carried them up and laid them out in a row on the flat stone roof. 'I'm afraid they're all dead,' I told Mother. '*All* of them?' she asked wretchedly. 'I'm afraid so.' 'Oh well,' said Mother, 'it can't be helped. We did our best . . .' She lifted one of the limp little scraps of fur and stroked it with one finger before replacing it, and said that she could only be thankful that she hadn't lost Shao-de as well, as she couldn't have borne that.

A pair of *nawar* beds, both fitted with mosquito nets, had been brought up and put in a section of the roof between two massive chimney-stacks joined by a brick wall and roofed, in order to make an open-sided *barra-durri* from which the original owner and his family and friends could sit and watch the sun go down, or eat their supper by moonlight. We had also been provided with a properly fitted out Victorian washstand, complete with china soap dish, basin and all the doings including jugs and cans of water. A bathroom had been put at our disposal on the floor below, and we had been given kerosene lamps and matches, and since Mother and I never travelled without a torch apiece, we couldn't have been better provided for. When Shao-de, ignoring that sad little row of white fur rugs and the plates of cat food, milk and water that had been provided for her, wriggled under the mosquito net and ensconced herself at the foot of Mother's bed, I returned her babies to their basket, and pushed it under the washstand.

There was a rolled up *chik* spanning the front of the *barra-durri*, probably for a curtain that could be let down when holding *purdah* parties, and Mother and I rinsed out our sweat-soaked clothes and pinned them to it, knowing they would dry within minutes. Having done that, we said our prayers (we had much to be thankful for!), fell into our beds and were asleep in seconds. It had been a long, long day, and I hoped that we wouldn't oversleep too badly.

We needn't have worried. It can't have been more than two or three hours later that we were woken up by a crash of thunder, and almost on its heels a blinding flash of lightning, and then all Niagara Falls seemed to descend on our rooftop. Mother and I were out of bed and paddling in a lake within seconds. I heard her screaming something through the uproar, and was only able to translate it because the same thought had occurred to me: the *chik*. Together we groped for the rope catches that held it, and with the aid of our torches freed it and felt it unroll and fall with a *wump* into the two or three inches of water with which the roof was awash.

If it had been just an ordinary split-cane *chik* it would have given us little protection, but as luck would have it, it was a lined one, and the stout cotton cloth with which it was lined was thick enough to keep the lashing rain from soaking our beds and most of our belongings. We were also fortunate in that the wind was blowing away from the enclosure, for had it been blowing in the opposite direction nothing could have saved us from being drenched. As it was, though our hair and our nightgowns were soaked in the minute or two it took to release the *chik*, our beds escaped a wetting by inches and we pushed them back into the enclosure as far as they would go. Having removed our nightgowns and wrung them out, we scrubbed ourselves dry with face-towels and crawled back into bed, starkers.

Fortunately, it was one of those freak storms that blow up without warning out of nowhere, and only last for a very short time. Our hosts, a storey below, slept through it all, and the coolness that it left in its wake was so pleasant that Mother and I fell asleep again almost at once. We woke to another day of heat and blazing sunlight, and the incredible sight of eight small white balls of fur racing around on the roof!

I couldn't believe my eyes for a moment or two, because only last night I would have sworn they were all as dead as that proverbial mutton. Not a heartbeat or a twitch or the faintest sign of life. I should have remembered that cats have nine lives. This lot had obviously only shed one of them, and still had eight in their paws. It was a most cheering sight.

But though we were plus eight kittens we were minus the various items of clothing that we had washed and pinned on to the rolled-up *chik*. The gale that had propelled that brief and furious storm across the country had torn them away and scattered them all over the landscape, and though we retrieved the larger items, such as my cotton frock and Mother's dress and petticoat, which could be seen from a long way off, stranded among the thorny twigs of the occasional kikar tree, the smaller items, bust-bodices and panties, probably ended up in the next county and were seen no more.

The storm that had cooled the air had also laid the dust for miles around, so the rest of the journey made up for the previous day's purgatory as the land became higher, wetter and greener, until in the end the road became a tunnel of shade through avenues of jacaranda and flame trees.

Bangalore was looking its best and living up to its reputation as one of the most delightful stations in the Deccan, and we were both sorry to leave it, after a short visit during which Mother painted several pictures. Before we left she unloaded the majority of the kittens on to their bespoke owners. The remainder were promised to people already in 'Ooty',* the favourite hill-station of South India, where we too were bound by way of Mysore where we were to stay with a great friend of Mother's, a Muslim lady whose husband held an important post in the Government of the princely state of Mysore.

We stayed with the Begum and her husband for a few days and were shown all the sights of Mysore and given a tremendous party by our kind

* Ootacamund.

hosts, at which Mother mentioned to a group of the guests that we would be driving to Ootacamund in a day or two. Being asked if she was familiar with that road, she admitted that she knew nothing about it, but that it couldn't be worse than the one to Bangalore! 'Oh, couldn't it!' retorted one of the guests, and all of them laughed. Which made Mother inquire apprehensively what was so funny about that? Well, practically everything, they said . . .

For one thing, the road would take us straight across the Mysore Ditch, a wide strip of virgin jungle which was more or less a nature reserve, since on it only the ruler of Mysore (or by his permission any friend or special guest) was allowed to shoot. 'And you've chosen a bad day to drive through it,' they told her, because a friend of the Maharajah's had been given permission to shoot a tiger there on the very next day, which meant that what with beaters and the noise of rifle-fire and general kerfuffle, the tiger population, together with the rest of the animals and birds who resided in the 'Ditch', would be thoroughly stirred up and on the move. In fact we were likely to see a good deal more livestock than usual. However, it was not the tigers that were a problem, but the elephants. But we wouldn't have to worry about them until we came to the first black milestone.

'*Black milestone?*' echoed Mother hollowly. 'Why black milestones?'

'Oh, didn't they tell you about them?' replied a chorus of guests. 'That means you are in elephant country.'

'But why *black*?' quavered Mother.

That, she was told, was because the wild elephants in the Ditch, having taken a dislike to the white ones, had uprooted them as fast as they were set up; until in the end the exasperated PWD had decided to try black ones lettered with white, which worked a treat. 'As soon as you see a black milestone, you'll know you're in elephant territory. So watch out!' warned one of our fellow guests gleefully.

'But *why*? What for?' asked Mother.

'For elephants, of course,' they told her. 'If you see any on the road, stop at once. And if they start walking towards you, get out of the car and hide – there are a lot of culverts on that strip, and with luck there'll be one you can get into.'

'Oh, *nuts!*' said Mother, suddenly deciding that they were pulling her leg. 'I'm not going to let you scare me. Why would an elephant want to attack me?'

'Well,' said these Job's comforters, 'only to mention a recent case, there was a chap – he's a dentist in Ooty – who stopped when he saw a single wild tusker standing by the side of the road browsing on a tree that overhung it. He waited a bit, but he was in a hurry, and there was plenty of room behind the elephant for his car to pass. Besides, the creature was not even looking his way and was being so leisurely about nibbling leaves, that the dentist got the impression that it was going to be a long time before it moved off. So he decided to take a chance. He released the brake and drove forward as cautiously as he could, and when he was near enough (the tusker still not having paid any attention to him) he put his foot on the accelerator and whipped past at a high speed. But that solid-looking, leisurely lump had also got into top gear. It too could move like a streak of light, and as the car shot past it put out its trunk, and in the chap's own words, "ripped off the roof of my car as neatly as if it were picking a lily-pad".' The victim had streaked away, lidless, and hadn't paused to draw breath until he was well out of range of the last black milestone.

The guests had endless stories of encounters with elephants in the Ditch, but I shall only tell one more, because I think it's funny, though it can't have been in the least funny for its victims. A party of holiday-makers, *en route* for a cool summer break in Ooty, saw a group of elephants on the road ahead of them, and obeying the rules, stopped at once. Only when the creatures began to move towards them did they hastily abandon their car and take refuge in a convenient culvert, from where they watched the group move slowly up the road until it reached the car. Apparently this particular herd had never seen a car at close quarters before, for they surrounded it, touching it cautiously with the tips of their trunks, removing various objects from inside it and, finding these not edible, tossing them aside.

All might have gone well if one of them had not touched something that was exceedingly hot and caused it to retreat sharply with a squeal of alarm. The entire party backed off for a moment, eyeing this strange thing that had just bitten one of them. They might at that point have decided that discretion was the better part of valour, but for the curiosity of one of the female elephants who chose that moment to stretch out her trunk and touch the horn.

Horns in those days were intended to be good and loud, and this one gave an excellent account of itself. It was too much for the elephants. This strange thing could not only bite if one touched it, it could also yell defiance. Accepting the challenge they charged as one, and tore it to bits. Kicking and squealing, they got angrier and angrier when they got the bonnet off and burned themselves savagely on the over-heated engine.

Fortunately, they had forgotten the humans who had scuttled out of it and were crouched in hiding watching, horrified, the destruction of their car, not daring to creep out until some time after the herd had abandoned their battered enemy and moved off into the jungle. The trembling refugees were picked up by a bus not long afterwards, and taken on to the next outpost of civilization.

Mother continued to believe that these stories, together with the black milestones, were an elaborate leg-pull, a belief strengthened by the fact that on checking up, she discovered that there was always a good deal of traffic on that road, including buses that ran at intervals of an hour and served both the forest and Dâk bungalows as well as the occasional small village. So that when we started out on the last leg of our journey to Ooty we were both in the best of spirits.

For a long way our road ran through typically South Indian scenery, and it was almost mid-morning by the time we left the lush greenery and flat cultivated fields of village India and began to twist and turn up the low slopes that would eventually take us to the cool blue heights of the Nilgiri Hills.

We were driving up a short steep slope towards the crest of a low ridge when I became aware of movement higher up on the slope and immediately ahead of us. I was trying to make out what it was when Mother, looking to her right, gave a gasp of horror and said: 'There's a black milestone!' in almost the same moment that I said: 'There's a tiger!' Mother, still staring to her right, not only did not hear what I said, but had begun to slow down as we came out on a straight stretch of road on which, directly in front of us, a tiger was crossing.

I have yet to see a live one in any zoo that looked as magnificent as this one. It not only looked enormous, but its colouring was brilliant – bright golden red, chalk white and ebony black. It strolled across the road, not making the least effort to hurry, and merely turned its head and gave us a cold stare, as though to say: 'Gatecrashers, I presume!' before walking haughtily and unhurriedly into the jungle.

I have never felt so small. Or so scared. That creature looked quite large enough to turn our tiny Baby Austin over with one swipe of its paw; and as Mother slowed, I began frantically winding up the windows on my side and imploring her to 'hurry, *hurry*!' The tiger (who had made no attempt to hurry) averted its gaze and removed itself into the scrub. But I was afraid that it might change its mind and come back and attack us, and continued to urge Mother to step on it and to wind up her window. Mother obediently stepped on the accelerator and asked me what was I getting into such a panic for? One black milestone didn't necessarily mean there were elephants nearby. 'Not elephants,' I said. 'That tiger.' 'What tiger?' said Mother.

Believe it or not, she hadn't even *seen* the tiger! It had crossed the road right in front of us, so close that we could have almost reached out and touched it, but she had been so hypnotized by the sight of that black milestone that she had slowed down, still staring at it. She had been quite sure that the whole story of the milestones was a leg-pull, and, seeing one, had been so startled at finding it was true that she couldn't focus on anything else.

I am thankful to say that we saw no more tigers, and not a single elephant on the rest of our drive through the Mysore Ditch. Later on Mother was invited by His Highness of Mysore to attend a *keddah*, which is an elephant drive in which a herd of wild elephants will be located and driven very slowly and cautiously, so that they do not become scared and break back, by men on the backs of tame elephants, through the jungles of the Mysore Ditch towards an enormous enclosure somewhere in the forest, where they are trapped and led away to be tamed and turned into working elephants. Kipling has written a wonderful description of a *keddah* in a story called 'Toomai of the Elephants', which is one of the tales in *The Jungle Book*. You should read it – if you haven't already done so.

I would have given anything to be invited to watch a *keddah*, but alas, only a very few white people get the chance, and I wasn't as lucky as Mother. However, she took a lot of photographs, and described it all to me, which I suppose was the next best thing to seeing one myself. Nowadays, when engines and electricity have almost eliminated man and animal power, and the once-great forests of the world are falling with frightening speed to the assaults of chain-saws, I don't suppose there can be all that much need for working elephants, except for use on ceremonial occasions, and very soon, if it has not happened already, the world will have witnessed its last *keddah*. However, I did have one more jungle experience during that summer in Ootacamund.

A syndicate had been formed to run a series of 'walks' through the Mysore Ditch on elephants' backs. You either spent the previous night in a nearby forest bungalow, or got up in the small hours in order to reach the starting point by first light. Sitting in rough-and-ready *howdahs* on the back of pad-elephants, parties of four to six sightseers would start off at a word from the *mahout*, who would be sitting on his animal's neck with a knee tucked under each of the leathery fan-like ears, and away they would go, to drift silently through the fringe of the Mysore Ditch and see, in their natural habitat, the birds and beasts who inhabited that long strip of almost virgin jungle.

Those who were lucky might even see a tiger or a panther, though these Lords of the Jungle were apt to retire to some remoter spot for the day. The curious thing about those elephant-back walkabouts was that the other denizens of the jungle never appeared to notice any difference in smell or appearance between a tame elephant and a wild one, and never seemed to spot the clusters of humans on their backs. You would have thought that a *mahout* and half a dozen assorted sightseers would, between them, have given off the odd whiff of danger, and that the scent of the elephant lines would have clung about the tame ones. But apparently not. Your elephant drifted happily through the jungle, and not a bird or a mammal turned its head to look. I never saw another tiger (to tell the truth, I didn't want to. Twice was enough – it is very scary indeed to be in the presence of a wild tiger stalking through his own territory, take it from me). But I did see a leopard walking through the rustling grass as though he owned the place, a whole herd of bad-tempered wild buffalo, several kinds of deer, some of whom stopped and stared – not at us but at the leopard, who ignored them – and several nilgai, the big, blue bulls of the Indian forests. Monkeys of course, and any number of birds: peacocks by the score, and the beautiful and brilliantly feathered jungle-cocks, tree-creepers, woodpeckers, the black, long-tailed king-crows, and a dozen other species of bird life.

Bets and her baby, Richard, were in Ooty for the hot weather, as were many other people we had known in Hyderabad, and Mother spent most of her time sketching. Myself, I didn't find Ooty very paintable. It looked more like one of the midland counties of England, green and misty, with rolling downlands and a distant fringe of blue hills. I think that is why, when the Raj ended, so many people to whom this spelt instant retirement chose to spend their later years there. Ooty, to them, was the 'blue remembered hills' of the Housman poem and they thought – most of them wrongly – that it would always be like home to them.

I suppose it is because I didn't take to the place that I have almost no recollection of it. I can't even see it in my mind's eye, and all that remains of it is a memory of long avenues of eucalyptus, that decorative tree that Australians call 'wattle' and that legend says was brought to Ooty some time before the nineteenth century by a home-sick Ozzie who thought it might flourish there. Too right. It took to Ooty with enthusiasm, and it is sad to hear that India has been cutting down those beautiful blue-gum trees left and right. I am told that soon there will be none left.

The only thing I remember about Ooty is leaving it briefly to attend a party in Mysore. I'm quite sure Mother must have been asked too, because the invitation came from *Larla* Begum, and I am equally certain that Mother would have attended if she possibly could. But for some fairly pressing reason she was unable to accept. So I went by myself; and spent a fantastic few days in Mysore. For the Begum had asked us down to attend the festivities connected with the marriage of the Heir Apparent, a joyous event for which the old Maharajah, His Highness Sir Sri Krishnaraja Wadiyar Bahadur of Mysore, was throwing a truly magnificent party.

I had attended a good number of Indian weddings before, but never anything to compare with this one. All Mysore was *en fête*. Its palaces, temples and public buildings, and many of the private houses, were outlined in fairy-lights which were switched on as soon as darkness fell, so that night after night during the few days of celebration the city glittered like the diamond mines in Walt Disney's *Snow White*. I did not attend any of the special functions or dinners at which the old Maharajah was present, for His Highness was an orthodox Hindu. His caste did not permit him to eat with Europeans, though when it came to kingship and the good of his state he was broadminded enough to appoint a Muslim friend and fellow student of his boyhood as his Chief Minister. However, I was never made aware of being left out of anything and I remember every day as being planned out ahead and full of interest.

My first day began with a visit to the elephant lines, where the elephants who would be walking in the wedding processions were 'having their make-up put on' – literally! It was an enchanting sight, for the great creatures seemed to know exactly what was going on, and would hold out their trunks to make it easier for their make-up men to paint elaborate patterns on them. What's more, they appeared to appreciate the whole thing, and I was only sorry that no one gave them a full-length looking glass before which they could admire themselves.

The only trouble was caused by an endearing baby elephant, recently born in the lines, who was obviously becoming a spoilt brat, adored by both humans and elephants. He was deliberately naughty, and getting away with it every time. Well, not every time. When he knocked over yet *another* pot of paint, one of his elders and betters, losing patience, caught him by his little tail, hauled him close, and slapped him hard. Whereupon he bolted, squealing, to his Mum, who made a fuss of him, and then – most unexpectedly – gave him a good slap herself. At which all the *mahouts* laughed. I could have spent hours watching them.

I was taken to endless parties, one with the bridegroom's sisters, where for the first time I met Shri, the youngest sister, I believe, whom I was later to know well. She can't have been more than ten or eleven at the time, but she was an enchanting child and, I was to discover, very much better educated than I was.

Then there was another party after which the guests were taken to a wing of the palace where, in a series of gorgeously decorated rooms, the wedding presents were displayed. You've never seen such a collection of dazzling jewellery and bits of expensive bric-à-brac: though had I been asked to choose one item for myself I would have picked a sari. There must have been dozens of these, because I remember a whole very long table being given up to saris alone, every one of them a triumph of the weaver's art, and one of them designed by a genius. It's the only one of all those hundreds of glittering wedding presents that I can still remember quite clearly.

It was a Benares sari of silver gauze, hand-woven from every shade of silver you can imagine, from the brightest to the dullest, in a design of ostrich feathers. The silver changed colour as the light moved on it, and in some lights the feathers looked almost real, and as if they would move if a breeze blew on them. It was a fantastic piece of imaginative craftsmanship – and oh, how I coveted it!

There were any number of parties on the night of the wedding, and the Begum told me that it would be taken as a great compliment by the host and hostess of the one I would be attending if I wore Indian dress for the occasion. When I said that I was sorry, but I hadn't got such a thing, she laughed and said that needn't bother me, because she and the girls would be only too pleased to lend me anything I needed, which they did. Between them they produced endless gorgeous saris and bodices and any number of slippers and sandals and made-to-order-in-Paris high-heeled shoes for me to choose from, and we all had an uproarious time trying them all on and deciding which one we liked best. I tried on so many that I can't remember which we finally chose, but I do remember fancying myself no end in the winning number, and feeling exactly like Cinderella must have done before she arrived at that ball. The Begum's *ayah* and the one that had been temporarily put in charge of me for the duration of my visit smoothed my hair flat with some coconut oil and pulled it back from my ears into a knot of black silk that looked as though it was real hair, once the join between that and my own was concealed by a little wreath of jasmine flowers. They painted my eyes with kohl – most becoming! – and when they had finished making up my face, one of them added a *tilak*, a red caste mark between the eyebrows, as a final touch. And when I arrived at the party everyone pretended they didn't recognize me.

With the news that the *shadi* had been concluded and the procession was on its way, we all crowded out under the arches of the main entrance to the palace to watch it arrive. It was a really wonderful show against a night sky that was bright with fireworks, shower upon shower of gold and silver, bright pink, blue and viridian stars. The head of the procession took some time to reach us, headed by a double rank of men in gold-embroidered, bright-sashed uniforms and turbans, carrying flaming torches. Between them marched bands and prancing, wonderfully caparisoned horses, followed by more squads of marchers: men blowing on flutes, and priests and holy men in saffron-yellow and bright orange robes, the occasional elephant, painted all over with brilliant designs and draped in heavy, gold-embroidered housings – bearing, I presume, various senior officials of state or members of the family in gold or silver *howdahs*. It was difficult to make out faces in the flare of smoke from the torches.

And then at last the largest of all the elephants, wearing the most magnificent of housings heavily fringed with gold, and carrying on his back in a gold *howdah* the bridal couple. The procession halted under the marble porch, and, over the heads of the torch-bearers, as the elephant sank ponderously to its knees and a couple of palace servants hurried forward with a gold-plated ladder, I saw the bride. A slight, bowed figure, wrapped in a gold sari which was pulled so far forward that one could not catch a glimpse of her face, stood up and was handed down the ladder, and stepped back to allow her splendidly clad bridegroom to descend.

'Oh, good,' said the Begum on a deep sigh of thankfulness and satisfaction, as the groom and his bride disappeared into the palace. 'Now that that's settled, he can start looking about him for some really pretty little girl whom he can fall in love with!'

'*Larla!*' – I have seldom been more shocked, for I was still a child of Victorian parents, who had lived through the twilight of the Edwardian age. And though I knew that the aristocracy of that age had acquired a reputation for being incredibly 'fast' and immoral, this was not so of the middle classes. They remained prim, and believed strongly in faithfulness, true love and romance. Or at least, I did! The casualness, as well as the obvious relief in the Begum's remark horrified me.

'You are shocked,' said the Begum, and patted me consolingly on the arm. 'But why? – when you know very well that our marriages are arranged. And if even ordinary people arrange the marriages of their sons and daughters, how much more important must it be for members of ruling houses to see that the wives of their sons will make suitable mothers of future kings and princes?'

Well, of course I'd known that. But what with all the glamour and fuss that surrounded this particular wedding, I had been picturing some delicious princess hiding behind that concealing golden sari, and seeing the whole affair as a great romance. The Begum's heartfelt comment had brought me back to earth with a bump, and I could only hope that his bride would turn out to be pretty and witty and charming enough to make him fall in love with her, and that she would fall in love with him. After all, there had been plenty of precedents in the chronicles of princely India. The princess Pudmini was one example. It was written that she was the 'fairest flesh on earth', and her beauty had led to a war almost as famous and quite as murderous as that of the Siege of Troy.

It must have been some time during that season at Ooty that I returned to Hyderabad, this time as paying guest of a friend in the military cantonment of Secunderabad, which lies only a few miles to the north of Hyderabad city, while I fulfilled a commission to mural the walls of the main room of the Secunderabad Club. I don't remember how long I stayed there, only that it must have been the best part of a month, since there was a lot of wall space to fill. I have recently been fascinated to discover that those murals have been cherished and are in a truly marvellous state of preservation. The mother of one of my fans recently visited Secunderabad, and was allowed to take some snapshots of the murals, which her daughter sent on to me. They have come out beautifully, despite the fact that my medium was no more than good old Indian whitewash, coloured with little packets of powdered dye that I bought in the bazaar of Hyderabad city, some time in the late 1930s – I can't work it out nearer than that I'm afraid, though I think it *must* have been January or February of 1938. I also found time to dance and sing in a charity concert in the Club, and to fall madly in love with a professional heart-breaker named Clive someone-or-other.

I was, for the first time, completely bowled over. I convinced myself that here was the man I had been waiting for, and to heck with Prince Charming and Mr Right and the 'I'll be ready in five minutes! – no, make it three!' chap. The fact that he didn't fulfil a single one of the requirements I had mentally listed as absolutely necessary in my 'some-day-he'll-come-along' dreamboat (correction – one; he *was* in an Indian Service, Indian Army) was neither here nor there. I was besotted, and wouldn't have cared if he'd been a stoker on one of the ferry-boats that ran between Fishguard and Cork. However, he turned out to be yet another Don Juan of the type that women of all ages fall for in droves – heaven knows why, for he wasn't anything much to look at. Good old sex appeal, I suppose. It has a lot to answer for! And he didn't really like girls. He preferred older women; preferably married ones. (Well, I can see the point of that!) So although I couldn't pretend to be married, I pretended to be at least five years older than I was, heaven help me. It did me no good. He was temporarily without some adoring female, having been banished from his unit and sent off to the other end of India in the hope of putting an end to a liaison with the wife of his commanding officer before it became an open scandal. Or so he told me. I merely happened to be a useful stop-gap until another attractive married woman came along; which wasn't long.

I remember being heartbroken when I took the stage to do my cabaret turn at the Club and saw that his seat was empty (and that, worse still, so was that of a gay grass-widow who had begun to show an interest in him). I had designed my costume with particular care and was sure that I would look ravishing in it: all for his sake. And instead of being one of an enthusiastic audience who gave me a terrific hand, the only one whose praise and admiration I coveted had sneaked out as the house-lights went down and had seized the opportunity to take the next Mrs something-or-other for a smooch in the Club garden.

I recognized that this meant curtains for me. And sure enough it did. He dropped me like a cigarette stub and didn't even bother to put his heel on me and grind me into the dust. I don't know how I managed to get through the rest of the evening, only that it was worse, far worse, than that dance at the Srinagar Residency,* and that I cried my eyes out when I got back to bed, and nursed a sore heart and a terrible inferiority complex for months afterwards. How cross Tacklow would have been with me!

Mother, having given a successful exhibition of her watercolours, had returned to Kashmir, accompanied by Kadera and Shao-de, and I packed up my paints and said a fond farewell to my friends, taking myself and my broken heart back to Srinagar to join her.

* See *Golden Afternoon*.

✳ 7 ✳

Ranikhet

Chapter 26

~※◇※~

Judging from leaders in the press and the news bulletins on All India Radio, Europe appeared to be indulging in non-stop turmoil during the final years of the thirties. There was a civil war raging in Spain, marches and demonstrations by Brown Shirts in Germany, Black Shirts in Italy and London, and Red Flag wavers all over the place.

Edward VIII had abdicated after a reign of three hundred and something days, which had largely been spent in quarrelling. 'Ultimatums' and 'Demands' (usually 'final' ones) flew to and fro. Germany annexed Austria, which created a temporary panic that led to the British Navy being hastily mobilized and seems to have alerted everyone to the dangers of the situation, causing Neville Chamberlain, the British Prime Minister, to fly to Munich for a personal talk with Herr Hitler.

Chamberlain was not alone in believing that the piece of paper he brought back with him from Munich on that autumn afternoon (and which sold the Czechs down the river) would indeed guarantee us 'peace in our time' – if not, as he seemed to think, 'with honour'. The vast majority of us persuaded ourselves that we had avoided war by a whisker, and felt greatly cheered and enormously relieved in consequence; while too many people began to regard the MP for the Epping Division for Essex, Winston Churchill, as a warmonger, because he put no faith in Chamberlain's piece of paper. Having had a terrible fright, the rest of us relaxed and got on with our lives.

Brother Bill, together with umpteen other British officers of the Indian Army, took home leave, and he and Joy, who was expecting her first baby (already referred to as 'Timothy') sailed for England and her parents' home on the Isle of Wight, so that the Huttons could meet their son-in-law and introduce him to their friends and neighbours.

Mother was staying in Kashmir as a paying guest of old Mrs Wall, who had given her a small flat that was reached by a covered wooden bridge, and which Mother had managed to turn into a most decorative little home for herself. It had been built over stables which were now storerooms, and the view from its windows was charming even on wet days. Kadera had quarters within call, and all in all it could not have been a more attractive, comfortable and convenient place to live in. But Mother was still suffering from the effect that Tacklow's sudden death had had on her, and she continued to be dissatisfied with any place she was in, convinced that if she went somewhere else she would feel happier.

I couldn't have imagined a nicer place for her to live in, and when letter after letter arrived from her whingeing about the flat and everything to do with it, I sat down and wrote her a tough lecture, listing every one of the many advantages of her present perch, and rubbing in that 'for goodness sake, darling, can't you see that one day, *these* will be the "Good Old Days" . . . And what wouldn't we give to be back in them?' I was afraid, after I'd posted that letter, that I had overdone it and that it might only upset her. But, thank heaven, it worked. She actually took it in, and for the first time for many moons sat down and counted her blessings instead of dwelling solely on the drawbacks and the black patches of widowhood.

I had expected to be a paying guest at Mrs Wall's myself that year, but Bets wrote to say that her husband had been told that he would be transferred to the Lucknow branch of his firm in April, and that she and her two-year-old, Richard, were to spend the hot weather in Ranikhet, a small summer station among the mountains beyond Naini Tal. So couldn't I *please* spend the summer there too, instead of in Kashmir? She never knew, wrote Bets, where she would find herself posted next, and we might not have a chance of seeing each other again for ages.

Well, why not? Mother was comfortably settled in with Ma Wall for the summer, and there was no reason why I too should not spend the hot weather in the mountains beyond Naini Tal, where Mother had spent her first hot weather in India, and where Bill, her first baby, had been born.

Bets and her own two-year-old would be paying guests of a friend of ours, an Indian Army wife who as Connie Tallon had been a bridesmaid at Bets's wedding. She had rented a house in Ranikhet for the season and was better known at that time as 'Bogeen' – presumably because her home town was Dublin. Since Bogeen's sister had come out to India to spend the summer with her, there was no question of my being able to join Bets in the same bungalow. So I wrote and booked myself a room in a hotel before the available accommodation began to fill up.

I don't remember how I came to be staying in Government House in Lucknow towards the end of April that year.* Perhaps because it was the best place for taking off for Kathgodarm, which was as far as you could get by train if you were heading for Ranikhet. Tacklow and Mother had been great friends of the then Governor of the United Provinces, Sir Henry Haigh, and his wife, so I presume Mother must have written to Lady Haigh to ask if they would put me up for a few days on my way north, and see me safely off to Kathgodarm. In the event, Lady Haigh had already left for the Governor's summer residence, for the hot weather was beginning to make itself felt. She liked to leave for the Government House in Naini Tal well before Sir Harry, so that she could open it up and see that everything was ready for him, and could not endure the searing temperatures that were already reaching uncomfortable heights in Lucknow. She left a charming note of apology for her desertion, assuring me that Harry would enjoy having someone to talk to, and that he and 'the boys' – the ADCs I presume – would look after me and see me on my way, and that I must come to Naini Tal later on when the garden was at its best, and stay for at least a week or two.

There were no other guests at Government House. This surprised me, though it should not have done, since the period of breathless heat before the monsoon breaks is no time to go visiting. I had a suite of rooms whose french windows opened on to a deep, shady verandah that looked out across wide lawns to wilting flower-beds in which only zinnias and canna lilies flourished. Bougainvillaea was almost the only flower that revelled in the heat, and it fell in cascades of crimson, purple or white from the edge of the verandah above me.

I saw little or nothing of Sir Harry or his secretary, or of 'the boys', who were presumably kept busy with the sorting and packing of the piles of paperwork that would accompany Sir Harry to the hills. The grandiose, pillared house appeared to be empty, and it was very quiet, the only sound from outside being the creaking of a waterwheel that kept the lawns from drying up, and the maddening cry of the brain-fever bird, so called because its cry says: '*Brain fever! Brain fever! Brain fever!*' on an ascending scale. When

_____
* 1939.

it reaches the top it starts all over again from the bottom. Inside the house there was only the equally monotonous sound of the big, white ceiling-fans, swishing round and round in the hot stillness.

A house-servant in a spotless outfit of white, scarlet and gold would appear on silent feet half-way through the morning, bearing a frosted glass of *nimbu-pani* (literal translation: lemon-water) on a silver tray – a delicious drink which in Britain is called lemon squash and in general comes out of a bottle and in no way resembles its Indian original, which is made from fresh limes and lemons, sugared in the glass and topped up with ice-cold water or soda-water. Real *nimbu-pani* doesn't seem to exist outside India. Another and equally splendidly dressed retainer would warn me when I should go to the anteroom in which guests assembled to wait for His Excellency the Governor – or Their Excellencies if both were in residence – to join them for a pre-lunch drink, before leading them into the dining-room.

Since I was the only guest, and Sir Harry was not always able to appear on the dot, I used to bring with me whichever book I happened to be reading, and only put it down when I heard him approaching. The house was full of books. There were rows of them in every room. And since no one ever bothered me to do this or that, or go here or there, I had a field-day. For I am, and thanks to Tacklow always have been since the age of four, a compulsive bookworm. The only thing I am really frightened of is going blind. I could, I think, cope with almost anything else. But not to be able to read . . . ! How could I bear it? How does anyone? Non-stop 'talking books', I suppose.

I had been the only guest at Government House for several days when Sir Harry, hurrying into the anteroom before lunch, suddenly noticed that I had as usual a book in my hands and said, 'You always seem to be reading one of the Mutiny books. Is it a subject that particularly interests you?' I must have looked surprised at what I considered a silly question, and I said, 'Well, of course I am. I'm a Kaye!'

'Good Lord – how silly of me! Yes, of course you'd be interested – '*
Sir Harry talked about the Mutiny for most of that lunchtime, and afterwards opened a safe in which the Government House archives were kept and gave me a letter written in 1858, when the main fire of the

---

* Tacklow's first cousin, Sir John Kaye, wrote a contemporary history of the Mutiny which he called a *History of the Sepoy Rising*, and his *Kaye and Malleson's History of the Indian Mutiny* is still one of the best accounts of that bloodstained event.

Mutiny had been stamped out, though here and there a flame still flickered. It was a hand-written copy of the original which had been written by a girl who had come out to India to spend a season with her brother. She had been caught up by the Mutiny and spent close on a year captive in an Indian household in Lucknow, regaining her freedom only after the second and final relief of the beleaguered Residency and the fall of the city. She and her brother had been among the British who had taken refuge in the house of the Commissioner of Sitapur, from where they had escaped into the jungle when the sepoys who had been guarding the house joined the mutineers and attacked it.

The letter, telling her family of the murder of her brother and all that had happened to her, had been copied in spidery Victorian handwriting now yellowed with age, and sent out to Lucknow to be added to the Mutiny archives of the capital city of Oudh, the Province that Sir Henry Lawrence had done his best to keep peaceful and where, having failed, he had died in the besieged Residency.

I read that letter, and decided there and then that one day I *must* write a novel about the Mutiny in Oudh, and use that girl's story. It was all there. Handed to me on a plate by a girl who had lived through all the horrors of that rising and the terrifying day in which the Mutiny broke out in Sitapur, an unimportant district within the borders of Oudh.

Once again, as in the miracle year that had brought me back to India, when we had stayed on our way north in this same Government House, I was taken round the Mutiny sights – the battered Residency, with its cellars in which so many women and children had existed for day after day during the burning heat and the continuous gunfire of the siege, and in which so many of them had died. The shattered remains of the room in which Henry Lawrence had been killed; the cemetery with its more than doubtful labelling of graves, and the ruins of the Alum Bagh, the 'Garden of the World'.

I can't remember whether I left for Kathgodarm with Sir Harry and his party, yet I think I must have done, for I certainly didn't travel alone, but in company with several other people. We took the night train to Kathgodarm, which we reached in the dawn; a little station among the foothills on the edge of the plains.

The party I had travelled with from Lucknow, presumably the Government House one, was bound for Naini Tal. But since the little hill railway did not go as far as Ranikhet, I was transferred into a hired car and did the rest of the journey in that. I remember that car-ride with pleasure to this day. As hill roads go, it was much the same as any others I had travelled on: a gritty, dusty surface, edged on the outer side with a low dry-stone wall constructed from loose slabs of rock piled on one another, and winding and twisting in a manner that would once have made me car-sick, but which I had learned how to deal with. For one thing, I sat in the front seat beside the driver; and that makes all the difference.

On one side of the road the hillsides soared steeply upward, for the most part pine-clad, while on the other the ground dropped away to the foothills and the plains. Here, too, for a time, I could look down on to jungle. Most of it was tiger-jungle, which like that of the Mysore Ditch is not thick and green and tropical, but in general thin and lion-coloured and full of thorn and sal-trees, elephant grass and scarlet-flowered dhak trees. As our road took us higher and higher into the mountains, the trees dropped away; and presently, for miles in every direction, the hillsides were as bare as the back of your hand and sculpted all over by little shell-shaped fields, each one edged with a low wall of mud and stones and somehow reminiscent of the honeycombs of industrious bees. These hills too were part of the Himalayas. But they were not in the least like the mountains of Kashmir, or even Simla.

The trees began again as we neared Ranikhet, a green splash of pines, flowering trees and the roofs of houses, scattered along a high ridge, the far side of which overlooked a vast green valley whose far wall was rimmed by a rampart of mountains, among them the high white peak of Nanda Devi, surrounded by her attendant snows.

Ranikhet must, I think, be one of the prettiest of India's hill stations, and one of my many regrets is that I never kept any of my paintings of it. That is the worst of being skint and needing to earn enough money to live on. You are delighted when your work sells well, and it is only later, when things have become easier, that you regret not keeping just one or two of your own sketches. Another thing I had to economize on was films. I still only had my ancient Box-Brownie, and there were no colour films on the market as yet (anyway, as Bets has pointed out, we couldn't have afforded them if there had been!). So I have almost nothing to remind me of Ranikhet, apart from a few snapshots taken by other people, and one really good one of my great friend Jess Binnie. But apart from that, nothing tangible remains to remind me of the beauty of that little hill station.

Like many other summer resorts, this one was strung along the crest of a high ridge, and those houses that had failed to find a foothold on the top of it clung to the steep sides of the mountain as they do in Simla and Murree, Mussorie and Darjeeling. The buildings of the hotel in which I had taken rooms clung in descending layers to the southward slope, rather in the manner of a colony of swallows' nests, and consisted of two long rows of rooms, one below the other and separated from the next block by lawns and flower-beds. My room was in the lowest block, in the middle of the upper storey, and looked out on to a long communal verandah that was reached by a curving iron stairway at the near end.

The Ranikhet Club lay on the opposite side of the ridge, its tennis-courts giving the impression of being hacked out of the sheer hillside, and its windows looking out across that enormous valley to the white-topped mountain range on the far side. Often, during the months of the monsoon, the valley would fill up with mist, leaving only the lovely line of the snow-peaks to catch fire at sunset, as they used to do when I watched them from the verandah of our house in the hills beyond Simla, when I was a child. Only here they were even more spectacular, because they were so much nearer. So near that there were times when I felt I could almost reach out and touch them.

The white peaks that one looks out at from Ranikhet are merely the ladies-in-waiting to Nanda Devi, the Goddess of those snows, who stands in the centre of a ring of mountains that form the Nanda Devi basin. It is only at sunset and sunrise that you can tell which one is the goddess, for since they stand protectively around her, it follows that half of them are closer to you than she is, and therefore look much taller. But if you watch that glittering array of peaks at sunrise or sunset, you will see a single peak catch fire before the dawn, or hold the light while the rest are only cold silhouettes at sunset. That one is Nanda Devi.

The little town and its bazaar stood among pines and deodars and scores of a flowering tree that was strange to me. It was covered with pink and almost scentless blossoms, each one more than twice the size of any fruit blossom I knew, and the sight of the far snows seen through that foam of pink petals will stay with me always. Ranikhet was full of flowers. The hillsides were thick with wild balsam and cosmos, and the steep slope above the path that led down from the main road to the hotel had been planted with a mass of zinnias in every colour of the rainbow. I love zinnias, because they will brighten your garden when drought and heat have shrivelled almost every other flower that grows, and they thrive on the poorest soil and in the unkindest of temperatures.

I have tried and tried to grow them in England, but without success; they come up on thin straggly stalks and produce the smallest of flowers, and those only in the hot and angry colours that set my teeth on edge, instead of the huge and beautiful pale-coloured ones that are white or dusty-pink, or primrose-yellow — or any of the clear, soft colours. I persuaded the hotel *mali* to let me choose which ones I would like for the vase in my room, because his own choice was always for the reds, oranges and red-browns; and though he deplored my preference for the ones he obviously considered to be deadly dull, he gave in with a good grace.

Bets had taken up residence in the house with Connie, *née* Tallon (by then Mrs Tom Hughes), several weeks before I arrived, and had made friends with a number of that season's visitors. It was she who introduced me to Jess Binnie, who not only made my stay, but became a lifelong friend. I don't believe that anyone has ever made me laugh more than Jess. She was a jewel, and my only complaint against her was that she was also a dedicated and exceedingly good bridge player. Since I detest all card games, I would be deprived of her exhilarating company for large portions of each week. Jess was much too good a player to be left in peace by the bridge-fiends, and she made quite a bit of money out of the game, which is more than her opponents did! But when she wasn't playing bridge she spent a lot of time making me fall about laughing. It wasn't all intentional; it was just the tone of her voice and the way she phrased things that made you roll in the aisles; you could never repeat something that Jess said to you and make it sound funny. This was something that was uniquely Jess — I don't believe that she had any idea that she was doing it! It just came out that way. But knowing her gave me a hilarious summer.

It was Jess who suggested that I should try being a blonde, in order to test that theory that 'gentlemen prefer them'. Well she should know, for she had the most beautiful hair you ever saw, a natural ash-blonde, which is a hundred times better than being a golden or yellow one. Hers was that true, pale silvery colour that is a soft grey in the curves and curls and shimmers with pale gold highlights. She was also very slim, and she insisted that it was the combination of the two that made her such a success with 'the boys'. For there were no two ways about that. Men fell for Jess in droves.

'You see,' she explained, 'whenever I walk into a room in a strange place, the men turn round to have a look, and the minute they see my hair, and that I'm the right size, they sit up and take notice, and start straightening their ties. By the time I've got close enough to them to let them see that I have a face like a boot' (which was a *gross* libel) 'it's too late, because their brains have registered that I am an attractive blonde, and the dear saps are hooked. All I have to do is look them over and haul one in.' And it was true. At close range, her personality and her talent to amuse took over, and they couldn't care less what she looked like – they were hooked.

I knew that nothing I could do with a bottle of peroxide was going to produce the same effect that Jess produced so effortlessly, and I hadn't as yet seen anyone I would like to impress. But one fine morning, having nothing better to do, we walked off to the shops which adjoined the bazaar, found a chemist's and bought a bottle of peroxide and another of ammonia. And that afternoon, assisted by Jess, I sloshed peroxide and ammonia all over my head and covered it with a bathing cap, tied a towel over it, and waited the regulation time as advised by the chemist's assistant. I couldn't *wait* to turn myself into a pale gold blonde, and I remember the excitement with which I removed that towel-turban and rubber cap when the specified time was up . . .

Alas, the result was a disaster! Instead of a glamorous pale gold, my hair had turned an angry ginger-biscuit colour that was truly hideous. A second application only produced a depressing shade of Oxford Marmalade, and it took a third to achieve anything *approaching* the colour I had been aiming for. Jess was all for trying a fourth while I was about it; but by then I was exhausted, both mentally and physically. And anyway, we had run out of either ammonia or peroxide, I forget which (it was probably both). But Jess and the author of that crashing best-seller *Gentlemen Prefer Blondes* had been right. They certainly do.

On my initial appearance in the Club lounge, heads had automatically turned as members who were already seated there looked round in order to see if the newcomer was a friend, or, if a stranger, anyone worth taking note of – for this was, after all, the beginning of 'the Season'. My arrival had been briefly noted, but that was all. No one had taken a second look or bothered to stop talking. The difference this time was dramatically different. I might not have a sylph-like figure, but I was a young, blue-eyed blonde, and there was a distinct moment of silence as almost everyone in that long room stopped talking and took it in. 'Told you so!' hissed Jess, who had been sitting with a group of friends at the far end of the room, waiting for me to arrive.

She hailed me over to join her. The verdict on my refurbished locks was enthusiastic, and from then on I began to enjoy my stay in Ranikhet. I think we all did. Not so much despite the ugly, ominous war-clouds that were rolling up across Europe and the Middle East, but because of them. Because we were all, I think, aware that we were living on a knife edge, and that although the storm clouds were no more than a black line along the horizon, they could at any moment roll up and over us, and destroy us all. But since there was nothing we could do about it but pray, we might just as well eat, drink and be merry, and forget about tomorrow. What's more, apart from Kashmir, I couldn't have been in a lovelier place.

Chapter 27

~꓇꙰꓇~

One of the hotel guests had complained to the management about rats that (so she said) had taken to stealing the nuts and biscuits that she kept for her 'coffee mornings'. The management made apologetic noises, and took steps to deal with the problem by setting one of those large wire-cage rat-traps on the ground floor verandah of the block I was in, and baiting it with a bit of biscuit.

My room happened to be the one directly above it, and a few nights later, when the moon was almost full, I was awakened in the middle of the night by a small but irritating rattling noise that sounded like a piece of broken hinge or the end of a cane *chik* being shaken in the wind. It went on and on until presently, realizing that I had let it get on my nerves and that there was no chance of going to sleep again until it stopped, I got out of bed and went out, shoeless, into the verandah to investigate.

I had forgotten about the rat-trap, and as the night was exceptionally warm I had left my door open, and only had to part the curtains in order to step out on to the verandah. I stood there for a moment or two looking out at the black and silver world beyond the verandah railings and thinking how fabulous the hillsides looked by moonlight, before turning my attention to the source of that tiresome noise, and discovering that it came from somewhere on the verandah immediately below me. And also realizing, in almost the same moment and with a distinct sense of unease, that there was not a breath of wind stirring.

The night was so still that you could have heard a pine-cone drop in the woods behind the hotel. Which meant that whatever was making that irritating noise had hands – or paws? It was only then that I remembered the rat-trap, and was suddenly limp with relief, for I had had a swift and scary thought that it might be a thief trying to force a locked door or window. But of course it must be a rat – caught in that trap and scrabbling to get out. My bare feet can have made no sound on the matting as I walked to the edge of the verandah and leaned over the rail. And it *was* the rat-trap of course, and there was a rat inside it. But it wasn't the rat that was making the noise that had irritated me to the point of getting out of bed to investigate. It was a full-grown leopard, crouched there below me in the bright moonlight, with the trap and its frantic occupant between its paws. One paw held down the trap, while the other one was attempting to claw out the rat, shaking the wire cage to and fro. It began to growl very softly, deep in its throat, and all I could think of was that I had been sleeping with my doors and windows wide open, and it could have walked in on any night, for there was no door at the bottom of that staircase.

I stood there fascinated. Scared to death of moving in case the leopard might try and get at me in preference to the rat, though I knew it couldn't jump that high. But then there was always that open staircase . . .

I know that I made no sound and, as far as I know, didn't move a muscle. But either it caught my scent, or wild animals can sense the near presence of a human. For suddenly, its head came up and we were staring at each other in the bright moonlight. The rattling and growling stopped and the night was quiet again except for the scrabbling of that terrified rat. I remember noticing how the moonlight caught the leopard's eyes and made them glow like a pair of greeny-yellow moons. Then all at once it wasn't there any more. I didn't even see which way it went. It just vanished in a flash of spotted fur, and without the ghost of a sound. And there was only that rat-trap with a rat scrabbling wildly round and round inside it.

I woke the *chowkidar* (who naturally had slept throughout) and he took the trap and its captive away and went off to rouse some of his friends to patrol the approaches to the lower wing of the hotel. A day or two later a dog belonging to one of the hotel guests was taken by a leopard – presumably the one I had seen – and the bereaved owner organized a beat and succeeded in shooting the creature. But though I saw its body lying dead in a clearing on the edge of the forest, I never again slept with my windows wide and my door open while I was in Ranikhet. For an old *shikari*, who had helped set up the beat, told me a hair-raising story about a man-eating leopard which, in the years immediately following the end of the Great War, had terrorized a large part of the Gharwal and Kumaon districts, and according to Government records had been responsible for the deaths of a hundred and twenty-five people.

According to the *shikari*, the correct total was far larger than that, a verdict that was supported some years later when 'Carpet-Sahib', Colonel J. E. Corbett – the Jim Corbett who wrote a marvellous series of tiger books and gave the entire proceeds of the first one, *Man-eaters of Kumaon*, to St Dunstan's* – came up with a riveting book called *The Man-eating Leopard of Rudraprayag*. That book was first published in India in 1947, and I assure you that although at the time I read it I was nowhere near the hill-country in which that leopard had operated, when night fell I looked under the bed and in the cupboard and behind the curtains of my bedroom, to make sure that there were no leopards lurking there before I went to bed! It's that sort of book.

I remembered that night in Ranikhet when, a year later, I began to write a whodunnit set in Kashmir, eventually published as *Death Walks in Kashmir* and republished a long while later as *Death in Kashmir*. I started it with a girl being woken up on a moonlit night by a small monotonous sound that gets her out of bed to investigate. And when I finally came to write a Mutiny novel† I remembered the way that leopard's eyes had caught the moonlight and gleamed like a pair of green moons, and I put that in too – together with a host of other memories.

I don't remember when, in the course of that summer, Lady Haigh wrote to invite me over to Naini Tal to spend a week at Government House, and whether it was before or after I became a blonde. I think it was probably after, and that I must have been a bit worried about her writing to Mother to break the news, because I wasn't all that anxious to accept, and might even have invented some excuse if Jess hadn't told me I was behaving like a fourth-former with an inferiority complex. If she was in my shoes, she'd *jump* at it! Bets agreed, so I refurbished my distinctly scanty wardrobe and accepted.

An ADC arrived in one of the Government House cars to fetch me, and in spite of my qualms I had a truly enjoyable stay. Naini Tal, with its lake and its yacht-club and sailing boats, was the prettiest sight, and I was charmed by the entrance to Government House with its long, winding drive through woods, banked up high on either side of the drive with masses of hydrangeas in full bloom, not the shrieking '*deysi‡*-pink' colour,

* In aid of Indian Servicemen blinded during the war.
† *Shadow of the Moon*, published by Longmans Green, and republished by Viking.
‡ Indian.

but every shade of blue and mauve and lilac and that soft pinky-mauve like the best opals. And all of them with unbelievably large flower-heads – I've never seen such enormous ones before or since. The woods were full of them: and so was half the garden. The effect against the massed green of the trees that clothed the hillsides – for the *Tal* (lake) lies in a cup of the hills that rise up steeply on all but the side that looks towards the plains – was stunningly beautiful, and I fell out of the car, babbling with admiration.

I couldn't have done anything that pleased my hostess more, for it seemed that Lady Haigh had a passion for the multi-shaded hydrangeas (she, like me, disliked the shocking-pink ones) and was responsible for those in the garden and along the drive. She had even had a small notice pinned up in all the guest-bathrooms asking male guests to give her their discarded razor blades. These, when collected, were dug in around the roots of the hydrangeas in order to put iron into the soil, since iron helps turn the flowers blue. Too much iron and they are *only* blue. And no iron at all produces only *deysi*-pink ones. Lady Haigh had obviously struck the happy medium – with the help of all those razor blades which must have provided a terrible hazard in later years to unwary gardeners.

The week I spent in 'Naini' was a terrific success, at least from my point of view, and I was driven back to Ranikhet in the largest of the Government House cars, with the boot and the back seat stuffed full and overflowing with hydrangeas. *Dozens* of them. I filled every jar and pot and even a tin tub borrowed off the proprietor, with them. And the next day I photographed them with Jess and her lovely ash-blonde hair posing in the foreground to give them point. My Box-Brownie (I *think* it was still the Box-Brownie) came up trumps, and the result was so good that I had a really big enlargement done of it which I tinted with special photographic paint and will include in the book so that you can see both Jess and the size of the flower heads. But not, unfortunately, the lovely opal colours.

According to the latest films of the 1930s, and such magazines as *John Bull*, *Britannia and Eve*, the *Saturday Evening Post* and all that lot (now long defunct), the very latest way in which women were doing their hair was to pull it all up on top of their heads and, having first curled the ends into a handful of plump sausage rolls, skewer the lot on top with half a dozen bobby-pins. This fashion apparently only worked with blondes, for though research on thirties films and magazines showed scores of starlets balancing bunches of pallid-coloured sausages on their heads, I didn't find any girl sporting black or brown ones. Well, I was now a blonde, so why not have a stab at it?

The next time there was a Club dance to which I had been invited, I pressed Bets into service as a hairdresser's assistant, and spent the afternoon in strict seclusion and metal hair curlers. In those days you dressed up for dances and there was never any question of 'come as you are'. Women wore long dresses and men wore dinner-jackets and black ties, and that was that. I wore the two-piece grey evening dress that I had bought at Bourne & Hollingsworth and kept for 'best', and off I went to the ball.

That top-knot of bleached sausages (which I have to admit I thought was pretty hideous and would have combed out and restyled if only I had had the time) proved a wild success and gave me some of the greatest fun I had had since Tacklow died. There was never a shortage of personable young men up on leave in Ranikhet, and though the feminine section of the British holiday-makers remained more or less static, the male ranks were constantly changing, as those whose allowance of leave had run out left to go back to their regiments or their various jobs in the plains, and newcomers came up to replace them.

This turnover meant that there was always a selection of new faces to add interest to the season. But though August was more than half-way over, I had seen no one who caught my eye or caused me the slightest pang when we said goodbye. Tonight, though, when our party left the dining-room and joined the dancers in the ballroom, my attention was immediately caught by a newcomer who was standing at the far end of the room, hands in his pockets, idly surveying the dancers. He wasn't particularly tall, though that was probably because he was standing next to a man who was tall enough to make him look short, and I don't suppose I would have given him a second look if he hadn't happened to be the dead-spit of Brian Aherne, a British film star whom I much admired.

Intrigued by the likeness and wondering if anyone else had noticed it, I can't have been paying much attention to what my dancing partner was saying, for I didn't fail to note when Jess either introduced herself or was introduced to the Aherne double, and they started chatting to each other. I did hear when my partner informed me, somewhat sulkily, that one of my curls was about to fall down: instantly abandoning the poor fellow in the middle of the ballroom floor, I fled to the ladies' room in search of a comb and more bobby-pins. I was followed by Jess, who, seeing me leave, had hastily jettisoned her own partner* and ran after me to tell me that a new arrival who had joined the party she was with had asked who I was and did she know me? – if so would she please introduce me? 'Do you know what he said about you?' demanded Jess. 'He said, "I've been watching that girl, and I have to meet her. She's got *everything*!"'

Well, it may seem idiotic, but that extravagant compliment is one that I have always treasured, together with something that Roger wrote in the letter he sent me accepting the fact that I would never marry him: 'I have always thought of you,' he wrote, 'as a sort of Fairy Princess . . .'

Only a rather podgy girl whose brother persisted in calling her 'Fatty' or 'Old Piano-legs' can truly appreciate the value of such compliments as those. Pink with pleasure, I leapt to the conclusion that it was the Brian Aherne double who wanted Jess to introduce him to me and, dealing hastily with the recalcitrant sausage, I hurried back to the ballroom walking almost visibly on air. I was brought down to earth with a dull thump when Jess walked over to me, towing a man who bore no resemblance to Brian Aherne, and announced that she would like to introduce me to a newcomer to Ranikhet: George Something-or-other, who was up on a month's leave. It was, of course, the tall man who had been standing next to the Aherne look-alike, and they turned out to be great friends who had 'manoeuvred together' for some considerable time.

This was their first evening in Ranikhet.

Andrew 'Aherne', who was a bachelor, had fallen like a load of bricks for that ash-blonde charmer, Mrs Jess Binnie, and George, who had left his wife behind in England (or, more probably, Scotland) and was only interested in finding a temporary party and dance-partner to have fun with for the duration of his leave, found one in me. Together the four of us enjoyed an enormous amount of fun.

In the middle of all this fun and games, Jess fell ill and was removed to hospital for a few days. Andrew was inconsolable. George and I did our best to cheer him up, but he refused to be comforted and took to drink instead. I had the rest of this story from Jess, who regaled me with it when she was discharged. Andrew had visited her in hospital, bearing flowers and fruit, as did most of her friends. But this was not enough for

* *Dancing* partner – the word has now acquired another meaning.

him. Having refused to go partying with George and me, he had retired to his hotel room and got quietly sozzled, and at a late hour of night had been seized with the idea that he *must* say good-night to Jess.

If there hadn't been a full moon that night he would probably have come to grief long before he reached the hospital. But it was another white night, and since among India's many gods and godlings there is one, Bairon, who takes special care of drunks, Andrew, though sloshed to the eyebrows, arrived safely at his goal. Navigating down the long verandah on to which the doors and windows of a line of single-bed hospital rooms opened, he managed to end up outside the correct one, and our Mrs Binnie, abruptly jerked out of a healing sleep by the repetition of her name coupled with bangs on her door, realized with fury who was responsible for it, and called out to this sozzled and unwelcome Romeo, demanding that he leave *at once*.

'Can you believe it?' said Jess indignantly, recounting the scenario to me the next day. To make matters worse, her face had been plastered in cold cream and her hair had been in curlers: '*Not* the condition in which one would wish to appear before a devoted admirer – even one who's completely plastered,' said Jess. 'One has one's pride!' I saw her point. I wouldn't have liked the idea myself if I'd been in her shoes. However, since the lovelorn idiot continued banging on her door and yowling that he 'only wanner shay goo-nigh to you, Jessie; only shay goo-nigh,' and it was only a question of time before one of the hospital staff arrived hot-foot to inquire into the cause of this unseemly caterwauling, Jess nipped out of bed and, reaching the door, urged her admirer to go away *at once*! – 'Well, shay goo-nigh then.' 'Good-*night*, Andrew! And now for goodness sake shut up and go away before you wake the entire hospital: *please*, Andrew . . .'

But Andrew, having decided that he wanted to say goodnight to her, was not prepared to say it to a closed door. 'Wanna shee you Jessie . . . only wan' ter shee you so I can shay goo-ni . . .'

Jess, by this time getting desperate, realized that unless he saw her he was probably capable of maundering on for the rest of the night – or until he was taken away and locked up. So turning the key, she opened the door a crack and said: 'Well, you've seen me now. Good-*night*, Andrew! Now for pity's sake *shove off*!' But it was too late. The firm steps of an irate matron could be heard entering the verandah from the far end, and the next second a starched figure mounted the steps and became all too visible in the bright moonlight. Andrew waited not upon the order of his going. Giving the barely open door a violent shove, he pushed past Jess and shot across the room and under her bed with the speed of a startled rabbit, followed with equal celerity by Jess, who leapt into bed, pulled up the bedclothes and pretended to be asleep.

She had shut the door as Andrew shot past her, but had not had time to lock it, and the matron, opening it, stood in the doorway and, having allowed her steely gaze to travel over every inch of it that was visible to her (I presume she switched on the light or had a torch), asked Jess if everything was all right with her. Whereupon Jess gave up the pretence of being asleep, and sat up and said that everything was fine, thank you.

She told me that since a black bar of shadow covered that portion of the verandah on which Andrew had been standing, she thought it was just possible that the matron hadn't seen him vanish into her room, though she was obviously highly suspicious, for she stayed in the doorway making conversation. Jess said that she thought the woman was never going to leave, and that she could willingly have strangled Andrew, who passed the time by thumping the underside of her mattress, making it very difficult for her not to jump and say '*Ow*' every time he did it.

At long last, after raking the room with yet another searching glance, the matron left and Jess said she sat there in the darkness, holding her breath as she listened to the brisk receding footsteps. Not until she was quite sure that the coast was clear did she bang on her mattress and order Andrew, in a furious whisper, to come out at once, and get going while the going was good. Only to discover that the wretched man had fallen into a drunken slumber and was now beginning to snore. At which point she really *could* have murdered him and pleaded justifiable homicide. No jury, insisted Jess, would have convicted her. I don't think she knows how she managed to drag the dear boy out from under the bed and get him on his feet again. But she managed it at last (powered, I imagine, by sheer fury) and, with a parting shove, pushed him out of the room and into the verandah – straight into the arms of the matron, who was clearly a good deal more clued-up than she had appeared to be.

Jess's version of the episode, acted out for us later, was hilarious, though she kept on assuring us that it was all very well for us to laugh, but it hadn't been in the *least* funny at the time! Possibly not. But it had us shrieking at second-hand.

*

The four of us would picnic in the woods, and sometimes, lying out on the warm sunny hillsides, we would discuss the latest world news and the possibility of war. Jess and I were still inclined to be reassured by that 'peace in our time' speech, but George and Andrew were pessimistic. They took a poor view of all these 'scraps of paper' that were continually being signed by diplomats and heads of state. The British had signed a defensive agreement with Turkey – and Italy had responded by signing up with Germany. Yet another Anglo-Polish pact had been signed in London by von Ribbentrop; Prime Minister Chamberlain had reaffirmed our pledge to Poland, and Germany had appalled everyone by signing one with Russia (Nazism and Communism cosying up in the same bed? It was *impossible!*). 'Bits of paper,' said George scornfully. 'They'll tear them up in less time than it took to write them. You'll see!'

We celebrated my birthday with a picnic lunch in the woods and that night, with the addition of six or eight mutual friends, a dinner followed by a dance at the Club. A day or two later, invited by friends of George's, we left Ranikhet to spend a few days at Almora as guests of the Gurkhas stationed there, who were celebrating a yearly 'Week' in commemoration of some regimental triumph.

Almora was a small station roughly thirty miles from Ranikhet, along a narrow mountain road that winds and twists along the steep slopes of largely treeless hillsides that the sun has bleached to the uniform tint of a digestive biscuit. We were met by a Gurkha officer and put up in a large, two-storeyed wooden house that would have accommodated a far larger party and must have been the equivalent of a State guest-house. This makes me think that Almora and its surroundings must once have belonged to some small Hill Rajah, since the house was certainly far too large and rambling to be a Dâk bungalow.

The officer, having shown us to our room and told us that someone would collect us after we had had time to wash and unpack, hurried off to greet other arrivals who were apparently being put up in the houses of British officers which lay out of sight behind a curve of the hillside. Either Andrew or George (possibly both) had brought a bearer along, and this Admirable Crichton dealt with the unpacking, and chased up the skeleton staff that went with our outsize guest-house to see that cans of hot water were produced. And presently the young man who had greeted us reappeared and took us along to the cantonment proper, where we were introduced to the Colonel and his officers and their wives and the rest of their guests.

The whole cantonment was *en fête* and there were strings of flags and a large *shamiana*,* in the shade of which the guests sat down to a resplendent tea and were given a list of all the entertainments in store. These started with a large cocktail party that evening, for which we were allowed to disperse so that we could change into evening dress. No sooner was the cocktail party over than we were all ushered in to dinner. And when that was over, there was a dance, and I'm not too sure that there wasn't a 'Beating the Retreat' somewhere, for I have a fleeting memory of bagpipes playing 'The Road to the Isles'. But my recollections of that visit to Almora are very muddled and hazy, for it had been a very long day. The four of us gave up around one o'clock, and retreated, unobserved, to our commodious guest-house.

We all slept late the following morning. We would have slept even later if one of the Gurkha officers hadn't woken us with a top-priority message from HQ to Andrew and George, recalling them immediately to their unit. I remember George's face as he read it. And Andrew's. They stared at each other for what seemed like a long time and was probably only a minute, while their faces stiffened. All at once they no longer looked like the carefree happy-go-lucky pair of holiday-makers I had been laughing and partying with, but two much older people. Older and grimmer. George went to the window and called down to his bearer on the verandah below, telling him to see that there was enough petrol in the car and to pack the suitcases, because we had to get back to Ranikhet as soon as possible: '*Jaldi-se. Taze-jaldi!*' ('Quickly. Very quickly.')

'Why must we?' I asked. 'What's happened?'

'Don't be silly!' said George impatiently. 'War, of course. What did you think? Are you two coming back with us or would you prefer to stay here for the rest of the "Week"? – I'm sure we can arrange for someone to give you a lift.'

Well, naturally we opted for going back with them and seeing them off. After swallowing a hasty breakfast and making our apologies to our host, we returned to Ranikhet a good deal faster than we had come.

Once there, while the boys were rushing round the town settling accounts and paying bills, I painted a picture of a pin-up girl on the lines

* Marquee.

284

of the 'Petty Girl' who used to appear in the *Saturday Evening Post*, for George to take into battle with him. Not that I believed that there would be any battles. Just because a couple of Army officers on leave had been recalled to their unit it didn't mean that war was about to break out. It was just a precaution. But when I said as much to George (in an attempt to reassure myself rather than him) he told me not to be a half-witted ostrich, and asked me if I really thought that he and Andrew were the only ones who had been recalled. 'I'll bet you anything,' said George, 'that thousands of chaps all over the globe are being whipped back to their jobs this minute. We've all been expecting it for months. Don't you *ever* listen to the radio?'

'What about "Peace in Our Time"?' I said.

'Piece of paper!' sniffed George. 'I told you that before. If it hasn't been torn up already, it will be within a day or two.'

They left. And a few days later, on the third of September, we heard the tired voice of our Prime Minister informing the Empire that we were at war. The little piece of paper that had promised 'Peace in Our Time' had, after all, been torn up and consigned to Herr Hitler's waste-paper basket.

The announcement had been made at 11 a.m., Greenwich Mean Time. But Ranikhet did not hear it until much later in the day, and I don't remember how I heard it. I think someone in the Club must have told me, but I don't know who, only that I felt stunned and stupid. I went for a long walk on the road that looks down on the Club and, having passed the entrance to the hotel, goes on to meander round a steep, forest-clad hill that was a favourite walk of Bets's and mine, because it reminded us of Simla. Bets wasn't there to walk with me that evening, for she and baby Richard had left a week or so earlier to help WHP move house to his new posting in Lucknow. But today I did not miss her, because I wanted to be alone to think. And to remember . . .

To remember very clearly my six-year-old self asking Tacklow with a mixture of awe and disbelief if it was true that there was a war on *now*, this very minute. And being horrified when he told me that there was and tried to explain why. But I hadn't been interested in 'why'. Only appalled by the discovery that War – in other words grown-ups, *hundreds of grown-ups* killing each other – was not something that only happened in books or the tales that professional story-tellers told in the bazaars, but was actually happening *now*, in real life.

I remembered other things too. The wounded men who had been sent to recover from their wounds in various convalescent soldiers' homes in Simla. Mother and her friends organizing picnic parties for convalescent 'Tommies'. Rolling bandages for the Red Cross and knitting endless numbers of wool mufflers, balaclava helmets and fingerless gloves for the troops in the trenches. And Sir Charles's brother, in the guise of a tin-helmeted Hun, spreading mayhem among the amateur actresses who wore sashes labelled 'Belgium', 'Serbia' and so on in the course of a patriotic pageant on the stage of Simla's Gaiety Theatre.

The pageant, and any number of other fund-raising activities, had all been in aid of the 'War Effort' – the 'War to end War'. I suppose a good many people believed that. I certainly had. The 'Great War' had dominated my childhood. For one thing, if it had not broken out I would never have had that conversation with Tacklow, because Bets and I would, like Bill, have been back in England in a boarding school. Everything would have been different – even the songs of my youth. No 'Pack up Your Troubles in Your Old Kit Bag, and Smile, Smile, Smile'. No 'It's a Long Way to Tipperary', or 'Keep the Home Fires Burning' and all those others.

Yet the war that had brought such appalling sorrow and tragedy to uncounted thousands of people all over the world had given me a wonderfully happy childhood. It remained so clear in my memory that the gap between the past and the present seemed incredibly short. I had even set the opening chapter of my first ever novel, *Six Bars at Seven*, in the few weeks before the end of the Great War. My hero was a youthful Second-Lieutenant who, having fallen asleep in a bomb-damaged château 'somewhere in France', wakes up to find that a surprise attack, and a subsequent Allied retreat, have left him stranded in enemy-held territory.

If I could remember the Great War as clearly as that, then there must be any number of men who had fought in it and who were going to find themselves fighting again – many of them, this time, alongside their sons. How could they *bear* it? How could their wives and mothers bear it? Only twenty-one years ago! And now back again to those terrible trenches . . . It wasn't fair. It wasn't *possible*!

The sun had set and dusk was falling by the time I returned to the hotel, and though the sky still held some of the colours that had recently blazed there, they had faded now to a soft opalescence in which the first stars were barely visible, while the moon that had been full only a day or two before we left so light-heartedly for Almora was rising slowly from behind the ranges of the Gharwal hills. On the high bank to the left of the path that led down to the hotel's entrance, cosmos had replaced the zinnias of early summer, and the dusk was sweet with their distinctive, polleny scent.

I stopped on the path to sniff it nostalgically, and in doing so became aware of a movement among the mass of pink and white flowers above and a little ahead of me. Something or someone was making its way down the bank of cosmos, and since there was no breath of wind, and it was managing to move soundlessly through that feathery jungle, I stayed where I was; curious to see whether it was an animal – a jackal or a hill fox – or (remembering how Bets and I used to make secret tunnels through the cosmos at the Rookery) one of the children in the hotel.

It was none of them. And it was just as well that I had stopped when I did, because seconds later, still without making a sound, a full-grown leopard sprang down on to the path immediately in front of me. Checking briefly on seeing me, it gave me a long, yellow stare, decided that I posed no threat, looked away and took off again, crossing the path and disappearing down the slope with the speed and grace of a swallow.

The whole episode could not have taken more than a minute at most, and in all that time I don't remember hearing the slightest sound beyond the normal murmur of voices from the hotel and the servants' quarters behind it, and, occasionally, from the road above. Night falls so quickly in the East that by the time I dared to move again, the hotel, in which only a scattering of lights had been switched on when I started down the path, now glowed brightly from every door and window, while its grounds and buildings, which only moments ago had been grey in the dusk, were suddenly bathed in silver and blotched with black shadows as the moonlight gathered strength. There was no sign of the leopard, and I had no idea which way it had gone or whether it was lying low in one of those black, sharp-edged shadows. But with lighting-up time the hotel servants had begun to appear on the verandahs and paths, and what with the general air of bustle and activity that had succeeded that curious twilight interval, I managed to summon up enough courage to return to my room running into my room-bearer *en route* . . .

Still on edge from my close encounter with a leopard, I told him about it. But when I urged him to warn the other servants to be on their guard, he replied cheerfully that I had nothing to worry about. Everyone knew that there were very many leopards in these hills, and that they did no harm unless wounded or attacked, or with cubs. Since the Miss-Sahib was unlikely to meet one in that condition, she need have no fear; and having practically patted me on the head and said 'There, there – what a fuss about nothing!' he trotted away, leaving me feeling reassured but exceedingly small.

George and Andrew having departed almost as swiftly as the leopard, I dined alone and went to bed early. And so, for me, ended the day on which the Second World War began.

I don't remember how or where I met Rupert, but I imagine that it was, again, Jess who introduced us because his regiment was at that time stationed at Cawnpore, where the Binnie family were temporarily ensconced. But since Rupert too preferred blondes, he may well have introduced himself. A keen golfer, he managed to interest me in the game, and I took to it with enthusiasm. The course at Ranikhet was a paradise for beginners. It could have been designed with the 'Complete Rabbit' in mind since, provided one hits the ball, it almost can't *help* landing on the green, which is not all that far from the starting point, but slightly below it on the hillside immediately opposite you. The fact that between the player and the green lies a deep valley into which your ball will roll if you don't hit it fair and square doesn't really matter much, because you'll have to toil up hill and down without ceasing if you want to get round the course. But that first swipe (unless, of course, you miss the ball or merely top it) is almost bound to cross the grassy crevice at your feet, and land you somewhere on the flattened saucer of hillside that is waiting to receive it, giving you an initial surge of triumph that does wonders for your confidence. I actually became quite an adequate player. But only on that miniature switchback of a course among the mountains. When I tried playing it on the plains, I was a disaster.

I became very fond of Rupert, and there were times when I would have given almost anything I possessed to have a talk with Tacklow about him and ask for advice. But I always ended up realizing that Tacklow would have told me that I was quite old enough now to make up my own mind, and what about that test sentence: 'I'll be ready in five minutes.' Did that still stand? Had I tried it? Yes, of *course* I'd tried it! But somehow it didn't work any longer, for I still wavered. I was still in love with love, still hoping that some day, one day, that legendary Prince Charming would come riding past on his white horse and scoop me up off the pavement. That is, if such a person existed, which I was beginning to doubt.

Jess's husband, Steve, who worked for ICI, came up on leave and took Jess away on a trek to one of the famous pilgrimage places among the high mountains. And Bets too having left, I would have found myself with a lot of time on my hands if it had not been for Rupert, who filled the gap in my social life for the term of his leave. I discovered that being one of a twosome was not nearly as much fun as one of a foursome, or, even better, one of a crowd as I had been before the arrival of Andrew and George. Still, as half of a twosome I was never without a dancing partner.

Rupert escorted me to dinner-dances at the Club, played golf with me several times a week, drove me down miles of winding hill road to a popular picnicking spot on the river at its foot, where there were stretches of silver sand and deep, clear pools in which one could bathe. There, incidentally, he took the very first photograph of me as a blonde. This snapshot was to appear many years later on the back of one of my whodunnits.

I don't know if Jess was matchmaking or not, but she invited me to spend a week or ten days with her that cold weather, as soon as I could fit it in. The invitation ensured that Rupert and I would be seeing each other in the near future, *unless* (a word that must now be added to every plan) unless or until his regiment was sent off to the war. For the enemy had opened hostilities immediately and murderously, by torpedoing the *Athenia*, a British liner full of women and children, neutrals, non-combatants, home-going Americans who were hoping to take their children or themselves to safety until the war (if there *had* to be a war) was over.

I remember hearing the news of that tragedy only the day after Chamberlain's announcement that Britain and Germany were at war, and thinking what an unbelievably stupid thing for Hitler's gangsters to have done. If they didn't know that the passengers on that ship were non-combatants their Intelligence Department must have been staffed by boneheads. For there is little doubt that a similar sinking of a Cunard liner, the *Lusitania*, during the last war had helped to swing American public opinion in favour of supporting the Allies. To get in the first blow of this war by sinking a ship such as the *Athenia* must have sent a shudder through the entire world. Perhaps that was what it was meant to do? If so, it certainly showed us what we were in for: this was going to be a truly brutal war. And it was. It began with a brutal act, and ended with one – the atomic bomb.

Chapter 28

After Ranikhet, where the evenings and the early mornings had begun to hold an invigorating nip in the air, Lucknow seemed intolerably hot and dry. But I knew that once the cold weather set in it would return to being the city of which Kipling – who lived there as a cub-reporter – describing it in *Kim*, says: 'There is no city . . . more beautiful in her garish style than Lucknow, whether you see her from the bridge over the river, or from the top of the Imambara looking down on the gilt umbrellas of the Chutter Manzil and the trees in which the town is embedded.'

It was then, and I hope it still is, one of the leafiest of cities, and 'garish' is right. I don't think she could have changed very much since Kipling first saw her. The school that Kim attended, the famous La Martinière – which has the distinction of being the only school in the world to possess a Battle Honour – certainly had not. The Pardey house was quite near to it, and Bets and I used to walk past it of an evening.

It was while I was in Lucknow that some of our boxes, put into storage in Delhi a good ten years earlier, were sent for, under the mistaken impression that WHP would not be moved to another posting for at least three years. In the event, owing to so many of their young men having hurried off to enlist – WHP among them – the posting and re-posting of Burma-Shell staff became every bit as erratic as the Army ones. My brother-in-law, having failed to pass the Army medical tests, had supposed that his firm would leave him where he was for a few years. But it was not to be. Bets had barely had time to settle down in Lucknow before her husband was transferred to the Calcutta office. That was some time after I left them. And well after the boxes from Delhi had been opened.

There were not many of them, and only one was of any interest to us. It was a small tin-lined wooden box, additionally protected by Mother with a stout covering of that coarse cloth woven from hemp and known in India as *tart*, on which she had painted our names and a number. We cut the stitches and wrenched out the rusty nails in mounting excitement, for the contents of this one case were more valuable than rubies and we would not have swapped them for the Crown Jewels: Moko and Teddy! . . . Moko, my beloved life-sized monkey, who had once belonged to my brother Bill and had been annexed by me when Bill outgrew stuffed toys, and Teddy, the rotund, ginger-brown teddy-bear that was the joy of Bets's heart in the days when she and I played at being 'Mrs Jones and Mrs Snooks', and Moko and Teddy were our loved and obstreperous offspring.

They had been packed away carefully and brought out to India in the hope that one of these days we would get married and have children of our own to inherit these invaluable treasures. I had failed to do so and was considered to be firmly on the shelf. But Bets had a baby son, and now at last we could open that wooden box and hand over Teddy to the legal heir . . .

Too late, too late – we had been beaten to it by a different kind of bear, the voracious little insects that were known as 'woolly-bears'. Two or three of them must have sneaked in among the packing paper and proliferated at an alarming rate, chewing away at the contents of that box, thriving and raising families until there was barely anything you could recognize as the original contents. Certainly nothing that was re-usable. We almost wept at the horrid sight and ended up carrying the tin-lined box and what little was left of the contents – which amounted to barely more than a pile of dust, two glass eyes (Teddy) and a couple of boot-buttons (Moko), plus about a million little woolly-bear corpses and at least five million eggs the size of a grain of dust – into the backyard, where we gave poor Moko and Teddy a Maharajah's funeral, complete with piles of logs which we soaked in kerosene. It was a sad but most impressive send-off.

My only other memory of this particular visit to Lucknow is of being woken up in the middle of the night by the unmistakable roaring of a tiger coming, apparently, from the back garden. This would have scared me more than somewhat if I hadn't been warned about it by Bets, who told me that the tigers were actually safely behind bars in the zoo in which poor Angie had died, which was a long way off. But that when the wind was blowing from a certain direction, the sound travelled clearly between a high, curved wall behind the tigers' enclosure and the wall at the bottom of Bets's garden. This explanation reassured me, though not entirely. (I still used to wonder if, *this* time, one of the tigers hadn't managed to escape?)

Since Cawnpore was not much more than fifty miles from Lucknow I had fixed a date with Jess for my visit to her, and one of Bets's friends offered to give me a lift there. The Binnies had a charming bungalow, and they and the faithful Rupert gave me a lovely time – a good deal more enjoyable than my last one in Cawnpore, with Gerry Ross.

I had not seen Mother for some months, for she had been in Srinagar throughout the spring and summer, and she had not taken it at all badly when I wrote to break the news that I had become a 'bottle blonde', merely observing that she wasn't sure that it would suit me, and that Sandy would have a fit: 'You know how prim and proper he can be!' (Sandy had invited us both to spend the winter with him.) She didn't mention the matter again and I began to feel a bit anxious as to how she would react when she actually saw me.

There was also another consideration, one that had never occurred to me when I sploshed on all that peroxide. The expense. I had thought I looked terrific for the first week or ten days of being blonde, but at the end of that the roots of my hair began to look distinctly grubby as it grew out and grew darker and darker and more obtrusive. Had I been able to afford visits to a professional hairdresser once every ten days, or, better still, once a week, all would have been well. As it was, I had to buy more peroxide and ammonia, and deal with it myself, and after a while it began to look dull and strawish, because it's difficult to paint peroxide on to one's own head without sploshing it all over the place, and it wasn't too long before I ended up as a platinum-blonde, which didn't suit me at all.

So what with one thing and another, I decided that the aggro involved in trying to stay a blonde was simply not worth it, and I made an appointment with Jess's hairdresser to turn me back to being mouse-brown. The girl was a bit apprehensive, since the dyes she possessed did not include the colour I was after, but in the end I persuaded her to let me mix together several of the ones in stock – something that she was convinced wouldn't work.

'Whoever *heard* of such a thing! Oh well, if you *insist*, but I take *no* responsibility for it so don't blame me if it turns out to look like streaks of different colours – or bright blue or green.' She need not have worried. It was a terrific success, and couldn't have looked glossier and in better condition. When Mother saw it she was so impressed that she actually played with the idea of dyeing her own hair, which by now was rapidly becoming white. 'I always thought,' said Mother, 'that dyed hair looked dull and dead and obviously dyed. But yours looks simply wonderful! *No one* would guess that it's dyed.'

Bill and Joy, complete with a baby daughter called Suzan, were back in a bungalow in Delhi and invited me to pay them a visit to be introduced to my first niece. Bill, like so many Indian Army officers, had been on home leave when a letter like the one that had ordered Andrew and George to return to their units immediately was delivered to Bill at his in-laws' house on the Isle of Wight, where he and Joy had been staying. It arrived, I gather, with the effect of a bombshell, since Bill (like me) had been putting far too much faith in those 'bits of paper' that George had been so scathing about. This bit of paper could *not* be torn up.

It had been headed: MOVEMENT ORDERS I O M O I India Office S W I. P A R T I. (Regular Officers on leave or duty.) And it notified Captain W. Kaye, IA, that he was to report not later than twelve noon on the first of September 1939, to the Movement Control Office, Command Headquarters, Chester, where 'no official accommodation would be available' (find your own, in fact!). Furthermore: 'No arrangement can be made for your family to accompany you; nor can any information be furnished as to when they may be able to return to India or Burma.'

Joy did not waste time wringing her hands. She and any number of devoted wives, many of them pregnant and others, like my indomitable sister-in-law, with very new babies (her first-born, Suzan, was barely six weeks old!), realized immediately that this meant war and that the moment it was declared they stood little or no chance of rejoining their men. They therefore descended on the shipping offices in droves and grabbed any berth available on any ship going east, even if it meant travelling steerage.

Nothing was going to induce Joy to be parted from 'Beloved', and that was that. The only ship that had a few spare berths was an Italian one sailing from Tripoli, and the minute Bill left, Joy packed a small holdall with anything that Suzan might need, plus the minimum in the way of clothing for herself, took the next ferry boat from the island to the mainland, and caught a train to Dover. She got herself across the Channel and to Paris, where, she said, there was a most unhelpful British Consul – I presume the poor man must have been badgered to death by anxious young wives bent on being *vivandières* and sticking to their men. In the end she managed to get on to an overcrowded train – a series of them, I think – that eventually landed her in Italy.

Joy said the journey across France to the Italian border was sheer hell, made more so by the French, who could not, she insisted, have been unkinder or more unhelpful. She had not expected this from people who were our allies, and had begun to dread what it would be like in Italy. But the Italians couldn't have been nicer to this convoy of exhausted British women who (very properly, in their opinion) were following their husbands.

From then on, their entire journey was comparatively trouble-free. Joy actually made it back to India before Bill. Quite an achievement, I reckon, and worthy of a medal; if medals were given for this type of thing. If they had been, a good many women could have lined up for one, the equivalent of the Victoria Cross going to a girl whose name I can no longer remember. She, like Joy, realized at once that the recall of her darling husband meant war, and she didn't wait to find out if she was right. She was expecting her first baby in the near future, but that didn't stop her from taking off at top speed for London and the India Office, where she wheedled them into giving her one of the last passages in a cargo-boat leaving within a couple of days for Calcutta, via the Atlantic and Pacific route. She caught it, and set off, and a day or two after war was declared the ship was torpedoed. Luckily she was among the survivors, and no sooner had they landed than she was back at the War Office and, I gather, making such a nuisance of herself that if only to get rid of her they wangled her a berth on a ship going east via the Mediterranean. She embarked again. And was torpedoed once more . . .

Put ashore in some Mediterranean country, she managed, for the third time, to get herself on to a ship that took her through the Red Sea and across the Indian Ocean, via Ceylon, to Calcutta – where she learned that her husband's regiment had been moved to Quetta – roughly 2,000 miles away on the far side of the sub-continent. Undeterred, she caught the next train and arrived in Quetta . . . to find that her telegram to her husband had crossed one of his telling her to stay put, because the regiment were about to leave for – guess where? – Calcutta! She was just in time to travel back there with him. And half-way across India that baby, doubtless fed up by all this fuss and bother, and deciding that enough was enough, jumped the gun and arrived unexpectedly, but in excellent form, in their railway carriage, its entry into the world being assisted by its father and the Regimental MO.

I never heard the end of that story, and frankly, I don't want to, in case that girl's man was one of the many who never came back from Burma, or wherever it was that his regiment was sent. I do hope and pray that he survived. But if he didn't, at least he and his young wife had a few days together and he had been able to see and hold his child.

Bill's return journey was far less exciting, though it had had its moments. Arriving as ordered at Command Headquarters in Chester, in company with a horde of I A O s,* he and they were sent by train, on 2 September, for an 'Unknown Destination', which turned out to be the SS *Duchess of Bedford*, one of several liners that had been commandeered to take 2,000 military and civil officers back to India. The *Duchess* was docked somewhere on the Clyde, and did not sail until 5 September. By that time war had been declared and the *Athenia* had been torpedoed. But no one was allowed off the ship, or to communicate in any way with friends or family ashore. Bill, who had been put in a dark and pokey four-berth cabin on D-deck, was greatly relieved when he was suddenly moved up to a larger and more comfortable one on B-deck, thereby evicting a Lieutenant Hamilton because Bill, being a Captain, outranked him.

Their darkened ship, by this time in convoy with ten other liners and escorted by seven or eight cruisers (and later, off the south coast of Ireland, a battleship), moved out late at night, silently and with every light blacked out. Legend has it that as they moved down the Irish Sea they met the Irish mailboat with all her lights ablaze, and that the shock she got at finding herself at dead of night in the middle of a ghostly convoy of warships put years on her Captain and crew.

The voyage in those overcrowded ships was hideously uncomfortable and not without its exciting moments, for the convoy was twice attacked by enemy submarines, one of which was said to have been sunk. Lifebelts had to be worn at all times, and since blackout conditions were the rule, all windows and portholes were shut between darkness and dawn (the latter being kept hermetically sealed throughout the entire voyage). According to Bill, the temperature between decks in the Red Sea in September could not be imagined.

Docking at Bombay on the 27th, they found that the Taj Mahal Hotel

* Indian Army Officers.

had been turned into an Officers' Mess. It continued to be used as one for several days while these flocks of homing pigeons were sorted out, provided with rail warrants, and booked on to trains that would take them to their various destinations. As one of them wrote at that time: 'The three or four delightful days that most of us spent there, largely at Government expense, fully made up for any inconvenience we may have suffered on the voyage.'

An example of the way in which the Taj and Bombay 'pushed out the boat' for the passengers of the *Duchess* was a dinner and dance which included a cabaret show and ended with the management offering a magnum of champagne as a prize for the best performance by an amateur. A large number of enthusiastic amateurs, all of them pleasantly inebriated, entered for the contest, which was won hands down by the young Lieutenant who had lost his berth in the cabin on B-deck owing to the superior rank of Captain Bill Kaye.

This entrant for the Magnum-stakes put on a performance that was described to me by a dear friend, Robbie Barcroft, as one of the best he had seen in years. 'He was as tight as an owl, of course,' explained Robbie, 'or he wouldn't have done it. He just got up and strolled across the ballroom with a glass of champagne in one hand, asked the leader of the band if they could play some fairly recent dance tune, and when the chap nodded, got up on the stage, grasped the microphone in the other hand, and began to sing some exceedingly *risqué* songs in French. Only it wasn't French. It was some rubbish that he made up as he went along that sounded *exactly* like French, and he sang it as someone like Maurice Chevalier might have done in a late-night cabaret in Paris. It was the gestures and the expression which made you think he was saying something terrifically *risqué*,' explained Robbie. 'He'd pause and look at the audience as if it was unbelievably shocking, and they fell about laughing at cracks that he hadn't made, in a language that they didn't understand. It brought the house down. I laughed until my jaws ached. We all did. He could have taken twenty encores if he'd wanted to, and he won easily by a unanimous show of hands. It was a splendid end to the night's entertainment!'

On the morning after my arrival in Delhi I made my way to the office of a man in Intelligence, who had worked under Tacklow, and asked if I could be of any use in the way of war-work in that Department. I thought perhaps I could do something in the way of propaganda. Line drawings. Posters, perhaps? He had seen some of my murals in the Secunderabad Club, and had bought several of my 'little pics' at art exhibitions, and I ended up being engaged to do illustrations in a propaganda magazine aimed at the Middle East – on the same terms that Tacklow, long before I was born, had been given by Field Marshal Lord Kitchener of Khartoum, who wished him to produce and edit a magazine for the Indian Troops. The terms being: 'Find your own time and no pay.'

Well, that suited me, because it would not restrict me to staying in one place. Provided they always knew where I was they could send me a list of the material they needed and the latest day on which I must deliver. The only snag, which I discovered later, was when they asked for weapons to be illustrated, for I was not familiar with guns of any sort, and had to get hold of photographs to copy. As far as I remember the illustrations were always in black and white, with the occasional extra line-block in red on the cover, or the heading of a story. A list of subjects that needed illustrating arrived a few days later, and I laid in a supply of my favourite hot-press paper, indian ink, mapping pens, pencils and rubbers, and anything else in the art line that might soon become scarce or unavailable if the submarine war intensified.

Mother had done the same, buying her paints and paper from Lamberts the Chemists in Srinagar before she left Kashmir to join me in Delhi. We spent a few days there together and then, accompanied by Kadera, for whom we had to get a passport and presumably a visa, we set out on our travels again, war or no war. This time, via Bombay, for Persia.

❋ 8 ❋

Persian Interlude

Chapter 29

Sandy had been posted as Vice-Consul to Khorramshah in Persia and wanted his bungalow (which he described as 'a tip') taken in hand and turned into something more fitting the home of a Vice-Consul.

Funds were on hand for this purpose, and he wanted us to come for the cold weather and to stay on for as long as we liked after we'd 'tished the place up'. I think we were both enthralled by the idea of living in Persia; and equally enthralled by the prospect of taking the Vice-Consulate in hand. So we accepted joyfully, setting out on a small coastal steamer to travel, via a brief stop at Karachi, up the Persian Gulf to the oil town of Abadan, which stands at the mouth of the Shatt-el-Arab waterway.

It was a slow and idyllic voyage. No shred of cloud or breath of breeze came to ruffle the glassy blue of sea and sky as we steamed across the Gulf of Cambray, past the little Portuguese islands of Daman and Dui and the long western shores of Gujerat and Cutch, to cross the Tropic of Cancer and steam up the Gulf of Oman past Jask and through the Strait of Ormuz, into the Persian Gulf and some of the most godforsaken country I have ever seen.

It probably doesn't look nearly as bad now, because the oil-rich countries have, I am told, made miles of the desert lands bloom like the rose, with the aid of desalination plants and such-like modern inventions. But, at the time I am writing about, the hills and the mountain ranges behind them were grey and bleached and lifeless. Not a speck of green or even the skeleton of a dead tree broke the miles of waterless rock and shale. Nor was there any colour in it – just grey. Ash-grey, as though the once liquid rock had only recently cooled.

A more desolate and inhospitable land I have yet to see. And just to make the landscape even less alluring, the sea here was no longer blue, but green with the dull green of over-boiled spinach, and alive with water-snakes – hundreds of them, weaving and writhing through the

301

water in which, on the previous days, there had been platoons of jellyfish, families of smiling, frisking dolphins, shoals of shimmering unidentified fish and flights of flying-fish.

I asked the ship's Captain if the Gulf was always full of snakes, and he said no, only at certain times of the year, and probably only after a particularly large hatch of them. He himself had only seen them in this quantity once before in all his years of plying those waters, and didn't care if he never did so again. He believed, he said, that they were considered a delicacy among some of the Gulf people.

We ran out of the 'snake belt' eventually, not far from the little island of Bahrain – then an almost barren and practically unknown dot on the map – and passed through a fleet of fishing boats whose occupants called out greetings to us and held out their outstretched palms in the manner of beggars soliciting alms. But when I remarked acidly that they couldn't possibly catch a coin at that range, the Captain laughed and said they weren't begging, they were showing off their day's catch. 'Oh, fish,' I said. 'Nothing so ordinary: pearls,' replied the Captain. One of the neighbouring islands was the headquarters of the Gulf's pearl fishery. Not a very big one, but its pearls were greatly prized.

One casualty of that dream-like voyage was Mother's anti-rheumatic charm, which had not only cured her rheumatism but, we were to discover, ensured that neither that nor any form of arthritis would ever trouble her again. That little white floret had died, as the doctor had told her it would unless it had a glassful of fresh milk every day. And alas, after the first day, there was no fresh milk available until we reached Abadan. I have since been told that the doctor's magic floret was obviously only the germ of yoghurt. And I suppose this is so. Yet I have never seen anything quite like it; all the other 'seeds' of yoghurt have been much smaller than this one, and none have acted so instantly. Nor has the cure been permanent, as it was with Mother. I have a feeling that this curious organism must be the special yoghurt that some tribe or other from the wilds of Soviet Russia are supposed to live on, which enables them to live until they are a hundred and seventy or thereabouts.

Sandy, plus a horrid stink, met us as our ship docked in Abadan. He appeared to be in the best of spirits and, noticing that Mother held a strongly scented handkerchief to her nose (the stink met us from a good half-mile down the river), apologized for it, adding that she couldn't expect anything else from an oil refinery and that all the 'oil chaps' and their families didn't even notice it after the first few days. But it wasn't like this in Khorramshah. Which proved to be true, except on those occasions (fortunately rare) when the wind was blowing towards us from Abadan, and we would hastily rush round the house shutting every door and window, and lighting joss-sticks to try and counter that pervasive nastiness.

Sandy had brought his own car, and the Vice-Consulate one, complete with chauffeur, to take Kadera and the luggage. And off we went through tidy streets and rows of whitewashed houses with wide verandahs, each in its own square of garden shaded with flame trees and bushes of bougainvillaea and hibiscus. It looked like a typical colonial town, except for the tall blocks of offices and all the towering modern machinery that goes with a refinery. We saw a club house, complete with tennis courts and a swimming-pool, a hospital, shops – and then suddenly the desert.

Miles and miles of nothing but sand. No roads, no landmarks. Nothing to guide one. This must have been the kind of landscape that Shelley visualized when he wrote in one of his sonnets: 'boundless and bare, the lone and level sands stretch far away'. They did indeed. I remember remarking to Sandy that at least there could be no traffic accidents in a countryside as flat as a pancake in every direction, and with enough room for about a couple of hundred tanks to drive in line if they felt like it.

'You'd be surprised!' retorted Sandy. 'But then you don't know the Iranians.' He went on to tell me that there were more car crashes on the desert routes than there were on Calcutta's main street, Chowringi, any day of the week. When I protested, he explained that the local population all drove at top speed and with no regard for road rules (he said there weren't any) or, of course, speed limits. Every driver considered that with enormous stretches of desert to choose from, the other fellow could get out of the way.

They all, said Sandy, drove like Mr Toad, '*poop*-pooping!' on their horns while keeping a foot well down on the accelerator. It appeared to be a matter of personal honour not to give way to the other driver – even when it became clear that unless one of them did, they were indubitably booked for an almighty smash in which (depending on the size of the vehicles involved) anything between two and twenty passengers were bound to be killed and the rest badly injured.

Even when a driver did lose his nerve at the last moment, the move was just as likely to spell death and destruction, because with unrestricted space to manoeuvre in, one never knew in which direction the loser would decide to swerve. And then of course there was always the chance that both drivers would lose their nerve simultaneously, which could lead to a horrendous pile-up. But since in either or any case there was always the consoling thought that since one's fate is tied about one's neck from birth, and Allah has decreed that 'what is written is written', the whole affair was ordained from the beginning and so could not possibly have been avoided.

Sandy told us many tales of the reigning Shahanshah, Reza Shah Pahlavi, who had risen from being an officer in a Persian Cossack regiment to become Prime Minister of Iran, and from there, when the absentee ruler of the country had been deposed by the National Assembly, had been elected to take over the throne. Sandy was of the opinion that Reza Shah was just what the country needed, but that it would be interesting to see how long he would last the course. Because he had already trodden heavily on the toes of the Mulvies. 'The trouble with that chap,' said Sandy, 'is that he's as tough as old boots and does exactly as he pleases.'

Apparently the Imam of the largest mosque in Tehran had been criticizing the Shah's behaviour for some time past, under the mistaken impression that even the Shahanshah would not dare take action against a holy man. Reza had ignored the initial attacks, but when they became more and more insulting, he drove into Tehran, unaccompanied and armed only with a whip, and, marching into the mosque, dragged the Imam out into the middle of the courtyard, and flogged him, threw the victim down the outer steps and drove off – no one raising a finger to help or hinder.

Chapter 30

~꠹꠹꠹~

I can't remember how long it took us to drive across the desert from Abadan to Khorramshah,* though I must have made that journey many times. I only remember the relief of seeing greenness and trees and water again after those miles of greyish-brown sand. Sandy's house and the large and more pretentious house in which the British Consul lived were on the far side of the river as one approached Khorramshah from the direction of Abadan.

The house, when we reached it, was a sprawling and vaguely unattractive building, faintly suggestive of a Dâk bungalow, with the same flat roofs, high, whitewashed rooms and french windows opening on to stone-paved verandahs. The furniture was of the usual Army quarters pattern, and there was very little of it. In fact one might have been back in any cantonment house in India. Except for one thing. Here every room sported a hideous matting 'dado' that covered the lower four feet of the wall and was fastened to it by thin batons of wood in a criss-cross pattern, topped by a single thicker length of wood which managed to suggest a picture-rail that had slipped too far down the wall. I could see at once why Sandy had sent out that urgent SOS, urging us to come and make the Vice-Consul's house fit to live in. But when I said so, adding that we could make a start by stripping off those hideous matting splash-boards, Sandy shook his head sadly and said, 'No such luck.'

It seems that this was the first thing he himself had tried to do when he had first seen the house. Only to discover (as I did when I tried it) that those hideous splash-board things had a purpose. They were there to disguise the far more hideous stains of salt, leaching up from the ground: the Persians had never heard of such things as damp courses (nor had the British for that matter, not until fairly late in the day) and

---

* A'ba-*darn*. Khour-ram-*shah*.

305

the sand in this part of the Persian desert was full of salt. That was why it was so hard to grow anything in it, except along the river banks.

Later I removed a bit of splash-board to make certain I couldn't disguise it some better way. But the salt stains were beyond hope, all crusted and peeling, as though the walls had caught some terrible disease. Sandy said the surface had been scraped off many times and repainted, but sooner or later the salt won. Even the matting that hid the stains had to be replaced at fairly frequent intervals; but so far, it had proved to be better than anything else that had been tried. So we abandoned that, and gave our attention to the rest of the house. And I have to say, with pride, that Mother and I did wonders with it.

Almost *nothing* was available in that unalluring segment of the earth, and we had to make do with what little there was. We went down to the workshop where the furniture was made, and, sticking firmly to the idea of something simple, designed a sofa in three sections which, put together, made a large, curved and very comfortable piece of furniture on which five people could sit with plenty of room to spare, and six could sit without feeling squashed – very useful for parties. The chairs were made to match, and upholsterers were set to work to cover them with a heavy, white knobbly-surfaced material which was hand-woven locally, washed like a rag and was very cheap. An equally cheap form of carpeting was produced, I was interested to discover, by the prisoners in a local gaol.

Shaggy white sheepskin rugs were also obtainable locally, and since the only wall paint available in the bazaar was whitewash, we had a really lovely white drawing-room. I covered one door, the one that led to the hall and the dining-room, with a single slab of three-ply, and then muralled it with a Chinese-style picture of birds on a branch of a flowering cherry tree. And Mother had cushion covers made out of some remnants of the heavy white satin that we bought on one of our expeditions to Basrah, in the famous covered bazaar. The curtains were made of the same knobbly white material as the sofa and chair covers, and Syrie Maugham herself would not have been ashamed to own it.

The dining-room presented a more difficult problem, for facing the windward side of the house it got the full force of the monsoon rains, and here the salt stains came well above the wickerwork splash-board that was supposed to hide them. They crept above it in a series of odd-shaped streaks and blotches that were impossible to hide, since they leaked through any amount of over-painting. But looking at them one day, I suddenly saw the obvious answer, and instead of trying to hide them I turned them into rocks and tree-trunks and birds in the Chinese manner. It worked beautifully. So well, in fact, that I was to use the same trick again and again on the walls of Army quarters.

My bedroom too, 'tho' I says it me'self', was a triumph. The PWD office, who were in charge of painting and looking after official property, only stocked whitewash for walls, white enamel for woodwork, and aluminium paint for things like lamp-posts. Period. But they also provided the Consulates with such necessities as ink. Red ink, added to a pailful of whitewash, produced a charming shade of apple-blossom pink, with which I covered the walls and ceiling – plus the usual wickerwork splash-board of course.

The ceiling, for some reason, had been criss-crossed with flat wood batons, which I painted with the aluminium paint, and having also painted a large sheet of brown packing-paper with it, I cut out aluminium stars and stuck one in the centre of each square. The effect was charmingly frivolous, and somehow suggestive of Columbine and Pierrot. So, remembering a small black and white poster I had seen and admired in my art student days, I did a suitably pastel-coloured mural in the space over the fireplace, depicting a coy, pink-skirted Columbine being serenaded by a colourful Harlequin in a flowery setting of blue-green, decorative trees and daisy-spangled grass.

All the rest of the woodwork – dressing-table, chairs, bedstead, windows – was painted with aluminium, and to set it off I made two little artificial Chinese-style blossom trees, one to stand at each end of the long, low bookcases against the wall on either side of my bed. The tree-trunks and boughs were dead twigs selected from bushes in the garden, stuck into small pots and also painted with aluminium, and the pink petals and buds were modelled out of fresh bread, stuck on to the twigs with glue from a glue-pot on Sandy's office desk.

Bread makes a marvellous modelling material if squeezed between your fingers until it's the right consistency. And if you wait until your flower or whatever is dry, it takes watercolour paint beautifully. Best of all, it lasts a surprisingly long time, hardening into something that could almost be china – and if you've got any colourless nail varnish (I hadn't, worse luck) it will last for years.

Sandy was delighted with his house when we'd finished with it. And so was the PWD, because since the whitewash, ink, aluminium and white paint were all items that came out of stock, the expense was minimal, for Mother and I had done nearly all the painting ourselves. We struck at doing the ceilings, but did everything else, and the bill for the country-made curtains, covers and druggets was astonishingly modest. So were the satin ones that we bought in the covered bazaar in Basrah. Those last were the only furnishings we did not obtain locally. No one would believe that the Consulate funds had not been heavily drawn on when Sandy gave a large party to celebrate the metamorphosis of what had been, let's face it, an essentially hideous house. Even the husbands approved, while as for their womenfolk, they 'ooh-ed' and 'ah-ed' and refused to believe that this was not the result of official privilege, and a bottomless purse provided by the Foreign Office for the decoration of their overseas Consulates.

Several of them appeared to take it as a personal grievance, and one woman in particular informed me acidly that it was all very well for people like us, who had the use of the Consular launch and could go shopping in Basrah whenever we liked and didn't have to worry about bills, whereas ordinary people such as herself . . . etc., etc. When she had quite finished, I told her exactly what the decoration of my bedroom had cost, item by item, including the covered bazaar curtain-material. At which she merely said crossly that she couldn't have done any of it because in the first place she never would have thought of it, and in the second, if she *had* thought of it, she couldn't possibly have done the mural; adding bitterly that I was merely lucky in that I could draw and paint: 'Because most of us can't, you know!'

The complaint about the use of the Consular launch and our supposedly frequent visits to Basrah was anything but true, for Sandy got the use of the launch only when the Consul did not need it, and then one way only, Basrah to Khorramshah. Never vice versa. This meant that we only visited Basrah on those occasions when for some official reason or other the Consul had gone up by launch but would not need it to come back in for some time, so that it would have been returning empty. This did not happen very often. This was just as well, since the city of Basrah lies in Iraq, several miles beyond the borders of Iran where, in those days, the Iranian officials who manned the border post demanded that any European crossing into Iraq should be provided with no less than *seven* photographs of themselves, in addition to filling in a lengthy form on which you had to give your surname and all your given names, date of birth, place of birth, etc., etc., plus the same for your parents, and, believe it or not, your grandparents.

The whole business of crossing the frontier merely to spend a few hours in Basrah (though Sandy generally had some business with the British Consul there) was a lengthy and humiliating one. Our passports and our pack of seven photographs were handed over to an Iranian guard, who would keep us waiting for some time. Sandy would hand over the passports, one at a time, and the guard would take them without a word, stare at our faces and compare them with the ones in the passport before putting out a hand for the next. Finally the packs of photographs were handed over and the forms to be filled in were given to us. While we struggled with these, the senior official (who sat throughout in a chair in the wooden hut that did duty for a border post, his feet on the table) went through the passports examining the photographs one by one and commenting on them to the couple of assistant border-guards, who would look at them over his shoulder and laugh loudly whenever he laughed.

When the senior official felt he had wasted enough of his valuable time on us, he would take up our passports and throw them out of the open door of the hut on to the ground, from where, as the guard made no move, our chauffeur would descend from the car and pick them up. After which we were allowed to cross the border into Iraq, where the Iraqi officials glanced at our passports, stamped them, and handing them back waved us politely through.

On a later visit we were accompanied by a Frenchman, a friend of Sandy's who had business interests in those parts, and who showed us (too late to be of much use to us, I'm afraid) how to shorten these ridiculous shenanigans considerably. He wrote his surname and his Christian names in the correct slot, but drew a long diagonal line across the rest of the form. The border officer bristled at once and demanded the reason for this action, and the Frenchman said in a hushed voice: 'Illegitimate!' At which the Boss and his assistants visibly melted, and murmuring 'Ah, M'sieur, but how sad!' they patted him consolingly on the back and passed him through with no more fuss.

Basrah, what little I saw of it, remains in my memory as a pleasant town full of mosques and shade trees, busy streets and, in the suburbs, familiar East-of-Suez-style houses with flat roofs and whitewashed walls, and gardens full of poinsettias, canna lilies and bougainvillaea. It was the vast covered bazaar that drew us there, and Mother and I could have spent hours in it if our time had not been dictated by how long the car journey from Khorramshah had taken us this time, the hour the Consular launch would be leaving, and how soon Sandy could get through his official business and all three of us could escape after the inevitable luncheon party with friends or acquaintances. Any spare time that these restrictions left us we spent in the covered bazaar under the eagle eye – and wing – of one of the Consulate's Iraqi clerks, a jewel of a man who acted as a guide, interpreter and chief haggler.

There must be covered bazaars in many Eastern cities and I have seen a few of them myself, but none that held such fascination for me as the one in Basrah. The stalls that lined its winding ways made it into an ancient and far more attractive version of a modern shopping mall. It also had the advantage of looking like something out of the *Arabian Nights*, since most of it was covered with awnings of tattered canvas which let the sun shine through in a hundred brilliant shapes that patched the goods, and the shifting stream of turbaned or *bourkha*'d customers, with blobs and lozenges of gold.

Here and there a tear in the swagged ceiling-cloth would let in a long streak of sunlight, full of dancing motes that showed the atmosphere of the bazaar to be full of a hazy mist compounded of equal parts of the smoke of innumerable hookahs, dust, incense-sticks and fumes from the coffee-shops and purveyors of cakes and sweetmeats. The smell of the covered bazaar is not easily forgotten, an entirely individual mixture of the foul and the fragrant, for there were stenches as well as delicious scents, and one put up with the former for the sake of the latter.

Mother and I never stayed long enough to explore the bazaar, for we saw no point in wasting time on the stalls and shops which displayed goods that we knew we could not afford – carpets for instance, or jewellery. There were incredible glittering displays of the goldsmith's craft, earrings and necklaces, bracelets and brooches, chains and wrist-watches, ropes and handfuls of pearls from the Gulf, emeralds from the emerald mines of Swat, rubies from Ceylon – the island now known as Sri Lanka – and diamonds from Golconda.

We looked, but we did not buy. Our interest lay entirely with the cloth shops, for we needed materials for the furnishing of Sandy's house, and all the curtains and cushions and covers in it came from the covered bazaar. We also bought what we could for ourselves, because the material that made such an Aladdin's Cave out of every silk shop included offcuts from all the great Paris dress-shops. The head designers of such houses designed their own material and had it made up in limited lengths. Anything left over would not have been used again by the fashion-house that had ordered it, nor would they have allowed it to be sold locally. It was offloaded instead on to Arab traders in the Middle East, and one of the places where it ended up, to be re-sold at rock-bottom prices, was the covered bazaar in Basrah.

I still have several odd lengths that I bought there and never made use of. One (which I made into curtains for the 'Columbine and Harlequin' room that was my bedroom during our stay in Persia) was so pretty that Sandy paid for it himself, so that he could keep it for curtaining the guest-room of whatever house he would be occupying next. I think it cost him the equivalent of one shilling and sixpence a yard. I lined the curtains with heavy unbleached linen, also bought in that bazaar, to make them hang better, and they should have lasted him for years, but for a sad accident that befell them not long afterwards. By a curious fluke, Mother and I happened to be spending a few nights with Sandy, this time in Peshawar, to which outpost of Empire he had been transferred following his stint in Persia, and where he was again in need of a bit of help with the furnishing . . .

Sandy had already hung the Basrah curtains in the guest-room that had been allotted to me in his Peshawar house. This was a small, bare room that appeared to have been tacked on to the bungalow as an afterthought, since it was on a different level to the rest of the house and had to be entered by way of two or three shallow steps. Facing these, on the far side of the room, was a door that led into a small, Indian-style bathroom and beside it, filling the rest of the space on that wall, were three windows set side by side, making one oblong one. The windows looked out on to a short gravel drive that led out, over a culvert, to one of Peshawar's main side-roads. There was only one way of watering the public and private gardens that kept the city a green oasis in a largely barren land: an elaborate series of ditches that circled the cantonment area and threaded through it under a series of culverts. Once a week each section of these suburbs had its individual sluice opened, usually at night, so that anything that needed watering, lawns, flower-beds (Peshawar was famous for its roses), shade trees and gardens, was flooded to a depth of about three inches. This method is used in many arid countries, so I was familiar enough with it to recognize the sound of rushing water that awakened me out of a sound sleep on my second night in Peshawar.

Lying in the dark and listening to it, I got more and more irritated by the noise and began to work out what I would say in a snarky letter to the Municipality, complaining of being woken up by the uproar and being quite unable to get to sleep again.

I remember tossing and turning and pulling a pillow over my ears to shut out the maddening sound, and my imaginary letters of complaint grew more and more acidulated, until suddenly, after a good hour of this I lost my temper. After a brief angry struggle with my mosquito net, I swung my feet clear and jumped out of bed. To land in over a foot of cold water!

It gave me the shock of my life and I did one of the stupidest things I could have done in the circumstances. I groped under my sodden mosquito net and turned on the switch of my bedside light. One is always warned not to muck about with electricity when in a bath, and I was in one all right. Almost up to my knees. Luckily, I came to no harm. I realized that the roar of water that had been driving me crazy was coming from a point much nearer to me than the culvert. I waded across the room and opened the bathroom door. It was a mistake . . .

The room appeared to be full of water, and I had a lightning vision of a wall of water on which leaves of Bromo lavatory paper floated like lily-pads, before the whole thing fell on me like the Red Sea falling on the hosts of Egypt. It swept me across the room to end up on the steps, and I managed to crawl up them, soaked to the skin, get the door at the top of them opened and, again without pausing to think, turn on the lights.

My room opened into the hall, and there was less water here, only a few inches, just enough to launch Sandy's treasured Persian carpets, which looked very pretty floating about on the surface of the flood. Sandy looked equally pretty when I banged on his bedroom door and he came paddling out wearing pale blue short-legged pyjamas, with his yellow hair all ruffled from sleep, just like Little Boy Blue. I remember telling him so. He was not amused. But fortunately, the sight of my duck-pond strewn with leaves of Bromo suddenly struck both of us as funny, and we spent the next half-hour in intermittent attacks of helpless giggling, which made it difficult to explain what had happened to Mother and Kadera and Sandy's bearer, who shot out of different doors and found themselves splashing in shallow water.

It wasn't anything to do with the Municipality after all. It was the pipe that brought the cold water into my bathroom – the hot was still carried in kerosene tins. It had broken somewhere near the ceiling, and if only I hadn't been sure that it was water intended for the garden, I could have stopped it – or rather, got Kadera and Co. to do so – almost as soon as it started. As it was, it left a horrid high water-mark on the wall of my bedroom and a worse one on the Basrah curtains. It didn't do much good to the furniture or Sandy's carpets, either. Sandy gave me the stained remains of those charming curtains, and I cut off the stained halves and kept the rest for years, using them for short windows and cushion covers and things like that. But to get back to Iran/Iraq . . .

The return journey from Basrah to Khorramshah was always by river in the Consular launch, probably because the prospect of another humiliating delay at the Iranian frontier, and the production of yet *another* seven photographs apiece, was too much. Instead, we took to the water and went home far quicker than we had come by land, as the Shatt-el-Arab raced towards the sea. Mother used to take surreptitious pencil notes, for Iran at that time was paranoid on the subject of spies, and any foreigner taking photographs or sketching was instantly suspected of making maps for sinister reasons. Not that there was anything much to sketch or photograph, except for groves of date palms wherever there was a village and endless miles of desert and wonderful sunsets.

The useful thing, to me, about that stay in Persia/Iran, was that it gave me hours and hours of leisure, which I filled most usefully – once the muralling of Sandy's house was finished* – by writing the murder story that Fudge and I had concocted on the stormy afternoon in the Andamans, marooned on the tiny island of Ross. I had meant to write it before, but there had never seemed to be enough time. Now there was all the time in the world. I borrowed an office table and chair from Sandy, bought several students' pads, a handful of pencils and a couple of rubbers from a shop in Abadan, and shut myself away in my starry-ceilinged bedroom for the best part of every day until I managed to get *Strange Island*, the title I gave to my second whodunnit and (if you count a couple of *Potter Pinner* books and *The Ordinary Princess*) my fifth book.

I knocked off work for a brief interval in order to fulfil a promise that

* Mother did a lovely 'Peter Scott' on the wall above the fireplace in her bedroom.

I would paint some frivolous murals on the walls of the Khorramshah Club's lounge and dining-room for Christmas. Since these rooms were often used for parties and the occasional dance, the silly winter-sporting figures that skied and tobogganed round the room were only intended to be temporary, and the plan had been to repaint them once the New Year's partying was over. But the Committee must have got attached to those light-hearted creatures frolicking around their rooms, for many years later, while talking to a war correspondent who had been covering the Iraq–Iran war, I learned that the only house left standing when the Iraqi forces had finished pounding Khorramshah with the heavy guns was the one with the figures of skiers painted on its walls. After all those years . . . and they were only painted with poster-paint on to whitewash! Everything else, including the palm trees, had gone and nothing else was recognizable. I had seen photographs of the devastation on television newsreels, and could not believe that this was once a place I had lived in, and that somewhere underneath those piles of blackened rubble were the remains of my starry-ceilinged room and that flirtatious Columbine.

I managed to finish the second draft of my Andaman story, and to meet a jewel of a woman who not only offered to type it for me in return for one of my pictures, but could actually read my writing!

9

Raja Santosh Road, Calcutta

Chapter 31

~✸✕✕✸✕~

I don't remember anything about our departure from Iran, or the return trip down the Persian Gulf to Bombay where, upon landing, the first thing I did was to post off a copy of *Strange Island* to the publishers. That done, I returned to the Taj Mahal Hotel, where Mother and I had tea and sat around talking and making plans until it was time to leave for the station, where Mother and Kadera saw me on to a train for Calcutta before catching the night mail to Delhi themselves, where Mother was to retrieve the Beetle — on loan to Joy for the past few months — so that they could drive the rest of the way back to Srinagar.

Mother had suggested that I go back with her to Delhi, breaking the long journey by spending a night or two with Bill and Joy and taking a Calcutta train from there. But since all I had ever seen of the south, or of the east coasts of India, was that drive to Bangalore and Mysore, a few weeks in Ootacamund and that short and crowded week of the Mysore wedding (I didn't count Hyderabad as the south), I couldn't resist the chance to see more. In those days one could buy a ticket on a through train from Bombay to Calcutta, via Bangalore to Madras, and from there along the eastern shores of India, touching at such towns as Vizagapatam and Calinapatam, and Cuttack in Orissa.

The journey took three nights and the best part of four days as we chugged and puffed and loitered down one side of India and up the other, and I spent most of my waking hours with my nose glued to a window, gazing, fascinated, at the countryside we were passing through. Most of the towns were disappointingly shoddy. But the scenery was a delight. There were hills and plains, high lands and low, rivers and waterways and groves of coconut palms, hibiscus and flowering trees, alluring glimpses of silver sand and a glassy sea coloured emerald and turquoise and ultramarine, pale jade in the shallows and fringed with chalk-white foam.

Forty years later, almost to the day, I made the same journey in reverse, from Calcutta to Bombay, only this time by air. It took about forty minutes, and I could see nothing below but a map, mainly light brown, splashed here and there with pale green. As we neared Bombay I saw a curious, shadowy smudge on the map and realized that it must be the *ghats*, that deep and entrancing crack in the earth's surface that almost all trains from Bombay must pass through. And, looking down on that smudge, I thought what a lot modern airborne tourists must miss.

Mark you, those train journeys had their drawbacks, and mine to Calcutta was no exception. The carriage was hot and gritty, and became more so every hour. And as we got further and further south, a majority of the people on the platform and in the third class carriage spoke Tamil or Telagu, and I found that I could not talk to them except in sign language and scrambled Hindustani.

Fortunately the food posed no problems, because at any stop where there is not a railway restaurant there are always one or two licensed vendors of local dishes which in general are far nicer than the imitation English dishes served in the platform restaurants or the dining-cars on trains. And since I could identify most of the food on offer (largely vegetarian and always served up on a banana leaf) I only had to point. Which brings me to the main drawback of long-haul train journeys: your fellow passengers . . .

This must always be a toss-up if one is travelling alone, and this time I had the bad luck to find myself cooped up in a two-berth sleeper with one of those women who, like Nancy Mitford's 'Uncle Matthew', hated 'Abroad' – which in their case seems to begin half-way across the English Channel. This poor creature was a rabid example of the type. I've never been able to understand why on earth they do it – marry someone in Foreign Service, I mean.

This tedious woman gasped with horror at the very idea of eating *gobi bharwan*, or *dahi aloo** – or even *chuppattis* and plain rice! – from a 'common food vendor' on a station platform. I mustn't *dream* of touching it or I'd get terrible stomach trouble, even cholera! I tried to explain that I'd been self-inoculated against bazaar food since the days when Bets and I used to steal handfuls of roast *chunna* from the food shops in Simla's Lucker Bazaar, or be given *jellabies*, hot and crunchy and oozing with honey,

* Spiced courgette and potatoes with yoghurt.

318

by some kind-hearted shopkeeper. But my carriage companion would have none of it. 'Bazaar' food was poison, and that was all there was to it.

She herself had come prepared with enough packaged and sterilized food, bottled water and pasteurized milk, to feed an army for a week; and she had brought with her a spoilt and exceedingly badly behaved eighteen-month-old daughter who howled, screamed and whined practically non-stop, threw her sterilized food about and paid not the slightest attention to her mother's repeated threats to smack baby if baby didn't stop doing so. Baby knew darn well that mother wouldn't do anything of the sort. And so did mother. So I don't know why she bothered. Was I glad to lose them at Howrah! But apart from their company, and the dust and the grit, it was a memorable journey. I wouldn't have missed it for anything.

It was great to see Bets again. She had been waiting for me on the platform, and as she drove me across Howrah bridge and through the busy streets to her flat in a suburb of the city, she filled me in with all her news since she had left Lucknow. WHP had been turned down for the Army, it having been discovered in the course of his medical that he had only one kidney. Bets was reticent on the subject of her home life, just telling me that young Richard, now approaching his third birthday, could, though looking like one of the heavenly choir, invent some of the most disastrous ways of amusing himself that she had ever conceived of. His usual excuse being: 'You never told me *not* to!'

Bets said that unfortunately her imagination came nowhere near covering the variety of things that she had 'not thought' of telling her angel-child not to do. Once, finding a saw that workmen had left unguarded, he had tried to saw off the legs of the dining-room table in order to bring it down to a more accessible height.

Bets was certainly busy, WHP was in the office for the best part of every day, and she had Richard, and lots of friends, and plenty of work to keep her occupied. Her mornings, and more often than not her late afternoons as well, were taken up doing pastel portraits. Hal Bevan-Petman, who was at one time – as I once read in one of those lavishly illustrated monthly American art magazines – 'unquestionably one of the finest pastel artists of our generation', was a great friend of our family's and, though he had refused to teach Bets, he had for some time allowed her to sit behind him while he was doing one of his pastel portraits (provided she didn't make a sound and his sitter didn't object) and watch how he did it.

Bets had found those sessions invaluable, for she had picked up any number of tips, and her own pastel portraits improved mightily. She became what she referred to as 'the poor man's Bevan-Petman' and, though she could not command the prices for her portraits that Hal could, she did very well, and orders poured in. There always seemed to be a sitter in the room she used as a studio.

Calcutta, in the hey-day of the East India Company, when magnificent Palladian-style mansions were being built every day and the Park Street Cemetery was little more than a third full, must have been a magnificent city. It was still fairly impressive when I first saw it in the autumn of 1927, though its main street, Chrowringee, was beginning to look pretty tatty.

As for the slums that had crept up behind its prosperous façade, the less said about them the better. But its zoo and its public gardens, the leafy suburbs where the rich Indians and prosperous *Sahib-log* lived, and its two golf clubs – the Royal, and the one at Tolleygunge (which, together with a racecourse, a club-house, complete with ballroom, billiard rooms and an indoor swimming-pool, lay a mile or two beyond the outskirts of the city), not to mention the pleasant 'Saturday Club' – had few equals East of Suez.

I had thought Calcutta a splendid city on that wonderful day when I found myself back in the beloved land of my birth and childhood. Every yard of the city – every inch, if it came to that! – the squalor as well as the glamour, had spelled 'home' to me. But now, seeing it again after another and even longer gap of years, it seemed far more crowded. There seemed to be twice, or even three times as many people on the streets and in the bazaars as I remembered. In all other aspects, the city seemed unchanged.

WHP and Bets had a large ground-floor flat in a two-storeyed block of flats surrounded by green lawns and flower-beds that were walled in by trees. The flat immediately above us was occupied by an American businessman and his wife. I didn't see much of him, since he left for his office early and came back late. But Louise Rankin was not only a charmer, but a cook who could have beaten Escoffier at his own game. Cooking was her hobby, and her husband avoided as many invitations as he possibly could, on the grounds that he could see no reason for 'dressing up in his soup-and-fish' to eat indifferent meals in other people's houses, when the best cooking in Calcutta was right here in his own house! This excuse was regarded as fully acceptable by both friends and acquaintances.

Louise's contribution to the local war effort was *An American Cookbook for India*, dedicated 'to housewives in India', while its profits went to the Indian Red Cross Society and the St John's Ambulance Association, India. It was an invaluable book and must have made a packet for the charities she named, since it sold out almost at once and had to be reprinted in a hurry. I managed to acquire a first edition, and so did Bets, who would soon be driving ambulances for St John's herself, and both of us bought extra copies to give as presents to 'memsahibs' newly arrived in India and unfamiliar with the ways of Indian cooks and kitchen-matters.

The few months I spent in Calcutta were among the most hectic that I can remember of my India days. I had barely arrived in the place when who should drop in to greet me but one of my best Delhi friends, dear Marcia Mariden, and before I knew where I was I found myself roped in to help with a monster fête in aid of something or other to do with the war. I've forgotten what, there were so many of them: the Red Cross; St John's; Buying-another-Spitfire, or another Bomber; Help for the Wounded or help towards acquiring more weapons of destruction, which sounds silly looking back on it, but was the best that many of us could do at the time. I was put down to help with an art stall, and asked to contribute a few large and gaudy poster-sized pictures to be auctioned at the conclusion of the fête. I painted half a dozen 'Cocktail Girls', in the style of the 'Petty Girl' pin-ups, on large sheets of three-ply wood. Cocktails and cocktail parties were a great feature of the 1920s and 30s, and a clutch of Calcutta businessmen bid against each other to acquire the 'Cocktail Girls' in the interests of patriotism, and because they thought it would be amusing to hang them up in the private bars of their own houses.

My glamorous pin-up girls were knocked down for enormous prices, and the fête, like most of these fund-raising affairs, proved a riotous success and raised a great deal of money. It also brought me into contact with a great many people I might otherwise have never met, and for the rest of my stay in Calcutta there was never a dull moment.

Bets and I were invited to do the scenery and costumes for a production of Sir James Barrie's *Quality Street*. This entailed hours of shopping in the Crawford Market – an enormous covered bazaar in which all the material we needed could be bought for a song, and where Bets and I spent many hectic hours. We designed all the costumes in pastel colours, with the exception of the leading man's, and even his coat looked charming by itself. But when we came to put them together at the first costume rehearsal, we were disappointed with the total effect, which was too wishy-washy, and were wondering what to do about it when I had a brainwave . . .

I had recently seen a London play designed and dressed by Motley with a Regency setting. There was one scene that was surrounded by an oval wreath of flowers. I thought we could manage the frame of flowers by designing a permanent set that would stand in front of the curtain, and be shaped like a wide doorway, edged by a wreath of large formalized flowers. We tried it out with one of the theatre's old safety-curtains, on which we drew and painted the flowers, and cut out and discarded the centre doorway.

It couldn't have looked better, for we matched the colours of the flowers to any of the costumes we wanted emphasized. It really was the prettiest of stage sets. The youthful performers rose to the occasion and made a great success of the run, and I found myself being inveigled into acting in Calcutta's prestigious Amateur Dramatic Society in a run of *The Barretts of Wimpole Street*. I played the flighty niece who flirts with her dour and forbidding Uncle. It's what I believe is known to actors as a 'cameo' part; which means that you're on for a total of five minutes – if that! However, it was great fun to play, but I'm afraid I trod on the designer's toes within a very short time.

He had designed dresses for the Barrett women and their servants in exactly the drab colours that you felt the father of that oppressed family would have approved of. But the flighty niece had obviously never been oppressed in her life, and was used to parties and gaiety. Yet this spoilt, flirtatious snippet had been given a dress in the drabbest of drab-coloured materials, and might have been a schoolmarm or an elderly housemaid.

I registered a strong protest, and the producer, who didn't care what his actors wore as long as it was in period, unexpectedly backed me. 'Yes,' he said, 'now that you mention it, that girl should wear a pretty dress, if only to underline the deadly life of her cousins.' The designer was furious, and rehearsals stopped while the cast argued the case. They all agreed with me. Until, that is, my opponent pointed out that there wasn't any time to make another one, or – more importantly – any money. The costume department had already exceeded their budget, and a new dress, needing new materials and hours of extra work, could not be afforded. The cast nodded gloomily and agreed. It was at this point that I remembered Bets's smash-hit performance as *Lydia Languish* in the Simla Theatre only the year before. She was certain to have kept that costume, and all we had to do was adapt it. So, keeping my fingers crossed, I said I would provide my own costume, free. This settled the matter; and since Bets still had her Lydia costume, which hardly needed any alterations, I wore this, plus a very fetching bonnet with yards of matching ribbon that Bets and I manufactured to go with it. Great success!

In between all this I did quite a bit of work for All India Radio, and lined up, together with half Calcutta, in answer to an urgent appeal for blood donors, only to be told by a harassed and over-worked matron that my blood was of such poor quality that it was no use to the Blood Bank, and of very little use to me, so not to report again please. This lowering piece of news was handed to me in a manner that suggested that I should have known it from the first and refrained from wasting their valuable time. But I have to admit that having made the gesture, it was a relief to find that I need not donate a pint a week in future.

I also had my photograph taken by one of my Calcutta friends, Sidney Ralli, whose husband was in Ralli Brothers, one of the best known firms in that city of businessmen. Sidney became a great friend, and still is. Her photograph shows me wearing a huge hat which was, actually, the tail of the silver fox fur that I bought with my very first *Potter Pinner* cheque, and had made into a cape. It was very much in the style of the early Cecil Beaton, and was reproduced again, much to Sidney's amusement, on the cover of the American hardback edition of one of my whodunnits nearly half a century later. Remembering the success of my photographs of Jess with stacks of hydrangeas and a silvery curtain, Sidney and I went shopping in the Crawford Market for a background for the photograph, and returned with a length of cheap silver gauze and a dozen of the huge paper and tinsel flowers that are a feature of Indian festivities. Both made a successful appearance in this photograph.

It would not have occurred to me that one could use such gaudy and obviously artificial flowers as a decoration in one's own house, if I had not seen how effectively Nancy Caccia had used their Chinese counterparts in her house in the British Legation in Peking. So when a mutual friend of Marcia's and my parents, J. B. Taylor, the head (I think) of Grindlay's

Bank, suggested that Marcia and I do up the Bank House – a huge white-walled 'John Company' edifice – we incorporated, with great success, a good many of those artificial flowers in the décor. We had the greatest fun decorating that enormous barn of a house, and in return we got asked out to a great many of his lunch and dinner parties.

Our Calcutta mornings used to begin with *chota-hazri* (small breakfast) just as the sun rose behind the long veil of smoke from a thousand cooking-fires and the mist off the Hoogly river. By the time it had risen above both, and set the garden and the trees and the wasteland beyond them a-glitter with dewdrops, we were ready to pile into the car and drive out to the zoo.

Early morning – the earlier the better – was the best time in which to visit the zoo, for it was then the peacocks would screech to each other and parade up and down the gravel paths and the dewy lawns, their shimmering tails spread wide. The peacocks and many of the birds were not behind bars, and they seemed to know very well which side their bread was buttered, and stayed where they were safe and well cared for. Even the creatures in cages appeared well-fed and contented, as they stretched out in the early morning sunlight, the tigers and leopards licking their paws and looking exactly like outsized pussycats.

Chapter 32

~※🐦🐦🐦※~

All India Radio asked me to do a series of playlets based on the war news. The idea was that every Friday night someone in the AIR newsroom (where the day's news-flashes were received and handed on to newsreaders and newspapers) should select two or three of the latest and hottest items and hand them over to me to turn into short playlets. I would only have an hour in which to write them, and after that only just enough time for the cast to read through them once before going on the air. This called for quite a lot of quick thinking on everyone's part, not only mine! Bearing that in mind, I selected my team of amateur actors with considerable care, impressing on them that for the next couple of months at least they would have to keep Friday nights free. All India Radio provided a brilliant shorthand typist and assured me that they would be able to produce copies of the script for us 'in no time at all'. And we were off!

The project worked very much better than I thought it could. I would arrive at the AIR building, armed with a block of lined paper, several sharpened pencils and an india rubber, and would be handed the two or three typed items that the AIR decided were the most important. Sitting in a secluded corner I would read them and decide how best to make them into plays that my team could manage. I used to take any female parts that I thought I could manage myself: hospital nurses; women caught in an air-raid or a bombed munitions factory, or reading a letter from a soldier. But in general there were more men involved than women, and I had a couple of good ones. One youngish and one well into his sixties, and both of them very good at accents. As soon as I had decided on my plots and scribbled the dialogue down in pencil, I would ring for my shorthand typist, who would appear with the speed of a diving duck. And having read the playlets to her, I only had to walk across the road to a nearby eatery, where the team would have collected, and while we were eating our supper, outline the plots to them and allot the parts.

Such was the efficiency of the AIR staff that quite often carbon copies of the script would be brought to us before we had even stopped eating; and they never failed to be handed to us the moment we returned. Clutching them, we were hurried into an inner room where we ran through the scripts at speed, did a couple of voice tests, and were on the air. I don't think that the AIR paid their contributors very much in those days, but as the entire team had donated their earnings to one or other of the war charities, I imagine that the Indian Red Cross (or whoever) were handed a tolerably useful subscription.

The impromptu playlets, based on the last-minute news of the war, were not the only thing I wrote and directed for the AIR while I was in Calcutta. They wanted something patriotic, so I wrote them a one-act play-let called *England Awakes*. It was a ghost-story really, and strongly influenced by my fond memories of a children's play that had been performed in Simla's Gaiety Theatre in the early years of the First World War.

The setting of my one-act play was London in the blackout, and the action began with a terrific bang that was meant to be a bomb falling somewhere near Westminster Abbey, followed by the clatter of falling masonry and, very far away, beyond Vauxhall Bridge and on the other side of the river, the wail of an air-raid warning. The voice of an air-raid warden with a strong cockney accent speaks into a patch of silence: 'Strewth, wot a bleedin' row! Nearly broke me eardrums that did. Loud enough to wake the dead. You all right, Nobby?' A second voice says he is and that he must be getting along. You hear its owner's footsteps retreating and the sound of falling rubble fades away and there is a moment of silence. Then someone says quite softly: 'To wake the dead.' The first speaker says: ''Alt! 'Oo goes there?' and the newcomer says, in a Liverpool accent, that men call him the 'Unknown Soldier'. Then one after another the great ghosts of the past come out of the Abbey and speak their bit: Queen Elizabeth, who defied the Spanish Armada; Raleigh, Drake, Frobisher and Nelson; the Duke of Wellington and old Queen Victoria. They all make speeches on the lines of 'never give in!' It ended with St George and the 'God for Harry!' battle cry.

Unlike the newsflash playlets, this one had to have a bit of rehearsal, mainly because of the sound effects. It turned out to be a great success, and was repeated no less than four times 'by popular request'. I took two of the parts myself: Elizabeth I and Victoria, and was delighted to discover that although the two sounded properly autocratic, the voices were quite different. I had worried over how to sound like an old lady who had just celebrated her Diamond Jubilee, and had practised various degrees of croakiness, none of which seemed right, until I had a brainwave – by no means an original one I am told, though I'd never heard of it before. I stuffed my cheeks with pieces of sponge, and that, together with the pitch, worked beautifully.

I continued to do the news playlets until I left Calcutta some time towards the end of March, to join Mother, who was back with old Mrs Wall. I had meant to make straight for Kashmir, taking the Frontier Mail from Calcutta to Rawalpindi, and from there by bus to Srinagar. But J B had invited me to join Marcia and her family, whom he had asked to spend a couple of weeks with him in the Bank House on Bombay's Malabar Hill. That beautiful green garden of a hill – once so full of flowering trees but already being built over by the modern white houses of merchant princes – was where I had once seen and never forgotten the fishing fleet sailing out into a long-ago sunset.

Marcia urged me to accept, and since there was really no reason why I shouldn't I set off to Bombay with the Marindens, this time by a shorter route which entailed a couple of changes at stations where we were royally entertained by bank managers pushing the boat out for the boss.

Bombay as a guest in J B's house was quite an experience. He seemed to throw luncheon and dinner parties, and grand dinners from which the entire party would go on to dance at the Taj Mahal Hotel or some other night spot, almost daily. And oh, the saris worn by J B's Indian guests! Marcia and I used to drool over them, and moan to each other over our own *darzi*-made evening dresses. The women were so beautiful and so *soignée*. Their men were as well-groomed as their wives, and almost as good-looking.

It was at a dance in the Taj ballroom that I saw one of the four most beautiful women I have ever seen: a slim and enchanting Parsee girl wearing a chalk-white Molyneux dress and a single, wide diamond bracelet – an item of jewellery that was once almost part of any rich or pretty woman's party-going apparel.

J B's wife, Betty,* had decorated the Bank House *à la* Syrie Maugham:

---

* J B's wife disliked living in places like Calcutta, Delhi and Bombay. She much preferred their home in England, and had gone on strike and stayed there. Which probably accounts for his tendency to chase women around tables.

that is, 'all white' with only touches of colour. The only room I can remember in detail was the guest bedroom allotted to me, and I was charmed by it. Like Aunt Peg's all-white bedroom in Shanghai, only not as large, looking-glass had been used to give an illusion of size, and since it was an L-shaped room with two windows, one facing towards the sea and the other towards the garden, it seemed at least twice as large as it really was. Betty, explained JB, had done all the décor of the house astonishingly cheaply. She had bought all the furniture in the 'Chor Bazaar' (Thieves' Bazaar) – a well-known source of second-hand junk – and had it spray-painted in matt white. The curtains, cushions and upholstery were all of different materials, some shiny, some rough surfaced, but all in white, as were the shaggy, raw-cotton rugs. The vases and ornaments were of pottery, some white and others the colour that went with that particular room – in the case of my bedroom, turquoise blue – and instead of flowers there were sprays of skeleton leaves, dried leaves, or spray-painted branches. The whole effect was not only attractive but astonishingly cool, which was what she had aimed for, since Bombay's climate is notoriously unpleasant.

In the city itself the temperature was already well into the eighties, but up on Malabar Hill it was still pleasantly cool, and I was sorry to leave it and exchange my ravishing white-and-turquoise room for three days in a hot and dusty railway carriage, with no Marcia to talk and laugh with. But it was high time I got back to Kashmir and did some paintings for the spring Art Exhibition, if I didn't want to run out of money. Besides, there had been an embarrassing evening when Marcia and Jocelyn had been dining out with friends, and JB and I had been dining *à deux* at the Bank House. I had rather enjoyed the prospect of a peaceful evening and not having to dress up and go dancing for a change, and for a time all had gone well. But when dinner was over and the servants had finally gone back to their quarters, the conversation suddenly took a most unexpected turn, and before I knew it I found myself behaving exactly like one of those nit-wit heroines of the Silent Screen days, who, having misread the motives of the elderly villain, winds up being chased round and round the dining-room table.

The situation looks absurd enough on the screen – unless it's being played for laughs with someone like Charlie Chaplin doing the chasing. But in real life, it's merely deeply embarrassing. I've never felt so silly in my life, and I could have strangled JB. Which I probably would have done if he'd been quicker on his feet and hadn't put away so many glasses of wine at dinner. Fortunately for everyone, the Marindens arrived back unexpectedly early from their dinner – their hostess having been smitten with a migraine or something of the sort – and broke up this ridiculous round-and-round-the-mulberry-bush nonsense.

We had not heard the car-wheels on the gravel but we heard Marcia's unmistakable laugh, and JB stopped and said: '*Damn!*' and I fled out by a side-door and up the stairs to my bedroom, where Marcia came in to tell me why they had had to leave their dinner-party so soon. When I told her how grateful I was for her hostess's misfortune, and why, she shouted with laughter, and said didn't I *know* that JB was a well known 'fatal scuffler'? He tried it out on all his girl-friends.

'And you'd be surprised,' said Marcia, 'how many women have allowed themselves to be caught!' It was all his wife's fault for hating 'abroad' and leaving him high and dry: 'He never looks at anyone else when she's around, but when he gets left on his own for months on end, he gets restless, and starts putting in a bit of practice.' Poor JB. He really was a dear man, not like the general run of fatal scufflers, and we remained on the best of terms. All the same, I thought it was time to leave for Kashmir.

JB, Marcia and Jocelyn and an assortment of friends came to see me off, and stacked my carriage with books, flowers and ice, boxes of chocolates and baskets of fruit. And despite that awkward interlude I felt truly sorry to be leaving, while at the same time delighted to be going back to the Punjab again. And to Kashmir.

I had arranged with the bank at Rawalpindi to book me a front seat in a bus going to Srinagar (having discovered that I didn't get car-sick provided I sat in the front seat beside the driver, when travelling in a car or a bus). I can't say I enjoyed that part of the journey, for scenically lovely as most of it is, I cannot feel happy when being driven at top speed on a winding mountain road cut into the side of an almost perpendicular gorge, at the bottom of which – a sheer drop of 500 feet below the outer edge of the road – rages a foaming torrent, while a third of the inner side is overhung by terrifyingly unstable-looking rocks. To be honest, I spent a good deal of the drive with my eyes shut, praying.

The last part of the journey, however, is mostly on the level, and by the time we left the gorges and reached Baramullah, a town that stands in the doorway of the valley and from where you can see the twin mountain ranges that wall it in on either side, the air suddenly became sweet with the faint, elusive fragrance of irises – the tall, yellow-bearded purple or white ones that grow among the gravestones in the Muslim cemeteries, and spread out from there across the valley floor between the fruit trees and the poplars, and whose scent has always seemed to me to be the smell of spring. And all at once I was conscious of feeling wildly, gloriously happy, drunk with happiness, because I was back once more in beautiful Kashmir, and it was spring again.

I have never forgotten that quiet evening and the drive from Baramullah to Srinagar city, through the long avenue of Lombardy poplars that line the crest of the embankment upon which the road runs, raised a little above the level of the valley floor against floods. (I tried to describe it when I wrote a whodunnit that I had intended to call *There's a Moon Tonight* – the one that ended up as *Death in Kashmir*.) The last of the daylight had almost left the sky and the first stars were out by the time we reached the bus station and the end of the journey. And there was Mother waiting for me, with Kadera to cope with my luggage. Presently we were driving up to the Walls' house in Sonawar Bagh, and I was being hugged and kissed by Ma Wall and dear 'Tugboat Annie' and her husband the Colonel, as though I were a prodigal daughter. What with Mr Wall's Australian terriers, Poppiter and Pippiter, leaping and yelping and trying to lick my face, and the servants beaming from ear to ear, it was quite a homecoming. An unforgettable one, followed by one of the *khansama*'s especially good dinners featuring my favourite dishes. And 'so to bed' in the familiar top-storey room I had stayed in so often before.

The air-letter that I had posted to my publishers at the same time as I sent off the manuscript of *Strange Island* had arrived with commendable promptness. But a month later the MS had still not turned up, so I sent off another, express, plus a separate letter to say I had done so. That letter too turned up, but not the MS, and my publishers suggested that this was probably due to 'enemy action'. But when a third copy – the last of the three carbons – failed to turn up, I realized that it was most unlikely that all three ships bearing a copy of *Strange Island* could have been torpedoed. It was far more likely that the Censor's Office had been unwilling to wade through that solid wodge of typescript in search of a possible code, and had merely stuffed each one as it arrived into an incinerator. So I asked my publisher if I could sell it locally and, permission being granted, arranged with Thacker Spink of Calcutta to publish it.

Which they did with the most unexpected speed. (Due, I suppose, to the scanty supply of publishing material in time of war.) It came out within a week or two of my handing over the top copy, and to the most gushing reviews. I can't *think* why, for the proof-reader had done an abysmally bad job. Typist's errors averaged fifteen to twenty a page, and whenever the print setters dropped or mislaid a paragraph and subsequently found it, they never wasted the missing bit. They merely shoved it in, with no explanation, at the end of the next chapter or wherever there was sufficient space for it.

I nearly wept when my free copies arrived. But I suppose that in time of war the reading public are not fussy. They liked the plot; failed to spot 'whodunnit'; and were intrigued by the setting. And in the end it made, and is still making me, a small but steady income. For long after it was out of print (and therefore my own property again) I needed to produce another book to fulfil a contractual three-book clause. Time was short, and I couldn't see how I was going to do it, since in those days I was 'following the drum', and always seemed to be packing and moving.

Remembering this long-forgotten mess of a book, I suggested that I rewrite it as a fictitious island off the coast of Mombasa. This was agreed with the publishers (I had an agent by then) and I spent a feverish two weeks rehashing the book, which, in due course, was flung in to plug the gap, retitled *Night on the Island*.

❧ 10 ❧

'There are more things in Heaven and Earth, Horatio . . .'

Chapter 33

~⋇⚡⋇~

Mother had managed to reserve our old *ghat* for us at Chota Nageem, and old Ahmadoo Siraj, who was beginning to show his years, was there to meet us and stayed to have tea with us and bring us up to date with all the gossip of the valley. Kadera and Mahdoo were there too, but the boat was not one of our old ones, because there were only the two of us.

The war news was still disheartening, yet here in 'far Kashmir', with none of my near and dear as yet involved in it, it still seemed to me as to so many others, 'a phoney war'. And sitting on the flat roof of our houseboat, looking around me at the beautiful, placid Dāl and the mountains behind Shalimar – at the almond blossom and wild iris and the shimmering line of the far snows – I remembered what Tacklow had said to me one evening at Pei-tai-ho. About the last Great War and the possibility of another one. A Second World War . . .

Tacklow believed that we should have bowed out of India in the early twenties, using an occasion such as the Prince of Wales's visit as an opportunity to do so gracefully. It wasn't, he said, as if we were making anything out of it any more, because we weren't; and in his opinion we couldn't *afford* to play at Empire-building any longer. It was becoming too expensive and the sooner we left the better.

I remember arguing hotly with him, shocked to the core at the very idea of 'giving up' the Empire and all that that would mean. I didn't want to *think* of such a thing. But Tacklow only reminded me a little impatiently of the endless times he had told me that we were in India on sufferance only, and that we'd promised to leave some day. Well, that 'some day', he insisted, was coming closer, and though he hoped very much he wouldn't live to see it, I might well do so. If there should be another major war, win or lose, once it was over we should have to give up India.

I had accused him of being an old Jeremiah, and put it down to the disillusionment he had suffered over the Tonk affair and his disappointment over China. Nor had I given any thought to it since we left. But I did now, and realized that he could be right, and that if he was, I was going to lose all this beauty, so much of which I had taken for granted. 'Win or lose,' Tacklow had said . . .

That same evening I made up my mind that while I still had it – while it was still here – I would follow the advice of one of my favourite poets,* who in a poem entitled 'Fare Well' had urged us to 'look [our] last on all things lovely, every hour'. Instead of fretting and fuming at being 'stranded in India' as so many were doing, I would thank God daily for letting me be one of the lucky ones who, in this violent hour, was able to spend my days in this paradise half a world away from the firing-line and the wail of air-raid warnings and the crash of bombs.

There were times when it didn't seem fair that, with my country embroiled in yet another murderous war, people like myself should be able to carry on living in much the same way as we had done before there was any thought of war. On the other hand, now that it had begun, there was no way I could get back to England even if I had wanted to.

Remembering Tacklow's many attempts to take part in the fighting during the First World War, I sympathized with the frustration of the British Indian Army men, all of whom seemed to be spending their time inundating Headquarters with letters begging for transfers to home units, or anywhere near the front line. They all seemed to think that the war would be over before they had a chance to take part in it.

When the war was over we who had not been in the thick of it – had never heard the sirens shrieking their warning of air-raids, had never run for cover when the bombs began to fall, or helped to dig in the smoking ruins for the shattered bodies of our friends and family and neighbours – found ourselves feeling almost as though we were from another planet, speaking a different language. Not that our men need have tried so hard to get themselves transferred back to one of the home-based battalions, because their own particular slice of hell was waiting for them in the Middle East and around the Mediterranean, in Libya and Crete, Sardinia and Monte Cassino. And after that in Burma and Malaysia, Singapore and Java and Hong Kong. Their turn came all too soon.

The only time I felt that I would give anything – anything at all – to

* Walter de la Mare.

336

be back in London was during that time when it really seemed that England was going to be invaded. Everything had gone wrong for us. Our troops had had to withdraw from Norway. Neutral Holland, Belgium and Luxembourg had been invaded. Rotterdam had been bombed into extinction and the Dutch forced to surrender. King Leopold of the Belgians had ordered his army to stop fighting and the British forces to withdraw from Flanders. The bulk of the BEF* were beaten back as town after town fell to the enemy, to be cornered at last at Dunkirk, from where the majority of them were evacuated in a spectacular rescue operation by the Navy, assisted by a fleet of little ships – sailing boats, Thames barges, tugs, motor-boats – every craft owned by those English who love 'messing about in boats' and spend their holidays doing so. Every fishing-boat and pleasure boat from every port on the south-east coast of England, and every cross-channel steamer, set out to pick up our defeated army off the beaches of Dunkirk . . . Close on 4,000 ships of every shape and size had, between them, snatched 335,000 men off those terrible bloodstained sands and brought them back home to a country that will remember their rescue long after the tales of victories are forgotten.

As Churchill reminded us, Dunkirk may have been a minor miracle, but it was also a major defeat. The rest of the world certainly saw it as such. Hitler made a ferocious speech in which he declared a war of 'total annihilation' against us. Italy declared war against Great Britain. Mussolini was not the only one to write us off after Dunkirk. The French had relied too heavily on their 'impregnable' Maginot Line, but in the event they did not have to put that impregnability to the test, for the Germans simply ignored it. They went round one end of it, and having chased the BEF out of Calais, advanced on Paris. And so sure were we all that Hitler would attempt to invade us that hundreds of schoolchildren were evacuated from London and frantic preparations were made to delay the advance of troops making for the capital.

It was only then, as I listened to the radio broadcasts, that I visualized the destruction of London and suddenly saw the streets and parks and historic buildings, Limerston Street and the little pub at the corner of the road, Park Walk, Battersea Bridge and that brand new – and to my mind hideous! – power plant on the other side of the Thames, invaded by

* British Expeditionary Force.

hordes of jackbooted enemy troops armed to the teeth and firing as they came.

My first reaction was total *fury* and a passionate regret that I too was not there and able to clobber one of them with any weapon that came to hand – a rolling-pin or a golf-club or a garden rake. *Anything* that one could hit with – *hard*! It would be worth dying just to get in one good clout at the so-and-so's. I genuinely felt that Churchill had been talking for all of us when he said that if they came we would fight them in the fields and on the beaches; even though I was aware – we all were – that there were appeasers in high places who were clamouring for a negotiated peace, despite the fact that they *must* have known that any peace terms would, at that time, have been dictated by Hitler.

I also remember hearing, with horrified disbelief, a popular young officer in a famous regiment of Indian Cavalry holding forth on this subject at a drinks party one evening. He was all for suing for peace before we were invaded because, according to him, it was only too obvious that we were hopelessly out-gunned and out-manned on land, sea and in the air, and the sooner we realized that the better. Why wait until London was reduced to a pile of rubble and a few thousand more men, women and children were dead?

There had been a chorus of protest. But not, as far as I remember, an ill-tempered one. Most of it was on the lines of 'Oh, come off it, old boy! You can't *really* believe that!' or 'You must be tight, old man!' I certainly never raised a squeak myself; kept silent, I suppose, by an inbred British horror of making a scene in public.

I acquired another beau at that party. Gordon was an officer in that famous Frontier-Force regiment, Queen Victoria's Own Corps of Guides. I had been fascinated by the history of that particular regiment ever since Tacklow had recited me a poem by Sir Henry Newbolt entitled 'The Guides at Kabul'. He had recited it to illustrate a shining example of loyalty and heroism on the part of a handful of Guides in 1879, who, against incredible odds, fought and died to the last man in defence of the British Residency in Kabul, and though I can't have been more than ten or eleven when Tacklow first told me that story, it made an enormous impression on me. A bit of the glamour of that tale seemed to me to have rubbed off on every member of that Corps.

Gordon too had been shocked at the opinions of the appeaser in our midst, and I took to him at once because he had announced loudly that he didn't know what the would-be quisling was so scared about, 'considering we were all lounging around sipping pink gins in perfect safety, several thousand miles removed from where the action was – and likely to remain so, worse luck, for as long as the Brass-Hats in Simla persisted in yammering about "Internal Security" and refused to let the bulk of the Indian Army off the leash'. Or words to that effect.

The defeatist officer did not take up the challenge, and I invited Gordon to have supper on our houseboat at Chota Nageem, where he took to Mother on sight and spent most of the rest of his leave in our company.

One of Mother's best friends in Srinagar, and quite one of the nicest people in Kashmir, was the wife of Sir Peter Clutterbuck, Chief Conservator of Woods and Forests in the State (the appointment was one of those in the gift of His Highness the Maharajah). Everyone knew and liked the Clutterbucks; including 'Tiger', the little heir to the throne, for whom Lady Clutter used to give children's parties.

He was an enchanting child, and Lady Clutter doted on him. I met him at her house on several occasions when she asked me to help at a children's party or chat up members of the little heir's entourage – who naturally had to accompany him everywhere. Many years later when he was grown up and married, I met him again when Bets and I were making a sentimental return journey to the haunts of our youth, and maharajahs had officially been abolished.

We were in Delhi, watching a performance of Indian dancing, and during the interval someone I had been talking to mentioned that a man standing near me was the son of the late Maharajah of Kashmir. I said: 'You mean that's *Tiger*?' and he heard me and whipped round and said: 'How did you know? Should I know you?' I said that he wouldn't remember me, but that I'd met him once or twice at Lady Clutterbuck's house in Kashmir, and he laughed and said, '*Dear* Lady Clutterbuck. I was so fond of her!' and we stood and talked for a little about the old days. It was good to find that the charming child had grown up to be such a very charming man.

Everyone loved Lady Clutterbuck. She was one of those rare people who seem to have no enemies, large, placid and comfortably upholstered, with an endearing sense of humour (she had been charmed at receiving a letter addressed to 'Lady Junglebuck'). Her friends and acquaintances were legion, and I don't suppose she was in the least taken aback when her *abdar* announced one afternoon, with some awe, that a well known holy man, a Yogi, had called and wished to speak with her. Would the lady-sahib receive him? Of course she would! She hurried out into the hall to greet the holy gentleman and ushered him into the drawing-room.

He had to come to ask her, he said, if she would be so good as to invite all her influential friends to a gathering in her garden, at which he would give a demonstration of the power of Yoga. No, no, he would take no payment. Nor did he wish to give a talk on the subject. He had learned that talking was of little use: it was better to see with one's own eyes, and he would wish, in these troubled times, to demonstrate that there were other resources than bullets and bombs.

He made such an impression on Lady Clutter that, despite some initial doubts, she ended by agreeing to the holy man's request, and the party was on. I don't know how I managed to wangle an invitation to it, for I certainly could not lay claim to being influential, and the majority of guests were of Mother's generation, not mine. But thank goodness I was asked, for I wouldn't have missed it for anything.

There must have been about thirty of us seated at little tables round two sides of the large lawn at Forest Lodge. Tea was handed round first, and when that had been dealt with, Lady Clutter introduced the Yogi, who told us that he only intended to demonstrate one aspect of the many that could be achieved by the study of Yoga. This was to prove that it is possible to see without the use of one's eyes.

Turning to Lady Clutterbuck, he asked her to bandage his eyes and ensure that he could not see, and Lady Clutter (who had not been briefed as to what precisely he meant to do, and had resolved to keep a watchful eye on the two *chelas** who accompanied him) thought she really had him. Bustling off to her kitchen, she got her *khansama* to mix some dough, and having watched him do so, collected one of Sir Peter's woollen scarves from the hall. Armed with the scarf and the ball of dough, she hurried back to the Yogi, and having turned the ball into a roll, laid it across his eyes and pressed it down with her fingertips, so that it sealed his eyes completely – 'I was sure he wouldn't have *thought* of anyone using a sticky mass of dough,' she said afterwards.

With the thick layer of dough in place, she tied her husband's scarf

* Disciples.

around the Yogi's head, making sure that the woolly material stuck to the dough, and having done that, led him around a bit so that everyone could see that he hadn't a hope of peeking out from under *that* bandage. He had only asked for two things in advance without explaining what they were for. One was a bag of flour which Lady Clutter had taken the precaution of borrowing, at the last moment, from the storeroom of one of her friends: 'Just to ensure there was no hanky-panky, dear,' she explained. The other was a blackboard and a piece of chalk which, again, she had borrowed at the eleventh hour from the Tyndall-Biscoe school in Srinagar. Having no idea what the flour or the blackboard were for, she had kept both firmly under her eye until the Yogi asked for them.

He now asked for the bag of flour, which he did not touch, merely asking Lady Clutter to select anyone she chose from the company around her, and ask him or her to make a small hole in the bottom of the bag and then walk around the lawn and the garden, allowing it to trickle out and leave a white line which, when the bag was empty, he would walk along. And that was exactly what he did.

He could not possibly have seen through that bandage. Or have forced open eyelids that were glued shut with dough. Yet he walked unhesitatingly along the white line that zig-zagged to and fro, turning and twisting and making complicated patterns on the grass; and watching him, there was no doubt at all that the man could see what he was doing.

When he had come to the end of that line, he turned on his heel, walked back to Lady Clutter and asked her if he might have the blackboard set up. That being done, he asked if anyone in the audience would write something on it, leaving enough room below for him to copy whatever they had written. Several people had a try at this in several different languages, among them French, German, Greek and Latin. And each time when they had finished, he picked up the chalk and copied what they had written. It was uncanny.

The third, and more ordinary, demonstration of his ability to see without eyes was one that is often done in provincial theatres by conjurors and thought-readers. He asked people in the audience to show him things and he would tell them what they were holding up. The only difference was that no patter accompanied this performance, and that he walked among his audience telling each one, briefly, what they were showing him. A pipe. A bandana handkerchief (he described it). A tie (ditto). A necklace, a watch, a ring. A cup and saucer off one of the little tables.

When he came to Mother, she took an unopened envelope out of her bag. (We had stopped on the way to the Clutterbucks to collect our mail from the Post Office and Mother had not yet had time to read any of it.) The Yogi told her what it was, and to whom it was addressed, and Mother said: 'And what's inside it?' At which point, and for the first time, the holy man came near to losing his temper with this unenlightened flock of sheep. He shook his head impatiently: 'Haven't I *told* you that I do not need eyes to see what you can see with yours? Do *you* know what is in that envelope?' 'I haven't opened it yet,' said Mother, 'so of course I don't.' 'Exactly,' said the holy man. 'I can't see what's inside it either. Not until you open it.'

Mother opened it and took out the contents, and that man described each item. There was a short note from Bets and several snapshots of Richard, taken in Ootacamund where they were spending the hot weather. 'Shall I read what your daughter has written?' asked the blindfolded Yogi in a distinctly sarcastic voice, and Mother, understandably shaken, shook her head and stuffed the note and the snapshots back into her bag, rather as if they might bite her. I remember feeling pretty shaken myself at the discovery that there are indeed more things in heaven and earth than are dreamed of in our philosophy. That man could see. There was no doubt about it at all. But a surprisingly large proportion of his audience on that afternoon persuaded themselves they had been the victims of mass hypnotism, which seems to me even more improbable.

Lady Clutterbuck told us later that it had taken the best part of half an hour to get the dough out of 'that poor man's' eyes and eyelashes, 'Not to mention his ears and the back of his neck, dear.' And although a lot of her guests had left donations on the letter tray in the hall (convinced that the exhibition they had witnessed must be in aid of some charity or other) the Yogi had refused to accept it, insisting that he was not a professional performer of tricks. He merely felt it was his mission to interest the 'unenlightened' in Yoga. Perhaps among all the Lady-Sahib's friends who had watched him that afternoon, one or two might be sufficiently interested to take up the study of Yoga. He sincerely hoped so.

Perhaps one or two of them did? I don't know. When one is living through a *Götterdämmerung*, one's mind is likely to be concentrated in a single direction.

*

It must have been in this same year, towards the end of May, that I had another odd experience. This time it was strictly personal to myself. I had been suffering badly from toothache, and our dentist, Mr Soni, told me that the cause was an impacted wisdom-tooth that must come out, and that he would have to give me gas, the sooner the better. An appointment was made and I duly presented myself at his surgery for the ordeal. Mother was away on trek, painting, but Mrs Soni, a red-haired Scotswoman of considerable charm and good sense, and a personal friend, accompanied the anaesthetist and stood by to lend a hand in case I didn't take to the gas. The dentist's chair faced a big many-paned window, on the far side of which hung trails of some sort of creeper falling down from the edge of a balcony above. I was looking at them when the gas mask was clamped on to my face and I heard the stuff hiss as it was turned on . . .

I was nine years old and sitting on my favourite seat in the drawing-room of the Rookery, the bow-window seat, from which I could look out across the gravelled drive and its wooden railings at all Simla, and the far away view of the plains laid out forty miles below.

I had an open book on my lap, but I was idly watching Bets, who was sitting on the edge of the verandah with her sandalled feet hanging down among the pots of scarlet geraniums lined up below. She was aimlessly kicking the flower heads, obviously bored, and presently she looked round and said, 'Oh, come on, Mouse. Let's *do* something!' The windows stood open, for the day was hot and cloudless and without a breath of wind, and putting my book aside I stood up and jumped down on to the verandah, turning my ankle in the process so that a loose blakey on the sole of my shoe stuck into the wood. (A blakey, for those who do not know, was a kidney-shaped piece of iron with prongs on one side, that could be hammered into the sole of children's shoes to prevent them getting worn down by wearers with a tendency to walk on one side of their feet.) The prongs of my errant blakey had fixed themselves firmly, if crookedly, into the wooden planks of the verandah, so I removed my shoe and used it to hammer the blakey hard into the wood.

'Let's pretty it,' said Bets, 'so that people will know that it's not here by mistake, and leave it alone. Then perhaps one day when we're grown up we can come back here and look at it.' So, we 'prettied' it. We pulled the petals off several geraniums and spent a happy interval rubbing them into the wood so that the blakey stood in the centre of a red circle and

343

we were sure that no one would think it was there by mistake. When we had finished Bets went off to wash her hands, and I climbed back into my seat and took up my book again, though I didn't read it. I just sat there, looking at the treetops and the roofs of the houses that covered the steep hillside below our drive, watching the kites, the common scavenger-hawks of India, that circled endlessly in the air above the Lower Simla bazaar and hearing their familiar call, pin-points of sound in the hot, lazy stillness.

I felt enormously happy because I was in a place I loved, and incredibly lucky because I was *me*, and able to look at it all. And then, even as I looked, a curious pattern of shadowy lines began to form itself in front of me, and I thought suddenly, 'How very odd! – I believe I'm dreaming with my eyes open. I didn't know you could do that . . .' The pattern became darker and sharper and the lines became bars and squares . . . and all at once, with a terrible sense of loss, I realized that I was looking at the trails of creeper on the far side of the window-panes in Dr Soni's surgery.

It took several minutes to take in that *this* – the surgery – was real, and that Simla and the Rookery was something that was over and done with long ago. And when it did I began to cry. I sat there with the tears trickling helplessly down my face while dear Mrs Soni patted and petted me, and told me that 'it was all over now'. Which was just exactly why I was crying. Because my happy childhood was over, and I was a 'grown-up', and Tacklow was dead, and I'd never be young any more.

It was one of the most desolate moments in my life, for I had just made the jump from childhood to my thirties, and I felt as though I had lost all the years in between. That I was *old*! I have often dreamt that I have gone back to some place that I used to know, and with people I knew. But though the people are always real, the places are not, and when I wake up I realize that they were in no way similar. But what I had just experienced had nothing in the least dreamlike about it. I had relived a small fragment of my childhood, exactly as it happened. So exactly, that I now knew how Mother had furnished the drawing-room. Which until then had not been one of the things that had been recorded on my private and personal video. What's more, I *knew* that it was all real. The smell of it. The feel of the hot morning in the hills. The shrill call of the kites that circled high above the bazaar. The scent of the pine trees in the woods behind the Rookery and the unseen banks of cosmos flowers, that were just coming into flower below the railings at the edge of the drive. I didn't find any explanation for that fragment of the past until a few years later, when I read Dunn's *Theory of Time*, which made sense to me. The gas obviously helped, and for a short while I had slipped back into the past and relived a happy, pointless fragment of it.

I wrote to Bets and asked her if she remembered the blakey incident, without going into any details; and she wrote back to say that now I had mentioned it, she did. Didn't we make a ring around it or something? Red paint, wasn't it? We had both of us seen a lot of Simla, and visited the Rookery on several occasions, yet neither of us had remembered the incident or thought to look to see if it was still there. And a very long time later, when we were both grandmothers and had a last chance to do so, there was no evidence that it had ever been there, because the entire verandah had been refloored.

Chapter 34

Mrs Lang, the Resident's wife, a dear old bun who strongly resembled the sheep in *Through the Looking-Glass*, was a keen amateur artist. She always took her painting-gear with her on the tours that were part of her husband, Colonel Lang's, official duties, and this year she invited Mother, whose sketches she much admired, to go with her: 'So that I can watch how you do it, dear.' Since these tours were treks which involved living in tents and moving on every two or three days, generally on horseback, Mother jumped at it, and it was arranged that I should stay at the Residency with the Langs' daughter, Joan Richardson, a dazzlingly pretty blonde who, if I remember rightly, was in the process of discarding her first husband.

During the next ten days I listened, riveted, to the tale of her latest love affair, of which I was given a blow-by-blow account. I couldn't help feeling that if only I were to abandon the 'whodunnits' (which needed careful thinking-out as well as a reasonable plot) and switch instead to 'Boy-meets-girl-loses-girl-gets-girl' romances, I could probably make a fortune. Inspired by Joanie's enthralling confidences I actually had a bash at it. But I discovered, as I imagine scores of would-be tripe-writers have done before me, that this form of literature isn't nearly as easy to write as you think. For one thing, you have to *believe* in it. You cannot write tongue-in-cheek about it. I *knew* I was writing something that I thought was sentimental and saccharine drip, and in consequence, all I produced was exceedingly bad and patently phoney drip that no publisher in their right minds would have accepted.

However, it all helped to pass the time very pleasantly during that stay at the Residency, and since Joan attracted admirers rather in the manner that a plate of sticky-toffee-pudding at a picnic will attract wasps, we never had a dull moment. As a result, I was invited to spend the Christmas and New Year holiday with Joan and her parents at the winter Residency in Sialkot, a cantonment town on the edge of the plains not far from the borders of Kashmir, where – since the few roads into that state are apt to be snowbound in winter – the Resident of Kashmir by tradition spent most of the cold weather.

Joan had invited several of her friends, including me, to spend the holiday in Sialkot, and I was able to accept with a clear conscience, since one of Mother's old friends had invited her to spend Christmas and New Year in Lahore, and had not included me in the invitation, and rightly. Mother really could not be expected to lug around a grown-up daughter wherever she went. ('Oh, we *don't* have to have that daughter of hers *too*, do we? It's high time Daisy made her paddle her own canoe!')

I had recently seen a good deal of Gordon, and had begun to think seriously of marrying him, urged on by Gordon himself and a number of mutual friends – mostly of my mother's generation, a group who appeared to dote on him. Gordon certainly had a way with the middle-aged and elderly, and he had made a great hit with Mother early on. I had told him again and again, in answer to his repeated demand to know why I wouldn't marry him, that I didn't love him. That I liked him and was fond of him. That he was a dear and that I knew exactly the kind of girl he ought to marry, but she wasn't me.

'Nonsense!' said Gordon. 'She's the image of you! And it doesn't matter, your not loving me now. You would one day, and I wouldn't mind how long I had to wait. Besides, they're sure to send us off to the Front one day. We can't be left hanging about like this for ever, and then if I were killed you would at least be fairly well looked after, instead of being as poor as a church mouse! You can't *afford* not to marry me, Moll. Do be sensible! You ought to think of your mother if you won't let me look after you.'

I thought seriously about being sensible. For some relationships were not going well in my family. WHP would never look after Mother when she was old, and nor would Bill – Joy had already said as much. So there was only me. I would have to be responsible for her. And she adored Gordon – he had made his number with her early on. But if you married someone for a meal-ticket and not for love, you'd have to spend your days feeling in his debt and making it up to him, which would be hellish. The sheer strain of living under an obligation to someone would be too much. Yet someone was going to have to look after Mother one day, and (since there was no National Assistance in those days) that someone was going to *have* to be me. I havered and wavered, badgered daily by pangs of conscience and the importunate Gordon, and finally lectured by my sister-in-law. Which turned out to be the last straw.

Bill and Joy had come up to Kashmir to spend a brief holiday on the Dāl, in the course of which they had met the persistent suitor, who had managed to sneak another few days 'casual' leave in Kashmir. Finding a sympathetic listener in Joy, he had unburdened his soul to her, and on the night before she and Bill left they sent a message asking me to go over and see them, 'p.s. *without Mother*' – an ominous footnote that could have caused great offence to Mother had she not, by the greatest good fortune, been dining at a *burra khana*, or Indian posh dinner, at the Clutterbucks' that night. So as it was, I did not mention that codicil, and went over to see my brother and his wife after supper. To be met by Joy – my craven brother having made himself scarce. For which one can hardly blame him, since his wife proceeded to haul me over the coals for my treatment of Gordon and my failure to see that in all probability he represented my last chance of finding a husband . . .

Considering my age, said Joy, and the number of seasons that I had been 'to put it crudely "one of the Fishing Fleet"', it was high time that I faced the fact that I was already on the shelf, and that if I didn't accept Gordon I would spend the rest of my life as an impecunious spinster. 'And I do hope,' said Joy, 'that you won't think I am being unkind. But in justice to my husband and my child, I have to warn you that you cannot count on any help, financial or otherwise, from us. Bill has to put his family first, and we both feel you should realize, here and now, that if you turn down this proposal, then you are on your own. I am speaking for Bill as well as myself . . .'

There was a lot more to this effect, plus a list of all Gordon's financial prospects, for, regarding Joy as an ally and a possible future sister-in-law, Gordon had listed these in some detail (down to the last aged relative whose Will was going to leave goods or property to 'dear Gordon') in order to assure Bill, through his wife, that he need have no fear of either Moll or her mother becoming a millstone round their necks in old age. (Always provided, of course, that I married the chap.) I was meant to feel that if I didn't I would end up in some charity-run home for the elderly and indigent, and though I murmured something about having written a couple of whodunnits and the first of a series of children's books, besides selling every painting that I had exhibited at the last art exhibition at the Club, this was brushed aside impatiently: *chickenfeed!*

An impecunious couple of in-laws with no home of their own were, apparently, as potentially lethal as those proverbial loose cannons on board a ship in wild weather, and Joy could only see us as a menace to the future peace and happiness of her marriage. My acceptance of Gordon would have solved all her problems, and she took my refusal of his proposals – which I could not see was any business of hers – as a personal blow against Bill and herself.

As for me, I sat staring at her (doubtless with a dropped jaw), unable to believe my ears and too stunned to interrupt the lecture. Damn it, I barely *knew* the woman. How dare she speak to me like this? I was on the verge of a major explosion when it suddenly occurred to me that she looked exactly like a truculent little London sparrow, valiantly defending its nest against a lurking magpie. Which, of course, was exactly what she was doing. At the moment there was only one hatchling in her nest. But I could almost see a clutch of little gaping beaks and Joy, every feather on end, wearing her wings out protecting her young. And quite suddenly I stopped being furious and exploded into helpless giggles. Which didn't help at all; it simply offended Joy, who said coldly that she herself could see nothing to laugh at in the situation. But having started to laugh, I couldn't stop, which though plainly lacking in tact was at least better than a blazing row and high words. I told Joy, between unstoppable explosions of giggles, that I would think it over, and departed, spluttering, into the night.

Joy never knew it, but her curtain-lecture had made up my mind for me, convincing me that I would rather spend the rest of my days on Joy's dreaded 'shelf' than marry someone I was not in love with. I knew that Mother was going to be bitterly disappointed (it was a pity that Gordon wasn't thirty years older; they would have made a perfect pair!). But he was not my cup of tea. I wanted something a good deal more stimulating, and if it didn't look as though I was going to get it, well, what the hell? I knew now that I could always support myself with my paintbrush and pencil. (And so, incidentally, could Mother, whose watercolours were getting better and better every day, and selling very well.) I couldn't see why Bill and Joy were so obsessed with the idea that the pair of us were going to be a ghastly and expensive burden on them one day. The effect of Joy's lecture on the necessity of snapping up Gordon's offer because 'at my age, I'd never get another' and would end up in some dim little bed-sit, was the opposite to what she had intended.

I gave Gordon a very final 'no' (courtesy of Bill and Joy, had they but known it), and he insisted that we 'remain friends'. Which doesn't often work, but in this case it did. Gordon went sadly off into the sunset, and that was that.

All I knew of Sialkot had been learnt from Sir John Kaye's *History of the Sepoy War*, and *Kaye and Malleson's History of the Indian Mutiny*, Vol. II. Which wasn't a great deal. They included the usual account of incompetence on the part of elderly, top-ranking, British Army Officers, and the refusal of those who commanded Bengal Army regiments to believe that their sepoy troops were not loyal to the core. This resulted in eventual murder, mayhem and bitter disillusionment. None of the details have stuck, but I was fascinated to discover that the house put at the disposal of the Kashmir Resident in Sialkot dated well back into East India Company days, and was said to be haunted.

I asked Mrs Lang what it was haunted by, and she said vaguely that she 'really didn't know dear,' except that it was something to do with the Mutiny year: 'I expect someone was killed here, dear; but no one seems to know who it was, and we never use the room they say is haunted, because the servants don't like to go in there, or the dogs either.'

Remembering the haunted room we had spent a night in at the Bower in Mashobra,* and how alarming it had been, I was relieved to hear that since this one was never used (it was barely more than an alcove off the big drawing-room) it could never have been used as a bedroom. Anyway, it had no bathroom and no outer door, and the only entrance to it was through a door in the drawing-room, which was hidden by a wall-hanging in the form of a long Persian carpet that looked as though it was merely part of the décor. But I was interested to discover that, like the servants, the dogs, of which the Langs kept several, would not go near it after sundown.

There were two doors – in addition to the french windows on the garden side – into the drawing-room from inside the house, and during the daylight hours the dogs used both impartially. But once the sun had set, none of them would use the one nearest the Persian carpet unless they had to, and then only at a run. And none of them would go within yards of the hidden door. I tried several times to take one of them up to

* See *The Sun in the Morning*.

350

it, but they pulled back hard against their collars and growled and bristled, and stuck in their toes. Colonel Lang, watching, laughed and said, 'It's no use. They won't go near it! I tried lugging them up to it when I first came here, but as I didn't want to break their necks or get sharply bitten, I gave it up. They don't seem to mind so much in the daytime.' So next day I borrowed the key, pulled aside the wall-hanging and went in, calling up the dogs to go with me.

They came. Not reluctantly, but very suspiciously, conveying the impression, as dogs can, of walking on tip-toe, growling the while, very softly in the back of their throats. They made no attempt to retreat, but went forward and sniffed the angles of the wall and every inch of the floor. It was a bright, cloudless morning and the sun was pouring directly into the little room through window-panes that no one had cleaned on the inside for some considerable time, so that although the outer side was clean enough, the grime on this one was so thick that no one trying to peer in could see anything. I know, because I tried. As for the rest of the room, the whitewashed walls appeared to be fairly newly painted and the dust on the floor was not particularly thick. I presumed that someone – Colonel Lang? – who did not believe in ghosts had seen to it that the room was kept reasonably swept and tidy. The dogs obviously didn't think much of it, for I saw the hairs lift along their backs. But I didn't feel anything at all. Standing there in that bare, white, sun-flooded little room, it was difficult to believe that anything really bad could have happened in it, let alone something so dreadful that it had left its imprint there, to creep out and re-enact the horror at night.

I learned from Sir John's *History of the Sepoy Rising* that because Sialkot had been stripped of British troops, who had been sent to other and supposedly more dangerous stations, many of those who had been left behind with few or no defences had been put to death, with the enthusiastic support of the criminals whom the Indian Regiments had released from the gaols, the riff-raff of the bazaars and – which is surprising – 'the servants from the houses and the bungalows of the English'. I find this last surprising because when I was researching for my 'Mutiny novel', *Shadow of the Moon*, I found that this was far and away the exception rather than the rule, and that again and again the lives of the English had been saved, at great personal risk, by their servants. I can only suppose that the English in Sialkot came out badly in this respect, and had been harsh and unjust to their servants. Though there is another side to that coin, as anyone who has read Rudyard Kipling's spine-chilling ghost story, 'The Return of Imray', will realize.

According to Sir John, in Sialkot 'From sunrise to sunset' the work of murder 'went on bravely'. Everything that could not be carried off was destroyed or defaced, with one 'strange and unaccountable exception' – the Christian church and chapel. Strange indeed, since the monuments in that church are to men killed in the battle of Sobraom, which was a resounding victory for the forces of 'John Company'.

No one knows why the church and the chapel escaped destruction. But I was told that when the Mutiny broke out in Sialkot, among the many who were killed there were the family who lived in the house that was now the Residency, and that their bodies were buried under the big peepul tree that still grows in the compound. Also that a mother and her young children, attempting to escape the killers, were cornered and butchered 'with great cruelty' in that little room off the Residency drawing-room – and that it is they who are said to return to it by night, hoping to hide there. I wouldn't know about that. But I do know that something or someone is there at night. And whatever it is, the dogs are afraid of it.

In spite of its Mutiny reputation, I thought Sialkot was one of the pleasantest cantonments in India. Day after day the weather was crisp and cold and cloudless, and every morning and evening one could see the Kashmir snows, orchid or vividly pink, lying along the horizon. At midday they were diamond white and glittering against a white winter sky, and among the trees in every garden, bougainvillaea hung in brilliant masses. Beyond the city the crop-lands were green with winter wheat, and though I do not ride, I would take my paintbox with me any morning that there was a meet for a jackal hunt or a paperchase and, when the riders set off, get down to work with my brush, surrounded by an interested and most complimentary audience of children: '*Waa!* That is the tree in thy father's field, Mustafa – look, the Memsahib has drawn it to the life – and there are the mountains!' One's audience had a habit of identifying everything one painted with cries of admiration.

Sialkot was full of men who would shortly be leaving for the Front – Middle East or elsewhere – from regiments such as the 14th/20th Hussars. It was difficult not to wonder for how many of them this would be the last Christmas they would see. But nobody spoke of war, perhaps because all of us thought of little else.

So many of the cheerful young men whom I dined and danced with that Christmas went off to war and never came back. But they stay alive and high-spirited in my memory, dancing until the small hours in the Club ballroom that Joan and I helped to decorate; galloping wildly to and fro on the polo ground while we cheered from the spectactor seats; setting off in a frosty dawn on a paperchase; pulling crackers or taking presents off the Christmas tree. Singing silly songs around the Club piano at three o'clock in the morning, and carols in that candlelit East India Company church. Among its many historic memorials is one that was raised to the memory of a Brigadier John Pennycuick, who 'entered the army as an ensign in the 78th Regiment, fought in fifteen general engagements, and after a service of 43 years, fell at the head of his Brigade at the Battle of Chillianwala, 13th January 1849. And his son Alexander, an ensign in HM 24th Regiment, who fell in the same engagement while defending the body of his father, aged seventeen.'

This is the church that Sir John Kaye says was, for some inexplicable reason, spared the looting and vandalism that befell the rest of the Sialkot cantonment, and, as far as I know, that memorial is still there together with the other plaques and monuments.

Having seen the New Year in with a final party at the Sialkot Club, I boarded the train to Delhi. There I was to spend several weeks working on murals on the walls of the many pre-fabs hastily erected for the use of troops on leave, or men convalescing from wounds, as well as a hospital in the new (and hideous) cantonment that had been built a few miles beyond the then limits of New Delhi, on a stark and barren ridge of exceedingly stony and unattractive ground. I remember dear Aud Wrench gazing long and thoughtfully at the enormity of those acres of raw, red-brick buildings, shaking her head and saying sadly, 'Oh well, only God can make a tree!' Nowadays I expect the whole place has mellowed, as New Delhi did, and has become a pleasant leafy suburb. Or merely been absorbed into the nearest portion of the city and become a part of it.

Bill, having achieved his exchange from the Gunners to the Department of Supply and Transport, was installed with his family in a bungalow in New Delhi, and Mother and I got our first look at her first grand-daughter and my first niece. Suzan, then around six months old, was already a young woman with a will of her own, and Joy warned us that we mustn't walk in on her too suddenly, because 'Suzi didn't like strangers'.

She had a starched English nanny, which impressed me; though remembering my own childhood I felt sorry for her. The nanny too told me to be careful how I approached her small charge, and the fact that Auntie Mollie had come to see her was duly broken to her gently by both. But these precautions did me no good. My niece, the prettiest little dot you ever saw corralled in a playpen, stopped playing with whatever toy had her attention and stared at me from under small, scowling brows for what seemed like a good two minutes before deciding that no, she *didn't* like strangers, especially this one! Opening a minute pink mouth to its widest extent, she proceeded to howl the house down. Joy swooped her up into a motherly embrace and eventually, defeated, handed her little darling over to Nanny, who whisked her away, still howling lustily, into the night-nursery. My tactful brother said, 'Oh, well, you know what they say, Moll: "Children and dogs, they always know; can't fool a child, can't fool a dog!"' and laughed as though he thought his daughter's reception of me was a tremendous joke. Anyone who has been blackballed by a baby will know just how I felt.

Delhi itself seemed unchanged by the war. But in the Secretariat buildings security had been tightened and unidentified strangers could not go far without being challenged. However, a friend of mine escorted me to the right office, where I handed in another bunch of black and white drawings and was asked if I could paint scenery. I imagine the official had camouflage in mind, for when I suggested that I might be able to brighten up some of the pre-fab buildings he said that sort of thing wasn't in his line, and directed me elsewhere. After spending some time in another office, I arrived back at the bungalow to be told by Mother that I'd had a caller, who, after waiting for the best part of half an hour, had got tired of waiting and left. 'Guess who?' she said. Believe it or not, it was Clive, the chap who had 'tossed me aside like a soiled glove'. Mother told me that Joy's nanny had been *most* impressed by him. 'Ooh, what a *lovely* young man!' she had said. 'Is he your daughter's young man? If he is, she's a lucky girl!' Shows he must have had something! But, oh, how wonderful to find that I honestly couldn't care less that I'd missed seeing him. Or if I never saw him again. We left for Kashmir on the following day in the best of spirits.

Chapter 35

⁓ᴪᴪᴪᴪᴪ⁓

Spring that year had been everything one expects of spring in Kashmir. The days were blue and sunny and the long line of the snows, seen through a mist of apple-blossom and reflected in the river and the lakes, was a page straight out of the Elizabethan poets – or the Americans who write the lyrics for the composers of popular love songs.

Mother and I spent a lot of our time out sketching, and I sent off what was to be the last batch of black-and-white illustrations to New Delhi, the propaganda people having found someone in the office who could do them, and decided that it was a great deal easier – and saved a lot of time and postage – to get the work done on the spot instead of at long range. I was not sorry to be done with having to hunt up photographs from old magazines when it came to having to draw weapons of war. But no sooner was I done with that job than the WVS* landed me with another: selecting and buying material for curtains, cushions and slip-covers for the countless windows, chairs and sofas in those aforementioned pre-fabs. They were urgently needed for the convalescent and wounded, and as recreation centres for soldiery on leave.

It was never very pleasant to go jaunting down to the plains during the hot weather, but this time I had the ill luck to hit a heatwave. We set out for Rawalpindi in an outsize Army lorry, my Punjabi driver and I, hoping to do the trip in record time, since the damage caused by the winter rains would have been repaired by now, and the monsoon had not yet broken.

The Srinagar–'Pindi road was looking its best and my driver handled that clumsy vehicle a treat, so that I soon stopped clutching the edge of my seat and shutting my eyes (my usual practice on that scary road) and did not have to resort to brandy or sea-sickness pills. The driver was a

---

* Women's Voluntary Service.

chatty individual, and I learned all about his family and his home town and his plans for the future. We were on excellent terms by the time we reached Garhi and paused in its small bazaar to buy fruit.

I slept a lot of the way after that, and didn't wake up until we stopped at Domel to pay the toll and have a cursory look taken at our luggage. But it wasn't until we reached Kohala, where another toll is demanded and one crosses the suspension bridge that takes one out of Kashmir and into British India, that the hot weather first made itself felt in a wave of muggy heat that made the valley feel like the steam-room in a Turkish bath. Luckily, from there the road climbs fairly steadily until it reaches Sunny Bank, from where a branch road some two miles long takes one up to Murree, while the main road dips down again towards the plains and the town and cantonments of Rawalpindi.

Once again, as we took the 'Pindi road, the heat met us like the blast from a furnace, and the air became hotter and hotter as we left the hills behind us and met the rocky levels where the trees give way to bushes and thorn-scrub and tufts of dry grass. Behind us the dust of our passage fumed up in a dense cloud that poured in between cracks and crannies of the truck, and though we shut every window, we could no more prevent the dust-clouds raised by approaching vehicles from half-smothering us than they could avoid being smothered by ours.

Fortunately, by this time it was nearing sundown and there was hardly any traffic on the 'Pindi–Murree road; which was a blessing. I suppose the heatwave, now in its third or fourth day and proving itself a killer, had driven people off the roads until after sunset. My driver's khaki uniform was dark with sweat; as was my own, made of grey *muzri*, a cotton material that is about the cheapest cloth obtainable in the bazaars (our higher echelon were all for saving money). Many of our better-heeled members preferred to provide their own uniforms, but people like myself accepted the ones on issue with gratitude. Which, on this occasion, proved a godsend, for had I been wearing a smarter and more expensive version of the uniform instead of a *muzri* one, I would probably have come down with a bad case of heat-rash or a lethal one of heat-stroke.

My driver pulled to the side of the road and once again requested permission to relieve himself, and as I too could do with the same, we descended, and disappeared behind the nearest bit of cover – of which there was plenty. When I came back to the lorry, without thinking I put my hand on the bonnet – and very nearly scorched my palm off. I swear you could have fried a steak on that metal, and I regretted that I could not take off my uniform and spread it over the bonnet, where it would have dried in under two minutes. However, since I had nothing under it except a pair of panties and a bra, I abandoned the idea and crawled reluctantly back into my seat – my uniform sticking to me as though I had been taking a dip in a swimming-pool full of glue.

We reached Rawalpindi around four o'clock, where a room had been reserved for me at Flashman's Hotel and where my driver (who had made his own arrangements for the night) dumped me, with the brief information that he would collect me again at seven o'clock the following morning. He gave a stern warning to the hotel room-bearer to look after the Missahib and see that she had everything she wanted, *tez jhaldi se!* – or Indian 'at the double!' He departed in a cloud of dust, and I was ushered into my room, which was possibly a degree cooler than the world outside, having been shuttered against the sun all day. As soon as the room-bearer had left me to my own devices, I stripped off my sweat-soaked clothing and made for the bathroom to wash off all the dust of that long journey. Heaven knows I ought to have known better, for we had had the same problem in Tonk. But I had forgotten. I turned on that cold tap, and putting my hand under it, got it practically par-boiled.

The water must have been near boiling point, for the metal water-tanks were on the roof, and for the past few days (and all of that one, with the thermometer hovering around 124 and the sun beating down on them) they had been absorbing heat. I let the tap run until the bath was almost full, in the hope that if left to itself for a few hours it might cool down. I suppose I had some supper, but if so I don't remember that. I do remember the *bheesti* sprinkling what must have been hot water over the stone floor of the verandah, and hearing it hiss. The water from the *mussacks* was also sprinkled all over the parched grass of the lawns and the gravel paths that surrounded the hotel, and for a minute or two the night air smelt deliciously of wet earth. But the darkness brought no alleviation of the heat, and I went in search of the manager, who lent me a couple of table-fans to help out the big white ceiling one.

I trained one of these on the bath and the other one directly on my bed – I didn't need a mosquito net, for the fans at least kept those maddening insects away.

It seemed like a good idea to dip my cotton nightgown in water before lying down in it, in the hope of getting some sleep. But it dried in seconds, and after that I fell back on dunking the sheets in the bath, wringing them out and lying down with the other table fan blowing directly on them. This was bliss for about five minutes, but not long enough to let one fall asleep. The room seemed to get hotter and hotter, and eventually, in the small hours, deciding that the night air must be cooler outside than the close heat of the room, I went out to walk in the shrivelled gardens. By now it was around two o'clock in the morning, and I crossed the brittle grass of the lawn outside my window, hearing it crunch under my sandals, to see what the thermometer on the tree in the centre of the lawn, which had been repeatedly watered, registered. The mercury stood at 103.

Well, that was a good deal better than the figure it had registered when I arrived, and feeling a trifle cheered I returned to the rooms and dipped a hand in the bath again. The water in it had had nearly ten hours and the services of a table-fan to cool it down, and though it was nowhere near cold it was nearly lukewarm. I got into it thankfully, and spent the rest of the night sleeping in it, which made my skin as shrivelled as an old washerwoman's. But it was wonderful.

The next day was another windless scorcher. But the heat had some advantages: the cloth-bazaar was half empty, so I got through my chores in half the time I would have done on a normal crowded day. Loaded to the roof with bales of material, I was able to avoid spending a second night in Rawalpindi. We made for the hills in the late afternoon, spent the night in a Dâk bungalow among the pines and got back to Srinagar in time for a late lunch next day.

Now that I didn't have to cope with any more 'propaganda illustrations', and the spring blossoming was over for another year, I decided that since the bank-balance was getting dangerously low, it was high time I got down to writing another 'whodunnit', this one to be set in Kashmir: time, the present, with a plot full of sinister Nazi spies scheming to pull down the Empire. I like to have a title for a book I'm working on, though it has often been changed by the time it gets to the printers – this one being a case in point. I had been charmed by a few verses in a back-number of the *Saturday Evening Post*, the last two lines of which I have used to start the next chapter.

Chapter 36

'And lilies blow and it is Spring. And there's a moon tonight . . .'*

Moonlight almost anywhere can be enchanting. But never more so than in Kashmir; and reading those lines I thought immediately that the last one would make a marvellous title for the book I had in mind. I still think so. But the publishers didn't, and they gave it a thoroughly pedestrian one. So I shall use it here instead.

I roughed out a plot, and did what I always did with a whodunnit – worked out a sort of grid for the chapters. You have to – or *I* have to – plant a clue in each chapter, so that when your villain is unmasked in the final one, your readers can think: 'So *that's* why George Blimp took twenty minutes longer to get back from the party than Gregory Blonk did! . . .' There has to be a reason why the characters behave as they do. In the case of the baddies, a sinister one; and with goodies (innocent but mistaken) just to provide an appropriate number of red-herrings.

That done, I replenished my stock of writing blocks and the usual supply of pencils and india rubbers. Mrs Wall loaned me the use of her late husband's desk and the little room that used to be his study, and I was off, determined to refuse all engagements until I had finished the book, and all unaware that this was going to be another case of 'Man proposes but God disposes'.

It had become a habit, ever since *Six Bars at Seven*, to count and write down in a ledger every day the exact number of words I had written. It may sound laborious, but it helped me to keep track of the length of each chapter and therefore the length of the book. I aimed at a minimum of 2,500 words a day. But if I could manage it I would write more than that

---

* I wish I knew who wrote that, but I don't. The lines have stayed in my mind all these years, but not the name of the poet. Perhaps someone will recognize them and tell me. I *think* the poem was called 'Guinevere'.

as a 'bank' on which I could draw if, for any reason, I wanted to take a day off to do something else.

I've always envied people who can write quickly. Me, I write at a snail's pace, and for every word I keep I rub out at least twenty. It's a slow process, and I only wish I could do what most of the true professionals do: set aside three or four working hours each day during which no one is allowed to disturb them, and live an active social life for the rest of the time. Alas, it does not work for me.

There's a Moon Tonight got off to a good start, and I often found myself doing a steady 2,500 words and up, without too much difficulty. I also found, with some irritation, that practice had not helped me to get started when I sat down to it each day. In an effort to defeat this, I made a point of leaving off work in the middle of a sentence and always at a sufficiently interesting part of the story to make it as easy as possible, next day, to pick it up from there and get started again.

The writing of the first two chapters of the book that ended up as *Death in Kashmir* was punctuated by the arrival of letters from Gordon, who was wildly elated by the prospect of being sent back to his regiment. The Guides had been whisked off to a war zone early on, but Gordon had been seconded to 'some dreary desk-job in Sialkot' (which was why he had been able to take those weekend holidays in Kashmir so frequently). He bombarded me with excitable letters, all of which included a plea that I would change my mind about marrying him. Couldn't I just get *engaged* to him for the duration?

Then one morning, to my horror, I found that his almost daily letter had been heavily censored. This not only showed that he had been breaking the wartime code of 'careless talk costs lives', but was a sharp reminder of something that darling Tacklow (who had been Deputy Chief Censor in India throughout the First World War) had mentioned not long before his death, at one of Buckie's lunch parties. Buckie had been discussing censorship versus security, and Tacklow had said that unfortunately, censors were only human, and that even the most trustworthy of them had been known to cause mayhem by passing on a legally obtained titbit of gossip ('in the strictest confidence') to his wife or a bosom friend.

I scribbled a hasty note to Gordon, warning him that his letters were being opened and read by a censor, but all I got in return was a flat refusal to believe that he had ever given away anything he shouldn't. Not even when he would be leaving Sialkot! (He said he didn't know that himself, and added a rude remark about 'dirty old men and peeping Toms'). However, after that he did at least stop criticizing – in detail and by name – the goings-on of certain senior 'brass hats' in charge of Movement and Control, confining his criticisms of these gentlemen to pen-and-ink drawings in the margins of his letter. Gordon would have made an excellent cartoonist.

His letters continued to be opened at intervals, but there were no more blacked-out lines, and there was far too much about the woes of his best friend in the regiment, one Goff Hamilton, who (in company with almost every officer in an Indian Army regiment still cooped up in cantonments) was spending every free moment, metaphorically speaking, battering on the doors of the mighty and badgering his superiors to let him be transferred to an active unit. Gordon, fuming on his friend's behalf, sent me an angry diatribe on the subject. Apparently those 'B——hatted B——s in Delhi (no names no packdrill!)' had not only turned a deaf ear to the poor chap's latest efforts to be let off the leash, but had arbitrarily returned him to – guess where? To Sialkot district! Just as he (Gordon) was about to leave it.

'Can you beat it?' demanded Gordon, exaggerating the timing of the appointment for the sake of drama and taking, as far as I can remember, at least four pages of writing-paper to give me his unexpurgated opinion of Fate and the Higher Command, who were obviously in collusion. No wonder his frustrated chum was going round 'like a bear with a sore head'.

I was faintly interested in the woes of the said chum only because he turned out to be the man who Mother had thought was 'just the one for Mouse if only he wasn't married'. He was also the chap who had lost his first-class berth on the *Duchess of Bedford* to my brother Bill and had later won the magnum of champagne presented to the best amateur floorshow by the management of the Taj Mahal Hotel. Apart from that, I had little interest to spare, and no sympathy, for either the domestic or the military woes of someone I had never even met, and was irritated enough to return an unnecessarily bad-tempered reply to Gordon's letter. It was something to the effect that his whingeing chum didn't know how lucky he was to be safely corralled in peaceful Sialkot instead of embroiled in some ferocious tank-battle in Italy or Abyssinia or wherever – while as for his wife's views on returning to India, she probably felt about that country as I did about China.

Gordon replied equally crossly that I was talking through the back of my head. And, after an interval of dignified silence, sent me a letter informing me that 'in case I hadn't noticed it' he was still in Sialkot awaiting his marching orders. Also that his chum had been granted a month's leave in Kashmir – 'as a sort of consolation prize he thinks, poor fellow' – and that he'd probably go fishing for most of it, but since he would be bound to go through Srinagar at some time or other, he (Gordon) had made him promise to look me up and give me lunch at Nedou's and take me out shopping to buy some expensive gift from him (Gordon), either as a 'goodbye' present or – if only I would change my mind – an engagement one. There was also a postscript to the effect that he hoped I would be kind to poor old Goff who, whatever I might think to the contrary, was going through a bad patch and needed cheering up. 'So no telling him how lucky he is to be in peaceful Sialkot, please!'

I replied suitably – I hope. I don't really remember, since I happened to be deeply involved in murdering imaginary characters during a fictitious ski-club meeting in Gulmarg, and was in no state to spare any interest, let alone sympathy, for Gordon's declarations of undying devotion (which I'd always taken with a large pinch of salt – and how right I was!), or the domestic problems of his friend, which seemed to me of minuscule importance when set against the frightening daily bulletins from the war zones and the tragic and harrowing casualty lists. I wished that I could have made the hoped-for last-minute gesture of sending Gordon off to the war feeling happy by saying I'd marry him. But it would have been a pretence, and if he came through safe and sound I'd have to explain that it was only a 'sympathy gesture' and that I'd never meant to go through with it. Which was not going to do much for his self-esteem.

It must have been about ten days after the arrival of that missive that I received another letter, postmarked Achabal, a little village known to all fishermen in the Raj and to most sightseers too, since the spring at Achabal is said to be the source of, among others, that excellent trout stream, the Bringi. The letter, a distinctly frivolous one, was from Gordon's friend, saying that he supposed I was aware of the purpose of his errand, and would it be OK by me if he were to pick me up at ten-thirty a.m. on 2 June and take me for a walk down the Bund in search of an expensive furrier and/or jeweller? It did not sound like the letter of a 'bear with a sore head'. But then the writer was not to know that Gordon had been giving him away.

No mention of standing me luncheon at Nedou's, you notice. However, that was just as well, since it meant that I would with luck be back at the Walls' for lunch and have the whole of the rest of the day free for writing. Lunching out always meant that half the morning and most of the afternoon went down the drain. I replied in an equally frivolous tone, addressed the letter c/o the Post Office, Srinagar (the only address given) and sat down to write enough words for my word-bank to enable me to take a few hours off come 2 June.

Just in case the shopping expedition took up more time than I expected, or involved a lunch at Nedou's after all, when the day came round I exchanged my working overall (you've no idea what a lot of pencil-dust gets strewn about the place when you are writing exclusively in pencil) for one of my prettier cotton dresses, and rather than waste valuable time sitting around with folded hands until the clock struck ten-thirty, I took Rudyard Kipling's advice and sat down to 'fill the unforgiving minute with sixty seconds' worth of distance run'. In other words, got on with my whodunnit, which had now advanced as far as the third chapter.

It went well that morning, and I was scribbling along at a great rate when I heard a man's voice in the hall and realized that the time had passed quicker than I expected, and that this must be Gordon's friend, Goff. Ma Wall was saying: 'Yes, this is the house; yes, she's expecting you . . .'

Hastily finishing the sentence I had been writing, I turned round to face the door. And there he was: Prince Charming in person. Mr Right at last! This was what I'd waited for. We stood and looked at each other for what seemed a very long time . . .

I can still see him clearly as he was at that moment. A tall young man with an engaging grin and eyes the exact shade of the rather battered green pork-pie hat that he had forgotten to remove . . . 'Who can explain it; who can tell us why? Fools give us reasons. Wise men never try . . .'

Many years later my American publisher and fiction editor, taking me through the manuscript of *The Far Pavilions*, protested that I had allowed my hero and heroine to fall for each other far too quickly, and insisted that the whole business of falling in love was a very much longer process. It was, he assured me, totally unrealistic to have Ashton and Anjuli do so in a matter of minutes. But since my father, and later I myself had done it *'between one breath and the next'*, nothing was going to persuade me to make my hero and heroine take any longer about it.

I don't understand it myself. This instant, mutual recognition that the French call a *coup de foudre*, and which can link two total strangers together as though by an almost visible flicker of lightning. And be durable enough to keep them in love with each other for close on half a century, *'until death do them part'* . . .

I still don't know what I would have done if there had not been a war on. You begin to think quite differently when your horizon is bounded by casualty lists. Or if Goff's marriage had been a happy one. I hope I would have had the courage to run like a hare while the going was good because I am a hundred per cent in favour of marriage. If it works, there is nothing that comes anywhere near it. But fate was kind to me and I was not put to the test. Because of Gordon's uninhibited correspondence, both I, and (I presume) a local representative of the Censorship Department, were aware that Lieut. Godfrey* John Hamilton's matrimonial barque had run aground on a familiar reef . . .

His wife had not settled down happily to the somewhat claustrophobic life of an Indian Army *'memsahib'*, in the little cantonment of Mardan† on the Empire's bleak North West Frontier Province. This cantonment was, by tradition, the headquarters and home of her husband's regiment, the Q V O‡ Corps of Guides. They had not seen each other for close on two years when she wrote to tell him that she was not coming back to India, and there had followed a harrowing correspondence. It was not a new situation: she had never wanted to live in the East and had thought from the beginning that she could persuade him to transfer to a British regiment. But Goff – who at an early age had fallen in love with the romance of the Guides and their history – could not contemplate leaving them. There had been long arguments which he thought he had won. But because of the war and long separation, and the birth of a daughter now well over a year old, whom he had not yet seen, it had cropped up again. This time it was no longer a problem to be discussed between them. This time it was an ultimatum: India was no place in which to bring up young children, and since his wife did not intend to try doing so he must choose between giving up the Guides and transferring to a home-based regiment, or seeing

* When he was very young he had a German governess who could not pronounce 'Godfrey'. She called him 'Goffrey' or 'Goff'; and the latter stuck to him for life.

† Ma'-*darn*.

‡ Queen Victoria's Own.

his wife and child for only part of one year in every three. (There were no passenger planes in those days, and though transport by sea was astonishingly cheap, it was slow, and home leave was granted only every three years.)

Goff had come up to Kashmir in a thoroughly angry, embittered and disillusioned frame of mind. He would, I imagine, have been only too ready to fall into the arms of almost *any* unattached woman who happened to be passing. And I can only be profoundly and eternally grateful that she happened to be me.

He still had a little more than two weeks of his leave, and he spent five days with me and then suddenly said that he would be going up to Gulmarg for the next week to stay with his CO's wife and to 'think things over'. I still remember those days as the longest in my life. Every hour of each one of those interminable days dragged by as slowly as a wet weekend in January. I didn't even know if he meant to see me again, and I found that I couldn't do any more work on *There's a Moon Tonight*, because my mind was a blank. Then, unannounced and unexpected, two days before I thought he might, he walked into the hall of the Walls' house and took me off to the Club.

There was never anyone in the Club ballroom at that hour of the morning, and we were crossing it side by side when he suddenly stopped and, turning to me, said, 'If I can get a divorce, would you marry me?'

I think I must have said 'Yes' almost before he'd stopped speaking, for fear he might change his mind. (*'I'll be ready in five minutes – no, make it three!'*) . . . 'No – one!'

It would be nice to finish this book with the four words with which Charlotte Brontë's Jane Eyre ended her story: 'Reader, I married him.' Well, I did marry him. But it wasn't as simple as all that. Jane Eyre's story came to a full stop with that statement. But ours, Goff's and mine, had only just begun. And so, too – though I had hoped against hope, and despite all Tacklow's warnings tried to make myself believe that it would never happen – began the slow, inexorable march towards the end of Empire and the tearing apart of the enchanted and enchanting land that I so loved.

Glossary

abdar	butler
Angrezi	English
Angrezi-log	English folk
barra-durri	open-sided outdoor pavilion
bhat	talk, speech
Bibi-ghur	women's house
bistra	bedding-roll
burra	large, e.g. Burra-Sahib, great man
butti	lamp
charpoy	Indian bedstead
chupprassi	peon
chatti	large earthenware water-jug
chokra	small boy
chota-bazri	small breakfast
chowkidar	watchman, caretaker
dâk-bungalow	resthouse for travellers; orginally for postmen (*dâk* means post)
darzi	tailor
dekchi	metal cooking-pot
dhobi	washerman, or woman
Diwan	Prime Minister
ferengi	foreigner
galeri	the little striped Indian tree-squirrel
ghari	vehicle; usually horse-drawn
gudee	throne
gussel	bath (*gussel-khana*: bathroom)
halwa	sweets
Jungi-Lat-Sahib	Commander-in-Chief
kutcha	rough, unfinished
khansama	cook
khitmatgar	waiter

Kaiser-i-Hind	the King (or Queen)
lathi	stout, iron-tipped and bound bamboo staff
Lal Khila	Red Fort
log (pronounced *low'g*)	people, folk
mahout	elephant rider
mali	gardener
manji	boatman
masalchi	washer-up, kitchen boy
maulvi	religious teacher
mufussal	countryside ('the sticks')
murgi	chicken
namaste	the Indian gesture of respect, greeting or farewell: hand-pressed palm to palm and lifted to the forehead
noker	servant (*noker-log:* servant folk)
powinders	tribe of gypsies who are always on the move
shikari	hunter
shikarra	canopied punt that is the water-taxi of the Kashmir lake
tonga	two-wheeled, horse-drawn taxi of the Indian plains
topi	pith hat – almost a uniform in the days of the Raj
vakil	lawyer